From Munich to the Liberation, 1938–1944

JEAN-PIERRE AZÉMA
Institut d'études politiques de Paris

Translated by
JANET LLOYD

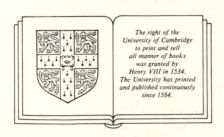

*The right of the
University of Cambridge
to print and sell
all manner of books
was granted by
Henry VIII in 1534.
The University has printed
and published continuously
since 1584.*

CAMBRIDGE UNIVERSITY PRESS

Cambridge
London   New York   New Rochelle   Melbourne   Sydney

EDITIONS DE
LA MAISON DES SCIENCES DE L'HOMME
Paris

Published by the Press Syndicate of the University of Cambridge
The Pitt Building, Trumpington Street, Cambridge CB2 1RP
32 East 57th Street, New York, NY 10022, USA
296 Beaconsfield Parade, Middle Park, Melbourne 3206, Australia
and
Editions de la Maison des Sciences de l'Homme
54 Boulevard Raspail, 75270 Paris Cedex 06

Originally published in French as *De Munich à la Libération 1938–1944*
by Editions du Seuil, Paris 1979 and © Editions du Seuil, 1979

English translation © Maison des Sciences de l'Homme and
Cambridge University Press 1984

First published in English by Maison des Sciences de l'Homme and Cambridge
University Press 1984 as *From Munich to the Liberation, 1938–1944*

Printed in Great Britain at the University Press, Cambridge

Library of Congress catalogue card number: 84-5828

British Library Cataloguing in Publication Data

Azéma, Jean-Pierre
From Munich to the Liberation, 1938–1944.
1. France – History – 1914–1940
2. France – History – German Occupation, 1940–1945
I. Title   II. De Munich à la Liberation
1938–1944, *English*
944.08   DC389
ISBN 0 521 25237 7 hard covers
ISBN 0 521 27238 6 paperback
ISBN 2 7351 0078 2 hard covers (France only)
ISBN 2 7351 0077 4 paperback (France only)

CE

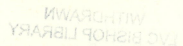

Contents

running out and a broken shield. The France of de Gaulle: a France united
in the fight, sovereign and restored. The France of the Resistance: an
insurgent, purified, new France. The France of the average man: freedom
and survival.

Illustrations

Foreword

In a contribution to the colloquium organised around the subject of 'The Liberation of France', Pascal Copeau, one of the leaders of Libération-Sud, observed without a trace of bitterness that 'any meeting between the protagonists of history and historians is likely to be difficult', and he went on to remark, more cynically, 'However, the historians may rest assured: it is they who are bound to have the last word.'[1] Historians nevertheless have their scruples. They have, with good reason, no illusions as to their objectivity. Especially in connection with those black years that for the French people who lived through them remain a period still charged with passion even today, and of which the younger generations in general retain a distorted image. Furthermore, they are faced with difficulties that are inseparable from all history of very recent years: the protagonists in and witnesses of the war have still not opened up all their archives. In France, a law passed in January 1979 has only recently made it possible to consult them. A number of obscurities therefore remain despite the fact that the documents confiscated from the defeated Germans together with the archives made available by the Anglo-Saxon allies have led to the publication of a sufficient number of scholarly works for it to be possible to proceed on firm ground. This book aims, first and foremost, to provide a review of the results already obtained and a strictly chronological plan has been deliberately adopted so as to indicate clearly the part played by accident. If it is particularly concerned with what happened in metropolitan France, that is because Jean-Pierre Rioux's book (the next volume in this collection) covers the events of what is called 'Overseas'.

The author was three years old in 1940 and is determined neither to preach nor to adopt the role of prosecutor. Nevertheless, he does not propose to act as a disembodied spectator, as he also has his own views to express. However, while this book makes no claims to objectivity, it does at least aim at impartiality to the extent that its author has had no personal scores to settle.

Abbreviations

ACJF	Association Catholique Jeunesse Française
AD	Armoured Division
ADD	Amis de Darlan
AEF	Afrique Equatoriale Française
AFN	Afrique Française du Nord
AMGOT	Allied Military Government of the Occupation
AOF	Afrique Occidentale Française
AS	Armée Secrète
BCRA(M)	Bureau Central de Renseignements et d'Action (Militaire)
BNCI	Banque National pour le Commerce et l'Industrie (Belgium)
BRAA	Bureau de Renseignements et d'Action d'Alger
BRAL	Bureau de Renseignements et d'Action de Londres
CDL	Comités de Libération
CDLL	Ceux de la Libération
CDLR	Ceux de la Résistance
CFLN	Comité Français de Libération Nationale
CFTC	Confédération Française des Travailleurs Chrétiens
CGT	Confederation Général de Travail
CLP	Comité de Libération Parisien
CND	La Confrérie Notre-Dame
CNR	Conseil National de la Résistance
CSAR	Comité Secret d'Action Révolutionnaire
FFI	Forces Françaises de l'Intérieure
FFL	Forces Françaises Libres
FNC	Fédération Nationale Catholique
FTPF	Franc-Tireurs et Partisans Français
GPRF	Gouvernement Provisoire de la République Française
JEC	Jeunesse Etudiants Chrétienne
JOC	Jeunesse Ouvrière Chrétienne
LVF	Légion des Volontaires Français
MLN	Mouvement de Libération Nationale
MNPGD	Mouvement National des Prisonniers de Guerre et des Déportés

MOF	Mouvement Ouvrier Français
MOI	Main d'Oeuvre Immigrée
MSR	Mouvement Social Révolutionnaire
MUR	Mouvements Unis de la Résistance
NAP	Noyautage de l'Administration Publique
NN	Nacht und Nebel (Night and Fog)
NSDAP	Nationalsozialistische Deutsche Arbeiter Partei
OCM	Organisation Civile et Militaire
OFI	Office Français d'Information
OMA	Organisation Métropolitaine de l'Armée
ORA	Organisation de Résistance de l'Armée
ORTF	Office de la Radiodiffusion-Télévision Française
OS	Organisation Secrète
PCF	Parti Communiste Français
PDP	Parti Démocrate Populaire
PPF	Parti Populaire Français
PSF	Parti Social Français
PTT	Postes et Télécommunications
RFA	République Fédérale d'Allemagne
RNP	Rassemblement National Populaire
SD	Sicherheitsdienst
SFIO	Section Française de l'Internationale Ouvrière
SMIC	Salaire Minimum de Croissance
SNCF	Société Nationale des Chemins de Fer
SNI	Syndicat National des Instituteurs
SOE	Special Operations Executive
SOL	Service d'Ordre Légionnaire
SPD	Sozialdemokratische Partei Deutschlands
STO	Service de Travail Obligatoire
TSF	Télégraphe sans fil

A Brief Chronology

A Brief Chronology 1938–39

Developments in metropolitan France

1938

20 January	No longer any socialists in the government.
10 March	Resignation of the Chautemps cabinet.
13 March	Formation of the second Blum government.
8 April	Blum resigns after another vote of no-confidence from the Senate.
10 April	Formation of Daladier government including no socialists at all.
12 April	Quasi-unanimous vote results in Daladier's investiture.
May	
3 June	SFIO congress at Royan.
21 August	Daladier tries to make the forty-hour week more flexible.
24 September	A number of reservists are called up.
30 September	Daladier's triumphal return to Paris.
4 October	Chamber approves the great majority of the Munich agreements.
27 October	Opening of the Radical Socialist Party congress in Marseilles.
1 November	P. Reynaud replaces Marchandeau at Ministry of Finance.
10 November	The Radicals cease to belong to the Rassemblement Populaire.
12–13 November	Publication of the first Reynaud decree-laws.
14–17 November	CGT congress at Nantes.
	Strikes and social confrontations, particularly at the Renault works.
30 November	Semi-failure of the strike launched by the CGT.
10 December	The Daladier government loses socialist support but finds compensations on the right.
24–25 December	Extraordinary National Congress of the SFIO at Montrouge.

1939

2 January	Daladier goes to Corsica and North Africa.
7 February	The government refuses an amnesty to the strikers of 30 November.
5 April	Lebrun re-elected as President of the Republic.
21 April	Fresh spate of Reynaud decrees.
27 May	Opening of SFIO congress in Nantes.
27 June	The Chamber adopts proportional representation.

International relations and the conduct of the war

1938

12 March	German troops enter Austria.
13 March	Proclamation of the Anschluss.
21 April	Hitler orders the Wehrmacht to prepare to invade Czechoslovakia.
20 May	Sudeten disturbances and Czech mobilisation.
June	
3 August	Beginning of the Runciman mission.
5 September	NSDAP congress at Nuremburg.
14 September	Henlein breaks off relations with Prague.
15 September	Chamberlain meets Hitler in Berchtesgaden.
21 September	Paris and London exert strong pressure upon the Czech government.
22 September	Chamberlain goes to Godesberg.
25 September	Daladier and Bonnet go to London.
29 September	Munich Conference begins.
30 September	The Munich agreements are signed. Anglo-German declaration of non-aggression.
7 October	Constitution of an autonomous Slovak government.
30 November	Anti-French demonstration in the Italian Chamber of Fasces and Corporations.
6 December	Ribbentrop signs an agreement of non-aggression in Paris.

1939

26 January	Barcelona falls to the Francoists.
10 February	Death of Pius XI.
27 February	Franco regime recognised by Paris.
2 March	Election of Pius XII (Cardinal Pacelli).
6 March	Destitution of Mgr Tiso by the Prague government.
14 March	Hacha goes to Berlin.
15 March	German troops enter Bohemia.
16 March	The Slovaks place themselves under the 'protectorate' of the Reich.
28 March	Fall of Madrid.
29 March	Poland rejects the demands of the Reich.
31 March	Great Britain pledges itself to guarantee the integrity of the Polish territory.
7 April	Italian attack against Albania.
13 April	France and Great Britain guarantee the independence of Greece and Romania.

Developments in metropolitan France (continued)

28 July	Promulgation of the Family Code.
29 July	Prorogation of Chamber of Deputies by decree.
25 August	*L'Humanité* and *Ce Soir* are seized.
27 August	Censorship is established.
31 August	The Council of Ministers refuses to follow G. Bonnet. France will support Poland.
1 September	General mobilisation.
2 September	The Chamber votes military funds.
13 September	Minor ministerial reshuffle.
26 September	Dissolution of the PCF and its organisations.
1 October	The new Groupe Ouvrier et Paysan (Worker and Peasant Group) insists on a parliamentary debate on peace.
4 October	Thorez deserts.
8 October	Arrest of PCF deputies.
November	

International relations and the conduct of the war
(continued)

30 April	The Soviet Union proposes a military alliance to France and Great Britain.
22 May	Signature of the 'Steel Pact'.
23 May	Hitler orders the Wehrmacht to prepare to invade Poland.
23 June	Mutual Franco-Turkish agreement of assistance.
July	
10 August	Arrival in Leningrad of French and British military negotiators.
21 August	*De facto* suspension of tripartite negotiations.
23 August	Signature of German–Soviet pact.
25 August	Signature of Anglo-Polish alliance.
	Hitler postpones the invasion of Poland.
30 August	General mobilisation in Poland.
31 August	The Reich claims Danzig and insists on a plebiscite in the 'corridor'.
1 September	German troops invade Poland.
2 September	Italy breaks off its mission of mediation.
3 September	First Great Britain, then France, declare themselves to be at war with Germany.
6 September	French troops enter the Sarre.
17 September	The Red Army invades Poland.
27 September	Warsaw falls.
28 September	The Reich and the Soviet Union carve up Poland between them.
30 September	French divisions pull back.
6–12 October	Failure of a white peace.
3 November	The American Congress votes a new law of neutrality.
30 November	The Soviet Union attacks Finland.

A Brief Chronology 1940–44

Developments in metropolitan France **Internal resistance**

1940

1940

20 January	The Chamber votes to disqualify the communist deputies.
19 March	Daladier's policies are strongly attacked in the Chamber.
20 March	Daladier resigns.
22 March	The new Reynaud government only just wins a vote of confidence.
3 April	Communist ex-deputies sentenced to prison.
9 May	The cabinet resigns.
18 May	Ministerial reshuffle. Philippe Pétain is appointed vice-president of the Council.
19 May	Gamelin is superseded. Weygand is appointed commander-in-chief.
5 June	Last reshuffle of Reynaud cabinet: de Gaulle appointed Under-Secretary of State for National Defence and War.
10 June	The government leaves Paris.
13 June	The Cangey Council of Ministers; violent clash between supporters and opposers of an armistice.
15 June	In Bordeaux, Chautemps proposes enquiring about armistice conditions.
16 June	The Council of Ministers rejects the plan for Franco-British union. Paul Reynaud resigns. Pétain replaces him.
17 June	Pétain forms a cabinet. He asks for armistice conditions.
19 June	In Paris the Central Committee of the PCF seeks

17 June   In Brive, Edmond Michelet distributes tracts protesting against the request for an armistice.
In Chartres, Jean Moulin attempts suicide rather than sign a dishonourable statement.

xviii

External resistance and the governments of Algiers
1940

International relations and the conduct of the war
1940

12 March	Signature in Moscow of Finno-Soviet peace treaty.
28 March	Meeting of Supreme Inter-Allied Council: the French and the British agree not to sign any separate peace treaties.
9 April	Beginning of 'war of encirclement'. Denmark and Norway are invaded by German forces.
10 May	Beginning of the German offensive in the west. Invasion of Belgium and Holland.
13 May	*Panzer* divisions cross the Meuse, in particular at Sedan.
15 May	Capitulation of Dutch army.
27 May	Leopold III orders Belgian troops to capitulate.
28 May	Franco-British forces are lifted off Dunkirk.
4 June	Collapse of the Dunkirk pocket.
6 June	The French lines of defence are breached.

17 June De Gaulle reaches London.
18 June First *Appel* to the 'Resistance'.
24 June All the able-bodied men of the Ile de Sein join the 'Free French forces'.

10 June	Italy enters the war on Germany's side.
14 June	German troops enter Paris.
22 June	In Rethondes, the French plenipotentiaries sign the Franco-German armistice agreement.

28 June De Gaulle is recognised by the British government as 'the head of the Free French'.
22 July Rallying of the New Hebrides.
August Arrival in France of the first agents of Free France, with the mission of setting up intelligence networks.

25 June	The armistice becomes valid.
3 July	'Operation Catapult': the French ocean-going fleet suffers serious losses at Mers el-Kébir.
2 August	Japan demands bases in

Developments in metropolitan France (continued)

	to bring out *L'Humanité* legally again.
21 June	Departure of the *Massilia*, bound for Casablanca.
23 June	Laval and Marquet enter the government.
29 June	The government leaves Bordeaux for Vichy, via Clermont-Ferrand.
2 July	Convocation of National Assembly in Vichy.
7 July	Philippe Pétain gives his agreement to the Laval plan.
9 July	The two Chambers decide, with quasi-unanimity, to revise the constitutional laws.
10 July	Private, then official, sessions of the National Assembly. Large majority votes in favour of full constitutional powers.
11 July	Philippe Pétain promulgates the three first Constitutional Acts founding the French State. In Paris, Châteaubriant publishes *La Gerbe*.
12 July	Promulgation of Constitutional Act no. 4 instituting Laval heir apparent. Ministerial reshuffle.
30 July	Law to 'francise' the administration. Institution of the Chantiers de la Jeunesse.
August	Rejection of Déat's proposal for a 'single party'.
7 August	The Reich places three departments in the east under the rule of two Gauleiters.
13 August	Dissolution of all 'secret societies'.
16 August	Establishment of 'Provisional Committees of Organisation'.
29 August	Creation of the Légion Française des Combattants.
6 September	Ministerial reshuffle. The parliamentarians are almost all eliminated.
7 September	Weygand becomes the government delegate-general to French Africa.
10 September	Creation of the Central Office for the Allocation of Industrial Products.
17 September	*L'Oeuvre* reappears in Paris.

Internal resistance (continued)

20 June	E. Achavanne sabotages the Wehrmacht's telephone communications near Rouen.
23 June	Vieljeux, mayor of La Rochelle, refuses to show the French flag.
7 August	Publication in the occupied zone of J. Texcier's *Conseils à l'occupé*.
29 August	Frenay drafts a plan for a Secret Army.

External resistance and the governments of Algiers (continued)	**International relations and the conduct of the war** (continued)

Developments in metropolitan France (continued)		**Internal resistance** (continued)	
	Rationing is introduced for all principal foodstuffs.		
27 September	In the occupied zone, the occupying power promulgates decree on the Jews.		
3 October	In Vichy, the Council of Ministers produces a 'Statute' on the Jews.	3 October	Raymond Deiss brings out the first number of *Pantagruel*. Jean Lebas distributes *L'homme Libre*.
5 October	Round-ups of communists in the Paris region.		
11 October	Speech by Pétain containing overtures to the Reich.		
13 October	The general councils are replaced by 'administrative commissions'.		
22 October	Meeting between Hitler and Laval.		
24 October	At Montoire, Hitler and Pétain agree upon the principle of political collaboration.		
30 October	*Message* from Philippe Pétain urging the French people to support State collaboration.		
1 November	Jean Luchaire publishes *Les Nouveaux Temps*.	11 November	Demonstrations by students and schoolchildren in Paris. Christian Democrat militants form the Liberté movement.
9 November	Dissolution of national professional organisations.		
14 November	Franco-German 'compensation agreement'.	16 November	*France-Liberté*, the ancestor of *Franc-Tireur*, puts down roots in Lyons.
16 November	Law reforming limited companies. Expulsion of some 70,000 people from Lorraine.		
2 December	Law on the corporative organisation of agriculture.	2 December	Christian Pineau brings out the first number of *Libération-Nord*.
13 December	Palace revolution in Vichy: Laval is sacked and arrested. Déat is detained in Paris.	15 December	First number of *Résistance* produced by the Musée de l'Homme group. The OCM is set up in Paris. The first steps of Ceux de la Libération.
14 December	Flandin becomes Minister of Foreign Affairs.		
25 December	Darlan meets Hitler near Beauvais.		

1941		**1941**	
22 January	Creation of the National Council.	22 January	First number of *Valmay* published by R. Burgard.
27 January	Members of the government are obliged to swear an oath of loyalty to the head of the French State.	28 January	Frenay resigns from the army to devote himself to his Movement for National Liberation.
February	*Le Juif Süss* is shown at Parisian cinemas.	February	The Musée de l'Homme group is decapitated.
1 February	The RNP is founded by Déat	14 March	The MOI is reinforced.

External resistance and the governments of Algiers (continued)

International relations and the conduct of the war (continued)

1941

29 January	FFL raid on Mourzouk.
10 February	A column from the Chad surrounds Koufra.
March	Rémy founds the Confrérie de Notre Dame.
2 March	Koufra falls.
14 March	The 1st DFL is engaged in Eritrea.
8 June	The FFL enter Syria.

1941

26 February	Rommel's Afrikakorps is engaged in Libya.
11 March	Promulgation of the 'bail-loan'.
15 March	Italo-German offensive in the direction of Egypt.
3 April	Anti-British *coup d'état* in Baghdad.
13 April	German troops enter

Developments in metropolitan France (continued)

Internal resistance (continued)

	and Deloncle.	
7 February	*Je Suis Partout* reappears.	
9 February	Law controlling seed-corn and harvests. Flandin resigns: Darlan is appointed vice-president of the Council and Minister of Foreign Affairs.	
10 February	Darlan replaces Laval as heir apparent.	
26 February	Murphy–Weygand agreement on supplies in North Africa.	
14 March	Creation of the allowance for retired workers.	
29 March	Xavier Vallat is appointed General Commissioner for Jewish Questions.	30 March The first Comité d'Action Socialiste (Committee of Socialist Action) is set up in Nîmes.
April	The daily ration of bread drops to 275 grams.	*La Voix du Nord* appears.
12 April	Ruling on divorce.	14 April In Lisbon, Loustaunau-Lacau contacts an emissary from the Intelligence Service.
17 April	Creation in Paris of the Trade-Unionist Propaganda Centre.	
8 May	Further German order relating to the Jews resident in the occupied zone.	15 May Creation of the National Front.
13 May	Interview between Hitler and Darlan in the Berghof.	26 May Beginning of the strike by the miners of the Nord and the Pas de Calais.
14 May	Foreign Jews in Paris arrested.	
27–28 May	'Protocoles de Paris' are initialled in Paris. The daily tribute is raised to 300 million francs.	
2 June	Second 'Statute for Jews' published in Vichy.	
3–6 June	The Council of Ministers refuses to sign the 'Protocoles de Paris'.	9 June End of the miners' strike.
14 June	National congress of the RNP.	7 July First number of *Libération-Sud*.
22 June	PPF Congress in Villeurbanne.	14 July *Défense de la France* is launched.
7 July	The collaborationists want to create a 'Legion of French Volunteers against Bolshevism'.	
18 July	A big meeting is held in Paris to support the LVF. Pucheu becomes Minister of the Interior.	
24 July	Declaration of allegiance from the cardinals and archbishops of France.	
26 July	Marx Dormy is assassinated	

External resistance and the governments of Algiers (continued)

International relations and the conduct of the war (continued)

	Belgrade.
22 April	The Greeks capitulate.
11 May	German planes in transit via Syria.
27 May	The British fleet sinks the *Bismark*.
31 May	First massive RAF raid on the territory of the Reich.
22 June	The Wehrmacht invades the Soviet Union.
	Damascus is taken.
14 July	Armistice of Saint-Jean-d'Acre.
16 July	Smolensk is taken.
10 August	Churchill–Roosevelt meeting and signature of the Atlantic charter.
25 August	British and Soviet troops enter Iran.
9 September	Beginning of the siege of Leningrad.
19 September	Kiev falls.
16 October	Odessa is taken.
20 October	The Soviet government leaves Moscow.
3 November	The fall of Koursk.
16 November	Beginning of the battle for Moscow.
7 December	Pearl Harbor.
	The Japanese enter Malaysia and Thailand.
8 December	The United States and the United Kingdom declare war on Japan.
20 December	Failure of the German assault against Moscow.

External resistance column:

25 July	De Gaulle–Lyttleton agreement on the Middle East.
29 August	Honoré d'Estienne d'Orves and two of his companions are executed.
4 September	First Lysander operation.
12 September	Jean Moulin crosses the Spanish frontier.
24 September	Establishment of the Comité National Français (French National Committee).
27 September	Catroux proclaims the independence of Syria.
6 November	Yvon Morandat is dropped by parachute in the southern zone.
27 November	Catroux proclaims the independence of the Lebanon.
24 December	The Free French forces rally Saint-Pierre-et-Miquelon.

Developments in metropolitan France (continued)		**Internal resistance** (continued)	
	in Montélimar.		
12 August	The 'Evil wind' speech.		
14 August	The (antedated) creation of the special courts of justice. The oath of loyalty is required from high-ranking civil servants, soldiers and magistrates.		
22 August	Promulgation of the 'Order on Hostages'.	21 August	*Fabien* assassinates Moser, the Minister designate of Marine Affairs, in the Barbès *métro* (the underground).
27 August	Colette's attack against Laval and Déat.		
4 September	Doriot departs with a contingent of the LVF.	5 September	The National Front is set up.
5 September	Marcel Gitton is killed. Inauguration in Paris of the exhibition 'The Jew and France'.		
16 September	Execution of 10 hostages. Refugees are allowed to re-enter the 'prohibited zone'.		
4 October	Promulgation of 'The Charter of Work'.		
13 October	Institution of 'family parcels'. Definitive break between the RNP and the MSR.		
22–23 October	Execution of 98 hostages, 27 of whom are shot at Châteaubriant.		
1 November	The weekly paper, *Le Rouge et le Bleu*, comes out in Paris.	1 November	The 'Combat' movement is founded in Grenoble.
20 November	At the Reich's insistence, Weygand is recalled from Africa.	20 November	The first *Cahiers du Témoignage Chrétien*. The first number of *Combat*. *Franc-Tireur* is published for the first time.
1 December	Pétain and Goering meet at Saint-Florentin.		
12 December	750 Jews of French nationality are arrested in Paris. Official birth of the Service d'Ordre Légionnaire.	5 December	Execution of Gabriel Péri.

1942		**1942**	
9–12 January	Negotiations between Benoist-Méchin and Abetz.	19 February	The Editions de Minuit publish *Le silence de la mer*. Lecompte-Boinet founds
19 February	Beginning of the Riom trial.		
1 March	Opening in Paris of the exhibition on 'Bolshevism against Europe'.		Ceux de la Résistance.
3–4 March	Heavy Allied bombing of Boulogne-Billancourt claims many victims.	28 March	Christian Peneau reaches London with a mandate from his comrades to negotiate with Free France. Birth of the FTPF. The 'K source' becomes
15 March	Law on the black market.		
26 March	Meeting between Pétain and Laval in the Randan Forest.		operational.
27 March	Departure of the first convoy	16 April	In Paris, a demonstration by pupils of the Lycée Buffon.

External resistance and the governments of Algiers (continued)

International relations and the conduct of the war (continued)

1942

1 January	Jean Moulin dropped by parachute.
17 January	Birth of the BCRAM.
February	Leclerc controls the oases of Le Fezzan.
3 March	Admiral Muselier leaves the French National Committee.
April	Moulin creates the Bureau d'Information et de Presse. Brossolette reaches London.
May	Rémy meets an emissary from the PCF.
26 May	Beginning of the assault

1942

21 January	Rommel counter-offensive in Libya.
15 February	Singapore taken by the Japanese.
16 February	Occupation of Sumatra.
8 March	Capitulation of Java.
21 March	Fritz Saukel is appointed 'general planner for the recruitment of labour'.
27 March	British raid on Saint-Nazaire.
4 May	Beginning of the battle of the Coral sea.
5 May	The British land in

Developments in metropolitan France (continued)

of 'racial deportees'.

5 April   Official installation of the Gestapo in the occupied zone.

15 April Riom trial suspended indefinitely.

17 April Giraud's escape.
Darlan's resignation.

18 April Constitutional Act number 11 creates the function of 'head of the government'. Laval becomes the head of the government.

29 April Giraud in Vichy.

4 May   Lachal succeeds Valentin as the director of the Légion des Combattants.

6 May   Darquier de Pellepoix is appointed General Commissioner for Jewish Questions.

18 May   Germany insists on the transfer of skilled workers to the Reich.

29 May   Jews resident in the occupied zone are obliged to wear a yellow star.

16 June Meeting between Laval and Saukel: the principle of the *Relève* (the Relief Programme) is accepted.

22 June Laval broadcasts a speech announcing the Relief Programme and publicly declaring his desire for a German victory.

16–17 July In Paris, 'Operation Spring Wind': the so-called 'Vel' d'hiv' round-up.

18 July In Vichy a law institutes the Tricolour Legion.

28 July Franco-German aeronautic agreement.
Appearance of *L'étranger*.

August   Foreign Jews from the southern zone are handed over to the Nazis.

11 August Arrival in Compiègne of the first convoy of prisoners freed in the 'Relief Programme'.

19 August Compulsory military service in the Moselle.

25 August The *Bureaux* of both Chambers are obliged to cease all activities.
Compulsory military service

Internal resistance (continued)

1 May   Patriotic demonstrations in a large number of towns in the southern zone.

6 May   E. d'Astier de la Vigerie reaches London.

18 May   Gouin has Blum's mandate to go to London.

29 May   The first number of *Le Populaire* appears in the southern zone.

16 June Publication of the first *Cahier* by the OCM,

22 June Publication in the underground press of Charles de Gaulle's message as reported by Pineau.

14 July Further demonstrations, in particular in Marseilles.
Arrival of a new generation of militants in Libération-Sud.

25 August Diffusion of Monsignor Saliège's diocesan letter protesting against the persecution of the Jews.

External resistance and the governments of Algiers (continued)

	against the entrenched camp of Bir Hakeim.
11 June	Koenig's forces manage to break through.
July	First meeting of the Comité Général d'Etudes created by Jean Moulin.
14 July	Free France becomes Fighting France.
28 July	Reorganisation of the Comité National (National Committee). Philip becomes Commissioner of Internal Affairs.
August	The BCRAM becomes the BCRA and takes charge of political action in France.
September	Brossolette returns to London, taking Charles Vallin with him.
23 October	'Cherchell Conference' between General Clark and emissaries from the 'Group of Five'.
2 November	Giraud–Murphy agreements.
7 November	Mobilisation of the conspirators in Algiers and Morocco.
9 November	Giraud arrives in Algeria.
15 November	On the basis of 'the deep agreement' of the Maréchal, Darlan assumes power in North Africa.
22 November	Clark–Darlan agreements.
23 November	The AOF rallies to Darlan.
27 November	Gaullian manifesto of P. Brossolette. Rémy–Grenier interview. Gaullists arrested in Algeria.
30 November	La Réunion rallies to Fighting France.

International relations and the conduct of the war (continued)

	Madagascar.
6 May	End of American resistance in the Philippines.
8 May	The Wehrmacht launch a new spring offensive in the Soviet Union.
21 June	Tobruk falls.
2 July	Sebastopol falls.
18–20 July	The Anglo-Saxon strategists plan 'Operation Torch'.
9 August	Gandhi and the leaders of the Congress Party are arrested.
18 August	Failure of the Anglo-Canadian raid on Dieppe.
4 October	Beginning of the Battle of Stalingrad.
22 October	Montgomery's counter-offensive in Egypt.
3 November	Rommel is defeated at El Alamein.
5 November	End of the fighting in Madagascar.
8 November	Beginning of 'Operation Torch'.
9 November	Suspension of the fighting in Algiers. Laval meets Hitler in Berchtesgaden.
11 November	The armistice is extended to Algeria as a whole and to Morocco.
13 November	The American military authorities enter upon the 'Darlan deal'.
19 November	Beginning of the Tunisian campaign.

Developments in metropolitan France (continued)

	in Alsace. German 'Gonio' vehicles enter the free zone.
4 September	Publication of the law relating to 'the use and orientation of manpower'.
October	Politico-literary event: *Les Décombres*.
4–8 November	Congress of the PPF.
11 November	'Operation Anton': the Wehrmacht enters the southern zone. Déat launches a revolutionary National Front.
12 November	Weygand is arrested by the occupying power. De Lattre is taken prisoner.
16 November	Pétain relieves Darlan of all his official functions.
17 November	Constitutional Act number 12 gives Laval the power to sign laws and decrees on his own.
18 November	Gibrat, Barnaud and Auphan resign. Introduction of the single salary allocation.
27 November	'Operation Lila': the armistice army is disarmed; the fleet is scuttled in Toulon. The daily tribute is raised to 500 million francs.
December	The film *Les visiteurs du soir* is shown in Paris.
8 December	First night of *La reine morte*.
28 December	Dissolution of the Tricolour Legion.
29 December	Gounot law on family associations.

Internal resistance (continued)

4 September	Beginnings of the NAP.
8 September	Frenay and E. d'Astier de la Vigerie reach London.
20 September	First number of *Les Lettres Françaises*.
23 September	Death of Charles Debarge. In London, decisive conversations between Frenay, E. d'Astier de la Vigerie, Passy and de Gaulle. General Delestraint becomes the head of the Secret Army. Publication of the first number of *Résistance*, edited by Renet-*Destrée*.
16 October	First tract of the non-communist Resistance to be signed by a political party. Establishment of a committee for the co-ordination of the movements in the southern zone. Creation of Action Ouvrière. Establishment of the NAP-*Fer*. The first *maquis* in the southern zone are set up.
December	Officers from the ex-armistice army found the OMA.

**External resistance and the
governments of Algiers** (continued)

**International relations and the
conduct of the war** (continued)

4 December   Darlan creates the Imperial
             Council.
10 December The Comte de Paris arrives in
             Algiers.
24 December Assassination of Darlan.
26 December Execution of Bonnier de La
             Chapelle.
             The Imperial Council
             appoints Giraud civilian and
             military commander-in chief
             in North Africa.

| **Developments in metropolitan France** (continued) | **Internal resistance** (continued) |

1943

1 January	Closure of the Uriage leadership school.
24 January	Destruction of the old port of Marseilles.
30 January	Creation of the Militia.
16 February	Three classes of men are conscripted for the STO.
1 March	Suppression of the demarcation line for 'full' French citizens.
21 March	Cardinal Liénart declares that to leave for the STO is not a conscientious duty.
26 March	Ministerial reshuffle in Vichy.
April	The weekly ration of meat falls to 120 grams.
4 April	Another heavy bombing raid on Boulogne-Billancourt, with many casualties.
5 April	The French State hands Blum, Daladier, Mandel, Reynaud and Gamelin over to Germany.
24 April	Death of the first Militia man to be killed by the Resistance.
2 June	Creation of the Militia *Franc-Garde*.
21 June	Rally of the Militia men of the RNP in the Coubertin stadium.
17 July	Congress of the Collaboration group.
August	Crisis at *Je Suis Partout*: Brasillach and his friends leave the editorial staff.
8 September	The Wehrmacht occupies the ex-Italian zone.
17 September	Speer and Bichelonne agree on the creation of *Speer-Betriebe* in France. Extremists publish the 'plan for French national retraining'.
13 November	The Reich forbids Pétain to broadcast. The head of the French State ceases to exercise his functions.
27 November	In Paris, first night of *Le Soulier de Satin*.
1 December	Doriot receives the iron cross.

1943

18 January	Arrival in London of Grenier, representative of the PCF and the FTP to Free France.
26 January	Fusion of the three principal movements of the southern zone: the birth of the MUR. *Maquis* take root in the northern zone.
15 March	In a letter to de Gaulle, Blum, in the name of the SFIO, declares support for the head of Free France, and at the same time defends the political parties.
26 March	The movements of the northern zone sign a 'declaration of the Resistance organisations of the northern zone'. The ORA, which has succeeded the OMA, is reinforced. The *'Service national Maquis'* is set up in the southern zone.
8 April	Long closely argued letter from Frenay to Moulin.
12 April	Daniel Mayer goes to London in the name of the SFIO.
17 April	The Perreux agreements: reunification of the CGT.
May	First number of the *Courier français du Témoignage chrétien*.
27 May	The CNR is founded.
9 June	Arrest of Delestraint.
21 June	Trap sprung at Caluire.
July	The movement leaders who are opposed to the presence of political parties in the CNR set up a Central Committee of the Resistance. An action Committee against deportation is set up.
14 July	Les Éditions de Minuit publish *L'Honneur des poètes*.
8 September	Election of G.Bidault as chairman of the CNR. A CNR office is set up. The first number of the *Cahiers de la Libération* includes what is later to become *Le Chant des Partisans*.

**External resistance and the
governments of Algiers** (continued)

**International relations and the
conduct of the war** (continued)

1943		**1943**	
13 January	Leclerc and Montgomery meet up.	*13 January*	Hitler's decree proclaiming 'total war'.
19 January	Peyrouton becomes governor general of Algeria.	*14–26 January*	Anfa conference between Roosevelt and Churchill; de Gaulle and Giraud are summoned to attend.
22 January	First meeting between de Gaulle and Giraud.		
27 January	Brossolette arrives in France: the 'Brumaire' mission.	*2 February*	Capitulation of Paulus' army corps at Stalingrad.
2 February	The army of Africa and the Leclerc column meet up.	*March*	Manstein counter-offensive.
12 February	F. Abbas' 'Manifesto of the Algerian people'.	*29 March*	The Mareth line is taken.
21 February	De Gaulle decides that the future CNR must include representatives from the political parties.	*19 April*	The uprising of the Warsaw ghetto.
		29 April	Meeting between Hitler and Laval.
23 February	Memorandum of the Comité National (National Committee) to Giraud.	*7 May*	The Allied forces enter Tunis.
		13 May	End of the Tunisian campaign.
26 February	Passy-*Arquebuse* arrives in France.	*10 June*	Dissolution of the Komintern.
1–25 March	Passy and Brossolette meet leaders of the movements in the northern zone.	*10 July*	Anglo-Saxon landing in Sicily.
		17 July	AMGOT is set up.
4 March	Jean Monnet arrives in Algiers.	*25 July*	Mussolini is relieved of his functions by the fascist Grand Council.
14 March	'Republican' speech by Giraud.		
16 March	Some of Giraud's entourage resign.	*26 July*	The Soviets launch a major counter-offensive.
17 March	The Comité National Français (French National Committee) insists that Giraud opens negotiations.	*17 August*	End of the resistance of the Axis powers in Sicily.
		8 September	Unconditional capitulation of Italy.
18 March	Guyana rallies to Giraud.	*12 September*	Mussolini is liberated by Skorzeny.
25 March	Catroux, representative of the (Comité National Français) (French National Committee), arrives in Algiers.	*25 September*	Smolensk is retaken.
		6 November	The Soviets recapture Kiev.
		12 November	Execution of Ciano and Balbo by the fascists.
12 April	Queuille arrives in London.	*29 November*	Beginning of the tripartite conference in Teheran.
19 April	Passy and Brossolette return to London. Jean Moulin extends the services of the Delegation.	*30 December*	The German lines are broken in the Ukraine.
7 May	Important report sent to London by Jean Moulin.		
14 May	Moncef Bey is relegated to Laghouat.		
15 May	Telegram sent by Jean		

Developments in metropolitan France (continued)

2 December	Maurice Sarraut assassinated.
4 December	Meeting between Abetz and Pétain.
18 December	Pétain accepts all the conditions imposed by the Reich.

Internal resistance (continued)

9 September	Uprising of the Corsican Resistance.
10 September	A detachment of the MOI assassinates Ritter, Saukel's adjutant in France.
5 October	End of the liberation of Corsica. Revers becomes the head of the ORA. Members of the Resistance plan departmental committees of liberation. François Lachenal publishes *Domaine française*, in Geneva.
11 November	Massive celebrations, some with tragic consequences, as in Grenoble. At Oyonnax, *maquis* forces parade through the town liberated for twenty-four hours.
25 November	Round-up among the students of Strasbourg who have been evacuated to Clermond-Ferrand.
29 December	Birth of the FFI.

External resistance and the governments of Algiers (continued)	**International relations and the conduct of the war** (continued)

	Moulin in the name of the future CNR, affirming the political primacy of Charles de Gaulle.
21 May	New instructions issued by Charles de Gaulle, accommodating the points insisted upon by the internal Resistance.
25 May	Meeting between Catroux, Monnet and Macmillan.
30 May	De Gaulle arrives in Algiers.
1 June	Peyrouton resigns.
3 June	Creation of the Comité Français de Libération Nationale (French Committee for National Liberation).
7 June	The CFLN is extended.
24 June	Martinique rallies to the CFLN.
1 July	Giraud leaves for the United States.
8 July	Probable date of the death of Jean Moulin.
23 July	Return of Giraud.
31 July and 4 August	The institutional rules of the CFLN are altered.
13 August	Pucheu is arrested.
25–26 August	*De facto* recognition of the CFLN by the Big Allies.
3 September	The ministers and the high-ranking civil servants of the French State will stand trial.
13 September	Shock batallions of the army of Africa land in Corsica.
15 September	Bollaert is appointed delegate general in France.
17 September	The decision is made to hold a meeting of a consultative Assembly. Military delegates to metropolitan France are named.
2 October	End of the dyarchy.
8 October	De Gaulle is in Ajaccio.
21 October	The Crémieux decree is re-established.
November	Nationalist demonstrations in the Lebanon.
3 November	Inaugural session of the consultatiave Assembly of Algiers.

Developments in metropolitan France (continued)

Internal resistance (continued)

1944

1 January	Darnand is appointed 'secretary general for the maintenance of order'.
4 January	Official suppression of the Chantiers de la jeunesse.
6 January	Philippe Henriot becomes secretary of State for Information and Propaganda.
20 January	Institution of expeditive court martials.
27 January	The Militia extends its activities to the northern zone.
February	First night of *Antigone*.
19–22 February	Repression of the mutiny in the Eysses prison.
16 March	Déat is appointed secretary of State.
	The Dordogne is put to fire and the sword by the B division.
2 April	The Ascq massacre.
9 April	'Red Easter' in the Jura.
10–25 April	Violent Allied bombing of the French territory.
26 April	Pétain in Paris.
28 April	Statement against terrorism by the head of the French State.
7–28 May	On German orders, Pétain tours the northern zone.
26–27 May	Violent Anglo-Saxon bombing of 25 large French

1944

5 January	The MUR integrate some of the movements in the northern zone and become the 'Mouvement de libération nationale'.
February	*Maquisards* go up to the Glières plateau.
21 February	Execution of 22 partisans of the MOI, condemned in the trial of the 'red notice'.
	Creation of the 'Corps francs de libération' by the MLN.
15 March	The CNR publishes a directive known as the 'programme of the CNR'.
26 March	With the aid of Militia men, the Germans launch an assault on the Glières plateau.
April	*Maquisards* go up to the Vercors plateau.
20 May	A mobilisation order goes out to *maquisards* who thereupon converge upon La Margeride.
6 June	The Resistance executes the various plans drawn up by the Allies.
7 June	Occupation of Tulle by the FFI.
	Proclamation of the 'Mauriac Republic'.
16–20 June	Dispersion of the *maquisards* after the fighting of Mont Mouchet.
18 June	Fighting round Saint-Marcel.

External resistance and the governments of Algiers (continued)

6 November	The CFLN is extended to include politicians and leaders of the internal Resistance.
8 November	Giraud becomes commander-in-chief of all the French armed forces.
16 November	Conflict between de Gaulle and the PCF over the choice of communist ministers.
27 November	De Gaulle decides to merge the special services.
10 December	French forces see action in Italy.
12 December	The Constantine Speech: de Gaulle announces greater Muslim integration.
18 December	Arrest of Flandin, Peyrouton and Boisson.

1944

11 January	Manifesto of Istiqlal.
27 January	Meetings between Churchill and E.d'Astier.
30 January	Programme of speeches by Charles de Gaulle at the African conference of Brazzaville.
31 January–2 February	Violent riots in Fez.
3 February	Bollaert and Brossolette are arrested.
7 March	In Algeria, order opening the first college to certain categories of muslims.
10 March	Instruction on the organisation of the Resistance. Parodi succeeds Bollaert as delegate general.
20 March	Execution of Pucheu.
23 March	The consultative Assembly pronounces in favour of the vote for women.
31 March	In Algiers, the COMIDAC decides upon a strategy of 'boltholes'.
4 April	Ministerial reshuffle: Grenier and Billoux enter the government.
8 April	Giraud appointed inspector general of the armies.
13 April	The 2nd AD embarks, bound for Great Britain.
15 April	Giraud withdraws to

International relations and the conduct of the war (continued)

1944

January	Massive air raid on Berlin.
5 January	Soviet troops enter Poland.
21 January	Leningrad is relieved.
25 January	In Italy, the Belvedere position is taken.
15 February	Beginning of the battle of Monte Cassino.
5 March	New Soviet offensive in the Ukraine.
4 April	Soviet troops enter Romania.
12 April	Abdication of Victor-Emmanuel.
13 May	End of German resistance at Monte Cassino.
4 June	Rome is taken.
5 June	Anglo-Saxon messages sent to the French Resistance.
6 June	Beginning of Operation 'Overlord'.
8 June	Bayeux is taken.
13 June	V1s fall on London.
14 June	American troops regain a foothold on the Marianne islands.
17–19 June	Conquest of the Isle of Elba.
23–24 June	Soviet offensive in the Baltic States.
26 June	Cherbourg is taken.
1 July	Conference and agreements of Bretton-Woods.
3–11 July	Battle of Minsk.
9 July	Liberation of Caen.
19 July	Saint-Lô is taken.
20 July	Assassination attempt on

Developments in metropolitan France (continued)

cities.

6 June	The *'Das Reich'* division sets out to 'exterminate the bands'.
8 June	Mobilisation of the Militia.
9 June	Hangings in Tulle.
10 June	The Oradour massacre.
13 June	Darnand becomes secretary of State for Internal Affairs.
20 June	Assassination of Jean Zay.
28 June	Philippe Henriot is assassinated by members of the Resistance.
5 July	Demonstration by collaborationist extremists.
7 July	Assassination of Georges Mandel.
12 July	Last council of ministers in Vichy.
5 August	Pétain disowns the Militia.
12 August	Laval meets Herriot near Nancy.
15 August	Departure of the last convoy of deportees.
17 August	Laval holds his last Council of ministers. The collaborationist press ceases to appear in Paris.
20 August	The Reich forces Pétain to leave Vichy for Belfort.

Internal resistance (continued)

3 July	Proclamation of the 'Vercors Republic'.
14 July	Popular demonstrations.
21–23 July	The Vercors 'bolthole' is attacked and demolished.
5 August	Liberation of Rennes.
9–11 August	Le Mans, Alençon, and Chartres are liberated.
14 August	Liberation of Dreux and Orléans.
15 August	Parisian police strike.
18 August	General strike launched by the trade unions.
19 August	Beginning of the Parisian uprising and occupation of the prefecture of police.
20 August	The truce is extended to Paris. Parodi is arrested. An emissary from Rol-Tanguy reaches the American HQ. Toulouse liberates itself.
22 August	Fighting flares up again in Paris. Eisenhower decides to have the 2nd AD move in.
23 August	Liberation of Grenoble and Aix-en-Provence.
25 August	Capitulation of von Choltitz.
28 August	Liberation of Marseilles.
29 August	Liberation of Nîmes, Montpellier, Narbonne.
30–31 August	Liberation of Rouen, Reims, Épernay, Châlons-sur-Marne and Saint-Dizier.

External resistance and the governments of Algiers (continued)

	Mazagran.
21 April	CFLN Order on the organisation of public powers in liberated France; women win the right to vote.
May	Commissioners of the Republic are named.
31 May	De Gaulle is invited to visit the United States.
2 June	The CFLN becomes the provisional government of the French Republic.
4 June	De Gaulle arrives in Great Britain; stormy meeting with Churchill.
6 June	Personal message from de Gaulle, calling upon the French to mobilise.
10 June	Koenig gives the order to limit action to guerilla operations.
14 June	De Gaulle lands on the beach at Courseulles; he installs F.Coulet as commissioner of the Republic at Bayeux.
6–10 July	Charles de Gaulle's visit to the United States and Canada.
1 August	The 2nd AD lands in Normandy.
9 August	Order re-establishing republican legality in metropolitan France.
23 August	The 2nd AD sets out for Paris.
24 August	The 'Leclerc' vanguard advances on the Hôtel de Ville.
25 August	The 2nd AD attacks German strongholds. Charles de Gaulle makes a tour from Montparnasse to the Hôtel de Ville.
26 August	Popular crowning of Charles de Gaulle.

International relations and the conduct of the war (continued)

	Hitler fails.
29–31 July	Avranches is captured after heavy fighting.
30 July	The Soviets reach the Vistula.
1 August	Warsaw uprising.
6–7 August	Failure of the German counter-offensive at Mortain.
10 August	Guam is retaken by the Americans.
13 August	Installation of the 'Lublin government'. German retreat in Norway.
15 August	Franco-American landings along the Provence coast.
19–21 August	American troops cross the Seine.
31 August	The Soviets enter Bucharest.

A phoney peace, a phoney war

In October 1938, in the immediate aftermath of the Munich conference, most French people were experiencing, in that salvaged peace, what Léon Blum called 'a cowardly relief'. Yet ten months later this phoney peace was to give way to a phoney war which a close analysis of the situation shows to have been its logical conclusion.

Throughout the years between Munich and the Liberation the French found themselves faced, often in dramatic fashion, by a double set of alternatives: whether to survive in a *pax germanica* or to make war; and whether priority should go to fighting the enemy from outside or to pursuing the internal conflicts that had been so marked ever since 1934. The burden of defeatism in the face of Hitler's Germany was thus aggravated by the deep political and social divisions that had been weakening the Republic ever since the great economic crisis of the thirties.[1]

How to be pro-Munich

Munich, a key reference for our contemporary history, a supreme insult in our political language, marks a decisive turning point in the destiny of Europe: while people believed that peace had been restored, the fact was that the Second World War was about to begin.

During that early autumn of 1938, it was impossible to be 'anti-Munich' with a light heart. It would have meant, in order to stop Hitler, risking war and its attendant slaughters as in 1914–18. A difficult choice but at least a simple one. Being 'pro-Munich', on the other hand, could involve different, even contradictory attitudes.

Fleeing in advance

During the twenties, the ruling coalitions had found themselves faced with two fundamental necessities: to keep the peace and to guarantee the security of the nation.[2] There were two opposed schools of thought as to how to fulfil this double task. The first sought to make France a policing agent for the Europe that had emerged from the peace treaties and, with a view to containing the 'Boche', placed its trust above all in military alliances: in the name of nationalism it did not exclude a policy of force, a policy symbolised by the occupation of the Ruhr. The second, prepared to accept a measure of revisionism under the control of the League of Nations, favoured a policy of peaceful coexistence with those who had earlier been conquered, so as to ensure peace and guarantee the country's security. The undeniable popularity of Briand stemmed in large measure from the fact that he succeeded in reconciling these two inclinations – although not without ambiguity: he managed to integrate Germany within the Locarno system placed under the joint guarantee of Italy and Great Britain while at the same time maintaining solid alternative alliances in the east.

The crises of the thirties upset this delicate equilibrium and tendencies became radicalised. In Germany, Hitler was carried to power on a nationalist, racialist and expansionist programme which planned, in the immediate term, to gather all the *Volk* of the German race into one great Reich and next to conquer its 'living space' – to the East – once it had come to a 'definite explanation' with France. Faced with these developments, those in power in France hesitated and tried out a number of policies in succession. They readopted the tactics of Briand but not with the same success: then, in 1932, they tried to form a kind of four-power directory (France, Great Britain, Italy and Germany), but the misgivings of the smaller powers and the demands of the Germans caused the project to founder. Finally, in 1934, Barthou, reverting to an earlier policy, planned a methodical encirclement of Germany. To this end it was necessary to strengthen the *Entente Cordiale* and keep Mussolini happy in his desire to maintain the status quo at Vienna. This policy resulted, in April 1935, in the 'Stresa Front', while in the East it was a matter of making an eastern pact which, to be effective, would have to include the Soviet Union, whatever the mistrust caused by the practices of the Komintern. So it was that in May 1935 Laval put his initials to a defensive Franco-Soviet pact.

The system was flawed, however. In 1935 the British, seeking to cut their losses, signed an Anglo-German naval treaty. As for Mussolini, he was prepared to stand guard along the Brenner Pass but only on condition that fascist Italy was recognised by her Stresa partners as a separate Mediterranean and colonial power. And the Stresa Front put up no opposition to the Ethiopian war. In the east, Poland, flirting with the Reich, proved a disappointment. In France, the alarm caused by the Bolsheviks was such that, despite the fact that the pact provided for no military agreement of any kind, the government delayed nine months before proposing its ratification to the two Chambers.

The decisive upset came between the summer of 1935 and the spring of 1936. In less than a year Hitler's Germany blew the safety valves applied in 1919 and undermined the Locarno agreement by reintroducing compulsory military service and – above all – by remilitarising the Rhineland. The bluff paid off: the French wavered, its protestations remaining purely formal even though its army's freedom of manoeuvre was substantially curtailed. The consequences were serious. How was such a rudderless government to be trusted? The Belgians withdrew from the French alliance and returned to a policy of 'independence'. Encouraged by this success, the Führer turned his attention to 'the question of Germans in foreign territories'. Austria was the first to be annexed, in March 1938, the Anschluss provoking no more than a measure of polite indifference punctuated by a few verbal protestations. France now found itself in a position that was, to say the least, ambiguous, for the Belgian change of heart and the construction of the Siegfried line made it difficult to come to the aid of her allies in the East, quite apart from the fact that, deducing their 'lessons' from the Great War, the 'big chiefs' were insisting upon a resolutely defensive strategy.

Such fleeing in advance can be explained first by the stresses arising from an *Entente Cordiale* considered by a succession of governments to be of the very first importance. The fact was that the French and the British did not see the German question from the same point of view. For one thing, the British, as islanders, considered themselves protected by the sea; for another, there were many financial and commercial circles in which it was considered desirable to make political allowances for the fourth most important client of the British economy. Finally, a fair number of the Conservatives, who were the dominant force in the cabinets of the period between the wars, considered that even a Hitlerian Germany was useful as a barrier in the path of Bolshevism. Neville Chamberlain, who had become Prime Minister after serving as Chancellor of the Exchequer, synthesised all these attitudes in what he called a policy of 'appeasement': a realistic appreciation of the situation dictated going along with Germany provided it behaved 'reasonably'. Faced with the remilitarisation of the Rhineland, as with the Anschluss crisis, His Majesty's government judged neither the security of France nor the balance of power in Europe to be truly threatened.

The ambiguities of pacifism

British policies carried all the more weight given that public opinion in France was profoundly disturbed by these new war threats. We should remember that the 1914 war exerted a decisive influence upon whole generations, producing a gut-reaction of pacifism without which the events at Munich would be incomprehensible. Veteran soldiers expressed it with their 'Der des Der'* which was simultaneously an appeal to enlightened patriotism, a rejection of narrow or jingoistic nationalism and a vehemently

---

* 'Der' is an abbreviation of *dernier*; thus 'Der des Der' means literally the last of the last. It was used a great deal during the First World War to mean 'the war to end all wars'. [Trans.]

declared will to prevent any recurrence of the barbarities of war.[3] Some literary and libertarian circles expressed these rejections with absolute slogans such as 'Servitude rather than war'. Furthermore, from 1935 onwards, the political map of pacifism became confused showing the, at first sight, somewhat surprising conjunction of a doctrinal brand of pacifism of social democrat inspiration together with a neo-pacifism loudly preached by erstwhile whole-hearted nationalists.

The 'sacred union'[*] had deeply divided the workers' movement and pacifists of a marxist inspiration. But in 1938 the PCF, while still accepting the Leninist theories of imperialist war, was counted among the war party by reason of the firm resistance that it favoured in the face of the aggression perpetrated by the fascist regimes. The SFIO, for its part, remained in principle faithful to the traditional pacifism of the Second International[4] just as it had during the twenties: the duty of the party was to take militant action to prevent a new war from crushing the working classes. And there were many militants (including Paul Faure, the secretary general of the party) who believed that no circumstances – even Hitlerism – could justify the violation of such a fundamental principle. They were opposed by the supporters of Léon Blum who, for their part, were convinced that Nazi expansionism made it necessary to undertake a painful revision of SFIO policies. The followers of Paul Faure were, however, in a strong position.

The traditional pacifists found altogether unexpected allies in the whole-hearted nationalists who had hitherto always been ready to cross swords with the Boche. This was a change of heart of some importance for it upset the balance of power. These converts to pacifism did not condemn war a priori and most of them remained convinced militarists. The reasons they gave for their selective pacifism rested upon the new socio-political situation: they now feared that a new conflict might – as in 1917 – provoke such turmoil that the whole western order would emerge from it fatally stricken. A war that was 'ideological' rather than 'national' would offer a springboard to the Soviet Union which was constantly lying in wait, for, as *L'Action Française* declared in March 1936, 'the Soviets need this war, to set off the universal revolution'. In France, the danger was all the greater given that the PCF, which had ventured out from its political ghetto, was singing the praises of Valmy[†] and even of Joan of Arc: even in the Chamber of Deputies it was said that 'We shall only accept the Franco-Soviet pact when there are no longer 72 Russian deputies sitting in our French Chamber'. In its most extreme form this neo-pacificism merged into defeatism: how, Maurras repeatedly asked, could such a 'dirty democrat' regime infiltrated

---

[*] In 1914 all political groups put aside their partisan interests and agreed to be represented in the government. [Trans.]

[†] In September 1792 the French Revolutionary forces defeated the Prussians at the Battle of Valmy and thus saved the Republic from invasion. [Trans.]

by 'Jews' and 'foreigners' dare to presume to wage war without knowingly planning the nation's suicide? That particular newly-adopted attitude, already detectable at the time of the Ethiopian war, was strengthened on the occasion of the ratification of the Franco-Soviet pact which was condemned by some 200 right-wing deputies chiefly on the grounds that 'the Russian alliance means war'; a headline in *L'Action Française* at the time of the remilitarisation of the Rhineland read: 'Above all, no war'. That wave of opinion grew following the victory of the Popular Front, swelled during the Spanish Civil War and broke at the time of the Anschluss. The 'great schism'[5] was complete; it was to have dire effects in September 1938.

'Peace with honour ... peace in our time'
These words were pronounced by the honourable leader of His Majesty's government as he left the aeroplane that had brought him back from Munich, brandishing a document countersigned by Hitler.[6] We are all aware of what happened next.

Within its 1919 frontiers, Czechoslovakia contained in the region of the Sudetenland a proportion of Germans regrouped in Bohemia that amounted to one fifth of its population. After 1933, these Sudeten Germans had voted massively for a party of Nazi inspiration under the leadership of Henlein. Its demands went far beyond mere administrative or cultural autonomy. Hitler saw these 'Germans in a foreign land' as the perfect instrument with which to undermine Czechoslovakia from within, her southern borders having been dangerously exposed ever since the Anschluss. In the face of his threats, the protection on which Czechoslovakia could call was twofold: a mutual Franco-Czech pact of assistance signed in 1925 and a Czech-Soviet pact concluded in May 1935 but which (at France's insistence) could only be applied once France had executed *her* obligations. Nevertheless, within four weeks Prague found itself trapped in a position of inextricable complexity.[7]

Hitler had drastically raised the stakes and thus, without striking a blow, had obtained from the British and the French more or less what he had demanded at Godesberg. A zone exceeding 30,000 square kilometres – that included almost a million Czech inhabitants – was immediately attached to the Reich; Hitler was now able to organise a plebiscite there without having to give any guarantees regarding the frontiers of what remained of the Czechoslovak State.

The French and the British had obtained their peace then.[8] Initially, it was a British peace: London took almost all the initiatives and went along with all the decisive deals (accepting that all zones more than 50% of whose inhabitants were German should be attached to the Reich). Furthermore, British policies displayed a remarkable continuity between the spring and the autumn of 1938: under no circumstances was the 'Czech question' to upset the policy of 'appeasement', whose economic and ideological bases we have discussed above. The best solution would have been to neutralise the troubled land of Czechoslovakia. In default of that, it was necessary to accept decisions which were, 'all things considered, reasonable'. The British Prime Minister was not at all sure that the Führer was a true gentleman but he was convinced that he would have to be trusted.

After that, it became a French peace: Daladier no doubt did make some attempts to limit the damage. (For instance, initially, he instigated the rejection of the idea of organising a plebiscite and forced the British to agree to guarantee the new Czech frontiers.) Overall, however, he conceded the essential points. (Since there was – in London – a plan devised by Beneš to avoid the worst, Daladier without argument accepted that zones where over 50% of the inhabitants were German should be attached to Germany.) And he allowed the British government to proceed almost entirely as it pleased. It is not too hard to account for such an attitude. Simplifying somewhat, the French politicians could be said to have fallen into three 'schools': first, those who declared themselves in favour of resistance and maintaining the 'eastern pact' – a tendency which lost many supporters as early as the beginning of September. At the opposite end of the spectrum were the partisans of 'appeasement'[9] who – following the example set by Georges Bonnet,[10] the minister of Foreign Affairs – were determined to 'accept any solution to the Czechoslovakian question that will avoid war'. The intermediate position was that of those who were resigned to capitulation, believing that – whatever the cost – it was necessary to secure a breathing space: all the indications suggest that Daladier was deeply convinced that – from every point of view – the French were not ready to face a war.[11] At all events, for the moment, those who believed in appeasement and those who sought a breathing space were united in their pro-Munich policy.

Twenty-four hours after the signing of the agreements, Poland was falling on the spoils, overrunning the Teschen region. Three weeks later, in a secret directive, Hitler was declaring his desire to 'crush all Czech resistance in Moravia and Bohemia'. It was quite clear from that moment on that the supporters of appeasement had lost their wager. The last shreds of French diplomatic policy disintegrated when the Soviet Union, which the pro-Munich press had described as 'having suffered the greatest defeat at Munich', also demonstrated its conversion to 'realism'. It was doubtful whether, in circumstances such as these, even the tactics of obtaining a breathing space were of any use; for there could be no certainty that even the (speeded-up) manufacture of Hurricanes and Spitfires could compensate for the elimination of an ally who also brought with her as a dowry three armoured divisions and several thousand aircraft. All in all, the verdict that Churchill pronounced a few years later remains vindicated:

'The government had to choose between shame and war. It chose shame and got war.'

Shame or relief?

For the time being, the French were relieved not to be at war and, to that extent, Munich represents an ending: it brings the post-war years to a close and is the apogee of the pacifism of the 'Der des Der!'

France had, with reservations, been much in favour of the Munich agreement. It was in Paris that its enthusiasm was most clearly expressed: Daladier was greeted as a hero; tension was followed by détente, flowers, emotion and the singing of the 'Marseillaise'. It was suggested that Chamberlain, the 'Lord of Peace', should be offered 'a house of peace on French soil'. *Le Petit Parisien* took the easier course of opening a golden book which received hundreds of thousands of signatures. The politicians were practically united: those who supported the Munich line by conviction were joined by those who did so opportunistically, including a number reputed to belong to the war party. Thus, Léon Blum wrote in *Le Populaire* of 1 October: 'Not a man or a woman in France can deny Mr Chamberlain and E. Daladier their rightful due of gratitude . . . We can all enjoy the beautiful, fine autumn sunshine'. On 4 October, a vote of confidence was passed in the Chamber of Deputies by 537 to 75 (73 communists, the nationalist Henri de Kérillis and the socialist deputy, Bouhey, who voted in defiance of the party whip). The government's declaration of 4 October won the approval of every member of the cabinet.

What carried most weight initially was – as we have already stressed – the gut or reasoned reaction of repulsion against war, against what Gamelin called 'a modern version of the battle of the Somme'. Louis Marin, who could not possibly be suspected of a luke-warm attitude, stated quite categorically on 1 October: 'On 28 September a sharp brake was applied to the frightful war party . . . We cannot possibly afford to offer the world a battle of the Marne every twenty years.'

Such reactions, to a large extent emotional and anyway exacerbated by the tension that had obtained the week before Munich, were effectively exploited by a number of activist minorities. They deployed every means at their disposal: urgent activity on the part of parliamentarians, general publicity and the posting up (on 28 September, with the aid of the PPF) of a defeatist proclamation by Flandin, pouring scorn upon 'the swindling of patriotism' perpetrated by 'hidden forces'; also a flood of articles in the press involving, among others, many organs of the extreme right, *Gringoire*, *Candide*, *Je Suis Partout*, *L'Action Française* and most of the so-called information press, including Bailby's *La Matin* and *Le Jour*. Much false information was spread and many threats were made.[12] As for the anti-Munich party, it formed a pressure group that was much less effective. While all of them were probably of the opinion that time was on Hitler's side and that, to save the peace it was necessary to be willing to risk a war, some were anti-Munich because they feared a rebirth of pan-Germanism while in the case of others it was above all because they were anti-fascist. However, this heterogeneity was of less account than the defections they suffered, in particular on the part of those who now supported the Munich policy out of opportunism. All in all, the left, which had nothing to gain from the progress of Hitlerism, wavered. The disruptiveness of Blum reinforced the pacifist section of the SFIO. The unity of the Confederal Bureau of the CGT failed to resist the pressure of events, while certain federations – for instance that of the post office and the SNI – served as the spearhead of attack for the 'Centre d'Action contre la Guerre' (Centre for action against war), set up in September. This was a regrouping of the 'Centre Syndical d'Action contre la Guerre (trade-unionist centre of action against war) that had been created in May and it included the vigilante committee of anti-fascist intellectuals and Pivertistes (anti-Stalinist communists), etc. A petition launched at the end of September collected within no more than a few days over 150,000 signatures in such circles as these. In the end, very few groups remained anti-Munich right the way through. The only ones that did were the PCF together with a number of federations from the CGT, the militants of the SFIO now regrouped behind Zyromsky, and a few figures from the right, in particular Henri de Kérillis who was now dragged through the mud by his former comrades and vilified as a 'paid lackey of Moscow and the Rothschilds'.

That point being established, it must be said the supporters of the Munich policies were of varying kinds. Some were opportunists, members of the war party who, when faced with Munich, nevertheless drew back from war. Léon Blum,[13] with his zig-zag reactions, is a good example: he lent his talents to the Czech cause even while congratulating Chamberlain upon going to Berchtesgaden; he was revolted by the Godesberg ultimatum but denounced as a 'crime against humanity' the rejection of an inter-national conference; he was pro-Munich on 30 September but thought better of it immediately afterwards. He himself cogently examined his own contradictory sentiments in an article published in *Le Populaire* on 20 September: 'War has probably been averted. But in conditions such that I, who have never ceased to fight for peace ... can feel no joy on that account and am torn between cowardly relief and shame.' Among these opportu-nists we also find, apart from Blum's supporters, a fair number of christian-democrats and conservative Jacobins such as Mandel.

Their inability to control the course of events assimilates them to a certain extent to those who favoured seeking a delay through Munich, for whom Munich represented a respite to be exploited in the best French interests. This appears to have been the underlying conviction of Daladier.

Scratch the surface there and you would find the veteran fighter – the man who had spent almost the entire war in the front line and who, on 9 December, claimed the satisfaction of having refused 'out of motives of firmness' to project the French into war and sacrifice another million or two French peasants.[14] However, he did not return from Munich feeling very proud of himself and the remark that Gamelin attributes to him sums up his position well enough: 'It wasn't brilliant, but I did what I could.' Quite a few radicals and independent socialists as well as a fraction of the nationalist right wing fit into this category.

Those who were in favour of Munich 'by conviction' were quite a different matter. These were truly partisans – from every point of view – of a veritable policy of appeasement. Their strategic experts were not without hopes of forging a third force which would make it possible to avoid consultation with both Berlin and Moscow. Many Italophiles were numbered among their ranks. The most machiavellian of them were counting on a neutralisation of both the Slav and the German peoples. This category included the right-wing radicals, the big battalions of conditional nationalists from the PSF, the Republican Federation and the Democratic Alliance, and also a sizeable proportion of Paul Faure's supporters from the SFIO.

Finally there was the extremist group who were to remain supporters of Munich come wind or high water – or at least until after the Prague coup.[15] They too claimed to be acting in the name of realism but it was a realism in which their ideological animosities were barely concealed. On 20 September, *L'Action Française* exclaimed: 'Peace, peace; the French do not wish to fight for the Jews, nor for the Russians, nor for the freemasons of Prague'. Analysing this attitude in greater depth, Thierry Maulnier, one of the better-known spokesmen of the young right, carefully spelt it out:

> The parties of the right considered that, in the event of war, not only was defeat or devastation possible for France but also that a defeat of Germany would mean the undermining of the totalitarian systems that constituted the principal bulwark against the communist revolution, perhaps against the immediate bolshevisation of Europe ... It is regrettable that the men and parties in France that held this opinion did not, for the most part, make it plain. For there was nothing inadmissable about it. I am even of the opinion that it was one of the principal reasons, if not *the* principal one, for not going to war in September 1939 (*Combat*, November 1938).

In the main, these people accepted, even preached the policy of 'a free hand in the east', that is to say the eradication of Bolshevism by Hitlerism. Such lines of thought found many an echo among a fair number of men of order as well as among those of the extreme right. And Mounier[16] was not mistaken when he wrote, after Munich, 'It is impossible to understand the behaviour of that fraction of the French bourgeoisie unless one can hear it muttering under its breath: Rather Hitler than Blum.'

Daladier's France

Daladier came to power in a France in which, nevertheless, the whiff of war was strong. It must be recognised that the man was popular and the regime appeared to find a new lease of life. But that was not enough to bring the crisis of the thirties to an end.

Pressures

When he agreed to form a government in April 1938, Edouard Daladier found himself in a more or less comfortable position. In January, a bitter altercation in the Chamber had brought Chautemps, one of the leading lights of the radical party, into confrontation with the communist Ramette and this resulted in a retreat on the part of the socialist ministers: the Rassemblement Populaire was in a bad way. After the collapse of a ministry of transition presided over by Chautemps himself, it fell to Léon Blum to show that a Popular Front majority was still viable. However, this second Blum ministry lasted barely five weeks. There were a number of reasons for this. In the first place, only a few weeks earlier Léon Blum had not managed to include in his ministerial team either Thorez or Marin: the spokesmen for the parliamentary right had – with one or two exceptions – declined his invitation for all the world as if national unity was the prerogative of the right and synonymous with social conservatism. Another reason was the hostility manifested against Blum personally; this had reached such a climax of virulence that, on 6 April, in the Chamber itself, cries of 'Death to the Jews' had broken out repeatedly. Finally, the Senate was waiting to 'get' Blum on the issue of his economic programme. His plan was coherent but interventionist, involving, in particular, a levy on capital. The senators surpassed themselves (47 in favour, 214 against) but even in the Chamber of Deputies it had been only grudgingly that full powers were granted him: it was not beyond the bounds of possibility that the next majority would be one of a so-called 'republican concentration'.

With the Blum option removed, Daladier, the official leader of the radical party, who had been Minister of War without interruption ever since June 1936, was invested on 12 April by 575 votes to 5. Neither the Chamber of Deputies nor the Senate raised any difficulties over granting him full economic powers. Both clearly had high expectations of him: all that remained was for him to make his choices.

The first thing he had to do was develop an economic policy. Following the early successes of the reflationary policies of Blum's first government, the situation had become a gloomy one: inflationary tendencies had reappeared and were being aggravated by protectionism and the relative stagnation of industrial production. The monetary and financial situation was even more precarious: the fact was that an increasing deficit was to be expected for public finances and also an increase in the floating debt, since 50% of the State's expenses were devoted to paying off the 1914–18 war and to preparing for the next one (a very significant increase in the armaments effort had been agreed as early as September 1936). Matters were not improved by an excessively high circulation of paper money nor by repeated appeals to advances from the Banque de France, following the failure of financial and monetary markets. On the exchange market, the franc, described first as 'elastic' and later as 'floating', was undergoing a marked depreciation. Chautemps' procrastinations had further weakened the relatively healthy situation left him by Léon Blum in June 1937.

On the political level, there was a rift between the 'collectivists' (that is to say interventionists) and the 'liberals', who were in favour of returning to a free trade economy. Two questions were the order of the day: exchange controls and – more importantly – the forty hour week that most wage-earners considered to have been an intangible victory of June 1936. There can be no doubt that many trade-unionists had over-estimated the mobility of the skilled work force and had created a number of bottlenecks through their inflexible application of the law. However, the employers had very little interest in the macro-economic consequences of the law: what was at stake at this time was something else, the cost of wages. Some employers wanted to pay as few hours as possible at the overtime rate and others were anxious not to diminish their buying power.[17]

Social problems were no less pressing. The climate remained extremely strained despite arbitration procedures. Ever since the unprecedented rout that the application of the Matignon agreements* had represented, the business bosses had been waiting for their battle of the Marne (to borrow Simone Weil's well-found expression). When that came about it would be possible to bring the militant trade-unionists on each shop floor to heel and, on a national level, break the 'trade-union power' which, for once, depended on the trade-unionism of the masses (in the spring of 1937, the CGT had four million members). As for the trade unions, which had been more or less on the defensive since Blum's government had fallen, they were determined at all costs to defend the social gains of 1936. In April 1938, 130,000 wage-earners from the private sector were on strike while a hundred or so factories were under worker occupation in the Paris region alone.

On a parliamentary level, finally, would it prove as easy as in 1926 and 1934 to dissociate the government majority from the electoral majority?

---

* Concluded on 7 June 1963 between the CGT and the employers, they gave official recognition to the unions and granted the 40-hour week. [Trans.]

The Popular Front had certainly lost some of its dynamic force but in the bye-elections the majority of electors – even when it came to a decisive vote – were still demonstrating their confidence in the coalition of the Rassemblement Populaire. Chautemps, who had been in power since June 1937, had tried above all to temporise. In April 1938, the new president of the Council resolved, in the first instance, to rally together radicals, socialists and independent socialists but, for super-subtle reasons of its own, the SFIO declined to participate; thereupon, in preference to a rather too limited coalition of the centre–left, Daladier settled for a government of concentration and handed out four portfolios to the right.

Daladier enjoyed a solid reputation as a Jacobin. Within the party he had – in opposition to the partisans of the national union (coalition government led by the right) – always favoured the strategy of a cartel of the left and he had become an advocate for the Rassemblement Populaire. Now, this party[18] was, to say the least, divided, reflecting as it did the contradictory sentiments of that part of the middle class, the notables of the provinces, for instance, who voted 'on the left' more to establish their distance from the reactionary and clerical group than in order to emancipate the fourth estate. These members of the third estate were mistrustful of the proletarian turmoil initiated by the series of strikes, and fearful of 'ideological' warmongering. Their feelings of reticence, which had become clear in the autumn of 1936 at the Congress of Biarritz, were played up by the right wing of the party which was becoming steadily stronger. It controlled an impregnable majority in the Senate, led by Caillaux, newspapers of renown such as *L'Ère Nouvelle* and *La République*, and a number of important federations – such as the Fédération du Nord led by Émile Roche – and it was in a position to produce an available leader in the person of Bonnet.

The demise of the Rassemblement Populaire

Daladier did not really have any definite strategy, to start with. Although he acted vigorously to put a stop to the occupation of factories, he claimed support from the majority of May 1936 and his first spate of decree-laws were inspired, rather, by reflationary policies. On 21 August, however, he opted for the first of his half-measures: in a broadcast address on the radio, he declared that he wished to 'get France back to work' and that he was authorising concerns working for the national defence to ignore the law on the forty hour working week.

By the autumn, people had made up their minds. Munich had provided the first impetus to that process: the communists' response of a negative vote was swiftly followed by the socialists' abstention over the granting of full powers. Daladier decided to take the initiative on the occasion of the radical congress which was held in Marseilles from 26 to 29 October and resulted in a triumphant success for him: he delivered a violently anti-communist speech and allowed the right wing of the party – which was determined to exploit Munich to the full – totally to dominate the congress. On 10 November, the radical part of the radical socialists officially ceased to participate in meetings of the Rassemblement Populaire.

In November this development was accentuated by the arrival of Paul Reynaud at the Ministry of Finance. After vigorously opposing exchange controls, he forced the initially reluctant government to accept a new economic strategy devised with the assistance of a cabinet of brilliant young technocrats: in order to relaunch the economic machine, it was necessary to rely first and foremost upon the mechanisms of a liberal economy, the encouragement of private investment and the recall of capital invested abroad since 1935. To these ends it was necessary to forego any further social measures and lift all 'interventionist' obstacles such as not only price-controls but also the restrictions on the terms on which employers recruited labour and the length of the working week. Finally, on the political level, it was necessary to administer a decisive psychological shock, take the plunge and squarely accept the fact that confrontation with trade-unionist power was now inevitable.

Thus, Reynaud's decrees lifted virtually all price controls, instituted a 'Hatchet Committee' to do away with budgetary appointments in the public services and, of course, tackled the forty hour working week. That law was not actually repealed but so many qualifications were introduced that it lost all meaning. And significant cuts were made in rates for overtime work. The militant rank and file reacted sharply and there were violent clashes, at the Renault works among other places.

The desired confrontation took place on 30 November.[19] At a meeting in Nantes, those attending the CGT congress unanimously condemned the 'poverty decrees' and decided in principle on a general strike. To put a stop to repression on the part of the employers, while still retaining control of the protest movement and aiming a warning shot in the direction of the government, the Confederal Bureau – not without hesitation – gave the order for a general strike, to be defensive and limited both in time (not to exceed twenty-four hours) and in space (strike action to take place on the spot with no demonstrations or meetings). Daladier, urged by Reynaud and the right wing of the party to adopt an intransigent position, refused to enter into any negotiations and resorted to extreme measures: the requisitioning of public services, the occupation of supply depots by troops, the use – for the first time – of tear-gas by the police. The measures proved effective; the day passed almost like any other and a fair number of strikers – some of whom were unconvinced of the timeliness of the strike – returned to work. To some extent, however, the strike was supported: among civil servants and white-collar workers the proportion of strikers was less than 10% but it was in excess of 50 or even 80% in the metal, chemical and building industries in the red suburbs. Nevertheless, through its lack of cohesion and firm objectives, it was a semi-failure that the government, with its extremely repressive measures, was to turn into a fiasco and exploit as such politically. Aided by the public authorities, the employers had won their Battle of the Marne: the Popular Front was well and truly dead.

Seen chronologically, the impulse that led Daladier to make his first move came from what he considered to be the insufficient productivity of factories working for the national defence. There can be no doubt that, after that, a good many of the more prominent members of the party tried to exploit to the maximum the popularity that Daladier had acquired at Munich. But his underlying motivations were of a socio-political order. It would seem that Daladier, who had carried the radicals into the Popular Front, was having second thoughts about the bases of the alliance. Speaking before the party's Executive Committee, meeting on 15 January 1939, he now rejected 'the alliance between the proletariat and the third estate' because, he declared – and the argument is not without force – 'if the third estate at any time gains the impression that it has been sacrificed and that in reality neither its ideas nor its efforts are respected, divorce is inevitable'.[20] The party was in duty bound to dispel the 'discouragement' of these 'middle classes, the backbone of democracy'.

By a remarkable effect of compensation, votes from the right[21] were now making up for those unforthcoming from the left. Foreshadowed on 17 June 1938 in a procedural vote, the majority of concentration was confirmed in the autumn and consolidated during the spring, with the PCF and the SFIO finding themselves isolated on virtually every political division. With the exception only of a handful of individuals, right-wingers had shifted from an attitude of expectancy to positive cohesion. To tell the truth – and this was Daladier's best parliamentary card – they hardly had a choice, so great was their fear that the coalition of the Rassemblement Populaire might be revived. Their efforts to rally were not simply tactical: the fact was that Daladierism offered a number of guarantees to the right-wingers. First – and this was fundamental – anti-communism: the PCF had been relegated to a political quasi-ghetto. This anti-communist trend was all the more significant given that the communist surge had levelled out and the Party was having difficulty in recuperating its losses from the autumn of 1938.[22] Another reason for satisfaction was the brake put upon the CGT. Claiming that the nature of the strike of 30 November had been political, the government justified a campaign of repression which it implemented with as much brutality as in 1920. That was glaringly plain in the private sector where – at a conservative estimate – 800,000 wage-earners were temporarily sacked; it was a way of systematically sifting out trade-unionists and 'ring-leaders'.[23] Then, in February 1939 again, Daladier, on the grounds of a lack of confidence, made sure than an amnesty for actions committed during the strike was rejected. Finally, the tactics of the Ministry of Finance facilitated the rallying of the right. Its policies were increasingly liberal, stripped of all 'demagogy' (with Reynaud insisting that an imperative choice had to be made between the 'social' and the 'economic').

The results obtained were encouraging: a few black areas remained, to be sure – if only on the level of employment – but wholesale prices had been stabilised and production was increasing. If the causes for this recovery – uneven but undeniable – are still a matter of controversy,[24] there can be no doubt that these policies enjoyed the support of the propertied classes as is demonstrated by the massive repatriation of capital, the sum total of which has been estimated at 35 thousand million francs (i.e. 25 thousand million new francs).

With the passing of time, Daladierism was gaining ground. The president of the Council was in a position to govern through decrees and votes of confidence. Here and there, there were grumbles about his 'dictatorship', but Daladier remained unconcerned. Furthermore, as from the autumn of 1938, electors approved his policies by plebiscite and meanwhile the radical party was winning new supporters. Now what remained was to make provision for the future. The right wing of the party got what it wanted: the return to proportional representation went a long way towards resolving the thorny problem of electoral alliances for the second term.[25]

The spring saw the beginning of a new, final stage. After the Prague coup, Daladier strove to create a climate of national unity. He took care not to clash openly with the socialists, was more ready to praise the 'voluntary efforts of the working classes' and meanwhile made open overtures towards the catholics.[26] To avoid spreading dissension, he persuaded Lebrun to be a candidate for the presidency of the Republic and ensured his re-election at the end of the first term; then, on 29 July, he decided to extend the Chamber of Deputies to June 1942. But he still had to agree to an armistice with the CGT and the extreme left and this he could not bring himself to do: so national unity remained incomplete.

A new lease of life for the regime?

The disasters of 1940 might give the conveniently simplified but misleading impression that the regime had been moribund already in 1939. That assessment deserves at the very least to be modified. Contemporaries themselves were under the impression that the regime had put itself to rights, firstly because vestiges of the undeniable renewal occasioned by the Popular Front still remained and secondly because Daladierism was better than a period of transition: so Daladier enjoyed great popularity. Many a Frenchman could identify with the portrait he painted of himself: 'I am a son of France, a bit rough but free and intending to remain so . . . a man who is first and foremost a sincere patriot, a patriot as those who used to be called "schoolmasters" taught him to be . . . a republican who understands the language of the humble worker . . . because he is himself the son of a worker and faithful to his origins'.[27] The average Frenchman dear to Herriot's* heart was, furthermore, grateful to him for having brought 1936 to an end without serious damage, as *L'Ère Nouvelle* of 1 November 1938 emphasised: 'The revolution of June '36 is well and truly over. It did not prove necessary to resort to a *coup d'état* or to a fascist movement to put it down. The simple exercise of governmental responsibility sufficed. President Daladier has done well by the Republic and the motherland.'[28] The decline of the extremist right wing was also evidence of the fact that the regime was behaving honourably. Certainly, as we have seen, the extreme right remained effective as a pacifist pressure group but for the time being it was no longer a serious threat to the regime as such: conspirators of the 'Cagoule' ilk (revolutionary right-wing group employing terrorist methods) had been dispersed; the French popular party which had been expected to be the 'great' fascist party was being torn to shreds by one split after another and *L'Action Française* was in political jeopardy. Equally significant was the electoral stagnation[29] of the French Social party despite its desire to play the parliamentary game: for many French people who in the past had come down on the side of resentful or violent opposition, Daladier and the radicals had taken the place of La Roque.

However, for reasons that have as much to do with the immediate circumstances as with the failings of a worn-out system, all this did not mean that the open crisis of the thirties was now a closed chapter; the relative erosion of the forces of the left was to be a significant factor in 1940. This was obvious in the case of the SFIO, the party that held such a pivotal position. It could muster a kind of unity[30] when it was a matter of condemning the economic and social policies of the government, but that was so as to mask as well as possible the particular profound dissensions that were undermining it, with everyone concerned wishing to step into Jaurès' shoes. Irreconcilable disagreement separated those who maintained that to fight against fascism – even by accepting the risk of war –was the only way of fighting for peace and those who countered that to fight for peace *was* to fight against fascism. Having narrowly carried the day at the Montrouge extraordinary congress in December 1938, Blum was obliged at the Nantes congress, in May, to resign himself to agree with Paul Faure on a compromise motion: it was the only way to avoid a clash. Ever since 1939 the party had been suffering cruel electoral reverses; by 1940 it was no more than a shadow of its former self. The crisis in the CGT was perhaps even more fundamental, for the divide that separated the pacifists from the war party to a large extent corresponded to the abyss that separated anti-

* Herriot had coined the phrase 'Français moyen' – Mr Average. [Trans.]

communists from communists. As early as October 1936 Belin, the joint general secretary, together with a group of his 'confederate' friends (ex-CGT), had launched a newspaper, *Syndicats*, to counter the thrust of the 'unitarians' (ex-CGTU). The latter had made so much progress (in less than two years they had acquired a majority in four new federations and in twenty or so new departmental unions) that by November 1938 they controlled just over half the voting delegates. Their success[31] stemmed not only from reasons of a socio-professional nature (the rising tide of the trade-unionist movement in the private sector had swollen the membership of federations already controlled by the unitarians in 1936) but also from their dynamism, their militancy which was attractive to young people sensitised by the Spanish War and the struggle against fascism. The partial failure of the strike of 30 November did the rest. In 1939 at least two CGTs were struggling for survival. The situation was such that the extremely anti-communist Dumoulin went so far as to write, in March: 'For our part, we wish no longer to limit ourselves to the vengeance-seeking trade-unionism of the past but to enter upon the path of a constructive trade-unionism that would not exclude collaboration with the employers.' In the spring of 1939 it still had perhaps 2,500,000 members; by May 1940, following a new split in September 1939, it could muster barely one million. The CGT by now carried no weight at all.

This weakening of the leftist groups was all the more alarming for the regime since a fraction of classic right-wingers – taking over from the extreme right – were, for their part, ready to step into the breach. Ever since 1936, these 'conservatives who had quarrelled with the Republic', as Stanley Hoffmann calls them,[32] had felt that indirect control of power was no longer enough, once the system had allowed an irruption – this time quite legal – of the extreme left and the 'collectivists'. For the time being there was, to be sure, nothing to be done about it but the time would come when it would be necessary to have done with this Third Republic and establish in its place not so much a fascist but an authoritarian and ultra-conservative regime, on the model of Salazar's Portugal. The defeat was to liberate such forces all the more easily given that they felt it had justified their temporary pacifism.

All in all, it was this violent confrontation between pacifists and the war party, together with the deep fears caused by 1936, which combined to leave the regime so fragile. And furthermore, the rejuvenation the regime had enjoyed in 1936 had not eliminated the flaws in the system (far from it). Despite what is often suggested, these stemmed not so much from the dislocation of the strictly constitutional machinery, rather from the mean-minded political practice of the successive generations of notables who had exclusively dominated the democracy that they controlled. When put to the test that democracy emerged as remarkably threadbare.

Die for some Polacks?

Barely six months after Munich, the French and the British were forced to face the facts: Hitler, who was decidedly no gentleman, had torn up the scrap of paper from Munich and was playing with fire. It became necessary to resign oneself to war, but the manner in which it broke out caught everyone by surprise.

The illusions and disillusions of the Pact of Four

As the Munich agreement was trampled underfoot, Paris sought to exploit the Pact of Four.[33] The climate clearly favoured compromise. For some – Daladier among them – it was a question of consolidating the respite gained; for others, Bonnet for example – the Franco-German *entente* needed to be firmly strengthened: this was the 'new spirit'. These policies were symbolised by a pact of non-aggression. Ribbentrop came to Paris on 6 December to sign it, despite the anti-semitic frenzy of the 'Night of Glass'.[*] He was welcomed with great pomp. Furthermore, in a private discussion with the arrogant minister of the Reich, Bonnet indulged in a number of dangerous confidences: he waxed loquacious about 'indifference with regard to the East', a phrase that Ribbentrop understood or interpreted as a pledge.

But these policies were soon brought up short. Paris reacted strongly to Rome's announcement, on 30 November, of its claims to Nice, Savoy, Corsica and Tunisia. The Prague coup finished off the 'new spirit'. Skilfully exploiting the rivalries between the various nations, Hitler contrived, in less than a week, to persuade the Slovaks to place themselves under the protection of the Reich and turned Bohemia and Moravia into a 'protectorate'. It was clearly no longer simply a matter of freeing the *Volksdeutsche* from oppression but of domesticating the Slavs. For many of the pro-Munich party this was the end of their illusions: pan-Germanism was rearing its threatening head again. A few days later, Lithuania was obliged to give up Memel; and Mussolini, not to be outdone, invaded Albania on Good Friday.

This double Italian and German offensive split the Munich block. Daladier, while still trying to buy as much time as possible, was determined to abandon 'not an inch of our territories nor a single one of our rights'.[34] Bonnet's influence was on the decline and the secretary general of the Quai d'Orsay, Alexis Léger, was turned into a kind of second Minister of Foreign Affairs. Firmness became the order of the day: it was aboard a warship that Daladier visited Corsica, Tunisia and Algeria to reaffirm the French

---

[*] The Nuit de Crystal took place on 9 November 1938 when 'spontaneous' demonstrations were organised in Germany in which Jewish houses, shops and synagogues were looted and burned by the Nazis. [Trans.]

presence. Guarantees were offered to Poland, Romania and Greece; to win over Turkey, France ceded to the Levant the sanjak of Alexandretta, a territory that had been under litigation for the past twenty years or more; above all, Paris strove to persuade London to conclude a defensive alliance with Moscow. In France itself the extremely germanophile France-Allemagne Committee was dissolved and the future ambassador, Otto Abetz, who had been over-prodigal with 'cultural' funds, was prevented from returning to Paris.

Resolution and pressures

With the exception of the extreme right and a number of impenitent pacifists, the politicians and public opinion were in favour of this firmness and, significantly enough, condemned the article entitled 'Must we die for Danzig?' published by Déat in *L'Oeuvre* on 4 May, in which he declared: 'French peasants have absolutely no desire to die for the Polacks'. Inveterate pacifists were now not nearly so well received and, during the last days of the peace, were quite reduced to impotence. On 2 September only Bergery, in the Chamber of Deputies, and Laval, in the Senate, tried to oppose the war.[35] The only demonstration of any significance was the circulation of a tract produced by the libertarian Lecoin entitled 'Immediate Peace' and signed by about thirty intellectuals (Giono, Alain, Margueritte), trade-unionists and politicians; all the latter, however, – led by Déat himself – subsequently renounced their signatures. Frenchmen were not setting out on a fresh and joyous war any more than they had in 1914. The difference was that in 1939 there had already been 1914. The most prevalent feeling seems to have been a mixture of resolution (to have done with it, once and for all) and resigned surprise (according to opinion polls, the first ever conducted in France, the majority of French people in 1939 thought that war was increasingly inevitable but were at the same time putting off the evil day). At all events, there was no defeatism worth mentioning.[36]

Yet Munich had been more than a mere parenthesis. In the main, in fact, there was no break in the continuity between the choices of the pre-war period and the various positions adopted subsequently, up until 1942: anti-Munich nationalists were to be quick to enrol in the Resistance, 'conditional' nationalists[37] were to seek desperately for a third way between Berlin and London; neo-pacifists were to be divided between State collaboration and the collaborationists; and the Blumists, who outnumbered the Paul-Faurists, were to find themselves in the ranks of the clandestine Socialist Party. It should be added that not all the hard-line pacifists had disappeared: Maurras' followers were making their stand within the frontiers of France itself and sacrificing the Poles (despite the fact that the latter were no vulgar 'dirty-democrat' Czechs) for, as Maurras

himself wrote on 29 August: 'After three partitions, Poland died once but
was resuscitated. So long as France survives, it will always be resuscitated
... In difficult cases it is the child who must be saved; well then, let us save
France first, if we want to save the future of Poland.' As for Flandin and his
friends, they were pressing for 'imperial withdrawal', while Paul Faure, for
whom Poland was not worth 'the death of a single wine-producer from the
Mâconnais', was pressing for disarmament and economic collaboration.
All in all, a policy of firmness could include plenty of variations. Many of
those now rallying to such a policy were 'conditional' nationalists still
seeking a way out that would make it possible – ideally with the help of Italy
– to resist pan-German expansionism while maintaining intact the *cordon
sanitaire* flung around the Soviet Union.

The staggering events of the summer of 1939

By the spring of 1939 tension was already high. After a period of
neighbourliness, German–Polish relations became strained. The Poles had,
after all, been determined ever since 1920 to resist any intrusion whether
from the Soviet Union or from Germany. They accordingly refused to
comply with the Reich's demands: there could be no more question of
ceding Danzig than of admitting that the roads and railways that crossed
the 'Polish corridor' were outside their territory. Thanks to the existence of
the Franco-British guarantees, relations between Warsaw and Berlin
practically ceased and meanwhile violent incidents occurred in Danzig. It
appears to have been in May that Hitler decided to 'settle the Polish
problem' (and that included the Baltic States); if it came to armed conflict,
military operations would – because of the weather – have to begin before
the autumn.

The development of the situation depended largely upon the attitude of
the British. Following the Prague coup, the champions of appeasement had
been obliged – whatever the cost – to modify their strategy. While it had not
turned them into warmongers (negotiations with a view to reaching a
'gentlemen's agreement' went on right up to the last days of the peace),[38]
they were no longer prepared to tolerate any other use of force. This is why
London decided to offer the States which appeared most directly threatened a 'guarantee' which would, in theory, suffice to make Hitler draw
back. Meanwhile, however, the British did not relax at all in their profound
distrust with regard to the Soviet Union. The latter had been fearful of the
consequences of a western strategy that encouraged Hitler to feel that 'his
hands were free in the east' ever since 1937 and was now taking its own
precautions: in March, in the course of the 18th Congress of the CPSU (b)
(Communist Party of the Soviet Union (bolshevik)), Stalin had seen fit to
emphasise that the Soviet Union was not prepared 'to pull chestnuts out of
the fire' for the sake of the fine bourgeoisies of the West.

It was, precisely, the Soviet Union that was becoming the stake in a last rush to form alliances.[39] The French and the British were – in theory – the better placed to win. Nevertheless a full four months passed before any plan for a political agreement was produced, and even then no military agreement was envisaged.[40] The delay was, to a large extent, imposed by the British who accepted the Soviets as auxiliaries but not as allies, as can be seen from the instructions given to Admiral Drax on his mission to Moscow: 'The British government must not enter into engagements that would tie her hands in any circumstances.' It is true that in the meantime the Germans and the Soviets had reopened communications;[41] these first contacts, bedevilled by a reciprocal distrust, had been in no way conclusive. At the end of July, however, as soon as the tripartite military negotiations were announced, Berlin upped the stakes.

The game was played out during the first fortnight in August and the Franco-British did not play their hands skilfully.[42] Their delegation reached Moscow – taking their time – with no mandate to adopt any position on the question of the passage of Soviet troops through the territories belonging to Poland and Romania. On 16 August, after four days of talks, Vorochilov refused to go any further so long as there was no 'decision on the issue of cardinal importance for the Soviet party, namely on the question of the passage of Soviet troops through the territories of Poland and Romania for joint actions of the contracting parties against the common enemy'. The negotiations remained in a stalemate from 18 to 21 August, the day when Daladier, anxious to come to some conclusion whatever the cost, authorised General Doumenc to 'sign in the best common interests'.[43] Too late: 'somebody', as Doumenc noted, was already expected. That somebody, as we know, was Ribbentrop. It was no doubt Franco-British procrastination that provoked the Soviets, with two irons in the fire already, into playing their German card on 17 or 18 August. As for Hitler, he wasted no time; he hurried on negotiations and, as soon as he could, concluded a commercial treaty that would be very useful in the event of a blockade. Ribbentrop, who had arrived in Moscow on 23 August, settled the outstanding questions in less than a day and, that night, Stalin in person, 'knowing how much the German people love their Führer', declared his delight at 'drinking to his health'. Also being celebrated was the signature of a pact of non-aggression valid for ten years which, by forbidding the signatories to join any group of hostile powers, put an end to the tripartite negotiations. A secret protocol, in an appendix, determined spheres of influence and, in particular, sketched out a fourth division of Poland along a Narew–Vistula–San line. Hitler – with his fundamental opportunism – had scored a decisive point against the dumbfounded French. Thanks to the pact, the Reich would not have to fight, as it had in 1914, on two fronts. As for Poland, it fell even more easily. All the same, it proved more difficult to gauge the deeper motivations of Stalin and Molotov. The tactics decided upon certainly tallied with the prudent line of constructing socialism in one single country. However, the thesis of gaining a respite – necessary and secured in 1939 – was to a large extent invalidated by the disasters of the year 1941. There is good reason to wonder whether, as in the early thirties, Stalin did not in every respect miscalculate the forces of Hitlerism and did not mistakenly over-simplify in seeing fascism as the ultimate transformation of inter-imperialistic contradictions. If that was not the case, it has to be admitted that in the end he decided in favour of the deal that seemed most advantageous in the very short term, namely that which annulled the treaties of 1919–20.[44] At all events, the immediate effect of the pact was to plunge most communist militants – particularly in France – into the most profound disarray.

There can be little doubt that the German–Soviet pact accelerated the outbreak of war.[45] If we are to believe the Secretary of State for Foreign Affairs, Weizäcker, on 30 July Hitler was still hesitating and suspending his decision until after the results of the German–Soviet talks. And a precise chronological study reveals that it was only after 20 August that Hitler initiated the war of nerves; on the 22nd he decided that military operations would commence on the morning of the 26th.

On the evening of the 25th, nevertheless, the Führer pulled back, suspending the implementation of the 'White Plan': during the day he had received two pieces of bad news: the evasions of Italy, which considered itself insufficiently prepared for a European war and – more importantly – the conclusion of the Anglo-Polish treaty of alliance. Hitler reckoned that it would, notwithstanding, be possible to isolate the Poles. Thereupon followed extremely complicated negotiations between Berlin and London, with Hitler brandishing now the stick, now the carrot.[46] When the Poles refused to accede to the German demands, tension rose to such a point that Mussolini, who was worried, proposed that a conference be organised for 5 September. While not turning down the proposal, Hitler was convinced that the British would not honour their obligations and at the last moment would abandon the Poles.

On 1 September at 4.15 a.m., the German radio station of Gleiwitz was attacked by German common-law criminals disguised as Poles. This 'armed attack' provoked a 'policing operation' of a quite exceptional kind, involving armoured divisions and bombers. The French had decided on 23 and 24 August what their position would be in precisely such an eventuality and on the 31st[47] they made good their undertaking: the Upper Council for National Defence and the Council of Ministers had refused to go along with Bonnet who, following the conclusion of the German–Soviet pact, had desired to 'slacken' the Franco-Polish alliance; a majority had been of the opinion that the army was ready and that any new German gains would create an irreversible situation of hegemony. The order for mobilisation went out on 1 September. Even then, two further days elapsed before Great Britain and France entered the war, both for military reasons (the need to protect the concentration of troops) and constitutional ones (war could not be declared without the assent of the two Chambers), and also on the pretext that the offer of Italian mediation was still viable. All in all, the position was not unambiguous, a fact the Poles bitterly deplored. On 2 September, before the two Chambers, the government contented itself with asking for a vote for the sum of 70 thousand million francs of extraordinary credit 'to tackle the obligations of the international situation', which amounted to semi-fudging the issue. On the evening of the second, however, the situation became clearer: at London's stipulation that, as a preliminary, the German troops should cross back over the frontier, Mussolini withdrew his proposal of mediation.[48]

Because of disagreements between the Home Fleet and the French general staff, the British and the French were not able to deliver a common ultimatum: on 3 September, the British Empire found itself at war at 11.00, the French empire at 17.00.

To cross the Siegfried line or to bomb Baku?

The war that the French entered upon was thus less sordid than its reputation has made out. The initial choices were not without a certain coherence.[49] But in the long run the non-war turned into the phoney war.

The initial choices

The French and the British, strategists and politicians alike, had taken up almost identical positions on two fundamental points: the war would be a long one and the outcome would depend upon the results of the economic war; for the present, no offensive should be launched on the western front. This strategy rested upon a triple postulate defended by the French general staff: in the first place, the fortifications of the Siegfried line and the Belgian government's refusal to abandon its policy of 'independence'[50] made any general offensive problematical and chancy. Secondly, a continuous defensive line was inviolable, fire-power being more effective than movement: the Germans would be broken either on the Maginot line or by the French battle forces deployed from the Ardennes across to the North Sea. This resolutely defensive strategy was in line with another fundamental preoccupation: there should be no repetition of 1914, 'the blood of France must be spared'. In the event of the Wehrmacht invading Belgium, the plan was to advance as far as an Antwerp–Namur line (this was the 'Dyle manoeuvre'). This was to avoid having the decisive shock of encounter take place on French national soil. Finally, in the opinion of all the strategists, time was on the side of the Franco-British: the English would be able to strengthen their expeditionary forces (they had so far sent only two divisions to the continent) whilst the Reich, already undermined from within and strangled by the blockade and the economic crisis, would capitulate.

For a while, this programme was, broadly speaking, respected. The rout of the Polish troops reinforced Gamelin's decision to mount in the Sarre no more than 'a phoney offensive' taking the form of 'reconnaissance and surprise attacks' (which levied a toll of 200 German dead). By 27 October, virtually all the 'conquered' territories had been evacuated. The Poles, crushed by the onslaughts of the Panzer divisions and the Stukas and shattered by the unexpected and brutal attack mounted in the east on 17 September by the Soviets, were abandoned to their unhappy lot. On the 27th Warsaw fell. By 12 October Poland had been divided up for the fourth time: it was a Soviet Poland with its 'German' territories annexed by the Reich and 'a government for the occupied Polish territories'. The élite corps of the Reich's secret police, the *Einsatzgruppen*, were detailed to carry out the physical liquidation of the entire intelligentsia and all the Polish notables. As for the other 'sub-men' (the Slavs), they would provide the new Europe with a 'cheap work force'. Poland's calvary had begun. Even as he launched a 'peace offensive' which was to remain without results, Hitler was setting 12 November as the date for the beginning of operations in the west. But weather conditions unfavourable to Luftwaffe action caused several delays: this was the period of the non-war. In the end, operations at sea were more decisive: despite its numerical inferiority, the Kriegsmarine with its 'pocket battleships' and its 'packs' of submarines enticed the Home Fleet into action.

It was principally at a diplomatic level that confrontation was taking place but the results obtained fell short of the efforts deployed. True, the Allies derived considerable satisfaction from the new 'law of neutrality' voted by the American Congress, which lifted the embargo on arms and war materials, thus giving considerable advantage to the maritime powers. Where Italy was concerned success was less spectacular: while she remained a 'non-belligerent', she was unhappy with the blockade. The fact was that Mussolini was hoping for defeat for the western democracies whose colonial spoils he expected to come his way. Finally, the Soviet problem loomed as large as ever. On 28 September, the 'Treaty of Delimitation and Friendship' consecrated the carving up of Poland, whilst according to the terms of the agreements signed in October 1939 and February 1940, the Soviet Union was supplying Germany with strategic materials, rare metals and petroleum (to the tune of one-tenth of the Reich's needs). Official pronouncements aimed against 'the false flag of the struggle for democracy' did not augur any better for the evolution of USSR strategy.

All in all, the situation in this *Kriegspiel* was far from incoherent[51] and the first results of the German 'Yellow Plan'[52] corresponded to the calculations of the French general staff. But the outcome of the campaign was to be decided elsewhere: the French 'big chiefs', unlike the leaders of the Wehrmacht, had foreseen everything except a mobile war (the French armies had at their disposal more than three times as many pieces of artillery but three times fewer anti-tank guns and half as many fighting aircraft). A strategy that left almost all the initiative to the enemy in this way was an arduous undertaking to carry right through from start to finish. Already the blockade was far from complete and France was running into many difficulties in mobilising its economic forces.

The fine days of the non-war

Initially, however, this unusual war seemed to be going well enough. The politicians[53] appeared to be unanimous, the ministerial reshuffle was quite well received[54] and Daladier seemed in control of the situation.

Supplies appeared to be getting through and the outbreak of war had caused no panic. Nevertheless, it was necessary to play a close hand and in particular increase the production potential while at the same time avoiding an extensive disordering of the economic machinery. Between September 1939 and April 1940, the State spent 700 million francs a day; if a serious price slippage was to be avoided, credit circulation would have to be slowed down and the 'circuit closed'; somehow or other a way would have to be found to soak up the widespread surplus of buying power. To keep 'prices stable', Paul Reynaud increased taxation (with deductions at source for wage-earners) and took out loans. But he was anxious – even as he did so – to promote a 'liberal war economy': exemptions from exchange controls multiplied, rationing was finally introduced and, in order to maintain 'the leverage of private initiative', derisory rates of taxation were introduced on the income and profits of the non-salaried. Right up until the spring, however, it seemed possible that Reynaud might still win out.

The trends in public opinion seemed more worrying, although there were not really serious grounds for concern as yet. There was no fear of a 'fifth column'.[55] The most dangerous of such French Nazis as there were was probably a little known publicist of the Grand Occident (a very small group of the extreme right), one Ferdonnet who, on Radio Stuttgart, repeated in French what Goebbels had already declared, namely that 'England was intending to fight to the last Frenchman'. Besides, many of the future collaborationists were too much put out by the German–Soviet pact to react at all: those who, like Labreaux, a *Je Suis Partout* journalist, were 'hoping that France would have a short and disastrous war' in the main kept such good wishes to themselves.

Developments in the PCF[56] were indubitably arousing graver concern. Initially, after the first moment of stupefaction, the leading party line repeatedly emphasised that the communists would be 'in the front line' to assure 'the country's security' and 'defend the liberty and independence of all peoples' and on 25 August the first issue of *L'Humanité* to be seized carried the headline 'The French nation united against Hitler's aggression'. It is also well known that the communist deputies voted in favour of the 70 thousand millions-worth of extraordinary credit.

As from 20 September, the PCF adopted a quite different line, imposed upon it by the leaders of the Komintern:[57] it endorsed the partition of Poland and denounced the 'imperialist war' with virulence, demanding an immediate halt to hostilities; meanwhile, the leaders of the PCF went into hiding and on 4 October Thorez[58] deserted, initially to 'somewhere in Europe' and later to the Soviet Union, to become a 'fighter against the imperialist war'. By the latter half of October, the PCF was putting about the new official line from the Komintern: not only was this an imperialist war ('the people of France have been assigned the mission of executing the orders of the bankers of London') but it was not even a struggle against Hitlerism. To quote Molotov, the party was determined to 'destroy the legend of the so-called anti-fascist nature of the war'.[59] However, that did not mean that it was the moment to preach 'revolutionary defeatism' in the strict sense of the term,[60] or to 'copy the directive of transforming the imperialist war into a civil war'.

However, this new type of pacifism produced no more than mediocre results. It is true that the organisation of the PCF was seriously affected by the repressive measures taken against it – and for a Leninist type of party that was a severe handicap. Retaliation measures were introduced even before it had declared itself pacifist. Already on 25 August, newspapers had been seized and on 26 September (following the invasion of Poland by Soviet troops), all organisations of the PCF or that obeyed 'the orders of the Third International' were dissolved by decree. After the end of the parliamentary session, a military examining magistrate on 8 October consigned to prison about forty deputies who were members of the new 'Groupe Ouvrier et Paysan Français' (French worker and peasant group) on the grounds of 'intelligence with the enemy'. And these measures came on top of the deep dissensions by which the Party was already riven. All the same, if it hadn't been for the systematic repression which produced reflexes of solidarity, defections might have been even more numerous (as it was, more than a quarter of the parliamentarian members left the PCF). At all events, the party machine was operating in neutral gear: the people who had been fighting against fascism ever since 1934 were loath to concede the possibility of 'neutrality' in the face of Nazism. It was only towards the end of the winter that the clandestine PCF, playing upon the aggravation of the economic and social situation, was able to recapture some of its audience in certain sectors of the working class.

From the non-war to the phoney war

The invasion of Finland[61] by the Red Army on 30 November speeded up events, for the Finns, while not rejecting mediation, defended themselves with determination and held off the Soviet forces. The Soviet aggression and the Finnish resistance provoked deep emotions in public opinion generally (a cry went up for 'aircraft and cannon for Finland') and set off a violent anti-Soviet and anti-communist campaign. Most of the parliamentary debates at this point were devoted to the disqualification of the members of the 'Groupe Ouvrier et Paysan Français' which was ruled on 20 February. A few weeks later 44 deputies were given prison sentences.

It was to a large extent these reactions that prompted the conversion of the general staff, the Quai d'Orsay and the politicians to a wider encircle-ment strategy.[62] Operations would now be carried out beyond the frontiers of France itself and at the same time efforts would be made to cut off Germany's strategic supplies (Swedish iron and Soviet petroleum). For-bearance with regard to the Soviet Union was less in order than ever now that she had become an 'objective ally' of the Reich. So operations were mounted in Scandinavia and preparations made to send a party of volun-teers to Baku (there were even plans to launch a pincer movement starting from Finland and the Caucasus). However, the British government temp-ered these excitable impulses. It was convinced that the Berlin–Moscow agreement would eventually go up in smoke and was anxious to deal as tactfully as possible with the Soviets. On 11 March, the first attempt to open an encircling front miscarried with the signing of the Finno-Soviet armistice[63] which, in the event, was to lie at the origin of the first political crisis of 1940.

Meanwhile, the internal situation had deteriorated, not dramatically but unrelentingly. On the 'front', the men were getting very exasperated, the leadership was confusing defensiveness with inertia and boredom affected every level. Efforts were made to involve the army in work in the fields, a thousand footballs were distributed, 'hot grogs' dispensed, a few rose-bushes planted along the earthworks of the Maginot Line and Maurice Chevalier was engaged by the army theatre. But all to no avail, morale had gone. Lassitude was increasing throughout what appeared to be an increas-ingly vain wait.

The lassitude felt in the front lines had varied repercussions in the rear.[64] The old rancour of the conscripted peasants – whose pay was a derisory pittance – again came to the surface in the face of the men in 'special postings' who, for their part, received a proper wage. And the economic situation was deteriorating too; the 'circuit' had not been closed: one third of the money distributed by the State was failing to find its way back into her coffers.[65] It had proved necessary to accept a *de facto* devaluation and – above all – it had not been possible to control prices.[66] As for wages, these had been virtually frozen,[67] while war-profiteering was ostentatious. Here and there people could be heard saying that 'they were not going to do themselves in just for the sake of the two hundred families* and the king of England'.

Daladier had also lost ground in parliament. Although he was President of the Council, National Defence Minister, Minister of Foreign Affairs and the chairman of countless committees, he found himself less and less in control of the situation. The political 'pause' came to an end. The right was now seeking above all to settle its scores with the Popular Front. Intrigues started up, a committee of parliamentary liaison was set up by the defeatists among whom were to be found Flandin, Montigny, Tixier-Vignancour, Laval and five socialists.[68] On 9 February, following a strong *pro domo* plea from the President of the Council, the Chamber, meeting in secret committee, was still giving Daladier's policies its unanimous approval. But he had become vulnerable; he was being criticised for governing by decree, for playing the dictator 'so as not to have to fight Germany' said some, 'so as not to have to fight the Soviet Union', shouted others.

---

* Originally the 200 principal stock holders of the Bank of France (the only ones entitled to vote). Gradually it came to mean a financial oligarchy. [Trans.]

2

The disasters of 1940

The year 1940 trails behind it a strange kind of notoriety: the most reputed French army since 1918 totally collapsed in a disaster which made the 1870 campaign look like an acceptable withdrawal. The war was lost by the military, by a high command outmanoeuvred in every domain. And the military crisis then turned into a political one that swept aside a regime sold out by its élite and delivered over into the hands of minority groups thirsting for revenge for 1936. The great majority of shattered and bewildered French people looked to Philippe Pétain in the hope of finding in him a paternal guide and in the armistice a relative measure of protection. But as from 25 June, the day on which hostilities ceased in metropolitan France, it was a completely new order that began.[1]

France goes off to war

An ambiguous political crisis

Less than six weeks after receiving renewed powers from both Chambers, Daladier tendered his resignation. The fund of sympathy upon which the Finns were drawing and the virulence of anti-Soviet feeling had placed him in an awkward position once 'heroic Finland' had been obliged to conclude an armistice. On 14 March, 60 senators manifested their dissatisfaction by abstaining. Five days later there was a total of 300 abstentionists in the Chamber; at this point Daladier decided to resign.

Paul Reynaud, president designate of the Council, who was pushed to the fore by the 'war party' decided that the best way to form a government[2] was to draw upon a judicious parliamentary mix: his cabinet included no less that 21 Ministers and 14 Secretaries of State (*Le Canard enchaîné* remarked humorously that Monsieur Reynaud 'had hired the Vélodrome d'Hiver for the first plenary session of the inner cabinet'). He had, certainly, admitted the socialists (without Blum) through the back door, and eliminated Bonnet, but the government lacked homogeneity and was in no sense a war cabinet. If he was to get as far as an investiture of office, Reynaud would have to take on the displeasure of some of the right wing who were critical of this 'cocktail mix of "Marseillaise" and "*Internationale*"', the dissatisfaction of the radicals and, above all, the manoeuvres of the partisans of a *paix blanche* in the West (which would bring the war to an end, without territorial modification in the west). That was a tall order. In the event, he owed his narrowly won investiture (268 votes in favour, 156 against, 111 abstentions) to an excellent speech by Blum, to Mandel who 'lobbied' for him and to Herriot who made it possible to delay the poll.

It had been an alarming session and the results of the voting could hardly have been more ambiguous: over half the deputies from his own party – the Alliance Démocratique – had voted against Reynaud, who was saved by the socialist votes. It was imperative to take some initiatives, but in what quarter? A fair proportion of the politicians were demanding that these should be against the Soviet Union. Furthermore, with Daladier still the Minister of National Defence, Reynaud did not really have his hands free. And was he, personally, the right man for the situation? Although he had been crowned with every success in his professional, political and social life, he nevertheless remained relatively isolated. His stand in favour of devaluation, his defence of the armoured divisions dear to the heart of Colonel de Gaulle and his membership of the war party had made him seem a relatively dangerous marginal figure. His touchy and over-confident nature had won him enemies as well as friends. Moreover, his whole set, starting with his busybody of a mistress, Hélène de Portes, was a target for criticism. He has sometimes been described as 'a man favoured by life',[3] successful in whatever he undertook; but he was not 'the man' for this crisis.

Relaunching the war of encirclement

It would be going too far to draw a systematic contrast between a cautiously defensive Daladier on the one hand and a constantly reckless Reynaud on the other.[4] Reynaud – who was not a First World War veteran – was a member of the war party and he was keen to cross swords with Germany as soon as possible. But they both – in mid-March at all events – favoured the same strategy of encirclement. Reynaud, it is true, added his own personal variation: being now convinced that time was not necessarily on the side of the Allies, he wanted to lure the Wehrmacht on so that it 'used up its men, resources, armaments and petroleum'. By concentrating upon two selected theatres of operation, the USSR and Scandinavia, it would be possible not only to cut off two fundamentally important economic routes (for Soviet petroleum and Swedish iron[5]) but also to force both the Soviet Union and the Reich to show their hands. It was, to say the least, risky. The British remained sceptical. On 28 March, a joint communiqué declared that each of the two allies 'made a mutual undertaking not to negotiate or conclude any armistice or peace treaty during the present war except by common agreement';[6] but the British responded to Reynaud's plan with a shower of objections and postponed all plans to invade or bomb the Caucasus. Following close consultations, Reynaud, who wanted to act quickly and, in his usual way, make a big splash, eventually wrung from the British an agreement to the effect that a Franco-British expeditionary force should hold itself in readiness to prevent the Reich from obtaining supplies of Swedish iron-ore.

Some alarming semi-failures

Hitler, who was still waiting for fine weather, had not initially included Scandinavia in his plans. Being now alerted, he decided to steal a march but without committing himself too far. The operation was carried out with brio: Denmark was occupied in less than four hours, Norway within forty-eight. The Franco-British were caught by surprise: it was ten days before the first Tommy set foot on Norwegian soil. Having failed to establish a bridgehead at Namsos, the Allies concentrated their attacks upon Narvik which eventually fell to them on 27 May. Four days later, the rout in France compelled the expeditionary force to pull out.

The record so far was not encouraging. In the first place, the trap set by Reynaud had rebounded against the Allies. Secondly, from a military point of view, the Germans had outclassed their enemies. The Kriegsmarine had been severely mauled by the Home Fleet but the Luftwaffe had made the RAF dance to their tune and had sunk plenty of His Majesty's ships.

However, these half-failures had not made much impression upon the morale of the French, who were hungry for action. Furthermore, Reynaud had confidently assured Déat that 'Germany had committed a colossal strategic error in sending its fleet to Norway', and he proclaimed to all and sundry that 'the iron route had been cut'. His own cabinet seemed to be giving him more cause for concern. Relations were not good between the president of the Council and his Minister of National Defence who only communicated with each other in writing and no Council of Ministers was able to meet between 14 April and 9 May. On that day, reckoning that he was not in a position to direct the war to his own liking and laying the blame for the setbacks in Scandinavia upon General Gamelin, Reynaud announced that the latter no longer had his confidence, while Daladier, for his part, defended the general. The conflict between the two was now an open one. Reynaud tendered his resignation to Lebrun who urged him – as a precaution – to keep this a secret. And the next day he indeed withdrew it, for the Wehrmacht had moved into action.

The Blitzkrieg hurricane

The French general staff were awaiting the German attack with confidence. It began on 10 May. Six weeks later in the stupefying lightning war, the

French army had disappeared lock, stock and barrel, crushed on all fronts.[7]

The breakthrough

With the return of fine weather, on 10 May Hitler launched an offensive in the grand style. The element of surprise was fully effective: the commander of the Dutch forces was obliged to capitulate in open country on 15 May and meanwhile the Belgians, taken by surprise, had allowed the Albert Canal to be crossed. Engaging immediately upon the Dyle-Bréda manoeuvre, Gamelin precipitated the Franco-British into the trap Hitler had set for them. The French battle corps and the only army held in reserve poured into Belgium while the Germans proceeded to implement their Manstein Plan, concentrating their greatest efforts upon the key positions of the Allies who were quite lacking in large-scale fortifications. After all, in 1934, Pétain had declared: 'After Montmédy there is the forest of the Ardennes. The Ardennes are impregnable if we take special precautions there ... As the front will have no depth, the enemy will not be able to engage action there. And if he does, he will be picked up as he emerges from the forests. So this sector is not dangerous.' On the strength of that opinion of his, the sector in question was held by troops with insufficient training and inadequate arms. Having passed through the Belgian Ardennes without difficulty, nine Panzer divisions, supported by élite divisions and in particular by fighter planes, pressed on towards the Meuse. There they established three bridgeheads, at Monthermé, Dinant and Sedan. By 15 May, the Germans had the way open before them at both Dinant and Sedan and three days later they reached the Oise.

After five days of fighting, the Germans had won all that they had tried in vain to obtain throughout the whole of the First World War: they had broken through the continuous front. A breach of 90 kilometres divided the French positions. But this strategic surprise was complemented by even more dramatic tactical deficiencies: once the 9th army had gone up in smoke, there was no reserve army to prevent the Germans from doing the unbelievable and attempting a sickle movement to surround the armies of the north which were pinned down in Flanders. The French were now paying for the mistakes of their 'big chiefs'.

The rout

The French High Command was inadequate on every count. 'In his Vincennes hide-out ... Gamelin ... was working out strategic reactions in his laboratory' (Charles de Gaulle). The commander of the north-eastern front, General Georges, seemed to have been struck with indecisiveness. Hunziger, who was in command of the 2nd army was, on 14 May, still reporting that 'the enemy's advance has been blocked'. Orders and counter-orders followed one upon another in such rapid succession that the 2nd armoured division eventually called up as a reinforcement was unable to reach the battlefield in good order and was destroyed before ever engaging battle.

The outcome of the French campaign was decided on 26 May when the last attempts to re-establish a continuous front failed. The French High Command in the end authorised the use of the armoured divisions, but three of these were swallowed up in the battle; although the fourth, under the command of Colonel de Gaulle, was successful in undermining the enemy position near Moncornet, it was unable to prevent the Germans from establishing three bridgeheads on the Somme and reaching the sea on 20 May. Forty-five Franco-British divisions were caught in the hoop-net of Flanders. The new commander-in-chief, Weygand, who had been recalled from the Levant, did attempt a new manoeuvre to allow them to break out, but it failed by reason of a series of contretemps, misunderstandings and disagreements between the French and the British.

The fate of the armies of the north became even more critical as the Belgians gave way. Once Leopold III had capitulated on 28 May, the Franco-British, with their backs to the sea, found themselves defending a kind of U position that was shrinking tragically all the time.

Impotence

Hitler then made two tactical mistakes: he called the Panzers to a halt, not so as to humour London – as has falsely been alleged – but in order to avoid getting his armoured divisions bogged down in 'the marshlands of Flanders' and risking a new battle of the Marne; secondly, he put his trust in Goering, who had been bragging about winning the day with the Luftwaffe alone – the Luftwaffe being, it is true, the most politicised division of the German armed forces. By dint of desperate efforts, the French and the British managed to turn this unexpected respite to their advantage. The Wehrmacht rounded up 50,000 prisoners, came into possession of considerable materials, shot down over 100 RAF aircraft and sank some 200 vessels; but 330,000 men – 130,000 of whom were French[8] – escaped from the trap.

Providential though it seemed, this success was at the very most no more than a retreat in good order. On the continent – now abandoned by the British expeditionary force – the situation was dramatic. To defend a front 280 kilometres long, stretching from the lower Somme to the Maginot line and backing onto a number of rivers and canals, Weygand had at his disposal no more than fifty divisions. To cap it all, on 10 June Italy entered the war. To Mussolini's wrath, her troops never managed to take over more than a few frontier valleys and half of Menton but they did at least pin down the Alpine army.

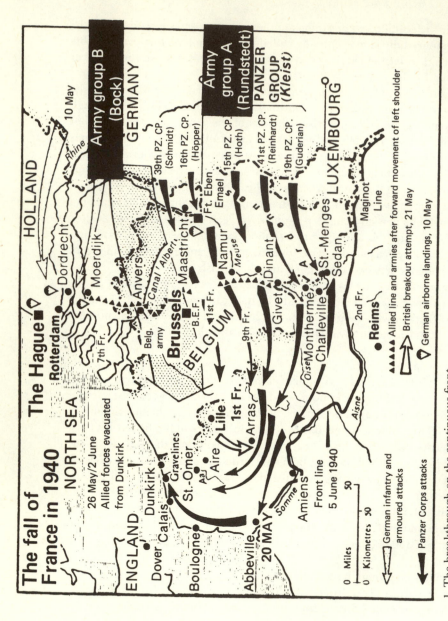

1 The breakthrough on the continuous front

Source: Liddel Hart, *Histoire de la Seconde Guerre mondiale*, Fayard, 1973, p. 70. Reproduced by permission of Editions Fayard

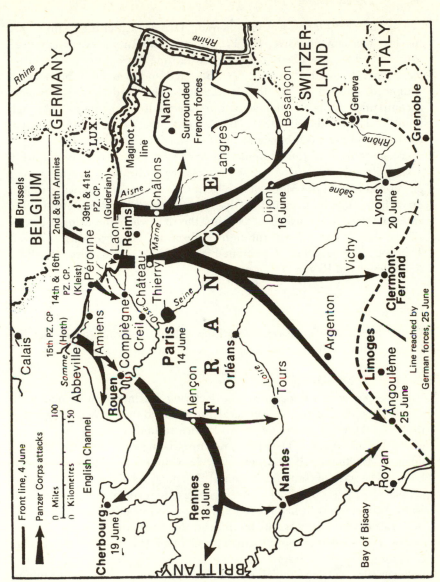

2 Blitzkrieg and the French rout

Source: Liddel Hart, *Histoire de la Seconde Guerre mondiale*, Fayard, 1973, p. 70. Reproduced by permission of Editions Fayard

35

The balance of forces was too unequal. Two days after the beginning of the last German offensive, the French positions in the west had been overrun and the lower Seine was lost. On 12 June, Weygand gave the order for a general retreat. Paris had been declared an 'open city': the German vanguard entered it on the fourteenth. The leader of the Reich, accompanied by Speer – his favourite architect – drove victoriously through it on the dawn of the eighteenth. By that date, the 'coordinated defence of the territory' had been blown to smithereens. The Panzers were ahead of everyone (during 16 June Rommel advanced 240 kilometres without firing a single shot), advancing on three axes: eastward to take the armies positioned behind the Maginot line from the rear,[9] south-eastward to join up with the Italian forces and, lastly, south-westward to gain control of the entire western seaboard. On 25 June, the day when the armistice took effect, the 'front' passed through Bellegarde, Aix-les-Bains, Voiron, Tournon, Saint-Etienne, Clermont-Ferrand, La Châtre, Montmorillon, Angoulême and Royon.

France adrift

In the face of the invasion, everything collapsed. France, just like the French refugees on the exodus routes, was falling apart.

The deficiencies of the politicians

Reynaud was nevertheless declaring his intention of making a stand. He sacked fifteen or so generals, superseded the secretary general of the Quai d'Orsay, Aléxis Léger, and twice reshuffled his cabinet, eliminating his adversaries (Daladier) and introducing men who had his confidence (Baudouin, Bouthillier and de Gaulle, who was appointed Under-Secretary of State for National Defence). As a show for 'the good people of France', he led his entire government to hear High Mass in Notre-Dame, where he had the relics of the protective saints paraded. At his side, rather like a prestigious figurehead, he positioned Philippe Pétain, whom he appointed vice-president of the Council. He chose Weygand as his commander-in-chief, despite his seventy-three years, not so much because he knew 'the secrets of Foch', but because he had the ear of the high-ranking officers. But he was much less sure of himself than he wished to appear. And he was less and less in control of the situation: it was in vain that he ordered a 'national storehouse' to be set up in Brittany and the transfer to North Africa of the most recently mobilised troops.

The machinery became totally jammed as from 10 June, the moment when the ministers and high dignitaries of State became obliged to set out on their own particular version of the Tour de France. On the twelfth and the thirteenth, they were scattering to the Touraine to a score or so of different castles. On the fifteenth, they were in Bordeaux, chosen in preference to Brest. It was during this migration that the government had to take its most dramatic decisions.[10] A thousand rumours were rife. Weygand, resolutely unperturbed, announced on 13 June that Thorez had installed himself in the Elysée! Emmanuel d'Astier de la Vigerie comes close to the truth when he describes Bordeaux as 'a South-American capital in which every public building sheltered a plot or a conspiracy.'[11]

The fate of the country was in the hands of twenty or so more or less representative individuals. It is true that the parliamentarians were not keen to remain in session without intermission and the most vociferous of them – with Lavel and Marquet at their head – expressed such defeatism that the president of the Senate, Jeanneney, warned Reynaud of 'the danger of exposing oneself to a collapse of the Assemblies, undermined as they are by defeatism, even more on the right than on the left'.[12]

Deep divisions soon appeared within this closed microcosm. The crisis, already foreseeable on 25 May, broke on 12 June at Cangey, after Weygand, an ex-officio member of the Council, had insisted upon an armistice. In Bordeaux, Pétain put himself at the head of the armistice lobby, a group that was growing from one day to the next. He gathered his supporters in his hotel, summoned Darlan (who had rallied to him) and Weygand, who left his general headquarters to attend. On the evening of 16 June, following two exceptionally violent meetings, Reynaud stepped down in favour of Pétain.

Now they had seen everything – everything but the France of the Revolutionary Year II (a year of great patriotic fervour against the invaders). Lebrun went about looking like 'Monsieur Prudhomme[*] lost in the palace of the Atrides' (Benoist-Méchin); Mandel, despite his reputation for firmness and determination, was not up to the situation; Jeanneney, a determined opponent of the armistice, got bogged down in an excess of legalism; and finally, although Reynaud managed to produce a premonitory diagnosis of the war, his behaviour was far less stable than his thinking.[13] He was no Churchill.[14] Furthermore, he was becoming entangled in the intrigues of an entourage won over to defeatism. Already in two minds – as can be sensed as early as 26 May – he was lacking in sang-froid during the decisive days of 15 and 16 June: he allowed himself to be taken in by the Chautemps manoeuvre[15] and, believing himself to be in a minority (voting was not customary in the Council of Ministers), he went off, without even consulting his friends, to tender his resignation to Lebrun, just as if no more than an ordinary ministerial crisis was involved.[16] Whether he wished it or no, he left the way clear for Pétain.[17]

---

[*] A character created by H. Monnier as a caricature of the narrow-minded *petit bourgeois*. [Trans.]

The great fear

For the non-mobilised French who lived to the north of the Loire, the year 1940 was first and foremost a year of exodus.[18] Bearing the lessons of the 1914 war in mind, the authorities had devised a plan of withdrawal for inhabitants (students, schoolchildren, etc.) of frontier regions, a plan which had functioned well enough in September 1939, given that time had not then been of the essence. But it was quite a different matter when it came to the onset of the German offensive: mixed up with Belgians fleeing southward, the people of the north tried to escape from the battlefield in conditions that were often highly dramatic.

The scale of these first enforced migrations still remained relatively modest so long as the Weygand line held. But as soon as it was broken, the roads were flooded by a tidal wave of humanity seeking to flee before the German advance. The decisive escalation came with the Parisian exodus which began as soon as the government's decision to quit the capital became known. At the lowest estimate, two million people, mainly the old, women and children, deserted the Paris region between 10 and 14 June, on foot, on bicycles, in the most unusual vehicles loaded with unbelievable bundles of chattels. In theory, they were making for the west, to reach the sea, or for the south-west, to cross the Loire which was believed to possess such great strategic virtues. But on 17 June, the last bridge in Gien was blown up, burying dozens of refugees who had remained deaf to the warnings of the soldiers in all their wisdom. With the Loire uncrossable between Tours and Nevers, most of these wanderers were brought to a halt in a zone encompassed by Melun, Sens and Pithiviers. Taking into account the movements that occurred in some areas of southern France, it may safely be assumed that, between 15 and 20 June, at least six million – more likely eight million – French men and women abandoned their homes. As in a system of communicating vessels, towns and market centres emptied and swelled: barely 700 inhabitants remained in Tourcoing, whilst Beaune-la-Rolande, a hamlet of 1,700 souls, became a 'town' of 40,000 nomads.

The phenomenon was part of the common experience of 'war miseries' with all the usual attendant violence and extortionism ('Come on, hand over your money, ten sous a glass [of water], two francs a bottle', peasants in the Beauce were heard to cry shamelessly) and looting too (many of the countless houses that were looted suffered less at the hands of the Wehrmacht than from the French themselves).

There were pressing enough reasons for flight. Among the inhabitants of frontier regions memories of a previous, particularly trying occupation were still vivid; others feared the fate of the people of Madrid or of the inhabitants of Rotterdam, buried beneath the bombs; and there were those who sought to escape the brutalities of a foe often depicted as 'the Hun' (and in point of fact, the Wehrmacht was not as *korrekt* as is often claimed: there were instances of the massacres of civilian hostages, several hundred in May in Oignies, fifteen or so on 14 June in Tremblay-lès-Gonesse, etc.). It was this great fear that made people risk joining convoys that might be bombed – as was the last train that tried to leave the station of Arras – and roads regularly raked by machine-gun fire. It should be added that the authorities responsible – where these had not already disappeared – were in no position to carry out the directives that the government had been so slow to formulate.

Choices were not necessarily governed by rational considerations, as can be seen from the behaviour of two villages in the Côte-d'Or no more than a few kilometres apart: of all the 220 inhabitants of Tichey, only one family of four left; in contrast, all 150 inhabitants of Bousselange took to the roads with the exception of one family that opted for collective suicide.[19] And what can be said of the nurses at Orsay who took it upon themselves to finish off their bed-ridden charges rather than allow them to fall into the hands of the enemy ... and was that really their only motive? Henri Amouroux has written quite correctly that 'a wind of madness was blowing over France'.[20] To some extent, the exodus stemmed from deep ancestral terrors similar to those that had worked upon the crowds of the middle ages or the peasants of 1789.

These civilian migrations did no doubt somewhat hamper French counter-attacks but the exodus did not play a decisive role from a military point of view since the outcome had already been decided before the June wave of movements began. At a personal level, however, it was a very heavy trial as is shown in particular by the thousands of children who went temporarily astray and the hundreds who were never found again. The political significance of the exodus is beyond question, if only for the reason that it was evidence of, to put it mildly, profound disarray.

For Philippe Pétain, hearing of the fate of the inhabitants of Bousselange, the exodus provided a moral and human justification both for the armistice and for a withdrawal within the boundaries of metropolitan France itself.

The people of France at a loss

On 17 June, the army, splintered and traumatised, heard the victor of Verdun declare in a radio broadcast speech: 'It is with a heavy heart that I tell you today that the fighting must stop.' Confusion increased tenfold. It was so bad that the maritime prefecture of Brest declared that it was all an enemy trick. It proved necessary to broadcast a second version – a quite incomprehensible one this time: 'We must try to stop the fighting.' But at that date fighting was still going on in places. The stand made along the Loire by the Saumur cadets, who had no thought of retreat, is famous. What is perhaps less well known is that near Lyons, the 1st regiment of colonial infantry defended itself with such determination that the Germans shot all the surviving officers and – spurred on by racism – flung the Senegalese soldiers to be crushed in the path of their tanks. It is true that with the approach of the armistice the situation almost everywhere else was much more simple: an ordinary German corporal captured the entire general staff of the 10th army single-handed, while at La Rochelle the following order went out: 'Disarm everybody. Collect all arms and keep them all together in a single place. Men and officers to report to head-quarters. Wait there without firing a shot or resisting in any way at all. Burn the documents. Officers who do not obey this order will be brought before a court martial.' In all this confusion, the Wehrmacht – in the period just before and just after the conclusion of the armistice – rounded up around 1.8 million prisoners.

The profound sense of disarray soon spread to the civil administration – wherever it still existed, that is. Once Herriot had ensured, on the eighteenth, that Lyons should be declared an 'open city', the example was soon followed by every city with more than 20,000 inhabitants. A mad rush ensued: in the Le Blanc region, former soldiers dug up the fuses that had been placed under the bridges; in Poitiers, the mayor marched out to meet the German troops, with a flag to the fore.

It is not easy to gauge the reactions of the French faced with the conqueror: there are so many contradictory accounts. Jules Jeanneney bitterly censured the people of Bordeaux for coming out to admire the Wehrmacht, 'crowds of them, strolling about, shameless';[21] but, as is well-known, on the fourteenth and the fifteenth Paris withdrew behind its shutters. It was 'Die Stadt ohne Blick'.[22] At least fifteen people had committed suicide there out of despair. The prefect of the Eure-et-Loir – whose name was Jean Moulin – cut his own throat rather than sign an announcement that was shaming to the French army. As Amouroux writes: 'Stupefaction, shame, terror, patriotic distress, hatred, relief, indifference ... it was all true'.[23] But what does seem certain, at least, is that the great majority of French people were not ready for a policy of total sell-out.

Was the war over?

The French campaign had been lost: on that point agreement was unanimous. But had France lost the war? This fundamental question elicited a number of totally divergent replies.

Capitulation or armistice?

Within governmental deliberations, it is true, the major rift had been between those who favoured an armistice and those who were for capitulation.[24] The latter course presented the undeniable political advantage of closing the score so far as the armed conflict was concerned, while leaving the political powers full latitude to continue the struggle in what-ever way they could. An armistice, on the other hand, offered the – short-term – advantage of concluding an official agreement between the two States and – in principle – limiting the powers of the conqueror; but even if it freed the army from its responsibilities, it most certainly limited the freedom of action of the government.

Furthermore, those who wanted an armistice would have to go back on the Franco-British agreement of 28 March which prohibited the conclusion of any separate armistice or peace. They could play up the inevitable frictions between the Allies, pointing in particular to Churchill's refusal to send extra RAF squadrons to France.[25] However, it was not possible in all good faith to proclaim that the British were laying down their arms and thus absolving France from her commitments.[26] In fact, quite to the contrary, London was making every effort to save the Franco-British alliance and made a number of solemn promises ('We shall never abandon the struggle until France has been restored in all its integrity and greatness'). Great Britain now took over a plan put forward by Corbin, Jean Monnet and Charles de Gaulle for Franco-British unity and the establishment of a common government, etc. Partisans of the armistice pretended to regard it as an attempt 'to turn France into a British Dominion' and forthwith gave their approval to the convenient evasion that the proposal formulated by Chautemps represented.[27]

At all events, Reynaud was not successful in winning over Weygand, who was devoted to the army, detested politicians and was, besides, extremely reactionary. To the president of the Council's exclamation: 'You will make the army capitulate, General ... You are here to obey', the commander-in-chief's dry rejoinder was: 'I am here to defend the honour of the army. You and the president of the Republic are seeking a transfer of responsibility. The government has taken responsibility for the war so it is up to the government to take responsibility for the armistice.' Speaking through Weygand, the great 'silent' majority was making itself felt and breaking the political pact tacitly recognised – ever since the Dreyfus affair – between the army and the nation. Weygand was no doubt sincere when he declared that 'the honour' of the army forbade him to capitulate in mid-campaign, but one may wonder whether that was his only consideration when he remarked to de Gaulle: 'Ah! If only I was sure that the Germans would leave me the necessary forces to maintain order.'[28]

Wait for peace here or continue the fight elsewhere?

Georges Mandel was not mistaken in the conclusion he reached on 16 June: 'The Council is divided; there are some who wish to fight and others who do not.' That was indeed the nub of the matter. Three days earlier, Pétain, for his part, had declared:

We must expect a French renewal to come rather from the soul of our country that we shall preserve by remaining on the spot, than from the reconquest of our territories using allied cannons, when and how it is impossible to foresee.... So the question posed at this moment is not whether the French government should or should not ask for an armistice, but whether the French government asks for an armistice or accepts leaving metropolitan France.... In my view, an armistice is the necessary condition for the survival of our eternal France.

It was already almost Vichy, national revolution and State collaboration. But at least that short statement had the merit of widening the terms of reference of the debate beyond the clash between the civil and military authorities.

While the 'defeatist' group led by Philippe Pétain scored a decisive point by declaring their ability to preserve metropolitan France, those who supported resistance backed by the Anglo-Saxon powers could offer nothing but blood and tears. The White House had offered no more than friendly words and Great Britain was in a difficult position. What was to be done in these circumstances? Leave for London, like the King of Norway, the Queen of the Netherlands and the Belgian government? Not many were in favour of emigration, but the Under-Secretary of War, Charles de Gaulle, was an exception. Most of those who opposed the armistice were in favour of establishing themselves in some part of the Empire, probably North Africa. As Hitler was playing with fire, allowing the Wehrmacht to approach rapidly towards Bordeaux, on 18 June Pétain was forced to agree to the transfer of part of the government to North Africa. But that operation never took place: pressure exerted by the regrouped extremists – led by Laval and Marquet – who had formed a 'Commune de Bordeaux', skilful procrastination on the part of the head of the government and the deliberate propagation of false news[29] won precious hours for the new regime. Only 26 deputies and one senator equipped with official orders signed by Darlan left Le Verdon on 21 June, aboard the *Massilia*.[30] Upon arrival in Casablanca they were, by government order, treated as suspects: Mandel and Daladier were forbidden to meet two members of the British cabinet; most of them were prevented from taking part in the polls of 9 and 10 July. As for Zay, Vienot, Mendès France and Wiltzer, they were soon to be court-martialled on charges of desertion. Meantime, the armistice had been signed and the *Massilia* became a trap closing upon all those who had opposed it. Anxious to do justice to his new functions as High-Commissioner for Propaganda, Prouvost, the proprietor of *Paris-Soir*, declared on 25 June: 'By fleeing from the responsibilities they had contracted with respect to the nation, they have cut themselves off from the French community.'

Long after all these events, those who championed the armistice continued to try to show that the base that North Africa offered had been logistically inadequate. But at the time, they were very little concerned by that, paying not the slightest heed to the warnings of General Noguès, the commander-in-chief in North Africa: 'The whole of North Africa is consternated by the demand for an armistice ... for it is impossible to govern in a climate of general scorn.'[31] After all, only a few days earlier, Weygand was on record as saying: 'The Empire ... childish nonsense', adding, 'If I am beaten here, England will not wait a week before negotiating with the Reich.'[32] The most urgent thing was to conclude a peace as soon as possible; for that is what it was to their minds: a peace. Lequerica, the Spanish ambassador in France, chosen by the French government as intermediary, conveyed the following communication to the German ambassador in Spain: 'I have asked [Baudouin] to specify whether he is speaking of conditions for an armistice or for a peace. He told me that armistice conditions were obviously a temporary expedient and that what the French government was interested in knowing were the conditions for peace.'[33] Meanwhile, at Rethondes, Hunziger was also interested in peace conditions. And one of the tasks that Pétain set himself on 11 July was 'to conclude the peace'.

Which to blame: a spirit of pleasure-seeking or deficiencies on the part of the 'big chiefs'?

Future developments depended on how the defeat was diagnosed. There can be nothing more illuminating in this respect than a comparison, virtually term for term, between the appeal by Charles de Gaulle, broadcast by the BBC on 18 June, and Philippe Pétain's broadcast on 20 June. Both in effect were taking stock, suggesting explanations and extracting lessons. In the eyes of de Gaulle, the battle had been lost through the fault of the High Command: 'The leaders who have been at the head of the French armies for so many years' had been taken by 'surprise' by 'the enemy's superior weaponry both on the ground and in the air'. As for Pétain, he blamed everything and everybody (except the big chiefs), including the famous spirit of pleasure-seeking: 'Ever since victory, our pleasure-seeking has been stronger than our spirit of sacrifice. People have taken more out than they have put in. They have tried to spare themselves effort; and today we have come face to face with misfortune.'

Philippe Pétain also nursed grievances of a military order: 'Not enough children, not enough arms...'. The demographic argument was hardly relevant since, as they confronted each other, the two armies were numerically equal. As for armaments, that thesis was hardly any more valid, although it is one that has died hard. It should be remembered that – contrary to what is often suggested – the French armies had at their disposal more armoured vehicles than the Wehrmacht and that some of them – the B tanks – were quite exceptional. It was in the air that Germany really did enjoy an appreciable advantage, thanks to its bombers and its dive-bombers, the much feared Stukas. But, on balance, the military potential of the two sides was about equal except that, in the case of the Reich, their war economy made it imperative that the war be a short one.[34] It should also be said that, contrary to a legend that some have found it convenient to encourage, 'on the whole the men did fight, and they fought well';[35] the 100,000 soldiers killed at the fronts in less than five weeks bear testimony to that.

What really counted was not so much armaments as the way in which they were used. As we know, the French High Command was stupefied by the successes of the enemy strategy. But it was the fact that they found themselves outclassed in every tactical domain that turned the strategic surprise into a rout for them. The Germans' war of mobility had pierced the 'continuous front'. Their manoeuvrability had made a mockery of static fire-power. Two postulates derived from the previous war and declared by the 'big chiefs' to be inviolable, were thus blown sky high.[36] The Germans' all-out mechanical power had upset everything. The *Schwerpunkt* tactic, involving a concentration both temporal and spatial of armoured vehicles and aircraft, had swallowed up the French tanks and aircraft, which had been deployed in small detachments, and had resulted in the fatal break-through.

Charles de Gaulle believed that the German mechanised forces that were for the moment victorious could soon be opposed by other mechanised forces both superior and better led. In his eyes, this was yet another reason why France should by hook or by crook contrive to remain in a war which he was convinced would become a world conflict. With the armistice secured, Philippe Pétain, for his part, was on June 25 inviting the French people to undertake an 'intellectual and moral retraining'.

Could the armistice win salvation?

An armistice to save France, an armistice that was the least of all evils, an armistice of betrayal: all three were currently accepted interpretations of an armistice that was – whatever the interpretation – decisive for the French people. The reason why the debate over it was charged with such passion is that, for one thing, the armistice agreement became, through force of circumstances, the necessary framework for four years of extraordinary Franco-German collaboration and, for another, the signing of the armistice marked the birth of the Vichy regime.

Tactical subtleties and forced hands

Once Reynaud had resigned, events moved fast. The new French government held out for only two conditions. The one was political: a sovereign French State had to be maintained; the other, military: the ocean-going fleet – which remained unvanquished – could not be handed over. Hitler, without hesitation and demonstrating considerable political acumen, seized upon the opportunity to neutralise one of the two Allied powers. As he put it to Mussolini on 18 June: 'Above all the French fleet must be prevented from reaching England'; ('a good solution might even be for the French fleet to scuttle itself'). To this end, the Axis powers had to 'ensure through negotiations that a French government continued to function on French territory' and at all costs had to prevent 'its flight abroad, to London, where it would continue to wage war'.[37] The survival of a French State presented other advantages too: it would guarantee the security of the troops of occupation and dispense the Wehrmacht from 'the disagreeable responsibility that would fall upon the occupying powers if they were obliged, among other things, to take charge of the administrative domain'. Curbing his belated ally's greed for extra territory, the Führer put off the distribution of spoils to a later date when Great Britain would have been brought to its knees. It was a clever move and Vichy, which was initially to congratulate itself on having 'wrung concessions' from the Reich, was only later and to its cost to discover the subtlety of the German trap.

The Reich nevertheless committed a tactical error by letting things drag on too long, so that the German embassy in Madrid telegraphed the following message: 'If the beginning of the armistice is deferred, the Reynaud faction ... could well regain the upper hand and the [Pétain] government would not survive being subjected to a threat from the German troops.' That warning was heeded and the operation was smartly executed. The French were a conquered power and to be treated as such. The delegation of their plenipotentiaries, headed by General Huntziger, assisted by four high-ranking officers and two important civil servants from the Quai d'Orsay, found itself on 22 June once again at Rethondes in the famous railway carriage whose destiny it clearly was to provide a venue for this kind of ceremony. Fully aware of the government's desire for haste in concluding an armistice and also of the state of mind prevalent in Bordeaux, the Germans were sitting pretty. Barely twenty-four hours after the start of negotiations, Keitel issued an ultimatum; a few hours later, on 22 June, the government gave Huntziger authorisation to sign the armistice agreement. The French plenipotentiaries then had to travel to Turin for a meeting with the Italians, who managed to show moderation. The armistice was to take effect as from 00.30 hours on 25 June.

Draconian measures

Out of the twenty-four articles that made up the 'armistice agreement' – 'to be valid until the conclusion of a peace treaty' – ten or more were designed to neutralise the French military potential: all troops 'except [those] necessary to maintain internal order' were to be disarmed, plans of fortifications were to be handed over to the Wehrmacht, war materials were to be delivered over intact, aerodromes passed into German control, etc. The naval forces, however, received more favourable treatment with the Reich agreeing 'to make no claims over the French fleet until peace has been concluded'. In the same article 8 it was stipulated that the ocean-going fleet was to be demobilised and disarmed under the respective control of Germany and Italy 'and that to this end it was to return to the ships' peacetime home ports'. It was this last clause that incited the British, who placed no trust at all in Hitler's words, to activate 'Operation Catapult'.

The Reich had also taken precautions of an economic nature. It had decreed a number of conservative measures concerning maritime commercial trade, the transfer of money and valuables and means of exchange. France had also to agree to 'the transport of merchandise in transit between the German Reich and Italy over the non-occupied territory'. Article 18 specified furthermore that 'the maintenance costs for the German troops of occupation on French territory should be charged to the French government'. This was the legal basis for what was in effect tribute that the French State was obliged to pay.

Finally, the agreement included a number of clauses of a more political nature. The most humiliating one obliged the French government to 'hand over, on demand, German nationals as indicated by the Reich government'.[38] Altogether in line with the tactics upon which Hitler had decided, the text included no territorial claims upon either the Empire or metropolitan France. However, France was cut in two by a 'demarcation line' between the zone that was 'occupied' and the zone that was, nominally, 'free'. Flung right across the country from the Lake of Geneva to the Spanish frontier, this new internal frontier passed to the east of Nantua, the south of Dôle, through Chalon-sur-Saône, to the south of Moulins, Bourges and Tours, to the east of Poitiers, Angoulême, Mont-de-Marsan and Bayonne and ended up at the Spanish frontier, leaving in the occupied territory all seaboards with the exception of the Mediterranean coastline.[39] The occupation, designed to 'ensure the interests of the Reich', was in principle temporary and linked with the pursuit of hostilities against Great Britain. Also in principle, the sovereignty of the French State remained intact over the whole metropolitan territory, but article 3 nonetheless stipulated that 'the French government should immediately invite all French authorities and administrative services in the occupied territory to conform with the regulations of the German military authorities and to collaborate (*zusammenarbeiten*) with the latter in a correct fashion'. For extra security, the conqueror carried off to Germany a million and a half political hostages who would have to remain 'prisoners of war until peace was concluded'.

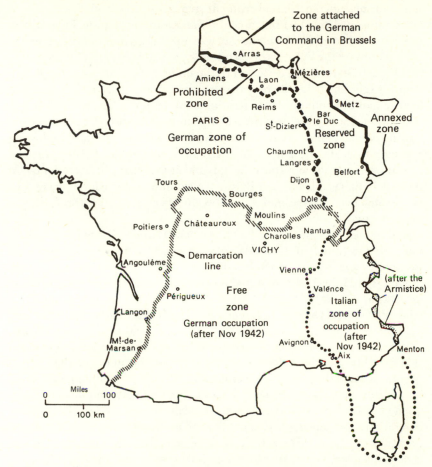

Zone attached
to the German
Command in Brussels

Arras

Amiens   Laon

Mézières

Prohibited
zone

Reims

Metz

PARIS O

German zone of
occupation

Bar
St-Dizier   le Duc

Annexed
zone

Reserved
zone

Chaumont

Langres

Belfort

Tours

Bourges

Dijon

Dôle

Poitiers   Châteauroux

Moulins

Charolles   Nantua

VICHY

Angoulême

Demarcation
line

Vienne

(after the
Armistice)

Périgueux

Free
zone

Valénce

Italian
zone of
occupation
(after
Nov 1942)

Langon

German occupation
(after Nov 1942)

Mt-de-
Marsan

Avignon

Aix

Menton

Miles
0   100

0   100 km

3 France split apart

Source: H. Michel, *La Seconde Guerre mondiale,* PUF, 1968, vol. 1, p. 190. Reproduced
by permission of Presses Universitaires de France

A 'diktat' or a golden bridge?

'France delivered up, pillaged and enslaved': that was how de
Gaulle, on 26 June, categorically condemned the *diktat* accepted by the
French government. All that the Germans had agreed to was not to seize all
French aviation and 'To take into account what is necessary for the life of
those living in the non-occupied territories'. They had rejected all the other
requests expressed by the French plenipotentiaries, refusing, most importantly, to modify the line of demarcation or to liberate the prisoners of war.
   While Philippe Pétain admitted that 'the conditions [were] severe', he
tried hard to show that 'honour [was] saved' since the air force and fleet had

not been surrendered, 'the government [remained] free' and 'France would be administered only by Frenchmen'.[40] It is quite true that the French were not subjected to a Nazi Gauleiter. It was a privilege that they owed not to the goodness of the Führer's heart but to a tactical calculation: the survival of a French State would better serve the immediate interests of the Reich. And for the time being there was every reason for Hitler to feel satisfied: France had been put out of the fighting for a decade or more, her fleet was neutralised and the Wehrmacht was in secure occupation of the bases from which it would launch an invasion of the British Isles which now, following the signing of the armistice, was extremely vulnerable. Besides, he had already decided not to respect the agreement that had just been signed: in August 1940, even before the Battle of Britain had started, he placed two Gauleiters over Alsace and Lorraine, in effect annexing three French departments.

Only much later, when the Reich was faced with total war, were claims made that in June 1940 Hitler had offered a 'golden bridge' to vanquished France. It was a thesis defended by a fraction of the Wehrmacht which judged that Hitler had committed a gross strategic error by not imposing direct control over the French Empire.[41] That was borne out by Churchill[42] who told General Georges in January 1944: 'All in all, the armistice helped us. Hitler made a mistake in granting it. He should have gone to North Africa and seized it in order to carry on to Egypt.' The *maréchalistes* exploited that weighty piece of evidence to laud the stubbornness of the French negotiators and the perspicacity of Philippe Pétain. It would not be correct for a historian to take retrospective speculations of that kind into consideration nor to accept as valid assertions that can be opposed by other equally peremptory judgements.[43] It should, at all events, be emphasised that the partisans of the armistice were looking ahead no further than to the conclusion of an immediate peace: and furthermore that the armistice gave Hitler the weapons he needed to deal swiftly with Great Britain. It was the British who, by winning the Battle of Britain, upset Hitler's plans and altered the distribution of the strategic cards in the game.

A decisive break with the past

For the next four years, the armistice was to provide the inescapable framework for the Vichy regime. It sanctioned the birth of that regime when, after a week of vacillation and uncertainty, it allowed Pétain to assume authority over the politicians: 25 June 1940 marked the beginning of a new order. It is not hard to understand why the leader of the government had spiritedly swept aside the objections raised by Lebrun and a number of ministers who judged the German *diktat* to be exorbitant. He was in an even better position to do so given that the majority, even (with certain reservations) the great majority, of French people approved of the ending of hostilities, objected to policies that sacrificed France and really do appear to have been feeling a mixture of shame and cowardly relief. At the opposite end of the scale, the armistice was giving rise to the first refractory responses: one such was the text circulated by Edmond Michelet on 17 June which, quoting Péguy, declared that 'those who do not give in are right and those who do are wrong'.

When the German conditions became known, the diplomat Charles-Roux urged the government to move to North Africa; Pétain's response to him was a 'Still at it, then?' to which there was no answer. What the armistice did in effect was ratify the metropolitan strategy to which the head of the French State was to cling for the next four years, come wind or high water.[44] It was a far cry from the imperial and world policies that de Gaulle immediately suggested.

In short, the armistice heralded State collaboration for which, given the force of circumstances, it provided a contractual basis. Through this bizarre policy of collaboration the French State was to attempt to liberate itself from the shackles it had accepted in June. But by so doing it was venturing into a formidable entanglement.

3

There you stand, Maréchal

'Here we stand, Maréchal. We, your lads, swear before you, the saviour of France, to serve and follow in your footsteps...' There can be little doubt that this remarkably naïve and foolish ditty (composed by A. Montagnard aided by C. Courtioux) was the most popular refrain of the year 1940. In the course of fifteen months or so, Pétainism became established, apparently wiping out 60 years of republicanism and relegating to the shadows all rebels and dissidents. But the 'national revolution'[1] also had its failures and – most importantly – it took place under the scrutiny of the occupying power. This officially-sealed collaboration between the French State and the Third Reich turned out to be a dangerous trick.

A phoney regime: the French State

As early as the end of June, the new team that had been installed determined to establish a 'new order'. The French State was officially born in July 1940: it was, in every respect, a most unusual regime.

Pétainism and the old order

The new regime diffused its official ideology through 'Messages' from the head of the French State and, initially anyway, he was very free with these.[2] To tell the truth, the strictly political education of Philippe Pétain was rudimentary enough; he was distrustful of ideological systems, preferring what he liked to call 'common sense'. It was from the army, which had formed him, that this solitary and dry-hearted man had received the handful of motivating ideas that he clung to so obstinately. The mutinies of 1917 and the war of the Rif had instilled in him a deep aversion for the extreme left; and the thirties had rekindled his anti-parliamentarianism, already exacerbated by his experiences as a minister.[3] Although he passed for a 'republican marshal' in the eyes of the left, his right-wing sympathies can be in little doubt. It had perhaps too easily been forgotten that – between the two elections of 1936 – he had spoken out in favour of the Rassemblement National, congratulating the extreme right group, the

Croix-de-Feu, for being 'one of the healthiest elements in our country'; at Verdun in 1936, he had stigmatised 'materialism' as an agent of corruption, concluding: 'It is high time that the French people got a grip on itself.' Deeply pro-Munich as he was, the declaration of war had done nothing to dissipate his defeatist pessimism.

In the view of the head of the French State, the first priority was for 'an intellectual and moral retraining': destructive individualism (that 'false idea of a natural equality between men') must give place to the true natural hierarchies ('the hierarchies of families, professions and communes'). Thanks to this return to 'reality', the 'true élites' were at last emerging from the false egalitarianism (for 'it is no longer enough simply to count votes, for some must weigh more than others'). The new élites would be formed by the work and discipline inculcated right from the start at schools from which 'purely bookish pseudo-culture' artificially shored up by rootless intellectuals would be banished. Only then could a truly national 'community' arise in which 'the spirit of pleasure-seeking' would dissolve away as would class conflicts and false divisions fomented by 'the shady alliance of international capitalism and international socialism'. For the rest, the economy that had inevitably been led astray by 'the powerful motivation of profit' would have to be 'organised and controlled' on the basis of 'trades and professions organised ... on a corporative basis'. This 'revolution' from the top that the head of State was resolutely inviting called for a 'hierarchical and authoritarian State ... in which consultation is a matter for only a few, one or two give the commands and, right at the summit, there is a leader who governs'.

So Pétainism was first and foremost a collection of right-wing ideas from the distant past with a coating of ingredients borrowed from the thirties. Its fundamental pessimism, sententious moralism and anti-democratic élitism, its refashioning of society with all the emphasis on organisation, and its defensive and inward-looking nationalism were deeply reactionary in the strictest sense of the term. It was a mish-mash – and on the whole an unoriginal one – of ideologies that had flourished at the end of the nineteenth century, with a dash of Maurrasism, although in fact this would-be regenerative syncretism was not over-much influenced by the Maurras system.[4] From the ideological upheavals of the thirties, Pétainism retained in particular the idea of a third way somewhere in between liberalism and State interference although it did not come down squarely on the side of a policy of planning, as was suggested here and there, or one of a 'corporatism' that was often invoked but seldom specified and that was in principle not a matter of State control. This basically authoritarian regime was nevertheless not fascist.[5] Pétain avoided the fundamental instrument represented by the single party system, power being in the first instance confiscated by a gerontocracy of conservative notables, which managed to

52   *There you stand, Maréchal*

avoid the social mutations inherent in any take-over of power in the fascist style.

The republican rout

The first objective of the new regime was to wipe out the Third Republic. By 10 July 1940, that was accomplished. It was an enterprise that was made easier by the weakness of the politicians who had either rallied eagerly to the new regime or faint-heartedly given in to it.[6]

Pétain's entourage had initially planned to send parliament off on indefinite vacation. But this half-measure was unacceptable to the extremists regrouped within the 'Bordeaux Commune' with Pierre Laval at their head.[7] Laval had a number of scores to settle but also a parliamentary past which he wished to see forgotten. In order to supplant his rivals and appear as the one man who was indispensable, he persuaded Pétain to support an ingenious idea: to get parliament to scuttle itself.

By dint of much manoeuvring, alternating promises and threats, he was successful in isolating those who had declared their opposition – who were uncoordinated and few in number anyway – and in rallying a number of powerful supporters: on the right, Flandin and on the left, one of Léon Blum's ministers, Spinasse, who was resigned to 'a crucifying operation'.

By 9 July, both Assemblies were ready to vote – with no more than four dissensions – for the principle of constitutional revision. The next day, the National Assembly was officially united by the end of the session dominated by a vociferous majority that was determined to abolish 'outworn formalism' and in which the opposition was unable to make itself heard.[8] With 468 in favour, 80 against[9] and 20 abstentions,[10] the National Assembly granted 'full powers to the government of the Republic under the authority and signature of Marshall Pétain, to the effect of promulgating by one or more acts a new Constitution for the French State. This Constitution must guarantee the rights of labour, the family and the motherland. It will be ratified by the nation and applied by the Assemblies that it creates.' By means of a few last-minute concessions, Laval's gamble had come off. Moreover, the manner in which the proposal was recorded had most explicitly dotted the 'i's and crossed the 't's: what the delegation of power boiled down to was giving to 'the government of Marshall Pétain full executive and legislative powers ... without restriction, in the widest possible fashion'. He was forbidden only to declare war without the assent of the Chambers. These would survive but their activities would 'necessarily be reduced'.

A number of irregularities undeniably took place in the course of this last session; but there was a certain amount of misrepresentation in 1945 when it was declared that it had amounted to a 'fleecing'. The 'victims' had in reality been consenting and Laval had been most explicit about what was to follow: 'Constitutional Acts' were to be promulgated and an heir apparent nominated. In his statement of evidence at Pétain's trial,[11] Léon Blum referred to the numbness, the sense of resignation and 'the fear of Doriot's* gangs in the streets, of Weygand's soldiers at Clermont and of the Germans who were at Moulins'. Divided as they were between cowardly relief, opportunism and a desire to be revenged on the Popular Front, the politicians sold out on the Republic. The regime had admittedly to sustain the assaults of a rejuvenated extreme right wing but that group could not, on its own, have strangled 'the Trollop'.† In the last analysis the Republic, left almost defenceless, was not so much attacked but rather delivered up by a mob of 'conservatives at odds with the Republic',[12] who had been terrified by 1936 and were determined to take their revenge, even if that meant cornering the paths of access to power. They were joined by men from the left, not only those who had been advocating a more authoritarian regime ever since the thirties, but also by 'republicans', radicals and socialists who moved across out of opportunism or pro-Munich pacifism. It would be erroneous to exaggerate the importance of the vote of 10 July, for the armistice itself was a much more decisive break with the past. But that act of hara-kiri well enough encapsulates the bankruptcy of a whole political system which is all too readily represented simply as an institutional problem. After all, Reynaud certainly possessed full powers at the time. What broke down was not just a regime of Assemblies but well and truly tattered democracy itself, crushed by military defeat and overrun by a pack of complacent notables.

Power in Vichy

To Marcel Astier's cry of 'Long live the Republic, anyway!', many voices (according to the *Journal Officiel*) had responded: 'Long live France!'.

In less than a week a veritable 'legalised revolution'[13] had taken place. Except for among the 'Free French',[14] there were not many voices raised at the time to challenge its legality. In the period leading up to the break of April 1942, ten 'Constitutional Acts' were promulgated, the first four on 11 and 12 July 1940. In the first Act, Philippe Pétain declared – and the procedure was clearly unusual – that he 'was assuming the functions of head of the French State'. In the second, he granted himself 'the entire range of governmental powers', concentrating in his own person all those that had formerly belonged to the President of the Republic and the Council of Ministers. In effect, his functions were legion: they were legislative 'in the Council of Ministers' (the latter being 'responsible to him alone') and he

---

* Doriot, a former leading communist, had become the head of an extreme right-wing movement. [Trans.]
† La Gueuse was a derisory nickname given to the Republic by the Royalists in the 1880s. [Trans.]

was to continue to exercise these even after 'the formation of new assemblies' in circumstances of 'grave external tension or internal crisis';[15] diplomatic when it came to negotiating and ratifying all treaties; administrative by virtue of the statutory power reinforced by the oath sworn 'to the person of the head of State' by all ministers, high-ranking civil servants, officers and magistrates; juridical, since he held the right to 'suspend' justice in the cases of high-ranking civil servants whom he could sentence on his own initiative even to 'detention in a fortified place'. On top of all this – and this innovation was no small matter – in Act 4 he assigned himself the right to designate his own successor as head of State. The truth of the matter is that he had a completely free hand.

He had never dissociated himself from politics. Even when he had already once been a minister and was twice more to be so,[16] he never swerved from a prudent line. With what was practically the detachment of a spectator, he had observed the noisy campaign launched by Gustave Hervé in February 1935 with the theme, 'It's Pétain we need' – a campaign orchestrated by the right-wing press and relaunched in March 1938 by Lémery and Taittinger. During the 'phoney war', while ambassador to Burgos, his name appeared on many possible ministerial lists but, even if he was a defeatist, he never played a factionist game.[17] There seems little doubt, however, that he considered himself available, as the last resort;[18] had he not already once before, in 1917, proved himself to be just that?

Having come to power – showing a considerable sense of manoeuvre in the process – he did not intend to be merely an ornamental figurehead; nor was he prepared to be another Monk.[19] As head of State, he wished to be kept informed of everything though written detailed reports: on 13 December, Laval learned to his cost that he should not be underestimated. The chief director of his civil cabinet had good reason to emphasise his 'political stinginess'. Age had, moreover, reinforced his authoritarianism and magnified his distrust. His ingratitude, which became proverbial, stemmed in part from his emotional aridity but also from his pragmatism.

The infirmities of old age – profound deafness and the strain he felt when subjected to any sustained intellectual effort – may have encouraged the idea that he was the prey of his entourage and in particular of his 'heirs presumptive'. Certainly, he was not able to control everything, but the fundamental orientation of internal politics and the attitude taken towards State collaboration truly were his own responsibility. Right up to and into the spring of 1944 he conducted himself as head of State. To claim, as is still sometimes done, that the lustreless Vichy episode was the result of 'an old man being misled' by Laval and a number of other boors is to play with words and twist the facts.

It was Philippe Pétain's intention to innovate. He wanted to govern as it were with a military general staff ('one who governs through three or through one hundred'). It was in the restricted Council or Small Council, which every morning brought together a few select ministers under the chairmanship of the head of State, that the main policy lines were – in principle – decided. The role of the other ministers and secretaries of State was rather that of high-ranking civil servants placed at the head of one ministry or another.[20] But in practice the situation was far more complicated and a host of other figures also had their say: the members of his (civil and military) cabinets, intimate friends (in particular, his personal doctor, Ménétrel), members of his political entourage (here, one Lucien Rouvier became increasingly important). The Hôtel du Parc – the seat of the French State – was a place rife with political manoeuvring,[21] intrigues and underhand deals.[22] For the rest, contrary to what is generally believed, the governmental life of the Vichy regime was an agitated one. There were no less than seven ministerial reshuffles between July 1940 and April 1942 and they took place in conditions that were, to say the least, original.[23] Vichy France was governed in a certain amount of confusion.

Old Romans and young cyclists

This distinction between the ancients and the moderns, for which we are indebted to Moysset,[24] is certainly simplistic but it fits the chronological pattern well enough.

Many were excluded from Vichy. Acceptance depended on being more of a *maréchaliste* than the next man. One feature in common united the motley crowd: a desire for revenge. Stanley Hoffmann described Vichy as 'the minorities' great revenge' while Bernanos, more savagely, called it 'the revolution of the failures'. The right, complacently expansive, offered a tiny place to the handful of trade-unionists who had followed Belin, the joint ex-secretary general of the CGT, now promoted to Minister of Work. The right-wingers were there in full force: slightly sobered extremists (Marion from the PPF, Saivre from the Jeunesses Patriotes, etc.), followers of Maurras (Alibert, etc.), solid reactionaries (Weygand, Xavier Vallat, etc) and there were also those who prided themselves upon their liberalism modelled on Romier of the Institute and *Le Figaro*.

It is perhaps not all that surprising to come across a fair sprinkling of the usual notables, members of the Institute (which consists of the five leading Academies of the Arts and Sciences) and of right-thinking milieux in government circles, but it is rather more so to find so very many generals and admirals[25] scattered around all over the place – in the Chantiers de la Jeunesse, the National Council, in charge of prefectures – although that does not mean that Vichy was, strictly speaking, a military regime. Professional officers[26] alleged – later on – that they had owed obedience to the legal authority and besides had sworn an oath to the head of State. But it should be added that most of them – including the future leaders of the

French 1st army – found it suited them very well: not only did they applaud the ends of the national revolution but the regime allowed them to steal a march on the civilians, the politicians and the parliamentarians.

But most remarkable of all was the infiltration of those who would today be described as technocrats: high-ranking civil servants or dynamic leaders from the private sector in the 'old-boy network', all products of the same Grandes Ecoles and Grands Corps.[27] Before the war these inspectors of Finances, graduates from the military academy (Ecole Polytechnique) and from the Ecole Centrale (engineers) had all participated in the same colloquia, met in the same select circles – such as the 'X-crise' founded by Jean Coutrot – and had written for the same quality journals, such as *Les Nouveaux Cahiers*. They had decided that it was imperative to shake free from the archaism of the economic and political structures of France. Paul Reynaud had made room for some of them but it was Vichy that gave them the chance to put their modernist ideology into practice and to win out over the neo-liberals. Thanks to Darlan, they were now extremely thick on the ground.[28] Among these 'Young Turks' were to be found not only Pucheu, a product of the Rue d'Ulm (the Ecole Normale Supérieure, another of the Grandes Ecoles) who had made his way up through Pont-à-Mousson, the Comptoir Sidérurgique (the major sales organisation of the steel industry) and Japy (a large industrial firm), but also Lehideux who had studied at the Ecole Libre des Sciences Politiques and been schooled as a 'manager' at Renault-Billancourt; Bichelonne, said to be the most brilliant product of the Polytechnique; and Barnaud, another Polytechnician who was an inspector of Finances and one of their most influential thinkers. All – or almost all – of them were decidedly to the right, élitists, devoted to order and rationality. The difficulties inherent in the situation gave these 'young cyclists' their chance and in some measure they took over from the old doctrinaire Romans, making Vichy a kind of posting stage between the immediate pre-war period and the fifties.

During the summer of 1940, the regime was seeking its identity in the midst of confusion and penury and meanwhile preparing itself for a *pax germanica*. Autumn saw a relative stabilisation; the fundamental choices had been made: Pétain came out unequivocally in favour of State collaboration. He pushed aside the proposal for a single party that had been quietly prepared by Déat[29] and contrived to ensure that the most aggressive of the right-wingers, who were drawing apart from the Vichy 'reactionaries', left for Paris. With the parliamentarians eliminated,[30] the national revolution could be launched under the supervision of reactionary and doctrinaire notables such as Massis and Gillouin, who were all more or less won over to the doctrines of Maurras.[31]

The palace revolution of 13 December was followed by a period of relative confusion. On 13 December, in fact, Laval, the heir apparent, was himself sacked. His zeal for the national revolution was no more than moderate but he had seemed capable of conducting Franco-German negotiations satisfactorily. The trouble was that he wanted to conduct them in his own way. His enemies, of whom there were many, managed to convince Pétain of the jeopardy in which his heir apparent was placing the State: he was not presenting any reports; he was plotting in Paris, hand in glove with Déat who recently, on 2 December, had published a violent indictment against Vichy; and he was drawing Pétain into a trap on the pretext of presiding over the return of the Aiglon's body to Paris.* With Laval toppled, the conspirators of 13 December thrust forward Flandin who became Minister for Foreign Affairs. Although he had been one of the supporters of the abhorred parliamentarianism, his rallying to Pétain on 11 July had counted for something and his past record as an extreme supporter of Munich policies ought to have made it possible for him to renew negotiations with the Reich.[32] But he failed to please, being over-inclined to favour the old politicians: in the national Council[33] that he was trying to set up to overcome the misgivings of the hesitant, there were no less than 78 parliamentarians and former parliamentarians among the 188 notables that had been appointed. His inability to meet any Nazi negotiator, even of the humblest standing, sealed his disgrace. His moment of power was to last for less than three months.

It was now Darlan's hour (for he at least had managed to meet Hitler), an hour for which he had been patiently waiting. Although the son of a minister of the Third Republic and himself a former Minister for Marine Affairs with the reputation of a 'man of war' and a republican, he had – in June – managed to change sides at the right moment, bringing with him the navy that he had kept intact and well under control. Finally, he had been cautious enough to steer clear of clan rivalries. Having become heir apparent on 10 February 1941, he had acquired the Ministries of Foreign Affairs, Information and the Interior. This man,[34] apparently so thirsty for power, is a disconcerting figure. Possibly less intelligent than he believed himself to be, he was nevertheless not lacking in skill and he knew how to win Pétain's appreciation:[35] he plied him with written reports and never failed to consult him. Faithful to his reputation of an efficient pragmatist, he lost no time in relaunching State collaboration (and we know what a tragic aftermath ensued), thrusting the young cyclists to the fore. In response to the amazement of the director of the civil cabinet, who exclaimed: 'But you are bringing us the entire Worms bank', the admiral retorted: 'At least that is better than the sacristy fleas that surround you; no more generals, no more seminarists, but young chaps who know a thing or two, who will get on with the Fritz and keep our pot on the boil.'[36]

* The son of Napoleon I who died and was buried in Austria.

Was it really a revolution?

For the true Vichy men, the retraining of the French was to come not from outside but from a veritable national revolution. It was a revolution that was never completed both because of the war and also on account of its own inherent contradictions.

Settling old scores

For most Vichy men, making the *national* revolution meant setting the score right, first and foremost in respect of universal suffrage. The two Assemblies, whose survival was constitutional, were reduced to 'congrégations contemplatives' (congregations of spectators) (J. Jeanneney); the few informal meetings that had hitherto been tolerated were suppressed in August 1941 and the Bureaux des Assemblées were required to cease all their activities on 25 August 1942. The National Council that Flandin had set up to make up for the absence of any representative organ was placed in a position of liberty under surveillance and never met in plenary session. On the departmental level, the powers of the *arrondissement* and general councils devolved upon the sub-prefects and prefects assisted by 'administrative commissions'[37] which were forbidden to 'formulate wishes' and whose members, who were appointed by decree, were drawn for the most part from the ranks of the 'apolitical' notables. At a local level, in communes of more than 2,000 inhabitants, municipal councillors and mayors were now appointed – a process that allowed for a considerable purge.

Meanwhile the problem of 'republican' personnel was tackled: some of those considered 'responsible' for the defeat were put out to grass and a number of 'politicians' who refused to rally to the new order were interned.[38] The upper echelons of the administration were 'made healthy'.[39] Freemasons, the henchmen of the devil, in the eyes of any good cleric, and in the eyes of everybody else[40] the backbone of the deceased Third Republic, were also hauled up to be disciplined: on 13 August 1940, the lodges were dismantled by virtue of a law affecting 'secret societies'; lodge dignitaries and those who had disguised their membership were banned from public functions. Finally, to decapitate what remained of trade-union power, a decree issued on 9 November 1940 made it possible to dissolve all interprofessional organisations at both national and departmental levels.

'Restoring France to the French' was the task that remained. That meant once more vigorously pursuing the hunt for communists – Moscovites and local French alike – and also tackling the worst of the 'metics', the Jews. It was an opportunity to be revenged for men like Dreyfus, Blum and Mandel and while so doing easy to pose as paragons of public virtue and find convenient scapegoats for the good French people currently so starved of nationalistic success. As from 3 October 1940 'Jews of French nationality' were made subject to a 'Statute', severely modified on 2 June 1941: they were thenceforth excluded from all elective and public functions, from the magistracy and from the army (except if they were veteran combatants); they could exercise no responsibilities in the cultural domain or the media. A strict quota limited their access to universities (3%) and also to many of the liberal professions (2%). Finally, 'to do away with all Israelite influence upon the national economy', all enterprises belonging to Jews could be Aryanised[41] by enforced liquidation or the appointment of trustees. It was alleged – later on – that this anti-semitism was not on racial grounds but for reasons of State. But the Statute was certainly based upon a strictly racial definition[42] since 'any person with three Jewish grandparents [was] considered a Jew'.[43] As for 'foreign Jews', a decree passed on 4 October 1940 gave prefects powers to put them under house arrest and intern them in special camps: by the spring of 1941, 40,000 had already been rounded up and crowded into camps at Gurs, Rivesaltes, Noé, etc. For many of them these camps represented the antechamber of death. The efficient coordination of all these measures was the responsibility of a General Commissariat for Jewish questions, created in March 1941 and initially entrusted to the extremely reactionary and ultra-xenophobic Xavier Vallat. It is worth pointing out that the Jewish Statute was the brainchild of Vichy and Vichy alone. Nazi Germany had not exerted the slightest pressure.

Building a healthy, disciplined and united France

It was necessary to restore the physical and moral health of a France emasculated by decades of 'pleasure-seeking'. First, from a physical point of view: it would be an open-air France; not the France of Léo Lagrange* with its dubious youth hostels and its outings in tandem undertaken on every demagogic paid holiday, but a France stepping out smartly, if not in step, saluting the colours and gathering round the camp-fires. The France of the *apéro* (the cocktail hour) was also a thing of the past. Permission to operate stills was withdrawn and 'dry' days were introduced (when no alcohol could be sold).

On the moral side, the first task, for reasons that were both social and demographic, was to consolidate the family, 'the basic cell of French life':[44] large families were encouraged, benefiting from a number of measures of tax relief; divorce was made more difficult and abortion was severely repressed.[45] Next, schools were totally remodelled: the intolerably independent Ecoles Normales were closed down, text books were revised, teaching transformed by the introduction of lessons in morality and classes for manual skills. In secondary schooling, to the end of reinforcing select-

---

* A socialist who promoted popular sport and who was the Under-Secretary of State for Leisure in Blum's government. [Trans.]

iveness, fees were reintroduced for the higher courses and the *lycées* provided classes only in the classic humanities.

'Leadership schools' were set up for the élite, inspired by the experience of the fiery Captain Dunoyer de Segonzac who took charge of the most famous one, at Uriage near Grenoble. Here, within no more than a few weeks, thanks to vigorous exercises and much ideological debate,[46] the directors of the Chantiers de la Jeunesse and high-ranking civil servants of the future developed a spirit of leadership and a new style of life.

To make sure that the national revolution was firmly rooted and to have done with 'individualism', it was necessary to re-establish a number of 'confidential networks'. This task was given to a particularly typical Vichy institution, the Légion Française des Combattants created on 29 August 1940. Its structure may not have been very original (local representatives were elected, national organisers appointed)[47] but the mission entrusted to it was significant: the legionnaire who was initially to 'collaborate' 'in the work undertaken by the public powers' a few months later became a 'national revolutionary' responsible for 'promoting, defending, if necessary imposing the national revolution'. It did not take the place of the administration but was given the honour of being the eyes and ears of the *Maréchal* throughout the land.

The regime – naturally enough – tried hard to enrol, discipline and model the young.[48] A general secretariat with considerable powers, in the charge of an engineer who was a Lyautey pupil, one Lamirand, undertook this task. It financed a number of individual initiatives such as the Compagnons de France created by Henry Dhavernas, which tried to mould the young refugees of the southern zone into 'an avant-garde for the national revolution'. But the greatest efforts were devoted to one of the best known of the Vichy ventures, the Chantiers de la Jeunesse. General La Porte du Theil was given the mission of finding occupation for the 100,000 or so young recruits who had never been sent to join the fighting units. Despite the displeasure manifested by the occupying power, the experiment appeared sufficiently convincing to be extended to all the young Frenchmen of twenty years of age in the southern zone, who were now to undergo a kind of national service lasting for eight months. Lodged far away from the towns and subjected to a quasi-military discipline, their time was divided between works of public utility – particularly in the forests – and schooling in the civic virtues. Although there was, strictly speaking, no official doctrine, the lessons were strongly impregnated with catholicism and even more by '*maréchalisme*'. Although Lamirand favoured a certain pluralism for youth movements, he stressed the importance of 'the civic and political element that it was the State's duty to provide'.[49]

Vichy was equally concerned to model people's minds by tightly controlling the media,[50] not only the national Radio[51] and the Office Français d'Information (OFI), which operated as an official agency, but also the printed press. The OFI's general secretariat had a number of ways of exerting pressure on the press: the simplest and most brutal was official censorship. It was niggling and, if we are to believe the journalists, usually exercised by petty tyrants who were not particularly bright. A slightly more sophisticated method was for the official services to dispense 'orientation notes' (themes that newspapers were strongly urged to develop) and, above all, a multitude of 'instructions'.[52] In a more discreet fashion, the French State also subsidised a number of newspapers published in the southern zone, above all the Parisian press that had withdrawn to the south[53] and now found itself in particular financial difficulties, failing to win new provincial readers.[54] On the whole this State take-over functioned efficiently. The journalists were no doubt not particularly happy about the snipping scissors of 'Dame Anastasie' (the censorship) and one or two of the dailies – *La Dépêche de Toulouse*, for example – engaged upon an undercover guerilla campaign against the services of the general secretariat. No doubt also, a number of papers scuttled themselves (*Le Jour-Echo de Paris* did so as early as March 1942), especially after an eruption of German 'supervisors', following the invasion of the southern zone (even *Le Temps* decided to close on 29 November 1942). In general, however, it seems reasonable to accept the view of Henri Michel and Claude Lévy: 'On the whole, the press was conformist',[55] 'right-thinking' and adopted a 'moralistic tone'.

French society still had to be welded into a unified whole. It was thought possible to achieve that end by organising 'professions on a corporative basis': this was thought to be the antidote, at last, against the combined iniquities of individualism and state interference. It was tried out in the domain of agriculture,[56] the area where class conflicts appeared to be the least bitter. As early as 2 December 1940, a law was promulgated 'relating to the corporative organisation of agriculture', commonly known as the law on 'Peasant Corporation'. The targets set were ambitious: 'to promote and manage the common interests of peasant families in the moral, social and economic domains'. The complex structure took the form of a hierarchical pyramid: at a local level there was a single syndicate with an elected syndic; above this, regional unions headed by an appointed council and one delegate. At the top, the National Corporative Council flanked by a permanent Council. In principle, the Corporation was supposed to regulate 'all the conditions of peasant life' and 'the entire agricultural economy' but, even at the regional level 'government commissioners' could 'refer all decisions taken to the minister'. This remarkable syndicate was open to 'all those who live on the land, whether they be workers, directors of enterprises or farming landowners'. It was not compulsory, but to benefit from a number of available loans it was necessary to be affiliated.

It was only much later, on 4 October 1941, after many ups and downs, that another law was introduced 'on the social organisation of professions'[57] for the 'industrial and commercial' sectors; it was better known as the 'Charte du Travail' (the Charter of Work). In theory, it instituted twenty-nine 'professional families' subdivided into five 'unique profess-ional syndicates' ('employers, workers, employees, superintendents and engineers, leaders of the administration and commerce'). Its structure was double: on the one hand vertical, with a pyramid of local syndicates, regional unions and national federations; on the other, horizontal, with 'social committees' composed of an equal number of 'employers, workers, employees and other categories'. In principle, these syndicates were com-pulsory and were 'called upon to keep themselves informed on all social and economic aspects of professional activity'.

Meagre results indeed

Seldom can there have been greater discrepancy between inten-tions and results, although there were one or two gains such as the introduction of the 'single salary', the minimum living wage and pension for retired workers.[58] In the main, the national revolution was no more than a sketchy blueprint[59] and the undertaking was full of contradictions as can be seen, for example, from the ever-increasing State intervention and the influence wielded by the great captains of industry.

In theory, the strengthening of authority at the top was supposed to be accompanied by a deconcentration at regional and local levels. But in fact the power of the prefects was consolidated and 'administrators responsible for public order and supplies' were introduced. Overall, non-conformists – or those considered as such – were quickly brought under control: for example, Uriage was soon subjected to niggling controls and obliged to dispense with a number of lecturers considered to be over-individualistic. The official policy of pluralism was so whittled down that even the catholic hierarchy became worried and as early as February 1941 issued a warning: 'youth united in the country's service, yes; a single version of youth, no'. The policies adopted in the agricultural domain are equally significant: not only were the resettlement of rural regions and the protection for family farms failures to a large extent[60] but also – and above all – in contradiction to the spirit of the law of 2 December 1940, it was the Minister who was pulling all the strings: the trade-unions themselves had so little power that even some of the champions of agrarian corporatism preferred to turn their backs on the official organisms or to resign. Furthermore, virtually from the very start the 'Peasant Corporation' was made into a State instrument for dividing up and collecting harvests and produce; and that soon had the effect of making the peasants keep their distance from an institution that practised coercive methods of a kind of which they had always been wary.

As is well known, the regime prided itself upon gathering all social categories under one banner. It had, after all, dissolved all inter-professional organisations, those of workers as well as employers; and had prohibited strikes as well as lock-outs. Yet it was a false symmetry since what it was in effect seeking to establish was one-way social peace. It was clearly not completely fortuitous that, in the event, the only concrete achievement of the Charter of Work was the establishment of 'social committees of enterprise' totally controlled by the employers. In a similar fashion, encouragement was given to 'mixed professional associations' under the wing of that past master of shock-tactics, Jules Verger. Meanwhile, wherever one turned there was a brutal clamp-down – at Renault, at Berliet, in the coal mines of the north and elsewhere too.[61]

On the evidence, once again, of official declarations, a new balance was to be introduced into the economy and society of the French people and measures taken to favour the artisans and the middle classes. The regime was even prone to congratulating itself on its anti-capitalism, priding itself on having reinforced State control over limited companies. However, there can be no doubt that in fact the real economic power lay in the hands of big business. In the event, the captains of industry turned out to be remarkably adept at using to their profit the official organisations that the situation had thrown up: on 16 August 1940, 'provisional organisational committees' were set up (by 1944 there were to be 234 of them). Their function was to assess the resources available, decide upon manufacturing programmes and, in general, to 'ensure a better functioning of whatever branch of activity was involved, in the common interest of both business and employees'; 10 December saw the institution of a 'Central Office for the Distribution of Industrial Production' charged with planning in relation to needs. As a general rule, management of these all-powerful organisations fell into the hands of the big employers and their own managers. It was thus that Pierre Ricard presided over the Committee for the Organisation of the Foundries and Auguste Detoeuf did so over electrical construction. It is true that the State retained overall control but, in the apparent interests of efficiency, it allowed the champions of big business a free hand.[62] In December 1941, it even assumed the right to close down businesses that were not sufficiently profitable.[63] Jacques Julliard certainly had good cause to call this 'a veritable golden age for French employers'.[64]

These contradictions in the national revolution stemmed in part from the pressures of the occupation which left their mark on the economic situation. The dislocation of the usual circuits of exchange and the obligation to pay a large tribute to the occupying power projected France rudely into an economy of penury.[65] Optimists hoped to maintain production at 70% of the 1938 level but by 1941 it became clear that this would not be possible. What with the German pressures on top of everything else, whether it liked it or not Vichy found itself with no alternative but to become an interventionist war economy:[66] it imposed tighter controls over foreign exchanges, taxation on prices and wages and stricter measures of rationing. In this economy of penury, it became even more important to 'close the circuit', to mop up any surplus buying power in order to check inflationist tendencies. Enforced savings were thus systematically channelled into State holdings[67] to the point where 40% of public spending was covered by such funds.

All the same, not everything can be blamed on the peculiarly difficult circumstances, for the national revolution had already revealed its limitations even before France became shackled to the total war in which the Reich was engaged. Most of its measures were limping compromises similar to the Charter of Work, which was returned three times to the drawing board only to produce a final text that pleased no one. In fact, so long as the verbal appearances were saved, the regime was quite satisfied to proceed on a day to day basis.

Pétainisms and Pétainists

In the last analysis the national revolution rested upon the assumption that it had won a consensus. In the early days, the regime made attempts to be persuasive – even as it applied the coercive measures mentioned above: this was the period that was known at the time as 'open Pétainism'. But, its opponents aside, there were a number of different ways of being a Pétainist and they were not all to stand the test of time in a similar fashion.[68]

Thus one can speak of a Pétainism by default: in effect, in the early days, the structures to contain its declared opponents had yet to be created or reconstructed. We should at this point open a brief parenthesis on the subject of the extremists[69] who, from their base in Paris, were beginning to criticise the Vichy 'reactionaries'. Still few in number, they were vociferous rather than truly dangerous. The principal danger seemed more likely to come from the left. But the PCF, which had lost its leaders in the repression and was still reeling in the aftermath of the German–Soviet pact, was struggling for its second wind. As for Daniel Mayer and those of his friends who remained Blumists, they were experiencing even greater difficulties in their attempts to purge the SFIO and set up a Socialist Action Committee. The remnants of the central trade-unions of workers[70] were showing extreme caution. Although many of the very first members of the Resistance came from their ranks, in general they were preferring to give ground: thus on 20 July, a national confederal committee of the CGT decided to modify the statutes, removing all references to the class struggle and introducing declarations on the subject of conciliation and arbitration to replace the articles on the subject of strikes.

So among the politicians Pétainism was quite healthy. Pétainists by conviction, transfigured by the 'divine surprise',[71] had been joined by others who had rallied from a number of quarters. The bulk of them came from the conservative and liberal right, men such as Bardoux and Flandin, for example. They did not approve of all the policies of the new regime, being in particular critical of the total disappearance of the representative system, but their misgivings gave way in the face of the re-established social peace, the appeal made to notables and members of the élite and the revenge taken for 1936. They were to expect much from Flandin's spell of power. The soft underbelly of the left[72] was also well represented: it included fringe figures such as Bergery, disillusioned men like Monzie and a fair number of neo-radicals from the right, led by Pierre Dominique. The classical left was also represented: on 30 March 1941, a group of radicals, some of them quite well known, Maurice Sarraut, for example, stated their approval of a 'Nîmes Declaration' which concluded as follows: 'We earnestly desire to serve France, grouped around you, Monsieur le Maréchal ... You give us grounds for hope.' Then there was a fraction – only a minority, it is true – from the socialist and trade-unionist left, which approved of the choices of Belin and Spinasse although not of everything else. While certain radicals seem to have been reticent to say the least, their benevolent willingness to wait and see meanwhile operated in favour of Pétainism.

The regime could also congratulate itself on the whole-hearted support of an important pressure group: the catholic hierarchy and practising catholics.[73] The defeat had given rise to virulent clerical repudiations fuelled by a summary providentialism: Mgr. Saliège[74] exclaimed: 'We ask pardon for having chased God from schools, pulpits and the nation, O Lord ... How would we have used an easy victory in 1940?' As for Claudel, representative of a militant strain of French catholicism, he noted on 6 July:

> After sixty years, France has been delivered from the yoke of the radical and anti-catholic party (professors, lawyers, Jews and Freemasons). The new government is invoking God and restoring the Grande-Chartreuse to the religious orders. There is hope that we may be delivered from universal suffrage and parliamentarianism; and also from the evil and imbecile domination of the schoolteachers who covered themselves with shame in the last war. Authority is restored.[75]

The hierarchy, as usual, had taken its time before declaring its official position in relation to the regime; in July and September 1941, the cardinals and archbishops of both zones had – in accordance with a well-tried policy – taken good care not to pronounce upon the problem of its legitimacy, limiting themselves to insisting that the faithful show 'a sincere and complete loyalism towards the established power'. But it immediately went on: 'We revere the head of State and ask that the union of all the French people should forthwith be made manifest around him.' In November 1940, furthermore, the primate of the Gauls, Cardinal Gerlier, had declared: 'Work, the Family, the Motherland: those are our three words' and had

Maréchal Pétain in front of the oak tree which bears his name in the Forest of Tronçais. Copyright: Photo Keystone

then exclaimed with no hesitation: 'Pétain is France; France is Pétain'. Over and above the satisfaction to be derived from the political and ideological situation, there were the numerous advantages that the French State had granted the Church, particularly in the vexed domain of education: legislation on congregations was considerably relaxed, religious instruction was reintroduced in schools as an option, municipalities received the right to grant subsidies to free schools and, for the year 1941, the State granted 'exceptional aid suited to the circumstances' amounting to 400 million francs. To be sure, not all bones of contention between the Catholic Church and the State had been resolved. The catholic hierarchy was demanding greater freedom of action for its youth movements and thought that the formula that one of the ministers for national education, Carcopino, defended did not go far enough. This was to favour 'religious neutrality in State schools and freedom of teaching for the nation'. The fact is that 'as always when in a position of strength, the catholics went all out to consolidate their own schools and to penetrate the public ones'.[76] On the whole, however, relations between a hierarchy that had been indubitably won over and the semi-clerical regime were altogether satisfactory.

In short, a groundroots movement of *maréchalisme* had arisen in a quite spontaneous fashion, fuelled by the profound traumas engendered by the defeat. Praise was given to the vigour of the head of State, his steadfast gaze and his classical profile. People participated in a communal cult of the Father, or the Grandfather, the Leader or worker of miracles. This combination of attributes brought him 2,000 letters a day. Propaganda was certainly encouraging such a personality cult: countless *maréchaliste* calenders and almanacs were produced, a peak near Chamonix was named after him, a 'Pétain oak tree' was consecrated in the Tronçais forest . . . There was even a curious paternoster going about which began 'Our Father, which art at our head. . .' and ended 'And deliver us from evil, oh Maréchal'.[77]

Work, the Family, the Motherland, for the children of France

'He is a fine old man, strong and straight as the Druids' tree; a limpid gaze illuminates his calm face, as limpid as his homeland's calm waters reflecting a patch of sky.

'His gait is firm, his head held high under the triple crown of oak; seven stars band his arm and the military medal lies on his chest, against his heart.

'He is Maréchal Pétain, our Maréchal, Father of all the children of France [who] . . . offers himself to France.

'Now he commands forty-two million crushed Frenchmen, one hundred and ten million men in metropolitan France and her colonies.

'Once again, for the second time, on the edge of the abyss he has saved a bruised but still living France.

'He is the sign of hope, the promise of new tomorrows.

'The earth grows green again in spring-time. . .

'He is our leader and our father; with devotion, intelligence, love and faith, he has brought the only balm that can restore France to her great destiny: the caring cure of Truth.'[78]

The popular fervour did not abate for a long time: in 1944, in the occupied zone at any rate, the arrival of Philippe Pétain could still attract large crowds. This groundroots version of *maréchalisme* was usually supported by a *maréchalisme* that emphasised the image of the staunch protector of metropolitan France, a figure to whom every virtue was ascribed. Much more fragile, on the other hand, was the image of *maréchalisme* associated with the national revolution: on 12 August 1941, Pétain, sensitive to the 'evil wind' that was starting to blow, chided those French people 'whose memories were so short'. Even after the events of 1942, there was still a Vichy neo-right wing which was unquestioningly Pétainist and resigned to State collaboration, but it was losing ground. *A fortiori*, the *maréchalisme* of the Pétainists who had rallied from other positions became increasingly dilute as the Anglo-Saxon successes multiplied.

State collaboration

The national revolution, with all its repressive measures, was the sole responsibility of Vichy, whose brainchild it exclusively was. In the main, the Reich showed no interest in it. Meanwhile, the armistice led to what Stanley Hoffmann has called 'State collaboration', a policy personally decided by Philippe Pétain. It opened a remarkable chapter in the history of Franco-German relations as it set off what has, with justification, been called a 'Franco-French' war. It was destined to divide the French people in all the more lasting fashion given that, in the view of many Vichy men, it was 'the enemy within' rather than the occupying power that had to be eliminated.[79]

The choices before Philippe Pétain, head of the French State

No sooner had the armistice been signed than Vichy found itself faced with a situation it had not foreseen: having failed to gain control of the English skies, the Reich indefinitely deferred the invasion of Great Britain and put off until later the conclusion of a peace in the west. From the very beginning, those in charge of the Reich's economy were in favour of exploiting the vanquished. In this respect, France, bound by the Draconian clauses of the armistice, became the most prized jewel in the whole of occupied Europe. The Wehrmacht, for its part, was concerned first and foremost to make it a reliable base; subsequently, overcoming its mistrust, it decided not to rule out a selective kind of collaboration if it could provide appreciable logistic support in the Mediterranean area. For the master of the Reich, the victory over France had to be a 'definitive' one. France would not be 'polonised' (Hitler's hierarchy did not class the French as *Untermenschen*). But, in conformity with his instructions of 9 July 1940, it would become a market garden for the new Europe ('a country of landowners that might eventually be responsible also for the supply of certain fashion commodities') and also its Luna Park. While the Führer was not enthusiastic about collaboration of a random kind, with his characteristic fundamental optimism he accepted it in principle, on opportunistic grounds, meanwhile setting strict limitations upon it, however. The Reich must profit substantially from it without making any concessions of a political nature. That set a check upon 'the German ambassador in Paris', Otto Abetz, one of the few Germans who wanted to turn Franco-German collaboration into the effective cornerstone of the new vassalised Europe.

Thanks to the armistice agreement, the Reich had a free choice as to the means of subduing the French State. The demarcation line, 'the bit in the horse's mouth', as one Wehrmacht leader put it, made it possible if need be to establish an economic stranglehold over the occupied zone; the official tribute paid as 'costs of upkeep for the German occupying troops' could be adjusted according to circumstances.[80] The prisoners interned 'pending peace' represented a remarkable reserve of political hostages. The Reich had, furthermore, seized a number of territorial pledges:[81] as early as August 1940, it had, *de facto*, annexed three departments in the east and established a line running north to east from the Somme to the Jura. This marked out a 'prohibited zone'[82] (which the refugees of the exodus were not permitted to cross) and it included an 'attached zone'[83] (the departments of the Nord and the Pas de Calais) which was controlled by the commandant of Brussels, placed under the brutal rule of General Niehoff. This area was barred to the ministers of Vichy and up until the summer of 1941 even high-ranking French civil servants retained no more than a derisory measure of power there. Worse still, in July 1940, a General Weyer was installed in the prefecture of Ille-et-Vilaine as governor of Brittany. Although this seems to have been no more than a false manoeuvre,[84] the territorial aggression was disturbing. Finally, as early as the summer of 1940, the occupying authorities cleverly made sure that the Vichy government, which was anxious to publish the same *Journal Officiel* in both zones, submitted all proposed laws and appointments to them for approval.

Faced with these very real constraints, Philippe Pétain chose not only economic collaboration – which seemed unavoidable anyway – but also political collaboration, the principle of which had been established at Montoire. There can be no doubt that this was the personal decision of the head of the French State.[85] It was not sympathy for the Nazi regime, which he mistrusted, that prompted him to make it; rather, a pragmatism that believed itself realistic. But he made two errors in his calculations: like a good many other theoretical strategists at the time, he was banking on a victory for Germany; at the same time – and this is more curious – he was sufficiently naïve to believe that through collaboration France would become a political partner on equal terms with the Reich; and that he, Pétain, would in exchange obtain political advantages that would promote the national revolution. That was the only thing that really counted for him. But he was becoming implicated in a system in which he would remain trapped to the last. Yet in this bargaining game, the French State had at its disposal considerable assets, in the shape of the Fleet and the Empire, even if these were vulnerable to unforseeable changes in the situation.

In a letter addressed to Weygand on 9 November 1940, Pétain claimed to be resolved to exclude all co-belligerence with the Reich. But he had already implicitly accepted a partial if not total reversal of alliances. It is true that, in the profound altercation dividing the French and the British, France could claim to be the injured party. As early as 16 June, the French fleet had become the pawn which could lead to a show-down.[86] Churchill, who knew nothing of the directives to scuttle sent out by Darlan,[87] placed no credence at all in Hitler's word[88] and was convinced that what was at stake was the survival of the British Isles.[89] On 3 July 1940, he launched 'Operation Catapult', with the aim of rallying or neutralising as many French warships as possible. In the British ports and the harbours of Alexandria the operation went ahead willy-nilly but at least there was not too much damage. In the Bay of Mers el-Kébir, on the other hand, Admiral Gensoul, somewhat high-handedly perhaps, refused even to consider the conditions proposed by the British Admiralty.[90] The English opened fire and the ensuing hostilities claimed 1,297 dead among the French sailors. The government did no more than break off diplomatic relations but the country as a whole was rocked by a violent explosion of anglophobia, with depressing effects.

It is true that, after the war, the Vichy men claimed that clandestine negotiations between Great Britain and the French State had continued all the time and that Pétain, even as he attended the Montoire meeting, was in truth playing the Anglo-Saxon game. This thesis of a double game has been much promoted but it does not stand up to a methodical examination of the facts.[91] It cannot be denied that, throughout the autumn of 1940, Churchill, using anything that came to hand and seriously concerned at the possibility of Franco-German co-belligerence, was not only receiving all those who claimed to be official emissaries from Vichy – in particular a university professor, Louis Rougier – but was also sending missives and messages not only to Pétain but also to Weygand. Thus on 31 December 1940, he urged Pétain to consider the possibility of the French Empire re-entering the war and suggested ultra-secret general staff consultations to this effect. No reply was ever forthcoming: not only had Philippe Pétain always been deeply mistrustful of the British but, above all, he was by now convinced that it would be a German peace.

Vichy variations

In Vichy itself, the Pétain line may not, strictly speaking, have been challenged but from a number of quarters pressure was at least exerted to modify it. In simple terms, two opposite tactics were suggested. There were some, partisans of 'the armistice, nothing but the armistice', who believed economic collaboration to be inevitable but were opposed to political collaboration. As time passed, they came to consider the latter increasingly dangerous from every point of view. Thus when, in November 1942, Laval declared that 'if the Anglo-Saxons are the victors in this war, it will mean Bolshevism', Weygand retorted sharply: 'I tell you yet again that the government, through its policies, is preparing the way for communism.'

Weygand was a typical representative of this attitude. In North Africa, to which Pétain had sent him as the government's delegate general, he, on his own authority, provided an umbrella for the clandestine stock-piling of war materials. Yet, committed to revenge though he was, he never wavered in his support for Pétain. In his view, as in that of a number of Vichy men who were both nationalist and anti-German, revenge could only come through an internal regeneration for which the national revolution provided the model.[92] Meanwhile, not only was dissidence rife in the army – and that was in itself unpardonable – but it was also undermining Authority, Order and the Hierarchy. That is why Weygand's loyalty to Pétain was unshakable and also why he did not respond to the repeated overtures of the British.

Others, alongside Laval, were in favour of quite the opposite tactics, of forging ahead regardless. Although he was pressing for an authoritarian 'republic', Laval was no more attracted to Nazism than Pétain was. He, like Pétain, fancied his own skilful foresight in the domain of *Realpolitik*. Meanwhile, he believed that the fate of the French State depended not upon the national revolution but rather upon its external policies. To him, it was quite obvious what these should be: the future Europe would be German, and it was of the first importance to ensure that France's place in that Europe would be as advantageous as possible. Instead of hedging one's bets, which would be not only unprofitable but criminal, it was necessary to take the initiative, engage in 'loyal' collaboration and force Germany's hand; France would then be in a more favourable position when the time came round for the spoils of peace. To these ends, he urged not only large-scale economic collaboration but also extensive political collaboration, not excluding open participation from the French State in the war effort of the Reich.

Between the line adopted by Pétain and that defended by Laval, there are considerable differences and there can be no doubt that under Laval's proconsulship collaboration – at least on the French side – thrived. It would nevertheless be mistaken to draw a categorical contrast between the Vichy of Pétain and that of Laval. Between the two there was no difference in kind: the starting point for Pétain, as for Laval, rested upon the same basic postulates and both the one and the other stuck to them right through and despite their rebuffs in the field of State collaboration. Besides, it was in May 1941, at a time when Laval was no longer in the government, that State collaboration reached its peak.

From Montoire to Saint-Florentin: the lure

State collaboration began at Montoire in October 1940 and reached its culmination in May 1941 with the 'Protocoles de Paris'. It had already run out of steam by December 1941 when the meeting of Saint-Florentin took place.

Throughout the summer of 1940, the leaders of the French State had done everything within their power to meet responsible negotiators from the German side. One point must, once again, be emphasised: it was Vichy, not the Reich, which requested these meetings, Vichy – logically enough – which was seeking State collaboration.[93] In Abetz, Laval discovered his most rewarding contact. But it fell to Pétain to make the first official overture. On 11 October, he declared himself ready 'to seek collaboration in every domain', provided that the victor would 'show restraint in victory'. Hitler allowed himself to be tempted: for one thing, he had been favourably impressed with the resistance put up by the Vichy forces at Dakar and, for another, before unleashing the Wehrmacht on the Russian steppes, he was trying hard to build up a complex structure to 'close the back door' in the Mediterranean area.

It was in Spain, on 22 October, that Hitler received Laval. Two days later, after disappointing conversations with Franco in Hendaye, he met with the head of the French State in Montoire. In their exchange of views, both parties showed great circumspection while agreeing, in principle, on collaboration between the French State and the Reich. The master of the Reich had received the victor of Verdun with much deference and had exchanged a handshake with him. The Propagandastaffel made sure that it created a sensation in France and, indeed, the world over. There were at least some, committed Vichy men though they were, whom this irritated (to put it mildly).[94] It was to assuage such 'anxieties' that had here and there broken out that on 30 October, Philippe Pétain made an all-out plea for political collaboration, staking on this all his authority of 'Father' and 'Leader'. The decisive step had now been taken.

So Vichy thought, at least. And the French State spared itself no effort: it proceeded to sign a 'compensation agreement' in which Germany took the lion's share, ceded French shares in the Yugoslav copper mines[95] and handed over to the Reich the gold that the Belgian government had earlier entrusted to the French government. Laval – but not Laval alone: Darlan, Hunziger and many others too – met with generals of the Wehrmacht to draw up plans to recapture the Chad from the forces of 'dissidence'. In return for these willingly granted concessions, the Reich made one or two gestures: for instance, it conceded that the French State could act as protective power over its own prisoners. However, at the same time, in November the two Gauleiters without warning expelled from Alsace-Lorraine 150,000 people who the Reich considered could not be assimilated; and on 10 December 1940 Hitler signed the order for the 'Attila plan' to invade the non-occupied zone in case of need. State collaboration clearly got off to a bad start.

The sacking of Laval ushered in a period of confusion. We have already indicated the deeper reasons for the palace revolution of 13 December which was concerned not so much with the bases of Laval's policies as with their modalities. But the astonishment provoked in public opinion by the abrupt dismissal of the Vichy man who seemed the most convinced architect of Franco-German reconciliation and the prompt reactions on the part of the Germans[96] lent this palace revolution an unexpected and, on the whole, disproportionate importance. It is that disproportion that explains the veritable ambiguity of this mini-crisis.

The Vichy government was meantime plunged into great embarrassment. However earnestly it proclaimed the purity of its intentions and Darlan assured Hitler, whom he met near Beauvais on 25 December, that nothing had changed in the policies decided at Montoire, Vichy proved unable to persuade Abetz[97] to lift his ostracism of Flandin, the new Minister of Foreign Affairs. It was the arguments of the Wehrmacht that resolved the situation. There was, as it happened, a fraction of the German High Command that was alarmed at the prospect of the Reich immediately setting up a second front, even before it had finished with the English in the Mediterranean. This group persuaded Hitler to accept at face value the many declarations of intent vouchsafed by Vichy so as to obtain a logistic support for Rommel's troops who were in difficulties in Cyrenaica and for the Iraqi insurgents who had mounted a successful anti-British *coup de'état* on 3 April. Pétain and Darlan rose to the bait. The Admiral of the Fleet, who was much struck by the amazing successes of the Reich in the Balkans, was, like Laval, out to secure a peace concluded at the expense of Great Britain that would safeguard the maritime power and colonial interests of the French. Three weeks of negotiations resulted in the initialling of the 'Protocoles de Paris': these included two technical clauses concerning Iraq and French North Africa, another 'of principle' concerning Dakar and the AOF and also a 'complementary protocol' of an extremely political nature, tacked on at the last minute. The terms of this agreement committed the

French State to providing appropriate logistic support for the Axis troops (the use of railways and airfields, delivery of materials, etc)[98] and it also declared itself prepared 'in principle' to turn Dakar into a support base for the Kriegsmarine. On top of all this, Darlan, who was out to win political concessions in exchange, had seen to it that the 'complementary protocol' specified that 'the German government should, by granting political and economic concessions, [provide] the French government with the means of justifying in the eyes of French public opinion the possibility of armed conflict against England and the United States'. This was going a long way, indeed playing with fire. But the admiral was, for his part, very pleased, congratulating himself on having wrung from the Reich more concessions than it had, in fact, ever granted: a reduction in the legal tribute, the rearmament of a dozen warships and the liberation of some 100,000 prisoners of war.

However, this latest burst of State collaboration was not maintained. In Vichy the *Protocoles de Paris* were severely criticised by Weygand who, supported by Boisson, the governor general of the AOF, bitterly reproached Darlan for having laid the Empire open to Axis penetration, thereby facilitating the sapping spread of dissidence and concluding a very short-term sell-out of France's overseas possessions. These were strong arguments and they undermined the confidence of the Vichy leaders. The French State then made a 'double or quits' move: Darlan demanded that by way of a political return, Berlin should re-establish the French State's total sovereignty over the entire territory. Such a claim to parity was intolerable to Hitler, particularly as the British had reconquered Baghdad and neutralised Syria and the Lebanon. Not only did he break off negotiations but he once again made it quite plain who was master: he demanded and obtained from Pétain that Weygand be recalled from North Africa.

The head of the French State can have harboured few illusions when he went to meet Goering at Saint-Florentin on 1 December 1941. The interview did indeed turn sour. The Nazi marshal berated him, made threats and curtly refused even to consider a French memorandum. The situation was such that Pétain felt in duty bound to reproach him:

> My understanding was that true collaboration implied treating on equal terms. If there is to be a conqueror set above and the conquered set below, there can be no more collaboration. All that remains is what you call a *Diktat* and we call the 'law of the strongest'... You can win the war on your own but you cannot make peace on your own. You cannot make peace without France. If you will not make a peace of collaboration, you risk losing the peace.

Philippe Pétain was beginning to realise that he had been swindled, that political collaboration with the Reich was nothing but a trap.

The record of fifteen months of voluntary collaboration was indeed disappointing, to say the least: it had just been a lure. The French State had received no more than a handful of crumbs in return for all the profit that the Reich had derived from the 'Montoire policy': namely, the official right to occupy and exploit a conquered country with hardly any of the disadvantages usually attendant upon such a situation. The inequality of the bargain was explained by an initial misunderstanding: namely, that in effect it takes two to collaborate and only the French State had been truly anxious for collaboration. At Montoire, Pétain (and the French people with him) had accepted all the risks. For Hitler, Montoire was but one of many incidents in a war which was about Europe, just a pawn in the Mediterranean game being played out with Spain and Italy. And the leaders of the French State, trapped in their gallocentricity, were to learn to their cost that in the eyes of the Führer, Vichy was of very little account compared with London and Moscow. The French had been duped in the bargain of political collaboration. Nevertheless, it had become a machine increasingly difficult to control to the point where even such an attitude as Weygand's seemed to have been overtaken by events. For Laval, straining at his leash, it seemed more imperative than ever to press forward.

The rebels

Both State collaboration and the armistice had immediately been rejected by those who very quickly identified themselves as rebels. In 1941 they still constituted no more than an ill-coordinated tiny minority. Nevertheless, it would be mistaken to underestimate their political importance: they foreshadowed future developments and the unification of a fighting France.[99]

Something had to be done

Those who had reacted with feelings of refusal and shame rather than of relief soon tried to 'do something' (C. Bourdet). As early as June 1940, General Cochet called upon the men under his command not to disarm; on 17 June, Edmond Michelet produced a tract in which, quoting Péguy, he declared that 'those who do not give in are right and those who do are wrong'; prisoners gave their guards the slip; on 20 June, an agricultural worker, Etienne Achavanne, cut the telephone wires of an airport occupied by the Wehrmacht; he was arrested and shot.

Contrary to what is generally believed, these spasms of defiance against the prevailing 'breast-beating' and defeatism were not prompted by directives from across the Channel. Resistance truly did have an original impulse within France itself. For one thing, liaison with London was extremely chancy: it was not until January 1941 that Frenay managed to relay – via Spain – the information that his movement had collected and it was October already by the time that Yves Morandat, the first emissary of Free

France, charged with an exploratory political mission, was parachuted into France. For another, there were many rebels who did not wish to be seen as *émigrés* and believed that most of the work would have to be done in France. When Daniel and Cleta Mayer told Blum that they wanted to get to London, he retorted bluntly: 'Over there you will be just two more individuals with no military skills who will have to be fed. Here, there will be work to be done. We must carry on with the war, reconstruct the party and direct it in the struggle against the occupying power and Vichy. You will be of more use here.'[100]

There is another generally accepted idea, namely that the first people to resist were marginal figures whose 'character' counted for more than their political commitment. It is true that a number of rebels – like Frenay and Emmanuel d'Astier de la Vigerie – were obliged to break with their families and their social and political milieux and become social adventurers of a kind.[101] It is, however, striking to note that these rebels came in the main from a number of particular schools of thought. There were many catholic militants – symbolised well enough by Edmond Michelet, the former president of the ACJF; many readers of *Sept* or *Temps Present* and also some of the popular democrat party (PDP) or the Jeune République. Many of them were to join the Liberté movement, founded in the autumn of 1940. Then there were the militants from the SFIO – those, at least, who, encouraged by Daniel Mayer, Félix Gouin, Suzanne Buisson and Lucien Hussel, had remained loyal or had rallied to the Blum line. In the occupied zone, the militant Jean Texcier was secretly distributing his *Conseils à l'occupé* (Advice for the Occupied) whilst in October 1940 the deputy-mayor of Roubaix, Jean Lebas, launched *L'Homme Libre* and in April 1941 Brigadier Jules Noutour created *La Voix du Nord*. And it was a group of socialists who started the Libération-Nord movement.[102] A number of trade-unionists both from the CGT and the CFTC also committed themselves, providing the inspiration for a 'Committee of Economic and Trade-Unionist Studies' which dissociated itself from Vichy and found active sympathy among a number of federations such as those of the railway workers and the postal workers.

But how?

The rebels all shared one belief: the war was not over, indeed it was just beginning. In January 1942, during the trial of one of the first of the northern zone's resistance movements known as the Musée de l'Homme, Léon-Maurice Nordmann declared before his German judges: 'Death is something risked every day on the battlefields; to my way of thinking we are still at war against you.' Such an assumption excluded *a fortiori* all forms of collaboration with the enemy. That being said, different appreciations of the situation soon emerged and to some extent they stemmed from political attitudes. They were not all fighting the same occupying power: many were still confronting the old hereditary enemy; for the militants of the left the target was also the products of the Nazi system. And in the early days there was another important choice to be made: should they go some way along the road with the Maréchal? Some thought that for tactical reasons they should, in order to win over those who in all good faith supported Pétain; others, in many cases those involved with the army at the time of the armistice,[103] believed that Philippe Pétain was playing a double game; others still were impressed by the renewal that the national revolution represented[104] and – according to Frenay's newspaper on 25 August 1941 – praised 'the excellent internal reforms that it announced', among them 'the suppression of all political parties'.[105] It was not until the spring or even the autumn of 1942 that those members of the Resistance who had been seduced by Pétain or the national revolution became both 'soldiers without uniforms and citizens in revolt',[106] falling into line with those who had opposed the Vichy regime without hesitation, in particular Libération-Nord and Liberation-Sud. In the meantime the French State had little by little interned or imprisoned many of those who had believed in Philippe Pétain's double game.[107]

The war was not over. Maybe. But how should it be waged, by military or by political means? Most of the rebels in the northern zone, perhaps because they found themselves in direct confrontation with the occupying power, wanted first and foremost to fight. Thus the Civil and Military Organisation (l'Organisation Civile et Militaire, the OCM) did indeed develop a civil section, under Blocq-Mascart, but it functioned just like a general staff commanded by active or reserve officers such as Arthuys, Heurteaux and Touny. In the southern zone, in contrast, the rebels were for the most part inclined to much more 'political' forms of action.[108]

Whilst most of the leaders of the more political movements planned to pursue their fight on an independent basis, even where the Free French were concerned, those who were looking first and foremost for immediate practical results were more inclined to join networks linked with the FFL or the British secret services.[109]

Everything – or almost everything – had to be started from scratch; nobody – at least hardly anybody – was equipped for this kind of struggle. The traditional élite groups were conspicuously absent, which certainly had the positive effect of stimulating new leadership but which was also a serious handicap in the early days of the Resistance. As for material means, they were quite derisory. Not much was said about armed combat and, in any case, arms, which had been confiscated by the army of the armistice, were in very short supply. Funds were low too: after four months of tireless fund-raising, Frenay had collected barely 14,000 francs: a pittance.[110]

In Pétainist France, stunned by defeat, such material conditions were of a kind to discourage even the most committed and reduce the rebels to a very small minority. The record for the summer of 1941, as assessed by Henri Noguères, was not brilliant. Statistically speaking, in terms of the French population as a whole, active members of the Resistance did not constitute even an appreciable minority. And what was more serious was that even 'passive' sympathisers were hardly more numerous. The great majority of French people were visibly more concerned to prevent a repetition of the horrors of war, to palliate the food shortages and to welcome home their prisoners of war than to carry on the struggle alongside the Allies.[111] In the northern zone, the risks that had to be run were considerable. In the southern zone, some people preferred first to try to explore all the legal possibilities. Thus, a man such as Monnier who was, if anyone was, anti-Munich and anti-Nazi opted to bring out *L'Esprit* again rather than join the team grouped around Père Chaillet who were about to publish the clandestine *Cahiers du Témoignage Chrétien*.[112] Others, among them Malraux, reacted with 'technical realism' and questions such as: 'Have you any money? . . . Have you any arms? . . . Right, . . . come back and see me when you have both'.[113]

It should be added that – apart from the communists – not many leaders of the Resistance were in a position to set up rapidly a truly popular organisation. They were not necessarily all as élitist as Blocq-Mascart who, in the first *Cahier* produced by the Organisation Civile et Militaire, wrote: 'It is up to the leaders to lead public opinion out of its disarray'. All the same, the non-communist leaders of the Resistance had relatively few contacts with popular milieux. Perhaps that was because many of them were either teachers[114] or else engaged in the liberal professions.

The first convergencies

In 1940, chance took a hand in a fair number of the choices made. It was in a train that Frenay made contact with Bourdet; one particular network was approached in preference to another because it happened to have the most roots in the area. As the months passed, differences emerged but also the first groups were formed. A schematic calendar of the course of events would be as follows: The summer of 1940 was a time when rebellion was a more or less symbolic matter; the autumn and winter saw the first initiatives; by 1941 the Resistance had taken root. By then two types of organisation were already operational: networks and movements. Claude Bourdet distinguished between the two as follows:

> A *network* is an organisation created for a specific military purpose, essentially intelligence, coincidentally sabotage and frequently also to help in the escape of prisoners of war, in particular pilots shot down by the enemy: these are what are called the 'escape routes'. A network is, by definition, in close contact with some organ of the general staff of the forces

for which it works ... The first objective of a *movement*, on the other hand, is to sensitise and organise the population as widely as possible. Of course, it also has concrete objectives ... but basically it could be said that it fulfils those tasks *over and above* its other duties, simply because it would be absurd not to make use of such means as well and because each of its members needs to feel committed in some concrete fashion. But it undertakes its tasks above all *in relation to the population.* It is *the population* that is its fundamental objective and preoccupation.[115]

Ever since June 1940, there had in effect been rebels who acted in a more or less individual manner. The case of Jean Moulin, who refused to put his signature to a document that was humiliating to the French army, is well known. Less well known perhaps are those of Vieljeux, a veteran officer, later deported, who, as mayor of La Rochelle, refused to show the flag; Paul Roche, shot for having sabotaged a telephone cable at Royan; Karp Israël who suffered the same fate for having raised a clenched fist as the Wehrmacht troops paraded through Bordeaux; and Paul Koepfer who set up an escape route and (on the night of Christmas 1940 alone) smuggled out 120 people who were in danger. During this same period, the militant socialist, Jean Texcier, was beginning clandestinely to distribute his *Conseils à l'occupé*, carrying recommendations such as: 'Display a fine indifference but keep alive the flame of your anger, it will come in useful', or 'Brother, wear your fine rebel's mask with care'.[116]

By the winter these rebels were getting themselves organised: sheltering prisoners who had had a lucky escape, collecting intelligence of every kind for a network just establishing itself; or copying and distributing tracts or even 'newspapers'. By October 1940, five newspapers had already appeared in the wake of what appears to have been the very first to be published by the underground press: Robert Deiss' *Pantagruel* (which ran to sixteen issues). All the major movements – or almost all – were soon to have their own newspaper,[117] the production of which, for many of them, constituted their principal militant activity. Those who were hungry for action sometimes felt frustration at such a situation – the Polytechnician Asher, for example (the future *Ravanel*). He would attend 'perfectly sympathetic meetings among perfectly civilised members of Lyonnais society, from which very little would emerge'.[118] Here and there, however, it was not simply a matter of propaganda. In Montpellier, Jacques Renouvin,[119] who had painted the words 'I shall not have collaborated' in blue methylene on the equestrian statue of Louis XIV, set up a number of commando groups that were prepared to take action against collaborationists. In Lyons, militants from the Franc-Tireur organisation and the JEC disrupted the showing of a Nazi film *Le Juif süss*. In the northern zone, German military installations had been subjected to continuous sabotage (in December, 1940, there were 51 cases in the departments of the Nord and the

Pas de Calais alone). The occupied zone had also been the scene of two demonstrations that were interesting in a number of respects: on 11 November 1940, in defiance of all prohibitions, schoolchildren and students, nationalists, 'Gaullists' and communists alike, had demonstrated against the occupying power,[120] holding the Champs Elysées for two hours before the German forces opened fire. On 26 May 1941, a strike began at Dourges, which by the time it ended, on 7 June, was to have involved three-quarters of the miners of the Nord and Pas de Calais. This was a quite exemplary operation: launched with quite specific demands (better wages and working conditions), it became increasingly political as it spread, and turned into a show of force against the occupying power.[121]

The initial stages were always laborious, risky and disappointing. Only a few of this minority of early rebels lived to see the Liberation; even fewer were spared imprisonment or concentration camps; as beginners, they took too many risks; and they were also the victims of betrayal. It was a denunciation that destroyed the Morpain group in Le Havre, a traitor who brought about the arrest and execution of the principal leaders (Vildé, Lewitsky, Nordmann etc) of the Musée de l'Homme group. Yet some organisations were successful in overcoming their initial handicaps. By 1941, intelligence networks of respectable proportions were operational. They included 'Interallié', an offshoot from the information service of the British army, the Confrérie de Notre-Dame set up by Rémy, and Alliance which, under the leadership of Loustaunau-Lacau, Faye and Marie-Madeleine Fourcade had already recruited a hundred or more valuable agents (one of the most intrepid of these was the engineering officer Schaerer who was finally caught in July 1941 as he was leaving a Kriegsmarine submarine with its plans in his pockets). Slightly later and with rather more hesitation, the movements also became organised.[122] In the northern zone, the Organisation Civile et Militaire (OCM) was an amalgamation of high-ranking officers and thinking civilians. Libération-Nord,[123] under the leadership of Christian Pineau, Robert Lacoste, Jean Texcier, etc., was recruiting in socialist and trade-unionist milieux. On 14 July 1941, Philippe Viannay and Robert Salmon brought out the first number of *Défense de la France* and were meantime recruiting among the students. In the southern zone, the movements that were to become the most important had already staked out promising claims. After trying his hand in La Dernière Colonne, a venture that came to nothing, a talented all-rounder, Emmanuel d'Astier de la Vigerie,[124] formerly of L'Action Française, a naval officer by profession and a journalist by inclination, set up Libération-Sud with the help of two teachers, Lucie Samuel and Jean Cavaillès. They sought support from the circles of the left and gained the backing of Léon Jouhaux. In Lyons, a group of militant catholics, Louis Cruvillier, Fernand Belot, Alfonse Drogou, Joseph Hours and the Jesuit

fathers Chaillet, Fessard and Henri de Lubac were expressing their spiritual resistance to Nazism in their *Cahiers du Témoignage Chrétien*, the first issue
of which appeared in November.[125] Also in Lyons, militants from La Jeune
République and a number of radicals grouped around an entrepreneur,
Elie Peju, a retailer of confectionery, Antoine Avinin, and a former municipal councillor, Auguste Pinton, founded a small movement called France-
Liberté. They made contact with Jean-Pierre Lévy, a leader working in the
textile business who, in a short space of time, managed to extend the
movement beyond the Lyons region. This led, in December 1941, to the
creation of Franc-Tireur.[126] Finally, Combat was born from the merging of
two movements. It was an interesting combination from many points of
view. Henri Frenay, an escaped serving officer, left the army, feeling
revulsion at the Montoire episode. He broke with his own milieu in order to
devote himself completely to a national movement of liberation which he
managed to keep alive thanks to the help of a remarkable militant woman,
Bertie Albrecht, and Claude Bourdet whom he had met quite by chance.
Frenay organised his movement on the model of a general staff office,
already thinking ahead to the possibility of turning it into the militant basis
for a future secret army.[127] A group of militant christian democrats,
Edmond Michelet, François de Menthon, Pierre-Henri Teitgen and Alfred
Coste-Floret had, for their part, set up Liberté, to fight politically, through
counter-propaganda, against the prevailing mood of defeatism. In November 1941, in Grenoble, these two movements merged to form Combat: and
in December 1941 the first issue of its newspaper appeared.

The communists: a totally committed Resistance?

Non-communist historiography has by now solidly established a
tradition of total segregation between non-communist and communist
rebels. There are, broadly speaking, two theses on the subject. The more
extreme suggests that communists did not start to resist until after the Nazi
invasion of the Soviet Union. The other, which is more moderate, maintains that *some* communists did join the Resistance, but not the PCF as such.
It is undeniable that both theses have been and still are exploited for
partisan purposes, often by politicians who in the main themselves left very
little mark upon the beginnings of the Resistance. It is equally clear that the
PCF, with its omissions, counter-claims and even falsifications[128] has
provided fuel for such polemics. Such records as are available to the
historians[129] are fragmentary and full of conflicting evidence. However, it
seems possible to come to two provisional conclusions: a number of changes
certainly took place in the PCF and they took place before June 1941. Tillon
tells us that there were by then – at least at a tactical level – not one but two
communist parties.[130]
Let us return to a rapid chronological survey of the PCF over what

Jacques Fauvet has called 'this equivocal summer'. The surge of Hitlerism had done nothing to alter the Party line,[131] at least as expressed in the underground *Humanité*. It maintained – as in the past – that it was necessary to 'subdue the imperialist gangsters', and if those gangsters had already been set to destroy each other, the most bitter blame of the PCF newspaper fell upon the 'City of London'. It went even further than that, however: in four successive issues, in July, it quite explicitly called for fraternisation (as in 1917?): 'It is particularly comforting in these unhappy times to see many Parisian workers on friendly terms with German soldiers, whether in the street or in the corner *bistro*. Well done, comrades, keep it up, even if it does not please certain bourgeois who are as stupid as they are harmful.'[132] This neutralist line confronted with the occupying power reappears – with a slightly different slant, it is true – in the appeal purporting to be dated 10 July.[133] This long analysis[134] of the situation that returns to the theme of class warfare declares war upon Vichy without reservation but is, on the other hand, totally silent on the subject on the anti-Nazi struggle. In this 'Appeal to the people of France', the directors of the underground PCF launched a violent attack against the betrayal on the part of the 'property-owning classes' and the politicians who were 'responsible for the war, the defeat and the occupation' (and they were all lumped together: Doriot, Blum, Laval, Jouhandeau, Daladier, Reynaud...). At the same time they took care to denounce 'the government of traitors and sellers-out set up in Vichy'. But they did so the better to justify their call for the establishment of 'a true peace' (to be followed up by 'the conclusion of a pact of Franco-Soviet friendship) and, since 'there can be no peace without the independence of all peoples', France wished to live 'in freedom and independence'. Salvation lay in setting up 'a government of the people' under the inspiration of the French Communist Party – the only party that 'had opposed the war' and remained 'the hope of the people of France'. There was no word against Hitler's Germany.[135] Strictly in line with this strategy, during the summer of 1940 the PCF, continuing to produce its clandestine newspaper, was urging its militants to organise unobtrusive meetings. At the same time, it twice approached the Kommandatur in attempts to win permission to produce *L'Humanité* legally.[136] But to crown all this, even as the talks took place, on 21 June, three of the communist emissaries, Maurice Tréand, Denise Ginolin and Jeanne Schrodt, were arrested by the French police and then, on the 25th, released on the orders of the occupying power. Meanwhile, here and there there were some communists who did not draw the line at mentioning anti-fascism: on 17 June, in the Bordeaux region, the order of the day given out by Charles Tillon was 'to fight against Hitler's fascism and the two hundred families'; in the west, on 22 June, Auguste Havet wrote that there would be 'no respite until the Hitlerian boots have been kicked out of our country' and in the Limousin Guingouin rejected any suggestion of neutrality. But these were isolated cases.[137]

During that autumn and winter, the two policies became clear. In a number of regions or sectors the anti-Nazi line was gaining ground. In the north, sabotage was going well and the mobilisation of resistance to the occupying power was progressing thanks to a number of astonishingly audacious young militants such as Eusebio Ferrari, Félicien Joly and Charles Debarge.[138] At the same time a group of intellectual communists and sympathisers, Jacques Solomon, Georges Politzer, Frédéric Joliot-Curie and Paul Langevin, were bringing out *L'Université libre*, making no attempt to disguise their aversion to Hitler's Germany and, on 11 November 1940, students from communist youth movements demonstrated against the occupying power. The 'official' line did not change, however. In the eyes of the editors of *L'Humanité*, the goal was still the same: peace, a peace that excluded both 'war under the aegis of collaboration and war under the aegis of so-called resistance to the oppressor' (from a special edition printed in January 1941). The British were perhaps attacked with less virulence while the subjection imposed by the Germans was denounced with increasing force, but neutralism certainly remained the line upheld in the face of everything. Similarly, far from building up a patriotic front strategy, the PCF was still bent on settling old scores. François Billoux and other imprisoned communists even wrote to Pétain requesting to be heard 'as witnesses at the supreme court of Riom'[139] and, meantime, *L'Humanité* was criticising the 'comfortable life' that, it claimed, Blum, Mandel, Reynaud and other men interned by the Vichy regime were leading. Only on one point did the 'Central Committee' modify its tactics: on 5 and 13 October, hundreds of militants were rounded up in the Paris region and after that semi-legality came to an end; to protect its militants, the Party began to try to set up its own 'Organisation Secrète' (the OS) solely, for the time being, for the purposes of protection.

As from December 1940, things began to change. On home ground, initially. *L'Humanité* began to make more forceful demands for 'the independence of France' even while, right up until June, it continued to defend its thesis of the double imperialistic war.[140] Although it took the occupying power sternly to task, as late as 20 June 1941, *L'Humanité* was also condemning not only the 'traitors of Vichy' but also de Gaulle and Catroux whom it blamed for the blood shed in Syria. Nevertheless, at the same time arms were being stock-piled and sabotage was increasing. It was a militant communist, Michel Brulé, who organised the big miners' strike in Dourges. And it seems clear that thenceforward many such actions were orchestrated by leaders such as Auguste Lecoeur, who were in direct contact with the 'Central Committee'. There was also activity on an ideological level:

March saw the publication of *Révolution et contre-révolution au XXe siècle*, Politzer's refutation of a lecture given in November 1940 by the Nazi theorist, Rosenberg; a month later Gabriel Péri brought out his paper: *Non, le Nazisme n'est pas le socialisme* (No, Nazism is not socialism). Meanwhile, the PCF was now holding out a friendly hand towards non-communist organisations: in April, at Toulouse, Marrane, acting in the name of the Party, made contact with Léo Hamon, the leader of a 'Gaullist' movement; on 15 May, the PCF launched 'the National Front, to fight for the independence of France' and henceforth the only people it rejected were those whom it regarded as 'capitulators and traitors'.[141]

From this chronological survey it is impossible not to conclude, with Charles Tillon, that there were indeed 'two parties, depending upon the region and local leaders concerned',[142] and for a Leninist party this was a relatively unusual situation. There is evidence to show that there were, among the earliest rebels, people for whom proletarian internationalism meant first and foremost anti-fascist solidarity, regardless of the fluctuations in the foreign policies of the Soviet Union. And it should be pointed out that they continued to consider themselves as communists through and through, not as militants cut off from their ideological sources of inspiration.

As for those – such as Duclos – who to the last clung to the line imposed by Stalin, their case is more complex. It can hardly be denied that the invasion of the Soviet Union by the Nazis brought about an undeniable shift in ideological statements; it also modified communist tactics (aggressive action against Wehrmacht personnel began in August) although, despite what is often still claimed today, this did not represent a total volte-face. Tillon puts it metaphorically: 'these courtiers of Soviet diplomacy' had 'dragged their feet up until May 1941'.[143] To find an explanation for these mistimings and contradictions, we must consider the situation from the two points of view simultaneously. As good Leninists, men of the communist machine ascribed a fundamental role to the Party and its reconstruction. At the same time, they knew from experience that there was a danger of the machine operating in a vacuum if it revealed itself incapable of winning over the masses. Yet again these party leaders were to find that there was no more than minimal agreement between popular aspirations and the edicts of the Komintern. The leadership therefore attempted first and foremost to restructure the machine that had been so disorganised by the repression, the war and the defections; and it was principally thanks to the militants that it was able to re-establish a number of points of contact. While so doing, it also tried to gain more time for manoeuvre (and it is easy enough to understand why it risked that bid for semi-legality), at the same time issuing an order of the day pressing for the formation of a 'popular government'.[144] The official line could not do otherwise than support the Stalinist strategic choices all the way. But meanwhile, the 'Central Committee' was conscious of the increasingly numerous body taking an anti-Nazi line.[145] It was ready to swing over to a different position if need be. Hitler's attack (of the Soviet Union) did away with the last outstanding contradictions.

These lengthy and round-about developments were to leave a lasting mark on the non-communist rebels of the early days of the Resistance,[146] either reinforcing their anti-communism or arousing determined defensive reactions. Nevertheless, the massive impact of the communists' entry into the Resistance, their efficiency and the audience that they won over by presenting themselves as the heirs of the soldiers of Valmy, was to affect the development of the Resistance movement inside France considerably.

The dissidents

Outside metropolitan France there were rebels who had also rejected the armistice. Vichy called them 'dissidents'. They called themselves the 'Free French'.[147] As yet they were more of a nuisance than a real threat to the French State: only a small number associated themselves with this particular venture and meanwhile, as we have seen, the resistance movements were developing quite independently. It was nevertheless in this first long march that Charles de Gaulle laid the foundations for his claim as a legitimate leader.

Rebellion and legitimacy

'At the age of forty-nine, I set out along the path of adventure.' It was not just because he happened to be the first soldier available and a general to boot. The adventure stemmed, rather, from a rift, a rebellion against what was considered the legal power, to which he was to oppose 'national legitimacy'.

As is well known, it all started on the morning of 17 June, when de Gaulle flew off from Bordeaux 'with no romanticism and no illusions', with a few secret funds and, at his side, a British guardian angel in the form of General Spears, who was anxious to bring back to England French politicians who were 'men of war' and also representative. The following day, he was allowed time on the radio and launched on the BBC[148] his first 'Appeal', the main lines of which he was to develop further during the days that followed.

In contrast to Philippe Pétain, he attributed France's defeat to mistakes of a military order. In his view, the armistice which strangled political power was a 'crime' against which it was legitimate to rebel. So it was necessary that 'somewhere ... the flame of the French Resistance [should keep burning]'. He, for his part, had chosen the path of exile, linking the destiny of Free France with that of the maritime and Anglo-Saxon powers which would eventually gain the upper hand. To Pétain's withdrawal within the boundaries of metropolitan France he riposted with a bet on world-wide involvement.

However, during these first crucial weeks, his behaviour was not altogether unambiguous. On 19 June, he wrote to Weygand and other 'veterans', undertaking to place himself under their orders if they would take on the leadership of the Resistance. At the same time, however, he was declaring on the BBC that, as a 'French soldier and leader' he was 'conscious of speaking in the name of France'. And while he claimed simply to be addressing those who could fight, 'French officers and soldiers ... , engineers and skilled workers in the armament industries', his 'appeals' nevertheless rang with deeply political overtones.

De Gaulle had set himself a goal: 'To bring back into the war not only Frenchmen but France itself.' He found an immediate ally in Churchill, who did not hesitate for a moment. No doubt he would have preferred to negotiate with Reynaud, Mandel or Daladier, or even with one of the 'big chiefs'. But for one thing, his emissaries had been unsuccessful in making contact with the statesmen of the *Massilia*, for another, the politicians as a whole were in a wavering state of mind and, finally, the military leaders were obeying the 'legal power'. Churchill, with an acute sense of opportunism, therefore wasted no time in recognising this general, a friend of Renault and a former member of the government who was at least anxious to fight as 'leader of all the Free French'; and on 7 August 1940, 'Free France' was recognised as representing France in the war and was provided with an advance of funds: the Free French were no longer 'a foreign legion within the English army'.

De Gaulle saw the Montoire interview as an unpardonable error. Thenceforward the person of the head of the French State no longer merited tactful consideration and it was clearly established that 'a French government no longer existed'. In these conditions it became necessary to ensure that France officially continued to take part in the war. To this end, de Gaulle took a number of provisional measures to be effective until such time as 'the representatives of the French people' should have their say once more: on 27 October 1940 he issued a manifesto from Brazzaville and promulgated a number of 'decrees', one of which set up a 'Council for the Defence of the Empire'.[149] He also produced a *Journal Officiel de l'Empire* and created an 'Order of the Liberation'.[150] All the same, Free France was tending – without the approval of His Majesty's government – to turn itself into a *de facto* government. Another step in this direction was taken on 24 September 1941, when it issued a decree creating a 'French National Committee'. This gathered under the presidency of Charles de Gaulle a number of 'committee members appointed by decree and responsible to the head of the Free French'. Later, in his *Mémoires de guerre*, de Gaulle was to remark, with reason: 'all in all, the committee was to be a government, with all the attributes and structures of one'.[151] In instituting this committee what the head of Free France was seeking in particular was a greater liberty of manoeuvre in diplomatic matters, but legal recognition was still a thing of the future.

Free France was all the more convinced of its right to represent the continuing French presence in the war, given that as early as 1940 it had taken possession of a number of territories – admittedly far-flung ones – in the French Empire: the New Hebrides, the *Comptoirs Français** in India, Tahiti and the French territories of Océanie, New Caledonia and French Equatorial Africa. The last was the finest prize: in August 1940 the Chad, the Cameroons and Congo-Brazzaville had been rallied thanks to the concerted action of a few colonial administrators and some audacious fighters.[152] It was not a rich harvest but it forced Vichy to keep the French Empire outside the Axis orbit through fear of seeing it succumb to 'dissidence'. Furthermore, it provided a seat for a government that was determined not to be simply a government in exile.

The first long march

The emergence of Free France was a laborious process and it was some time before it was in a position to play its part in the world concert.

For thinking people abroad who counted, de Gaulle was practically an unknown.[153] His career as an officer had certainly been an honourable one (Saint-Cyr (military academy), the war, three times wounded, left for dead and taken prisoner, three escape attempts and a period in the punitive camp of Ingolstadt, commands in Poland, the Rhineland, Lebanon, the War School); but it was not exceptional. There were one or two singular features to it however. He had initially passed for a product of Pétain's stable,[154] yet in one of his books,[155] he had defended some fairly heterodox theses, calling for a profound reform of the French military system, including a programme of mechanisation for the army.[156] But he had come up against the implacable opposition of Pétain and Weygand as well as the distrust of the left which was hostile to the idea of a 'professional army'. In 1940 he took command of the 4th reserve armoured division which saw illustrious service in the battles of Montcornet[157] and Abbeville and he was then, on 6 June, appointed by Reynaud to be Under-Secretary of State at the War Office.[158] Nevertheless, in France his reputation was rather slight.[159]

It was not a large force that had made its way to London and Mers el-Kébir and, later, joined the Dakar expedition, and the fighting in Syria was to stamp Free France with a lasting and detestable image of 'Anglo-Gaullism'. Some who had left metropolitan France – Jean Monnet for one –

* The five towns retained by the French at the end of the eighteenth century. [Trans.]

considered the plan to establish a *de facto* government premature and preferred instead to make their way to the United States, where they thought they would be useful. In London itself, Free France did not by any means manage to rally to it all those who had taken refuge in Great Britain. Some of them taxed de Gaulle with authoritarianism and saw his entourage as a group of extreme right-wing sectarians. These opponents published a daily newspaper, *France*, and also a widely read review, *La France Libre*. They included in particular a number of intellectuals – Raymond Aron[160] and André Labarthe, for instance – and socialist militants known as the 'Jean Jaurès group', centred upon Pierre Comert, Charles and Georges Gombault and Louis Lévy. Free France did not include very many well-known figures from either the civilian or the military sector: two parliamentarians (Pierre Cot and Pierre-Olivier Lapie) offered their services, as did a handful of civil servants and erstwhile members of ministerial cabinets (Georges Boris, Dejean, Diethelm, Gaston Palewski etc), one well-known university professor (René Cassin), and a few high-ranking officers (Catroux, Muselier, Legentilhomme, Larminat, Montclar etc).[161] The roll-call was somewhat sparse.

Fighting France, 'present in the fighting so as to take part in the victory' had soon been actively engaged in the struggle. The Free French forces (FFL) fought alongside the British in Libya and in Eritrea; and striking out from the Chad, they conquered a number of oases held by the Italians, in particular the Konfra oasis. But they suffered from a shortage of men. The 130 able-bodied men of the Ile de Sein had come to London in their fishing boats and a number of élite units such as the 13th Half-Brigade of the Foreign Legion under the command of Montclar had rallied to Free France; nevertheless the number of fighting men was still only 7,000 in July; and the Mers el-Kébir episode did not win it new recruits. After the AEF had rallied, the FFL may have numbered 35,000 men, a year later possibly 70,000.

There were plenty of set-backs. Except for here and there, the Empire had not come over. Several attempts had been necessary to gain control of the Gabon. Despite all this, the head of Free France convinced himself that the AOF was within his grasp and in September 1940, he won the initially reluctant Churchill over to his plan to mount an expedition against Dakar. It was a fiasco, however, and de Gaulle later admitted that those were perhaps his darkest hours. The operation had certainly relied too heavily upon improvisation but the principal trouble was that the Gaullists who landed there ahead of the main force were not successful in winning over either the army or the local population, and there were casualties on both sides. De Gaulle, sick at heart, was obliged to abandon the siege. Vichy did not miss the opportunity to declare that without the aid of the British the 'dissidents' were nothing.

It was a bitter pill to swallow and the defeat did nothing to improve his image in many Anglo-Saxon circles. Churchill had, it is true, meted out special treatment to fighting France and had supported its leader even after the Dakar venture. But he was not prepared to sacrifice the precious North-Atlantic Alliance to the passing whims of the head of the Free French. Moreover, old colonial rivalries were surfacing again: first in the Levant.[162] When Vichy was so imprudent as to authorise the Luftwaffe to land at Syrian airfields, it provided the British with the opportunity of setting to rights a Middle East that had been shaken by the revolt in Iraq and the loss of Crete. As for the Free French, they believed that this breaking of neutrality in favour of the Axis powers would have the effect of persuading Syria and the Lebanon to come over to the Allies without a fight. But that did not happen; they found themselves obliged to appeal for British reinforcements and even then hostilities continued for five weeks, causing relatively heavy losses.[163] The lack of logistic support obliged the Vichy high commissioner, General Dentz, to ask for an armistice. But the 'Franco-British agreement' signed on 14 July 1941 made the FFL propaganda aimed at the troops awaiting repatriation much less effective and, above all, made no mention of the fate of nations that had hitherto been placed under French mandate. There can be little doubt that the pro-Arab group in the Colonial Office sought to exploit the situation. De Gaulle made a stormy protest and in the end obtained 'an interpretative arrangement' and a letter stating plainly that 'In the Levant, France, of all the nations of Europe, should have a dominating and privileged position'.[164] Nevertheless, sparring continued between Catroux and Spears, the delegate of His Majesty's government, who was adept at playing off one nationalist movement against another. Relations with the United States immediately became cooler and soon deteriorated into psychodrama, despite the fact that the White House had decided to help countries that were resisting the Axis powers. The United States became 'the great arsenal for democracy' and on March 1941 offered to bail out the Allies with a loan to finance the war; in August 1941, Roosevelt and Churchill signed the 'Atlantic Charter'. However, Roosevelt had his isolationist lobby to cope with and, as always, was determined to proceed in a pragmatic fashion. Now, Free France was of much less interest to him than Vichy[165] which still held control over a powerful war fleet and a vast Empire. Furthermore, both the Secretary of State and Roosevelt himself considered de Gaulle to be ambitious, overweening and dangerous, especially since the ill-judged Dakar expedition. It was against this background of cooling relations that the affair over Saint-Pierre-et-Miquelon broke. It was to have lasting repercussions. Vichy was suspected of having installed a radio-transmitting station to guide the Kriegsmarine submarines. After a number of fruitless discussions, de Gaulle decided that it fell to Free France, and to it alone, to settle the problem. The islands were persuaded to rally to Free France without it proving necessary to fire a single shot,[166] but it stirred up a diplomatic storm[167] of what may appear to us to be disproportionate violence. In effect, it provoked a clash between de Gaulle, who was determined to 'lance the abcess without delay' and the White House, which was exasperated by this head of a government in exile who had the cheek to interfere in its strategies.

Once the Soviet Union was in the war, Free France managed quite rapidly to establish cordial relations with it; but the friction with the United States was a serious handicap to overcome, all the more so since Charles de Gaulle was still a long way from looking like the common denominator of all the different resistance movements.

Distant France

For many people, de Gaulle was still no more than a relatively obscure general who had taken refuge in London. His first radio appeals were seldom picked up, still less listened to, and the air time allotted to Free France's own particular programme, 'Honneur et Patrie', was relatively short in comparison with other BBC broadcasts in the French language. De Gaulle, for his part, could hardly have been less informed about the rebels in France and he was almost totally in the dark with regard to the movements that were being set up there. It was symptomatic enough that – up until 1942 – he limited himself to the most prudent of directives, pressing for no more than 'hours to take stock' or 'a national stand to attention'.[168] Whatever his claims to be speaking in the name of a bewildered France ready to respond to his appeals,[169] the truth of the matter was quite different.

Free France did at least manage to set up intelligence networks of a military type and the information that these produced was pooled by a kind of extended *deuxième bureau* (counter-espionage agency), placed under the authority of the Polytechnician, Captain Dewavrin-*Passy*. The first secret agents,[170] Renault-*Rémy*, Duclos-*Saint-Jacques*, Bersnikoff-*Corvisart*, Fourcaud etc had made considerable progress but transmitting stations were still very clumsy and the early days were hazardous. Already the corvette captain, Honoré d'Estienne D'Orves, and two of his companions had been betrayed by a double agent and shot, as many more were to be. By the autumn of 1941 only two large networks, the Confrérie de Notre-Dame and Brutus, were truly operational.

Many of the mutual misunderstandings between rebels and dissidents stemmed from obstacles of a technical nature. But political barriers also divided them. Many of the movement leaders saw de Gaulle as a creature of the right, a follower of Maurras.[171] Furthermore, most of those closest to him[172] were men who made no attempt to disguise their sympathy for an authoritarian regime, whereas the head of Free France had in fact turned down the services of Pierre Cot, admitting openly that he was 'too controversial a figure for it to be advisable'.[173] Furthermore, he had (justifiably) the reputation of governing in an authoritarian, if not solitary, fashion.[174] The last – and by no means the least – misgiving felt towards him was that it was not yet clear that he would be an intransigent defender of the Republic. Not that he was suspected of any luke-warm sentiments in respect of Hitler's Germany, but his inclination systematically to lump together the Third Republic and the French State was alarming.[175] After all, he had told Maurice Schumann that 'for reasons of a general nature' he 'hoped that the slogan carried by French town halls could be replaced by that borne by our flags, namely "Honour and the Motherland"'.[176] In short, if he was to win the confidence of a significant proportion of the resistance movements, de Gaulle was going to have to dispel all ambiguity in that respect and, above all, take account of their existence.[177]

France at the time of the Germans

It was not long before the occupiers were being compared to the Colorado beetles that were currently ravaging the potato fields. A popular story that went about was the one about the German who said to the Frenchman: 'You give me your watch and I'll give you the time.' And in the occupied zone it truly was the time of the Germans since the occupation authorities had seen to it that all watches and clocks were adjusted to the central European time zone. The collective memory of those years is a black one although the times were no doubt not uniformly dark: conditions varied from one year to another, from one socio-professional category to another and from one region to another.[1] On the whole, however, except for a minority of profiteers, these four years were hard ones to live through[2] and without doubt particularly unbearable for all those whom the Reich classed as 'sub-human' (*Untermenschen*).

The top of the basket

The Occupation, predictably enough, had its own temporary men of authority, its own masters greedy to taste the poisons and delights of power. It also had its own profiteers who – in many cases with complete impunity – did excellent business.

On the Vichy side

The capital of the French State[3] might have been mistaken for a capital in an operetta, with its spa surrounded by its white hotels. Official and unofficial personnel were all crowded into these luxurious but in the long run uncomfortable palaces, freezing in the winter and ill-suited to the housing of ministries. Bedrooms were converted into offices by day while by night they sheltered 'floosies' who drove the hotel staff to distraction. The Hôtel du Parc was the nerve-centre of the whole apparatus. This was where the leader of the French State put down his roots. Those who were superstitious were alarmed to see the Ministry for Colonies installed in the Hôtel d'Angleterre while others were bemused at the sight of the Hôtel

Helder, taken over by the Ministry of Marine Affairs, swabbing down its floors as if it was a warship in the Royal Navy.

The State 'cure' was not much fun. For one thing, the order of the day was austerity, if not virtue. Philippe Pétain imposed new rituals upon this spa life: the daily constitutional at 12.30, mass at the church of Saint-Louis, a parish that thereby acquired quite a fashionable clientèle, the running up of the colours at the Hôtel du Parc, etc. Apart from these, distractions were few but at least there were five or six cinemas which still showed a few Anglo-Saxon films and then there were the gala occasions – a multitude of galas held to support the numerous social works of the French State, but one was very much like all the rest. Otherwise Bridge, or exchanging tall stories of even the most unlikely kind. Sundays provided an opportunity to make excursions into the countryside to take the air and also to collect a few chickens and rabbits raised in the farms which the ministries and foreign embassies had divided out between them.

In 1940 the humblest garret cost a fortune; it is true that the new capital was surrounded by a motley local fauna described as follows by Du Moulin de Labarthète: 'beggers, ruffians, swindlers, women of varying age and varying beauty'.[4] As times became harder, the ranks thinned out; the better advised packed their bags and left. More rooms became available and even deeper gloom prevailed. Many officials were by no means unhappy to set off for Paris to inspect the services for which they were responsible there, on the governmental train that left Vichy every Saturday evening and returned the following Thursday morning.

On the Paris side

For those with money and discretion, life in Paris[5] was incontestably more amusing. The occupying power, for its part, had condescended to turn it into a place of recreation for its warriors on leave. For of course you had to get used to the idea that Paris was partly German. The banished tricolour was replaced by the Swastika flying alongside the Tuileries, over the Chamber of Deputies and the Palais de Luxembourg, a number of hotels and the Avenue Kleber which was requisitioned virtually *in toto*. And meanwhile, the Eiffel Tower was adorned with a gigantic V and the arrogant slogan: 'Deutschland siegt auf allen Fronten' (Germany victorious on all fronts). Furthermore, the Germans had their own restaurants, their *Soldatenkinos* (cinemas) and their own brothels. They felt not a bit out of place, indeed quite at home at the Tour d'Argent and in other temples of gastronomy which provided special menus in German for them. Up until the end of 1943, they did not lack for eating companions: a number of collaborationists,[6] racketeers of every kind, quite a collection of cultural personalities and people of the theatre who danced to please them, produced witty sayings and did the rounds of 'cultural' private views such as that of the sculptor Arno Breker which was attended in May 1942 by the cream of Parisian society. Sacha Guitry was keen enough on the company of Otto Abetz to be a frequent guest at the Embassy in the rue de Lille, while Serge Lifar was prepared to lay on spectacles at the Opera with Nazi trimmings. Tino Rossi, much fêted on Radio Paris, was the star of two gala performances given in aid of the prisoners, in June 1941 within the framework of an exhibition devoted to the theme of European France. The prisoners were also treated to concerts by Maurice Chevalier and Edith Piaf, this time in Germany, while Drieu La Rochelle, Brasillach, Thérive, Chardonne and a number of others went to Nuremberg to meet Goebbels. Cortot went off to play sonatas in Berlin; Albert Préjean, Robert Le Vigan, Danielle Darrieux and Viviane Romance were fêted on the other side of the Rhine, as were Derain, Vlaminck and Maillol.[7] There were some who gave free rein to their fascination with Hitlerian Germany – Alfred Fabre-Luce for instance, who was a little too ready in 1942 to publish an *Anthologie de l'Europe nouvelle*.[8] Meanwhile there were yet others who contributed to journals that were far from innocent,[9] *haute couture*[10] was anxious not to be found lacking and was dressing the whole of high society; ladies of fashion were said to be having grave problems however: when riding a bicycle, how was it possible to hold on to the handlebars as well as an outrageous hat and also prevent one's skirt from flying up? That was no doubt one of the few trials that they had to suffer. But in the end, it is not so much a matter of listing the reverse of a roll-call of honour which, at all events, would be far too long – rather of recognising that Parisian high society went on indulging itself without feeling too bothered about cohabiting with the occupying power.

In contrast, the 'Zazou' movement now sprang up.[11] It saw itself as reacting, in its own way, both against the moralism of Vichy and also the glibness of the local tyrants.[12] This movement, rather scraping the bottom of the barrel, orchestrated by young people, had cultural roots initially. It displayed a taste for American literature and films now banned and, above all, for jazz which *Je Suis Partout* was vilifying as 'Judeo (naturally!) – Negro–American' music that offered 'a taste of forbidden fruit' (Jean-Louis Bory). Along with this exaltation of 'swing' went a provocative style of dress: shabby jackets, narrow trousers and long flowing locks that were bound to anger the he-men who favoured the 'short back and sides' style. Police and collaborationists began to hunt down the Zazous as early as the autumn of 1942.

Ordinary Parisians were faced with worries of a more prosaic nature. Their overriding preoccupation was to bring home something for the pot. We shall have more to say about this presently. Meanwhile, even in circles of affluence, it was not unusual for guests to bring part of their dinner along with them, for gastronomic success depended upon the resources of the black market. The shortage of petrol also wrought havoc on the means of locomotion available to a Parisian. You could travel on a deformed kind of bus but it would run on *gazogène* in such a halting fashion that many people preferred the metro which was always overcrowded but warm in winter and which sometimes came in handy as a shelter in the event of an air raid. Otherwise you got on to your bicycle or – if you were in a hurry and had the money – you could take a *vélo-taxi*, a variably sprung and upholstered crate pulled by a professional latter-day cyclist. In the evening, you shrouded all the windows with care in conformity with the total black-out regulations and so as not to fall foul of the local air-raid warden.

Despite everything, Paris retained its reputation as the intellectual capital of France.[13] There was a continuous stream of first nights and literary events, just as before: the appearance of *La reine morte* established Montherlant as a dramatist; even more flamboyant was the first night, on 25 November 1943, of *Le soulier de satin* which Claudel had almost despaired of ever seeing staged, an occasion attended by all the appropriate intellectuals. In a different manner, the collection of patrons' signatures organised on 3 October 1942 at the Rive-Gauche bookshop, for Rebatet and his *Décombres*, was the talk of the town among collaborationist circles and a number of others too. But over these years there were some signs of the new wave that was to take over immediately after the war: Sartre as a writer for the theatre (with *Les mouches, Huis clos*) and also Camus (with *L'étranger, Le malentendu, Le mythe de Sisyphe*). Literary production gaily continued, despite paper shortages, and in 1943 the publishers' lists actually included more titles than in 1941. There were rather more new films than in the immediately pre-war period. As for the public, it kept up with all that went on. Not only were music-halls, *chansonnier* concerts and cabarets playing to full houses but a number of plays were box-office sell-outs, the cinemas were overflowing and libraries had never known so many readers. True, it was no doubt warmer in there than at home, but it really seems that the comfortable temperature was not the only thing that brought them, and that plenty of Parisians, whether or not they had time on their hands, went to forget the hard times for a few hours.

So was it wrong to 'sing' under the Occupation? It is not easy to be categorical upon such a matter for the relations of artists and writers to their times are so ambiguous. Certain purists, among them André Halimi who dedicated his book and his film to 'those who did not sing', were of the opinion that the only decent option was silence. But most of those who did 'sing' objected to such moralism which they condemned as puritanical. Besides, almost all those who later distinguished themselves in the Resistance – Aragon among others – had certainly published works that were not particularly committed. Some have pointed out that they did have to earn a living. Others – quite a few – are apt to add some patriotic observation to the effect that 'entertaining French men and women was the best way to prepare for more happy tomorrows'. But that is clearly rather overdoing it, for the vast majority of them continued to write, play and sing just as if the Occupation was no direct concern of theirs.[14] After the war, Jean-Paul Sartre acutely emphasised the profound ambiguity of the situation: 'I wonder if I shall be understood if I say that it [the Occupation] was both intolerable and at the same time we put up with it very well.'[15] At all events, one thing is certain: relatively few writers and even fewer actors and artists became closely or even remotely involved in the Resistance – intellectual[16] or otherwise.

In conclusion, let us consider the cinema under the Occupation.[17] It is an interesting subject in a number of respects. It seems fair to accept the overall view Joseph Daniel gave to the colloquium on 'The Vichy government and the national revolution': 'This cinema, often of brilliant quality but almost always conformist, aiming for neutrality and politically colourless, is a cinema of silence.' It is quite true that the film industry was thriving: it produced 220 long features and some 400 short ones; it discovered much new talent and confirmed the reputation of young directors such as Bresson, Autant-Lara, Clouzot and Becker. On the whole, cinema audiences did not fall for the Nazi culture trap[18] and the few films strongly impregnated with collaborationist ideology, such as *Forces occulates*, a diatribe against Freemasonry (and a very flat piece of work) directed – apparently – by Jean Mamy, was shunned by cinema-goers. Most committed films proffered a complacent kind of breast-beating or Vichy moralism but seldom ventured out of a morass of pious sentiments. We might mention *Le voile bleu*, the edifying tale of a widow (Gaby Morlay) who devoted herself body and soul to the education of adolescents who might one day become leaders, and *La nuit merveilleuse*, a rose-tinted remake of the familiar story of a birth in a stable with ox and ass in attendance, but this time the mother is a refugee in the exodus; and, in particular, *La fille du puisatier*, a film which ran to packed houses in Paris for 22 weeks. This story about a well-maker's daughter concerns an ordinary little slut who is inspired by the eruption of a redeeming sense of duty. Almost as if in response to a 'Message' from Philippe Pétain, an airman who has been reported 'missing' returns at just the right moment to make reparation for his fault (he had made the unmarried well-maker's daughter pregnant) and marry her, as he should. What with the censorship, however, the great majority of directors settled for themes of a less topical kind.[19] Some turned to history which on occasion did provide opportunities to introduce semi-subversive themes and dialogue. One such was *Pontcarral Colonel d'Empire* by Jean Delannoy; others escaped into fantasy (*La nuit fantastique* by Marcel l'Herbier); there were crime stories and *films noirs* which landed some of their authors in trouble at the Liberation, such as *Les inconnus dans la maison* made by Henri Decoin and, in particular, *Le corbeau* directed by Henri Georges Clouzot. Others still plunged into the literary past: *La Duchesse de Langeais* (Jean de Baroncelli), *Les dames du Bois de Boulogne*, which Bresson started filming in the spring of 1944 and *L'eternel retour* by Delannoy and Cocteau, while the alternative to this was 'poetic realism': *Les visiteurs du soir*, which came out in 1942 was the product of the Carné–Prévert–Kosma team together with an excellent group of actors, and it is a model of its kind. It could indeed be said that *Les visiteurs du soir* was the most representative film made during the Occupation.

'Au bon beurre'

This title, *Au bon beurre*, won success for Jean Dutourd. Despite an inverted kind of Poujadism too unrelenting to be altogether convincing, this book bears witness to the social mobility of middlemen of every kind, as in any period when the ordinary market fails to satisfy demand. The average Frenchman was particularly involved with the shopkeepers, butchers, dairymen, grocers, even the bakers who, thanks to rationing, now became new petty tyrants, feared and respected but inwardly cursed or at least envied. It is true that shopkeepers were not in a bad way,[20] but their profits were, in the end, negligible in comparison with the fortunes that were made in the higher echelons of the black market.

Alfred Sauvy[21] maintains that the role played by the black market was of small importance, particularly as the occupying power always, he claims, opposed it. It is true that economic collaboration left few lasting traces, but the few reliable sources of information that are available to the historian invalidate Sauvy's claims. Even if it is true that it was not in the interest of the Germans (who operated a quasi-legal levy on all French produce) to see some of that production go astray, they nevertheless, right up until the spring of 1943, systematically secured for themselves a certain percentage of products which they paid for at the recommended price. This was, of course, quite in conformity with the principle of booty-taking that was favoured by most of the Nazi dignitaries.[22] They thus set up a number of clandestine purchasing offices with commercial cover and unofficial protection. The first example seems to have been the 'Otto Bureau' run by Brandel, an agent of the Abwehr (counter-espionage), who managed thirty or more sub-offices operating on a rota system to buy up large quantities of the most disparate products – leather, furs, tools, etc. To increase profits, these outfits employed French touts. The report issued by the agency of economic control estimates that the value of purchases made by the 'Otto service' alone amounted to 50,000 million francs over the twenty months of its operations. That is quite a total! The records of up to 200 purchasing offices which stock-piled all these products in the warehouses reserved for them and then sent them on to Germany in special convoys have been analysed. Thus, between the summer of 1942 and the spring of 1943, cargoes included 72 tons (French tonnes) of frying pans, 10 tons of playing cards, 154 tons of footwear, etc. However, these lucrative offices had to be shut down after March 1943 when the French Minister, Bichelonne, sharply renewed his complaints to Dr Michel who was in charge of German economic services in the occupied zone: he told him that the anarchy engendered by the German black market would, as an immediate conse-quence, make it impossible for the French State to honour the agreements it had made with regard to deliveries to the Reich.

Analogously, and often with the connivance of the occupying power, a French black market had developed. Some of its beneficiaries eventually paid the price for their activities.[23] There was Szolkonikoff, known as 'Monsieur Michel', who despite his classification as a 'stateless Jew', enjoyed protection afforded by the highest German authorities as a result of which he made a profit of something like 2,000 million francs; and also 'Monsieur Joseph' Joanovici (who before the war had been a rag-and-bone man specialising in scrap iron), whose profits must have amounted to close on 4,000 million. This class of *nouveaux riches* included a bit of everything: some 'high society', some contractors from Les Halles, the director of 'a great and well-established' textile firm in the North who in one fell swoop sold the Otto Bureau 58,000 metres of combed wool at catalogue price, which provided him with the funds to set up 'a large factory of cotton materials in the Vosges', the director of a large Lyons hat-making company', etc.[24] Little men could aspire to grow bigger, to judge from the examples of Marcel and Ferdinand V. who ran a small string and packing business which progressed from a turnover of 8 million in 1938 to one of 112 million in the first seven months of 1944, once they had decided to specialise in the production of camouflage netting and sell it at catalogue price to the Wehrmacht.[25]

That is why the administration of economic control found that 'more and more commercial houses and industrial firms, attracted by the excep-tionally large orders, came round to selling their merchandise to German purchasing organisations which accepted the highest prices without too much argument. It is unfortunately all too clear that only these countless cases of French complicity made it possible for the German black market to lay France to waste to the extent that it did'.[26] Jean Delarue concludes his chapter on the black market with the following remarks:

> Twenty years later there remain only a few in the know who must sometimes be overcome with a feeling of revulsion when they read certain names in the financial reports or recognise certain faces in the society photographs, at the weighing-in at Auteuil or Longchamps, at gala first-nights or even ultra-'patriotic' functions. Sometimes elegant, often powerful, always well-heeled and confident, these people do not appear to be bothered by the unbearable stench of rot, poverty, tears and blood

which still rises from the ill-gotten millions which they continue to enjoy without regrets. Those were the Occupation's true profiteers.[27]

Down at the swede level

The average Frenchman and his wife and children living in a large town, with no cousins in the countryside and no income other than that of the ordinary man in the street, were cold and hungry. And as time passed, the more frightened they became.

Constraints and the D system

Every war imposes a number of constraints that are more or less hard to bear. The servitude and persecution inflicted by the occupying power obviously did nothing to improve daily life for the French people. Take as a single example the difficulties created by the demarcation line (see Map 3). In order to cross it,[28] it was necessary – right up until March 1943, that is to say five months after the southern zone had been invaded – to possess an *Ausweis* (a pass). And it was almost as difficult to correspond by the postal service between one zone and another: in the early weeks, one could only write on 'interzone cards' (a multiple choice of statements some of which could be crossed out). These were later replaced by 'family cards' (seven lines on which to write what one pleased) and then by ordinary postcards.

But poverty soon became the overriding concern: poverty occasioned in part by the suspension of the usual trading and the English blockade and in part by that lion's share seized by the occupying power. Quite soon it became impossible to find 'normal' shoes, and many other commodities were almost as difficult to come by: screws, diapers, panes of glass, soap, fats, and coal was worth its weight in gold, fetching almost as much as coffee. The French State soon found itself obliged to regulate[29] or tax foodstuffs and, above all, to establish quotas. As early as September 1940, bread, noodles and sugar were rationed; by the autumn of 1941, almost all foodstuffs were and also clothes, footwear, tobacco etc. One had to take great care of ration cards of every kind, with all their different coloured vouchers. It was strongly advisable to read the local press if one was not to be the last to hear that such and such a commodity would become available on such and such a day in quantities that varied in accordance with the eleven different categories into which French men and women were divided.[30]

One managed, by finding palliatives, if one could. Nothing was wasted; everything was saved and no one – or hardly anyone – would throw away so much as a cigarette stub. In the towns, people had soon learned to queue, arriving neither too early nor, above all, too late. Every old bike more or less reconstituted was wheeled out anew. The bicycle once more reigned supreme. The administration produced a stream of substitute products: wooden soles replaced those of leather. Housewives deployed incredible ingenuity to keep their pots on the boil, not without regrets at having to serve substitute coffee sweetened with saccharine. There was one vegetable that in particular symbolised this gastronomy of shortages, the swede (*rutabaga* in French), formerly known as the 'cabbage-turnip' (*le chou-navet*). It did not really fill one's stomach but townspeople who subsisted upon it have suffered from indigestion from it ever since. To improve the ordinary menu, the craftier used their balconies or cellars to raise rabbits, rather ricketty ones, it is true.

For the rest, it was a matter of depending on the D system: that is on the black market and its more or less efficient contacts. With money, one could find anything – or almost –, a broom (for which one would pay around 300 francs instead of 50), a 'real' tie (costing 1,500 francs, the entire monthly salary of a Parisian typist).[31] However, it was for food that most people turned to the black market – food, the prices of which varied from region to region[32] and from season to season. It is estimated that, as early as 1942, meat, milk and eggs were fetching on the black market between twice to five times the official prices, potatoes from four to five times as much, butter from six to eight times as much. The State itself encouraged the trend, for in the law of 15 May 1942, which established a code for the repression of illicit transactions, it excluded 'infractions that are committed solely for the direct purpose of satisfying personal or family needs'. And it does seem that quite a number of citizens who started off by being virtuous to the point of refusing to buy anything on the black market soon found themselves obliged to do so, although it became increasingly costly as foodstuffs grew scarcer and a number of clandestine stockpiles of supplies were seized. In the Basses-Pyrénées a kilo of butter cost over 250 francs in May 1942 and 350 francs six months later. Over and above official rationing there was a system of selection based on wealth.

The non-peasants tighten their belts

It was also very important to have at least some links with the countryside. In the immediate post-war period, the peasants were regarded by townspeople as sordid and egoistical grabbers. Let us not exaggerate however. For they faced difficulties too: in laying hands on sufficient seed, acquiring new farm implements, and enough cord for bundling, since sisal was in short supply. It is undeniable, however, that they were themselves consuming more than in the past;[33] it was one way of registering a protest against the German rake-offs and above all what were, in their eyes, the derisory prices at which the official organisation of general supplies was buying up a large proportion of their produce. Meanwhile, some were certainly glad to be able to reduce the 'city gentlemen' who had hitherto been so haughty towards them to a more reasonable frame of mind. Consider the words of Grenadou,[34] a peasant of the Beauce:

> Every week three fellows each drove off a cart drawn by two horses, loaded with two or three tons [French *tonnes*] of carrots which they delivered to the agricultural syndicate in Chartres. I was the only one who had grown carrots and they sold like hot cakes. We would drive through Chartres and people would run after us with their bags. I made money hand over fist. From time to time I would hide a calf under the carrots. That's where the black market started. But in Saint-Loup black-market prices were not twice or three times as high, as they were in Paris. We used to try to let the Germans have as little as possible. Beans that the Germans would requisition at 40 francs, we would sell for 50 francs to Parisians who would come to get them by train ... What with all the cows and calves that we killed during the war, there are enough skins buried in the garden to make shoes for a whole battalion. We did the slaughtering at home, in the evening. I would begin by cutting up the rump. Alice would put them on the grill and we would eat our steaks. While everybody else was hungry, talking about food, we were eating half as much again as we used to eat before the war. I got much fatter. I used to kill sheep too. I would provide meat for the authorities for Bridges and Roads, for the *gendarmes*, for the police superintendent ...

Not all French farmers were in a position to operate on so many fronts at once and one should certainly make distinctions between the scale of exploitation in the different regions and between the affluence of peasants in different parts of the country. But overall, statistics indicate that on one point at least Grenadou seems to have been right: food consumption among the peasants themselves really did double between 1940 and 1944.

Townsfolk, like everybody else, were cold, particularly during the winter of 1940. But the great majority of them also went hungry. Rations were constantly being reduced;[35] and in 1943, in Paris, ration cards ensured one of no more than 1,200 calories. Alfred Sauvy has calculated that on average a Parisian could count on between 1,800 and 2,000. But to reach that total, which is a maximum, one would have to have sufficient funds or to have preserved some rural connections. In 1941, it is true, the government gave authorisation for the sending of 'family parcels', the contents of which were subject to regulations and were, in principle, destined for relatives or friends. In practice, however, the receiver might be anybody.[36] It was also possible, provided one could afford it, to go to do one's shopping in the neighbouring countryside.[37] The system, with all its palliatives, con-demned to poverty low wage-earners in certain large centres (Paris, Marseilles, Bordeaux, Montpellier), particularly in the cases of couples with adolescent children and where the wife was not working.[38] It was above all such adolescents from working-class backgrounds or from the families of urban minor civil servants who sustained growth deficiencies to the tune of 20% both in height and in weight. It was also they who were the most affected by higher mortality rates caused by diseases attributable to undernourishment, such as tuberculosis.

Fertility and insecurity

In conditions such as these, one might have expected to find the birth-rate and, in particular, the fertility-rate going down and the death-rate dramatically increasing. However, such was not the case. The balance between births and normal civilian deaths certainly remained a negative one but the proportion was less high than was expected: around 500,000.[39] We even find a decrease in the mortality-rate[40] between 1941 and 1943 (from 17.4 per thousand to 16.3 per thousand) which it seems feasible to explain in terms of a relative physiological conditioning, on the part of the adults at least.[41] Even more surprising, perhaps, is the increase in the birth-rate (from 13.1 per thousand to 15.7 per thousand) due in large part to an upward surge in fertility, since, in 1943 – in contrast to the immediate pre-war period – the rate of generation replacement was certainly assured. Alfred Sauvy regards this fertility recovery as the result of policies towards the family that had been consistent ever since 1939. However, variations in the French fertility-rate over very recent years have taught us that explanations of that kind are quite inadequate and that it is never easy to distinguish the underlying causes at work. Besides which it is just as reasonable to claim that couples[42] were behaving as they did in 1942 because the war was over and lost as it is to claim that it was because in the end it would be won and lead to a better future.[43]

Whatever the explanation, the relatively high birth-rate was accompanied by a feeling of insecurity which, particularly in the towns, seems to have affected a good proportion of the population, namely the people who were most keenly and visibly affected by the presence of the occupying power: districts surrounded, round-ups, an ever-escalating system of controls, man-hunts in the country regions too, for those dodging the compulsory work service. This political insecurity contributed to the formulation of the general opinion, increasingly voiced as from the autumn of 1943, that there was a steady growing risk of civil war. There was also the fear that metropolitan France might once again become a battlefield in conditions such that the Nazis would exact terrible reprisals from the civilian population. Furthermore, in frontier towns and localities situated near marshalling yards or military targets the bombing suggested that there was worse to come. The air raids had, it is true, been going on all the time (Brest was bombed 78 times between September 1940 and May 1941); but they were becoming more deadly (the bombing of the Renault factories at Billancourt on 3 March 1942 claimed 623 deaths) and were provoking movements of collective panic; three-quarters of the population of Nantes scattered into the countryside after 16 September 1943 when the town had sustained a raid that had killed 1,150 people and the port had taken a hammering on two occasions ten days later. At Le Havre, there was an eighteen-hour exodus on the part of those who preferred to spend a relatively quiet night out in the open rather than be bombed in their beds. In 1944, at any rate, as soon as the sirens sounded the alert, everybody rushed for shelter in the 'classified cellars'. After the raids, the life-savers worked against the clock to pull survivors from the rubble or from cellars flooded as a result of smashed pipes. Including the victims of the German raids of 1940, an estimated 60,000 people died in the bombing.

The stokers of glory

This is the expression Pierre Brosselette used to refer to those obscure Resistance workers who are seldom remembered but without whom it could not have existed. I should like at this point briefly to consider the lives and deaths of those anonymous rebels.[44]

The 'other ranks'

It is impossible to assess the true number of French men and women who were involved, deeply or remotely, in the Resistance. It is possible only to state that 220,000 cards were issued to 'voluntary Resistance fighters'. There seems little doubt that up to and including the spring of 1944, members of the Resistance remained a minority. But were they just a tiny minority, as is so often claimed? I do not think so. It is my opinion that one should attempt to make a new estimate of the number of people who, in one way or another, at some time or other, helped those who were totally committed rebels. Many members of the Resistance have testified to the fact that, when on the run, they would knock at the first door they came to and be taken in and hidden by strangers who ran a heavy risk in doing so. Francis Closon escaped arrest one day through having met an adolescent who shouted to him: 'The Germans are over there; they're putting up a strong road-block'.[45] All these unknown individuals also played their part in the Resistance, even if they did not carry a stamped card. Without them the official Resistance could never have taken root. And there were enough of them for the Resistance not only to survive despite all the denunciations and betrayals but moreover to thrive like fish in water, to use the simile that has been associated with it ever since.

Jacques Soustelle paid tribute to all the 'stokers of glory' when he declared that 'in the Resistance there were no senior and junior ranks'. Without the devotion of all the 'other ranks', the liaison agents for example – a subordinate, thankless and dangerous yet fundamental role – neither the networks nor the movements could have existed. We should also stress the part played by the 'Maries of France with a hundred faces' to whom

Aragon has paid tribute: all the young women, companions or mothers who not only ensured supplies but were also, much more frequently than is suggested, active militants. The histories of some of these women are starting to become known.[46]

A rebel was not a James Bond

The collective memory of members of the Resistance tends to be a confused picture of secret agents, avengers and outlaws with something of the Western hero or the knight 'sans peur et sans reproche' about them, machine gun in hand, blowing up hundreds of factories and trains. A number of amazing, even fantastic episodes[47] certainly took place but they were the exception rather than the rule. The day to day reality was, in the main, much more down to earth and repetitive, although dangerous none the less. It should be emphasised that many members of the Resistance, often for family reasons, had not gone underground completely, but were for the most part leading double lives, continuing their professional activities alongside their militant existence, right up until the end of the spring of 1944. These semi-clandestine rebels, after or even during their day's work, were producing and distributing tracts and newspapers, receiving intelligence, collecting communications from secret 'letter-boxes' and also – but much more rarely – setting up sabotage operations.

The clandestine and the semi-clandestine alike were all familiar with hunger. They furthermore spent much of their militant lives covering many kilometres by bicycle or delivering propaganda material by one means or another. All of them lived in constant fear, fear of the doorbell that did not announce the milkman, of the black vans that spelt misfortune. The antidote to that fear came from those rare moments of relaxation that can arise even in the dangerous life of a militant. There may have been a few romantic idylls but a life of love was not always compatible with the security regulations inherent in the underground.[48]

Not many of them were prepared for a rebel's life; they had to be trained, accustom themselves to rigorous punctuality,[49] to seeking out discreet and anonymous meeting places – a relatively busy square, for instance – to arranging rendezvous, favouring houses with more than one exit,[50] to avoiding all 'letter-boxes' that had been blown, to shunning like the plague all comrades who had been arrested and released or who had escaped, until proof was established that they were not – unwittingly or not – being used as decoys by the Gestapo. Above all, they had to learn to be discreet, patient, suspicious and ... lucky. The braggarts, the show-offs, the vain-glorious were easy prey for Gestapo helpers whether German or French. It was easy to make turncoats of them and then use them as extremely dangerous 'plants'.

Among other remarkable figures, there were the radio operators, the famous '*pianistes*' who tinkered about with their sets to pick up the right wavelengths at the right times and make contact with London. It was usually while they were sending out no more than security instructions (since the genuine messages that had to be sent were usually too urgent) that many of them were surprised red-handed as they worked, picked up by detector vans. In principle, there was one key-phrase that was supposed to guarantee their broadcast as authentic and prevent the apparatus being used by German counter-espionage. But there were many disasters. Another somewhat mythical figure is that of the *maquisard*. We should beware of forming the wrong picture. Up until the summer of 1944, he would usually be a rebel on the move, living from hand to mouth, camping out in the forests in summer, sheltering in barns and isolated huts in winter. There were very few *maquis* groups of the kind organised by Guingouin, run on rational lines both sufficiently strict and sufficiently adaptable to be able to cope with any emergency.[51]

The hunt and the capture

Many rebels were eventually caught, the victims of bad luck,[52] imprudence,[53] but above all of treachery.

The Gestapo and secret services of the Reich managed to infiltrate networks and movements with a number of their own agents or 'turned' Resistance men. In November 1943, George Mathieu betrayed for money the Resistance organisation implanted in the University of Strasbourg, which had been moved to Clermond-Ferrand. On his release from the *Stalag* where he had been a prisoner, Henri Devilliers, who worked for Hachette, 'turned in' the Combat branch operating in the occupied zone. In November 1943, out of pure vanity and without even having been roughly used, Tilden, the radio operator, betrayed the leadership of the Confrérie de Notre-Dame network. The railway employee, Jean-Paul Lien, turned in 150 members of the Alliance network.

The great majority of the 'affairs' that were to rock the Resistance were the result of treachery. Particular mention should be made of the treachery at Caluire, if only because it led to the arrest and death of Jean Moulin.[54] Further up the line there was the treachery of Multon, the secretary of one of the MUR leaders; through him the Gestapo was able to lay its hands on a large number of militants of Combat – Bertie Albrecht among them; they arrested Delestraint and also René Hardy, one of the leaders of Résistance-Fer, whom they picked up in Chalon-sur-Saône. Hardy was interrogated and later released by the Gestapo. He said nothing of the incident to his comrades[55] and was invited to attend a meeting called by Jean Moulin at Caluire in the house of Dr Dugoujon, with the purpose of taking measures to palliate the arrest of Delestraint. On that 21 June 1943, the Gestapo were also at the rendezvous. The papers they seized told Klaus Barbie that he had captured *Max*. By the 23rd he had identified him as Jean Moulin. However, the chief torturer of the Lyons Gestapo 'interrogated' his prisoner in such a way that *Max* fell into a semi-coma and died in transit to Germany without having talked.[56]

Capture in effect nearly always meant torture. It would be pointless to go into details. Let us just say that the Nazis used every known means and, in particular, that they were the first to codify them in such a systematic fashion. That was another thing that Resistance members learned to their terrible cost. Rémy has, quite properly, written that 'nobody in the world has the right to judge without pity anyone who has talked after torture'. What was above all asked of one who was caught was at all costs to gain twenty-four to forty-eight hours, time enough for the warning to go out and the necessary links to be cut. Actually, so far as one can judge, the great majority of Resistance members arrested did hold their tongues or managed to bluff. In the end few betrayed their comrades. It is known that Gabriel Péri refused to save his life by writing a notice of betrayal on the eve of his execution, which took place on 15 December 1942: 'During that night I repeatedly thought of what my dear friend Paul Vaillant-Couturier so rightly used to say, namely that communism was youth for the world and heralded tomorrows that would sing ... ' To avoid giving away the slightest piece of information, some of those who carried the burden of the most important secrets chose to commit suicide. On 22 March 1944, Pierre Brosselette threw himself from the fifth floor of a building in Avenue Foch; Fred Scamaroni cut his wrists and wrote in the blood: 'I did not talk'. Jacques Bingen, Marchal, François Delimal, Gilbert Védy and others, too, swallowed their cyanide pill. Occasionally fate was kind. One of those condemned to death, André Devigny, after undergoing a day of torture, escaped from Montluc one night, showing quite remarkable composure.[57] In two months 19 members of the FTP dug a tunnel 40 metres long through which they escaped from the Royalieu camp in June 1942. In October 1943 it was the turn of 79 prisoners in the prison of Le Puy, who made their escape taking one of their guards along with them. Lucie Aubrac organised a remarkable operation to snatch her husband and 13 leaders of the MUR from the clutches of the Gestapo.[58] In March 1944, the RAF itself pounded the Amiens central prison in an attempt to rescue Resistance leaders due to face the firing squad (but this operation, known as 'Jericho', was not completed without losses). However, a more common fate would be at best a more or less protracted stay in a 'French' prison; or, more often, being shot as a hostage (as would be announced on a bilingual notice bordered in black and red), or execution in a German prison (in Cologne, Sonnenburg, Kehl, Fribourg or Brücksaal), or else slow death in an extermination camp, for most members of the Resistance who were deported were lumped together with deportees who were to be eliminated leaving no trace.

The uprooted

The people of Alsace-Lorraine who were Germanised whether they liked it or not may be added to all the prisoners and deportees of the Service du Travail Obligatoire (compulsory work service), who were forced to spend dozens of months away from home.

The people of Alsace-Lorraine transformed into 'Volksdeutsche'

Although the armistice agreement did not pronounce upon the fate of Alsace-Lorraine, the Reich was quite determined to turn the three departments of Moselle, the Upper and the Lower Rhineland into German marches once and for all.[59] For tactical reasons, it chose to annex the three departments *de facto* rather than *de jure*. And it proceeded to do so without waiting for the peace treaty so that by August 1940 they had become attached to the *Gaue* of the Reich and had been taken in hand by two Gauleiters, Bürckel and Wagner, two Nazis of very long standing. One month later, the sovereignty of the French State had been reduced to nothing. In Alsace, Wagner was counting on exploiting the autonomist movements which had recruited supporters among men of the right as well as among the curious 'Alsatian communists',[60] some of the leaders of which had already established contacts with the Nazis.[61]

The two Gauleiters were supposed – within ten years – to transform these *Volksdeutsche*, now considered ethnically as part of greater Germany, into model citizens of the Reich. By the autumn of 1940 they were expelling[62] all those considered undesirable or impossible to assimilate (Jews, naturally, and declared francophiles, as well as all those who had settled in the region later than 1918). These sections of the population were in part replaced by inhabitants from the Reich. At the same time, a careful programme of Germanisation was undertaken: it affected the economy, banks, insurance companies, company securities. The possessions of those expelled were confiscated. Teaching was also Germanised, becoming the monopoly of the Hitlerian State. Christian names, the names of streets,[63] towns and villages were all changed. Speaking French or wearing a Basque beret were both considered serious transgressions and those guilty could well fetch up in the Schirmeck camp. As for Nazification, that was undertaken more gradually. It was only in October 1941 that Alsace saw the creation of the first section of the Nazi Party. However, the Opferring (the Sacrifice Club) had already been set up and attempts were being made to attract the young to it. In

January 1942, the young were moreover compulsorily required to belong to Nazi youth organisations (Jungvolk and Hitlerjugend for the boys, Jung Maedel Bund and Bund Deutscher Maedel for the girls).

The failure of the Blitzkrieg aggravated the plight of the people of Alsace-Lorraine, starting with the young of both sexes who were made to serve a whole year of *Reichsarbeitsdienst*, a compulsory form of labour service for young people. Then, in August 1942, despite misgivings expressed by certain leaders of the party and the Wehrmacht, conscripts were mobilised from all three departments, as *Volksdeutsche*. There were 130,000 of these 'unwilling' conscripts; 40,000 were killed or reported missing and around 30,000 eventually came home wounded.[64]

In 1944, after four years of Germanisation, the achievements of the two Gauleiters were not impressive, even if they could boast of the rallying of a number of well-known autonomists and even if Wagner did pride himself on having recruited in Alsace some 25,000 whole-hearted members to the Party. In the two Rhineland departments the SS had recruited no more than 2,638 men. Declared members of the Resistance were rare. They were even more vulnerable than elsewhere and most were sent to the Schirmeck camps or even to that of the Struthof, while reprisals were exacted on their families, in particular those of so-called 'deserters'.[65] Strong-arm tactics had little effect on the resolution of the people of Alsace-Lorraine either in the case of francophiles and anti-Nazis or even in that of certain autonomists who came to realise that enforced Germanisation and Nazification meant the end of any hopes of autonomy.

The long solitude of the French prisoners

The disasters of 1940 had left about 1,850,000 prisoners in German hands.[66] About 1,500,000 had been put to work during the winter of 1940–41, of whom 940,000 survived to 1944. So half the prisoners had been placed on 'prisoner's leave' (in theory revocable), either directly in *Frontstalags* (camps improvised in France itself) or classed as *sick prisoners*, in the case of men of Alsace-Lorraine or even Bretons who had declared themselves to be autonomists. Others were placed on 'prisoner's leave' as a result of the processes of State collaboration: officers, veterans from the last war, the heads of large families; some were exchanged under the conditions of the 'Relief' programme or profited from particular liberal gestures on the part of the Führer.[67]

But the other half remained beyond the Rhine, distributed over 28 *Oflags* (officers' camps) and 69 *Stalags*. Most of the latter were run as labour *Kommandos* (there were about 82,000 of these at the beginning of 1941, each composed of between 6 and 1,000 men, administratively attached to 'base camps'.[68] Half the prisoners worked on farms, one third in mines and factories including those producing war materials. About 37,000 prisoners died in Germany: almost half of them killed in 1944 and 1945, victims of Allied bombs, epidemics and malnutrition.

On the whole, the prisoners felt not so much delivered over to severe warders but, rather, persecuted by police sergeants. It is true that the fate of prisoners varied considerably from one *Stalag* to another, that in some camps the roll-calls could last for as long as six hours and one was liable to be shot for venturing out of one's hut after curfew.[69] But at least the French were seldom treated as badly as the Russian prisoners who were considered by their captors as no more than human cattle.

That being said, prisoners were hungry, particularly during the winter of 1940 and during the last months of captivity. The usual fare was meagre: basically thin soup with a few swedes and scraps of meat floating in it. In these conditions, family food parcels truly were a godsend but the intervals at which they could be received were strictly regulated and the chances of their arriving intact were slight. After hunger, what the prisoners feared most, in winter, was the cold, especially in the camps situated furthest to the east, and the fleas and the lice which were constantly rampant despite regular delousing sessions. During the last winter typhus also struck. Above all, perhaps, they suffered from an emotional solitude; being uprooted became increasingly hard to bear as the months passed and matters were not greatly helped by the two letters a month (never more) that a prisoner was allowed to receive. In many camps, it is true, prisoners tried to organise their solitude, setting up orchestras, putting on plays and sporting activities. The teachers among them set up universities of a sort. Despite everything, there were some who fell for the countless *bouteillons*,[70] the irrepressible rumours always announcing an imminent general liberation. Then there were some who tried to make a break for it: about 71,000 escapes were successful between 1941 and 1944.[71]

In the autumn of 1940, the Reich had authorised the French State to be the protective power over its own prisoners but if the evidence of many prisoners is to be believed, the 'Scapini mission' which was supposed to defend their interests was more concerned with spreading propaganda than with improving their lot. That is why, in order to avoid the despotism of 'petty tyrants', when it came to negotiating with the '*Flick* sergeant' or settling problems with other nationalities in the same *Stalag*, the more responsible prisoners preferred to depend on their own organisation, choosing with care 'men they could trust' to be their spokesmen.

The Germans tried hard to indoctrinate the prisoners and to that end they brought out a paper called *Le Trait d'Union* (The Hyphen). Without success, however. Collaborationist propaganda similarly failed to make much impact. On the other hand quite a number of men – in the early days at least – were influenced by the Pétainist ideology disseminated through Cercles Pétain (Pétain clubs). The version of *maréchalisme* that they purveyed promoted a kind of 'passive patriotism' and at the same time encouraged rejection of the Third Republic, said to be the cause of all their misfortunes. At all events, despite the efforts of not only the German authorities but also Vichy and the collaborationists, in 1944 there were, at the outside, no more than 220,000 'transformed' prisoners.[72] On the whole, while the resistance organisations born in a number of *Stalags* and *Oflags* should not be overlooked, the most general feeling appears to have been one of disenchantment tinged with scepticism and irony.

The disappointments that awaited the STO men

Around 650,000 Frenchmen went off, either willingly or not, on compulsory labour service (the 'Service du Travail Obligatoire').[73] The propagandists of Germany and Vichy alike had sung the praises of the material advantages that awaited this particular category of 'uprooted men' in 'socialist' Germany. The reality, when they got there, was less rosy. The Reich needed manpower and it was not fussy about it. In general, State or private businesses came to draw quite indiscriminately upon this mass of available manpower that could be put to every kind of use, without, for the most part, showing the slightest concern for particular qualifications. Most of these men were installed in camps[74] which were faithful copies of those in which their prisoner comrades were held. And in many respects their living conditions were identical: a long working day (11 to 12 hours on average), a poor material environment and, to borrow Jacques Evrard's expression, 'the despotism of memory and the despotism of hunger'. Solitude and malnutrition made such inroads that in 1946 close on 60,000 of these people had to be treated for tuberculosis.[75] During working hours, as in the base camps, discipline was extremely strict and those who failed to observe it along with those who tried to leave the Reich were sent to disciplinary camps[76] where there were cells and 'punishment drill'. Some even ended up in concentration camps. 35,000 or perhaps rather more died in Germany,[77] some of them beneath the rubble of the bombed German towns.

The outcasts

No sooner was Hitler's Reich set up than it set about arresting, interning and confining all those – the Jews among others – whom it considered its ideological enemies. When total war broke out, the SS State was already constructing its world of concentration camps.

The Calvary of the Jews

For National Socialism, anti-semitism had been a prime weapon providing both a scapegoat and a handy source of exploitation. The Third Reich had reduced German and Austrian Jews to the state of non-citizens, meanwhile progressively herding them into what became the new ghettos. Nazi leaders hesitated until 1941 on the question of the ultimate strategy. In the autumn of 1940 they transferred 7,000 Jews from the Bade area to the free zone and some Nazis were drawing up plans to send all the Jews in Nazified Europe to Madagascar. But in July 1941 the Gestapo received the order to make a study of the 'final solution', the extermination of all European Jews. The principle was definitively adopted on 20 January 1942 at the Wannesee conference and in June 1942 the Gestapo section responsible for Jewish questions was required to plan the deportation of the Jews of France, Belgium and the Netherlands.

At a reasonable estimate, immediately prior to the war there were rather more than 300,000 Jews living in France, half of whom held French nationality and a quarter of whom had been born from French parents. As early as 1940 they were all hit by the new regulations introduced by both the occupying power and Vichy. The objectives of the Reich and those of the French State were no doubt not identical but both intended to turn the Jews into outcasts or semi-outcasts.[78]

Knochen, Danneker, Roethke and other leaders of the anti-Jewish Sonderkommando made the most of anything that fell to hand: they made use of the Vichy legislation,[79] stamping it with their own particular mark. Purporting to be 'Aryanising' businesses, they set about taking over Jewish possessions and immediately appropriated for themselves a large number of works of art which they seized 'to protect them'. In December 1941, this looting operation was further pursued through the medium of taxation – fixed at 1,000 million francs – imposed upon the Jewish community. Meantime, in the occupied zone they were imposing a systematic population census on the basis of a decree of 27 September 1940 which classified as Jewish all those who practised the Jewish religion or who had more than two grandparents who had done so. The great majority of Jews, French or otherwise, who had not yet lost all their illusions fell into the trap.[80] From May 1942, all Jews of six or more years of age were obliged to wear a yellow star prominently sewn onto their clothes. A few weeks later further vexing measures were introduced: Jews were now excluded from public places (cafés, theatres, libraries, swimming pools, fairgrounds and parks, etc.) and they were allowed to do their shopping only during the afternoons when there was hardly anything left in the food stores. By this time the first death convoy had already arrived in Auschwitz. The French State, for its part, did not go so far as to favour racial extermination but it did unremittingly enforce what Xavier Vallat, following Maurras and with the blessing of Pétain, was to call 'State anti-Judaism'. This xenophobic measure designed, according to its planners,[81] to have a 'phrophylactic effect', meant excluding Jews with French nationality from all public employment – or at least in the more important State departments of Justice and

Teaching. It also excluded them from serving as commissioned or non-commissioned officers and from the police force. It was furthermore to deprive them of all electoral rights. Vichy had also introduced a quota of 2% on entry to all the liberal professions and one of 3% for Jewish students. All Israelites were also now obliged to be reclassed as 'Jews' and their identity cards were stamped to this effect. French Jews no longer enjoyed full citizenship.

By 1941 a new stage had been reached. France became full of ghettos. On 4 October 1940 prefects in the occupied zone had been authorised to intern foreign and stateless Jews. In February 1941, 40,000 of them were crammed into the sordid camps at Gurs, Rivesaltes, Vernet, Noé, etc. from which they were transferred to Drancy in 1942 and 1943. The Nazis had themselves set up transit camps at Pithiviers, Beaune-la-Rolande and in particular at Drancy for all those that they had rounded up in 1941. On 14 May 1941, thousands of central European Jews had been arrested and interned. On 15 August an entire Paris *arrondissement* – the 11th – had been surrounded; on 12 December 1943 Jewish individuals of French nationality were apprehended and transferred to Royallieu: after three months of detention there one hundred were already dead. The rest, with a few exceptions, were sent off to Auschwitz. The French State was evidently incapable of protecting individuals of French nationality whom it claimed to be under its protection. The Occupation authorities even made sure that it was the French police that on 16 and 17 July 1942 provided the framework for 'Operation Spring Wind' in the course of which 12,884 Jewish men, women and children were arrested in Paris.[82] It was also under the supervision of the French State that round-ups of foreigners were organised during the August of 1942 all over the southern zone and that, in the January of 1943, French and foreign Jews were picked up during the destruction of the old port of Marseilles.[83]

It was in the spring of 1942 that the first convoys of 'racial deportees'[84] set off, bound for the 'final solution'.[85] A minimum of 75,721 people were despatched from France.[86] Of the 70,000 for whom there are reasonably accurate civil records, over 10,000 were children or adolescents of less than eighteen years of age.[87] Around 23,000 individuals were of French nationality[88] and 47,000 were foreigners. They left in 76 convoys, almost all from the station of Drancy-le-Bourget and almost all bound for Auschwitz. The first set out on 27 March 1942, the last on 31 July 1944. On arrival at Auschwitz, those – the great majority – judged to be of little physical use were immediately eliminated. The rest, the 'hand-picked', were exterminated in the course of forced labour.[89] Of the 28,754 'hand-picked' who left France (20,717 men and 8,037 women) about 2,190 (740 of them women) returned from Auschwitz. At a reasonable estimate less than 2,500 'racial deportees' from France survived, that is to say 3% of those who left.[90]

The demented world of the concentration camps

As well as racial there were political deportees, members of the Resistance, common-law deportees and people deported by mistake. It is almost impossible to describe this world of concentration camps governed by a demoniacal logic. All we can hope to do is provide an inadequate sketch[91] which will satisfy the questions of neither those who lived through it nor those who knew nothing of it.

The concentration camp was an intrinsic part of the totalitarian Nazi system. The Third Reich had opened the *Konzentrationlager* of Dachau, near Munich, as early as 1933. Enemies of the regime were isolated there, to be re-educated or, if need be, exterminated. As the dimensions of vassalised Europe grew and the number of the Reich's opponents swelled, the concentration system also assumed outlandish proportions.[92] As from the summer of 1942, these camps fulfilled a double function: they emptied the prisons and exterminated the ideological enemies of Nazism, at the same time providing the war economy of the Reich with an almost inexhaustible supply of well-nigh free labour that could be worked to the limit, in fact to death. Up until 1942 the plan was, by and large, extermination pure and simple. During 1943 the emphasis – except in the case of racial deportees – was laid upon forced labour,[93] often under the aegis of German heavy industry.[94] At the end of 1944 and during 1945 extermination took over once again, at least where the NN[95] and rebels were concerned.

Let us attempt to give some idea of the itinerary of the *Häftlinge* (deportees). In special convoys, they were crammed into cattle-trucks, 100 or 125 to a truck (designed to carry 40 men), where there was a total lack of everything, starting with air and space. It would take three to five days to reach their destination, during which time death would already have taken its first toll.[96] The SS would oversee the arrival organised by *Kapos* shouting 'Los, los, Schweinerei' (Faster, faster, you pigs) and wielding clubs. Then there would probably be a preliminary selection of those who were to be eliminated immediately. The rest would undergo a form of quarantine, crammed in three or four to a bunk, from which they would emerge shaven from head to foot, in some cases tattooed, and clothed in rags. (Only those who were detailed to work outside the camp wore the compulsory 'striped pyjamas' and caps.) The day would begin between four and five o'clock, slightly later in winter; time for a rapid wash, roll-call in all weathers lasting however long the SS chose, a first 'meal', then the departure of the *Kommandos* for a day of work eleven to twelve hours long (in theory, Sunday afternoons were a time of rest), punctuated by a 'lunch'; in the evening a third 'meal', then rest at last in sheds overrun by vermin.

To say that the *Häftlinge* were tortured day and night by hunger is to put it mildly: in all they had half a litre of some kind of slop in the morning, a litre of soup made from swedes with shreds of meat-scraps at midday, a litre of thin broth in the evening, one pound of bread a day with an occasional scrape of margarine. The Allies liberated skeletons whose average weight (for the men) was 45 kilos. Some – known as 'musulmen' – weighed less than 35. Then there was the cold in the winter, the fleas and the lice, above all the epidemics (tuberculosis, dysentery, typhus) to fight against which the deportees who were doctors detailed to work in the *Revier*[97] had no more than derisory means at their disposal. Death also came as a result of beatings, clubbings, 'sporting sessions' and solitary confinement. Some executions were public ceremonies – in particular in the cases of those who had tried to escape (who were almost invariably caught). Sometimes to the accompaniment of music, the hangings would take place in the presence of all the deportees, standing to attention. To save time, the Nazis sometimes used gas[98] in buses specially arranged for the purpose or more often in sham shower-houses which they would fill with Zyklon B, a gas with a basis of cyanide hydrate. The corpses would be thrown into common graves or burned on huge bonfires or in evil-smelling crematory ovens.

The SS commander of Mauthausen had not lied: the deportee did indeed enter a closed world organised around diabolically devised rituals and practices. At the top was the SS hierarchy with their skull and crossbones badges.[99] They were few in number and seldom mixed with the multitude of *Untermenschen*. They reigned through intermediaries, using a body of 'petty chiefs' most of whom were much to be feared, especially the *Kapos* and their seconds-in-command who were also in charge of the kitchen, the *Revier* and in particular the various labour *Kommandos*.[100] Most had been selected with care; the inherent advantages that went with their duties[101] usually ensured their obedience and efficiency. The master race knew how to divide and rule these strange field-towns[102] by playing upon the rivalries between the various categories and nationalities among the deportees.[103] There appear to have been relatively few camps and *Kommandos* where *Häftlinge* with better political or moral resources to draw upon managed to organise themselves sufficiently well to check the general degeneracy around them – a degeneracy that was not only physical but intellectual and moral as well. Most camps tended to be turned into a human jungle in which horror ceased to be in any way surprising. In some cases the choices to be made within this horror became unbearable, as in the case of deportee doctors at Ravensbrück who were obliged to kill new-born babies, pretending that they were stillborn, if the mother was not to be exterminated along with her child.

It may seem astonishing that in such conditions men and women managed to survive. It is true that not all the camps were – strictly speaking – camps of systematic extermination and that, except for the racial deportees and the NN, there were some moments of respite. But you had to be young enough and 'lucky' enough to be, for example, assigned to a relatively quiet *Kommando*. Except in the case of racial deportees, we do not know as accurately as we should wish exactly how many men and women were deported from France. The painstaking enquiries undertaken at departmental level by the Committee for the History of the Second World War overlap with the facts researched by M.Garban in Germany: they give an approximate total of 63,000 non-racial deportees of whom 41,000 were members of the Resistance.[104] The same sources indicate that the average death-rate – for non-racials – was around 40%.[105]

5

Relief operations

The fate of the war was decided between the summer of 1942 and the spring of 1943. At the end of the summer of 1942 the Axis powers believed they could win. The 'Battle for the Atlantic' was turning in favour of the Kriegsmarine's packs of submarines which were sinking hundreds of thousands of tons of shipping every month; the Suez route was open and the Afrikakorps had reached the slopes of El Alamein and the gates of Cairo. The Wehrmacht's second summer offensive in the Soviet Union had got as far as Voronej, Stalingrad and the edges of the Caucasus; and meantime the Dai Nippon in the Pacific and south-eastern Asia had never extended so far before.

Despite everything, however, American supplies were getting through to Great Britain and the Soviet Union. Rommel lost the battle of El Alamein and on 3 November 1942 was forced to beat a retreat; and soon after this the Anglo-Saxons were successful in their invasion of French North Africa. Above all, after fighting of hitherto unequalled violence outside Stalingrad, which had been under siege since September, the Wehrmacht suffered a defeat that was, in many respects, decisive. On 2 February 1943, being unable to prevent the capitulation of the 6th army, under the command of Marshal Paulus, it pulled back before the counter-attack of the Red Army.

The Allies had regained the upper hand over the Axis powers which now barricaded themselves within 'the fortress of Europe'. For the Reich, the fruitful and glorious days of the 'Blitzkrieg' were over; Hitler's Germany, too, was now plunged into a 'total war' which, despite everything, it was still counting on winning, chiefly by exploiting all its vassal nations to the limit.[1]

The evil wind

By the summer of 1941, the national revolution was already marking time. In a speech delivered in Saint-Etienne on 12 August 1941, the head of the French State made the following observation: 'For the past few weeks I have been conscious of an evil wind arising in a number of regions of

France. Minds are falling prey to anxiety, doubt is gaining a hold over the French ... the French people are falling victim to a veritable unease.' The regime itself was also changing. Persuasive Pétainism was being super-seded by hard-line Pétainism. But the decisive rupture for the French State came in the autumn of 1942. In November 1942, Vichy lost all – or virtually all – its means of bargaining. State collaboration, which had always been a one-way operation, was now to prove crushing for the French people. Disaffection with regard to the regime was increasing so rapidly that Laval had declared that he would like to 'make the French happy despite themselves'.

Relieving the guard

Laval had returned to power six months before the events of November. Contemporary witnesses and many historians have ascribed much importance to this relieving of the guard – an importance that seems to me exaggerated, although its effects should certainly not be under-estimated.

On 16 April 1942, then, Pierre Laval had been appointed 'head of the government', returning to the political scene from which he had been ejected on 13 December 1940. Darlan had finally proved a disappointment. He was sculling a single course to no very great effect. Despite all the efforts of the ADD (Les Amis de Darlan: Darlan's friends) who packed the administration, the popularity of the Admiral of the Fleet was low. His shock wave of technocrats had reduced unemployment and relaunched production, but food supplies were short and the black market was spreading. Darlan, who had eventually with the aid of the Reich managed to get Weygand relieved of his command in North Africa, had proved incapable of wringing from Hitler the slightest political concession in exchange.[2] The prisoners remained in their *Stalags* and France remained garrotted by the demarcation line. The Reich was not pleased either; the Führer had declared himself scandalised by 'the prostrating spectacle' offered by the Riom trial in which the accused had declared themselves accusers and had transformed this machination devised as an attack upon 'warmongering' into an indictment of the defeatists and those – Pétain included – who were responsible for the unprepared state of the French army. The trial had to be postponed indefinitely 'pending the collection of more information'.[3]

Ever since January 1941, Laval had been straining at the leash. What he wanted was not simply revenge for 13 December, but power. He was, in addition, deeply convinced that he – alone – could get through to the Reich. However, apart from Abetz, a few 'European' Vichy men and Doriot who, now that he was himself a minister, launched a press campaign in Laval's favour, not many flocked to support him. Anyway, Laval had always been a loner. Pétain was not ruling out a relieving of the guard, now that Darlan was clearly in deep water, but he envisaged this taking place under the aegis of orthodox and partisan *maréchalistes* determined to press on with the national revolution.[4] As for Hitler, contrary to what was generally believed, he distrusted Laval whom he regarded as the very model of a politician formed by the execrable liberal democracy.[5] It was Darlan himself who precipitated his rival's return to the political scene: to forestall – as he thought – any move on Laval's part, he took it upon himself to play up Roosevelt's dryly expressed distrust of Laval. Abetz was then able to manoeuvre to force Vichy to choose between the United States and the Reich. Pétain found himself willy-nilly obliged to recall Laval, hoping that he would at least lend new credibility to State collaboration; and in some Vichy circles Laval was even viewed with a certain amount of favour for not having brought any Parisian collaborationists along with him.

Pierre Laval[6] was not born with a silver spoon in his mouth: his father was a small village innkeeper and Laval became a junior schoolmaster in order to be able to pursue a higher education. His rural origins may perhaps account for his distrust of ideologies, his pragmatism and his unshakeable belief that everything was open to negotiation, his 'horse-dealer's mentality', as Blum would have put it. His peasant background had also imbued him with the gut-reactions of pacifism. His career at the Bar brought him out of obscurity and he even became sufficiently well known in socialist and anti-militarist circles to have his name entered in the 'Carnet B' (a list, drawn up by the army, of 'dangerous agitators and pacifists' who were to be interned during the war) among other left-wing personalities to be arrested when it came to mobilisation. He was elected as a deputy in 1914, lost his seat in 1919, then was re-elected in 1924. He had started his parliamentary career under the aegis of the SFIO but soon put a distance between himself and the party machine, taking his place first among the 'independent' socialists, then – after entering the Senate in 1927 – among the 'moderates'. He had also been elected mayor of Aubervilliers in 1923 and the belligerent municipal campaign he had had to lead against his communist rivals there had exacerbated his profound feelings of anti-Bolshevism. In 1925 he embarked upon a classic ministerial career as a result of which he served as president of the Council from January 1931 to February 1932. Although he was a skilful parliamentary manoeuvrer, he did not make his mark as an outstanding statesman.[7]

He became well known above all as Minister of Foreign Affairs, succeeding Barthou in this post; and he once again became president of the Council from June 1935 to January 1936. His dream was to become a second Briand, one of the few statesmen by whom he was truly impressed, and he thought he would be able to force a policy of *détente*. He tried to outmanoeuvre Stalin, made advances to Hitler with the aim of relaunching a policy of Franco-German collaboration, and meanwhile played the Italian card for all it was worth. But, all in all, his great European policies turned out to be confusing rather than productive: he had not succeeded in modifying Hitler's strategies in any way; France emerged from the Ethiopian affair more or less at odds with Great Britain and Mussolini, who was bitter, reckoned he had been duped.[8]

Four years of penance followed: the Popular Front was united in opposing his deflationist policies and his tolerance of factious cliques. He emerged from his parliamentary hibernation in September 1939 but during the period of the phoney war his attitude was not unambiguous. Although recognised as one of the leaders of the pacifist clan, when he headed an attack against Daladier in March 1940 it was only to reproach him for his bad management of the war. It was not until June 1940 that he really surfaced again, when he became an active member of the 'Bordeaux Commune' and, following one last false manoeuvre, eventually got himself accepted by Pétain by provoking and steering through the parliamentary hara-kiri.

In the spring of 1942, Laval's strategy was quite straightforward: France could expect salvation only from a relaunching of State collaboration. It was furthermore necessary to have his hands free and to protect himself against a second palace revolution.

He had no difficulty in obtaining the institutional guarantees that he sought. The Constitutional Act number 11 of 18 April 1942 stipulated that 'the effective management of both internal and external policies is the responsibility of the head of the government appointed by the head of State and responsible to him'. By distancing himself from the day to day direction of public affairs, Pétain definitely left his 'head of government' – a new title – a latitude of action that the events of November 1942 were further to reinforce.[9] But the head of government acted only through delegation and the same Constitutional Act required him to 'report his intentions and actions' to a head of State who intended to remain such[10] and was indeed considered such by the occupying powers and the occupied alike. So Laval, avoiding the blunders of the autumn of 1940, never failed to report to Philippe Pétain every day to discuss affairs of State. And even if the feelings of the two men towards each other were no warmer than before, they certainly declared themselves to be at one on the policies they were pursuing.[11] It was not until the autumn of 1943 that Pétain, conscious of the unpopularity of his head of government and trying to make capital out of the reverses suffered by the Axis powers, tried – in vain – to get rid of Laval.[12]

The new government was relatively stable.[13] Laval had settled for a mixed bag of ministers,[14] retaining long-serving Pétainists (Barthélémy and, in particular, Romier) or those of the Darlan team that he thought he could use (Benoist-Méchin and Bichelonne) but giving the difficult posts to the few men who were in his confidence (Finance to Cathala, Food Supplies to Max Bonnafous).[15] For himself he kept Foreign Affairs, Information and Interior (which occasioned the departure of Pucheu). He would tolerate few deviations from his own main line and ruthlessly pushed through business at the meetings of his Councils of Ministers.

While not fundamentally opposed to the national revolution, he judged it inappropriate – at all events unsuitable in the current circumstances. He did not support La Porte du Theil who was attempting to obtain some respite from the STO for the young people in the Chantiers de la Jeunesse and he definitively closed down the Uriage school.[16] His preference was, rather, for a more human, purer and stronger Republic[17] (sentiments that won him from *Je Suis Partout* the description of 'républicain musclé' (republican strong-man)). Rejecting his earlier right-thinking apoliticism, he now favoured 'effective repoliticisation':[18] he would have liked to extend political support for the regime, drawing upon the politicians and high-ranking civil servants who had hitherto been ostracised because of their past support for the Third Republic. With a similar purpose in mind, he also made contact with ex-leaders of the CGT.[19]

It went without saying that this 'Republic' would be an authoritarian one. Truth to tell, few material innovations were needed. Since August 1941, the French State had been striving to counter the 'evil wind': magistrates, officers and high-ranking civil servants had been required to swear a personal oath of loyalty to the head of State.[20] On 29 September 1941, the 'Council of Political Justice' had been instituted to establish the 'responsibilities of the political personalities of the Third Republic'; all political meetings had henceforth to obtain preliminary authorisation. But a veritable political police force had yet to be created. It was Laval who now instituted the Militia (la Milice).

Lemon-squeezer collaboration

In Laval's view, then, everything depended upon relaunching political collaboration. However, in the eighteen months since Montoire, much had changed. Furthermore, the Allied landing in North Africa had definitively ruined the foundations of Laval's strategy. State collaboration was henceforth strictly a one-way operation: the only course left was to haggle.

Laval was no more enchanted by the Nazi regime than before,[21] but he continued to believe that Germany would emerge victor from the war and that the peace would be a German one. At any rate, it would at all costs have to be a German peace in the east: as a Vichy man, Laval equated *Realpolitik* with anti-communism. It was an equation he expressed, in scandalous terms, in his announcement of the 'Relief' of 22 June 1942, the anniversary of the invasion of the Soviet Union: 'I desire victory for Germany because without it Bolshevism would establish itself everywhere. France cannot remain passive or indifferent before the immensity of the sacrifices that Germany is willing to make in order to construct a Europe in which we must take our place'.[22] And on 13 December 1942, he produced this recidivist statement: 'Victory for Germany will save our civilisation from sinking into communism. Victory for the Americans would be a triumph for Jewry and communism ... I, for my part, have made my choice.'

Convinced as he was that, ever since 13 December, Vichy had been pursuing policies of the utmost naïvety and that playing a cautious game could result only in tying one's own hands, Laval was again anxious to take the initiative and force Hitler to collaborate, so as to win France a privileged position in the German Europe. To this end, he came to agreements over contentious issues, offered French workers to the Reich,[23] invented the 'Relief' system, authorised the Gestapo to enter the free zone to rout out radio transmitting posts run by rebels, etc.[24] To him the time seemed ripe for another Montoire. It was, in all conscience, a serious misappraisal of the true nature of Hitler's strategy. It was at this point that the Americans landed in Algeria and Morocco.

It would not be exaggerated to select this date to close the chapter of State collaboration. After November 1942, the French State, now hardly more than a satellite, no longer commanded any real means of negotiation. This new turn of events not only compromised political collaboration but also made 'wait-and-see' neutralism an extremely risky business.[25] All that the French State could now hope to do was to attempt to minimise the damage.

For reasons already explained, North Africa had been left out of the armistice agreement. Weygand, during his African pro-consulship, had been at pains to maintain French Africa in a state of strict neutrality, defended by an army 120,000 strong. His only concession had been to come to an agreement[26] with Murphy, the American consul, which would make it possible to slacken the grip of the British blockade.

Vichy was caught by surprise by 'Operation Torch'.[27] The Anglo-Saxon landing seriously upset its strategy and, for a while, Pétain showed no hesitation as to the conduct to adopt, striving at all costs to defend the positions of the French State.[28] He sent a curt note to Roosevelt to the effect that nothing could justify such 'aggression', ending with the words: 'We are attacked; we shall defend ourselves', and meanwhile the French Admiralty was warning the armistice commission that it might have to use the ocean-going fleet. Darlan, who found himself in Algiers for quite fortuitous reasons,[29] received orders about which there could be no doubt: 'Order from the Maréchal: defend our territories.' The French State was all the more anxious to be seen to be resolute given that it feared the reactions of the Germans. At Abetz's instigation, the Reich had first offered aid,[30] then insisted on air support bases in Tunisia. Meanwhile Hitler, while willing to wait a while to let the situation become clearer, ordered the Wehrmacht to hold itself in readiness to launch 'Operation Attila', the invasion of the southern zone. Laval tried to gain time. He was quite ready to sever diplomatic relations with the United States and resigned himself to the arrival of German reinforcements in Tunisia, but he thought it necessary to propose to Hitler that overall negotiations should be resumed. He travelled to Munich in pessimistic mood but determined at last to obtain from the Reich political guarantees and concessions. Vichy had already committed itself to a tightrope act, tugged in opposite directions between two sets of negotiations unfolding simultaneously, one in Algiers between Darlan and the American military authorities, the other – which had to take priority – between Laval and Hitler. As early as 10 November, barely 48 hours after the Anglo-Saxon landing, the French State was overtaken by events and revealed itself incapable of staying the course. In Algiers Darlan, under pressure from the Americans, was also trying to gain time and cut the ground from under the feet of a non-*maréchaliste* movement of 'dissidence'. But he found himself obliged, unwillingly, to agree to a 'cease-fire' applicable in the first instance to the town of Algiers alone, then extended to cover the whole of Algeria and Morocco. He proclaimed that 'in the name of the Maréchal', he was 'assuming authority over North Africa' and he ordered that 'the strictest neutrality' be observed. At the same time he informed Vichy that 'it was impossible to do any better'. The French State, now thoroughly bogged down, had to put on some kind of a show: Pétain, who resumed his title of 'commander-in-chief' openly disowned his heir apparent: 'I issued the order to put up a defence against the aggressor; I stick by that order.' However, he meanwhile secretly let him know that this brutal rejection was unavoidable under the prevailing circumstance: 'You must understand that this rejection was necessary for the negotiations that are taking place'.[31] Reprimanded, still loyalist, but anxious to temporise, Darlan – without cancelling his cease-fire order – decided to become a 'prisoner of war'.[32] The negotiations in Munich were taking a disastrous turn. Laval soon realised that achieving another Montoire was out of the question. He was pushed into a defensive position and the first order he received was to let the Axis troops establish a bridgehead in Tunisia. In the end he agreed (putting the Reich in a position to proclaim that the Axis landing had been made 'with the agreement of the French government and at its request') although at the same time he pressed for guarantees as to the integrity of the Empire and necessary concessions in exchange etc. These verbal prevarications convinced Hitler that it was high time to launch 'Operation Attila', now renamed 'Anton';[33] the invasion of the southern zone fell on 11 November – a source of some satisfaction to Hitler who had quite a sense of timing.

In less than three days, the last illusions were gone: Hitler informed Pétain that 'much to his regret' he had given the order 'temporarily' to occupy the southern zone to prevent an Anglo-Saxon landing along the Mediterranean seaboard. 'Operation Anton' took place smoothly: in less than twenty-four hours the Italian[34] and German forces controlled the whole of the southern zone with the sole exception of the defensive region around Toulouse where most of the ocean-going fleet was stationed. On the orders[35] of General Bridoux, Secretary of State for War and a determined supporter of collaboration, the armistice army was to remain in its barracks. General de Lattre de Tassigny was the only – or virtually the only – one who refused to comply but he and the few hundred men who had followed him were soon surrounded.[36] Marshal Rundstedt had good reason to declare himself well satisfied: 'The French army is loyal and helping our troops; the French police is helpful and full of goodwill. In general the attitude of the population is indifferent, except in the regions of Marseilles and Roanne which are openly hostile ... '.[37] In Vichy, despite Weygand, who had been recalled for consultation and who insisted that they should 'stand firm' and despite Auphan[38] and a few others, Laval's line won the day: State collaboration continued; the army of Africa was to continue to fight in North Africa – in particular in Tunisia – against the Anglo-Saxons: it was necessary 'to continue to fight until you drop, in the interests of France and the Empire'. Care was taken, however, not to suggest an official military alliance with the Reich.

Meanwhile Vichy was losing political control over North Africa. However much Darlan and Noguès might have been tempted to go along for the time being with the Germans, they were obliged to recognise that 'the armistice had been broken' while 'French commitments had been fulfilled'. On 13 November, under pressure from the Americans, Darlan made some room for himself by announcing: 'I am assuming responsibility for the government in Africa with the consent of the American authorities with whom I have agreed to defend North Africa.' On the 15th he took a decisive step, declaring: 'the Maréchal is not in a position to communicate his deepest thoughts to the French people ... under these conditions I declare that all officers and civil servants of all ranks who have sworn an oath of loyalty to the Maréchal should consider themselves loyal to the Maréchal in executing my orders.'[39] In order to carry through the operation, he entered upon a veritable game of legerdemain, misrepresenting the gist of a further secret telegram sent by Auphan on the afternoon of 13 November which purported to read as follows: 'Maréchal and President in deep agreement but before giving an answer must consult the occupation authorities.' This famous telegram – known as the telegram of 'deep agreement' – which actually referred to a previous telegram sent by Noguès, in no way constituted an order to bring the army of Africa back into the war.[40] Besides, the President (Laval) never made any claim to have encouraged such a patriotic secession[41] (had he done so it would certainly have become known). The subterfuge was a little clumsy but Darlan was clever enough to make use of this 'deep agreement' of a 'beleaguered Maréchal' so as to appear as his legitimate representative. After the war the orthodox Pétainists fell in with Darlan's line, representing the 'deep agreement' as the crowning achievement in the 'double game' that, they claimed, Pétain had been playing ever since 1940. We have already said all that is necessary about that 'double game'. It is quite true that North Africa re-entered the war, but it did so in despite of Vichy.

During that month of November, Vichy had lost everything – or almost everything. The double neutrality favoured by Weygand himself had not withstood the pressure of the events. He himself was apprehended by the Reich security services and interned in Germany. It was Pétain who was the loser by it all. Not only had he been overtaken by events but, furthermore, having rallied to Weygand's line, he now found himself powerless, trapped in the machinery of State collaboration.[42] He nevertheless took care to rule out any possibility of co-belligerence.[43] Let us momentarily indulge in a flight of 'historical fiction'. Suppose Philippe Pétain had at this point gone to North Africa: in all likelihood, despite Montoire, despite the Protocoles de Paris, despite the excesses of State collaboration, he would have been treated with respect, hailed as 'liberator of the territory' and his name would have been given to more squares, avenues and schools than the late Monsieur Thiers' had ever been. But the logic of the system upon which the French State was founded proved too strong: Pétain remained and continued to the last to remain faithful to the strategy confined to metropolitan France that he had decided upon in June 1940. Laval, for his part, had still not seen the light. There can be nothing more revealing in this respect than the altercation that took place on 11 November between those two dyed-in-the-wool anti-communists, Weygand and Laval. To Laval's declaration, 'I am convinced that if the Anglo-Saxons are the victors in this war, it will be Bolshevism', Weygand retorted, 'I tell you once again that the government is preparing the way for communism'.[44] And that same day, Laval was still fantasising as follows: 'France ought to be treated no longer as a vanquished power but as an ally.' As if *he* had any say in the matter!

For the fact was that by now France was totally stripped: through Darlan's mediation, Algeria and Morocco were now placed under American protection. Tunisia was a battlefield and the AOF had rallied to Darlan on 23 November, after Boisson had convinced himself that the 'deep agreement' was valid. So nothing but scraps was left of the Empire. As for the armistice army, that had disappeared: on 27 November 1942, Hitler, growing increasingly distrustful, had launched 'Operation Lila'. It disarmed and then demobilised what was left of the troops of the French State. At dawn, the Axis powers tried a strike against Toulon:[45] most of the ocean-going fleet chose to scuttle itself.[46] It is true that a French State still did survive but only because the Führer judged that survival profitable to the Reich and, in any event, he held it entirely at his mercy.

Right up until the autumn of 1943, Laval continued to believe that it might all work out, that what he must at all costs do was continue to bargain. It took time for him to realise that he was being played along and that, thanks to his haggling, the Reich was now in a position to exploit France, the pearl of vassalised Europe, even more efficiently than before.

Laval had not detected the profound changes that had taken place in Hitler's Germany. During the heady days of the Blitzkrieg, Germany had remained a 'civilian sanctuary'. But from now on, in order to make good deficiencies in manpower and satisfy the imperious needs of the Wehrmacht, pressure was to be exerted upon the conquered countries so as to derive the utmost profit from them. France was to be no exception. Hitler, and many other high-ranking Nazis too, were quite decided not to make things at all easy for their hereditary enemy. On 13 December 1942 the Führer announced to the leaders of the Wehrmacht: 'French sovereignty will be maintained but only in so far as this serves our interests. It will be suppressed the moment it proves irreconcilable with military necessities.'[47] By continuing to maintain the French State, the Reich would obtain legally – and far more efficiently than by force – whatever it wanted and would be in a position to use the State apparatus to its own profit. As for Laval, he would be judged by his actions[48] and meanwhile, whenever necessary the spectre of the Parisian collaborationists would be brandished; in April 1943, he appeared still to be giving satisfaction, for Ribbentrop told an Italian dignitary that Laval, who had embarked upon his course 'for better, for worse' was the 'best possible option for the Axis powers'.[49] He was even granted a few concessions: the demarcation line was suppressed in March 1943; he was given authorisation to recruit 2,800 men to form the 'First Regiment of France' and a few thousand prisoners were liberated. That also explains why Hitler took care to inform Pétain on 28 April 1943 that he wanted Laval to remain in his post, even though he simultaneously refused to grant the latter's request that the collaborationist movements in the northern zone be dissolved. But there was a price to pay. The Reich expected the French State to collaborate on four counts considered as top priorities: it was to help to suppress 'terrorists', hand over Jews, transfer man-power to Germany and mobilise economic resources to an unprecedented degree.

Where repression was concerned, collaboration was already steaming ahead by the time Laval returned to the scene. After Moser, an officer in the

Navy, had been killed on 22 August 1941,[50] the French State complied with the demands of the occupying power, alleging that it did so in order to avoid the worst. It agreed to an extraordinary law. It was backdated to 14 August, for the sake of appearances, and was to take retroactive effect.[51] On 27 August, after a parody of a trial, a 'special court', hurriedly set up, sent three militant communists, who had already been sentenced to prison, to their deaths. The reputation of the French State, including its head who had explicitly given his approval to the entire procedure, was totally fouled. Two months later the Vichy Minister of the Interior, Pucheu, took further recidivist measures: he allowed a list of hostages due for execution, which to his mind contained too many former combatants, to be replaced by another partly of his own devising which, with very few exceptions, contained the names only of communists:[52] some of them were to be shot at Château-briant. Laval, for his part, gave his official approval to this repressive collaboration meanwhile, as usual, seeking to use it as a basis for bargaining. The Bousquet–Oberg agreements signed in August 1942, which were shortly extended to apply also to the southern zone, placed under German jurisdiction only those who perpetrated attacks against the army of occupation. In return, French services of repression were to collaborate closely with the security services of the Reich in their struggle against 'terrorists'. In that very month of August, the Gestapo, with Laval's agreement, launched the 'Funkspiel' operation: one hundred vehicles – about thirty of which were 'gonio' trucks – carrying Germans and hand-picked French policemen scoured the free zone, tracking down radio transmitters and 'pianists' (radio operators). The 'special brigades' were reinforced by French policemen who were feared as torturers just as much as the Gestapo men.[53] In fact, Oberg told Abetz how pleased he was with the 'exemplary attitude' of the French police and again in August 1943 his subordinate Knochen, while regretting a certain measure of vacillation, nevertheless still reckoned that it was proving effective against members of the Resistance, especially if they were communists.[54] It was at this period that Vichy, without too many protestations, handed over to Germany – among other political personalities – Blum, Daladier, Reynaud, Mandel.

In January 1942, the German authorities decided on the extermination of the Jews of Europe and their transfer to concentration camps. As mentioned above, there were about 300,000 Jews in France of whom 150,000 were of French nationality. Faced with the demands of the Nazis, Laval was evasive and tried to bargain: the Jews of French nationality – with the exception of those who could be 'denationalised' – would not be sent to Germany; in return, the French State would use its State apparatus to hand over all foreign or stateless Jews. This it started to do as early as the summer of 1942. In Paris, Darquier (known as Pellepoix), a rabidly anti-semitic extremist, succeeded Xavier Vallat as the head of the extremely pro-Vichy commissariat for Jewish questions. He took personal charge of 'Operation Spring Wind'. On 16 and 17 July about 900 teams of French policemen arrested 12,884 men, women and children[55] who were then transferred to Drancy and to the Vel' d'Hiv'* into which they were crowded in intolerable conditions. On 26, 27 and 28 August a sweep was carried out in the towns of the southern zone with further systematic round-ups and meanwhile the camps, in which foreign Jews – among other 'undesirables'[56] – had been interned since October 1940, were emptied. These people were now deposited at Pithiviers, Beaune-la-Rolande and finally Drancy, the ante-chamber for the extermination camps. Despite claims to the contrary,[57] the French State did collaborate – within the limits we have specified – in the 'final solution'. Indeed, through some aberrant twist of logic, it even went further than it needed in complying with Nazi demands. Thus on 6 July, Dannecker wrote to Berlin: 'President Laval has proposed that when the Jewish families in the non-occupied zone are deported, the children of less than sixteen years of age should be included; the question of children remaining in the occupied zone does not interest him.'[58] It should also be remembered that not all the Jews of French nationality did escape the death camps, for at least 23,000 were deported.

In order to win what was now the total war, the Reich desperately needed active manpower to replace the German workers drafted into the armed forces. The Reich was already using 'voluntary workers'[59] lured to Germany by propaganda and promises of high wages but there were not nearly enough of them for Germany's needs. Hitler therefore appointed as 'general planner for the recruitment of manpower' a former Gauleiter from Thuringe, Fritz Saukel, a regular Nazi with brutal and greedy ways who was nick-named 'the slave-trafficker of Europe'. His mission was to get as many workers as possible to Germany, whether of their own free will or by force. The demand he made to the French State during the spring of 1942 was for a '*single* contribution of 250,000 men' (150,000 were to be skilled workers). Laval thought he could soften the blow by having the transferred workers 'relieved' by prisoners who would be placed on 'prisoner's leave'. Hitler condescended to agree to the swap on condition that each prisoner would be replaced by three workers, whereas Laval had hoped that it would be on a one for one exchange. On 22 June 1942, Laval launched the 'Relief' operation which was given maximum publicity by the combined German and French propaganda services. On 11 August 1942 – for Hitler was in no hurry – in the station of Compiègne the first convoy of liberated prisoners[60] passed a train going in the opposite direction laden with workers bound for the factories of the Reich. Despite the fact that all the media were pressed into service, the 'Relief' did not enjoy the hoped-for success. Since per-

---

* The Vélodrome d'Hiver was a large Parisian sports arena which was also used for political rallies, and served as an internment centre during the war. [Trans.]

suasion proved inadequate round-ups and enforced factory closures took place in the northern zone. By December 1942 Saukel had (but for a few thousand men) obtained the tribute demanded. But Laval – and in particular the French people – were not at the end of their tribulations: the contribution paid turned out not to be a 'single' one after all; by the summer of 1942, Saukel was announcing that new 'action' was to be taken. Taking the initiative so as to protect itself against encroachments upon its sovereignty, on 4 September 1942 the French State promulgated a 'law on the use and deployment of labour' which introduced the sweeping mobilisation of all men between the ages of eighteen and fifty and all unmarried women between the ages of twenty-one and thirty-five 'to carry out all the work that the government deems necessary in the higher interest of the nation'. Saukel had no interest in legalities; what he was demanding in an increasingly imperious fashion was more human flesh and now there were to be no prisoner reliefs in exchange. On 16 February 1943, Laval drafted for two years three age-groups which, thanks to the post-war baby boom, were well packed ones: all men born between 1 January 1920 and 31 December 1922 were obliged to leave for Germany:[61] the Service du Travail Obligatoire (the service of compulsory labour), or the STO, had now been born. However much Vichy justified it with sermons about the need for solidarity between all categories of French people (for the 'Relief' had affected only the workers), backing this deportation of manpower with all its authority, it was in fact making an irreparable mistake. Saukel in turn was also forced to change his tune: after the first two 'contributions' as demanded, the general planner had at first boasted that, thanks to the efforts of Vichy, France alone had fulfilled the programme 100%. But from the autumn of 1943 onwards the Resistance struck back and the 'Saukel army' went to swell the numbers of the first *maquis* groups. It was to palliate the failure of the third and fourth 'Saukel actions' that the Reich's new Minister of Armaments, Speer, eagerly responded to the advances that the French Minister, Bichelonne, was making with a view to integrating the French economy into a 'European war economy'.[62] Speer tried to get the Nazi Party to accept a new policy for the exploitation of German Europe.[63] He announced that it was necessary to decentralise the war effort and transfer as little manpower as possible in order to increase profitability and productivity. Speer and Bichelonne rapidly reached agreement in their talks in Paris in September 1943: a large number of French businesses were to be classified as *Speer-Betriebe* (*S-Betriebe*): their labour forces would be excused transfer to Germany and they would receive priority for deliveries of raw materials; in return 80% (on average) of their potential output would go to the Reich. It was not at all a bad idea. At all events, the Speer system turned out to be more efficient than Saukel's round-ups.[64] It is estimated[65] that the total number of labour deportees – under the aegis of the STO – was somewhere between 625,000 and 700,000 persons. All in all, the Reich's exploitation of this labour force was remarkably successful. Jean-Marie d'Hoop has calculated[66] that, at one time or another, and for varying periods of time, 4.5 million French people worked for Nazi Germany; it can be estimated that at the beginning of 1944 they totalled 3,600,000 (40,000 volunteers, 650,000 in the STO, 900,000 prisoners used in labour *Kommandos* or as 'free workers', one million men in the *Rüstungs-Betriebe*[67] and a further million in the *S-Betriebe*.[68]

This mobilisation in France itself and the transfers to Germany were the most visible side to the systematic exploitation of the French economy. During the so-called Blitzkrieg period the Reich, having seized a considerable amount of loot, had more or less contented itself with demanding a tribute in a financial form, to be paid on the dot, every ten days, into a special account at the Banque de France. Certainly, we may reasonably surmise that at least half of it was used for purposes other than those envisaged by the Geneva convention – in particular to supply the German black market. The industrial potential had been exploited only with precaution and in particular, well-defined sectors: iron ore and bauxite, the construction of automobiles, aircraft and ships, and the chemical industries. Similarly, take-overs by financial intervention had been few.[69] But with total war, Hitler's strategy had changed drastically: France now, willy-nilly, was to provide the major part of the effort imposed upon occupied Europe. French agriculture was to feed even more Germans and French factories were to work harder and harder for the war economy of the Reich.[70] The financial aspect of the operation was subordinate since the exchange rate imposed by Germany as early as the summer of 1940 (1 RM = 20F) made it possible to acquire French goods at almost half price. Furthermore, the so-called compensation agreement, signed on 14 Novem-

State collaboration expressed in statistical terms[71]

1 *Payments of the French State to the Reich*

	% of the national French Revenue for 1938[73]	% of the GDP[72] for 1938[73]
1940	10.9	9.3
1941	19.3	16.5
1942	20.9	17.7
1943	36.6	31.3
1944	27.6	23.6

2 *Costs of the occupation and financing the Reich*[74]

	Revenues	Taxes and Debts	'Special revenue from foreign countries'
1940–41[75]	39,500	27,200	6,000
1941–42	50,000	32,500	11,000
1942–43	70,600	43,000	19,000
1943–44	73,300	35,000	28,000

3 *Total payments made by the French State and the GNP of the Reich*

	German GNP[74]	Occupation costs paid by France[76]	Total payments made by the French State[77]	Total payments expressed as a % of the GNP of the Reich	
1940	145,000	80,000	81,600	2.8[78]	3.0[79]
1941	156,000	121,500	144,300	4.6	5.3
1942	162,000	109,000	156,700	4.8	5.5
1943	170,000	194,000	273,600	8.0	9.1
1944	175,000	126,900	206,300	5.9	6.7

4 *French agricultural produce sent to the Reich*[80]

	Harvests 1941–42	Harvests 1942–43
Cereals	485,000	714,000
Fodder	458,000	686,000
Meat	140,000	227,000
Vegetables	98,000	107,000
Fruit	59,000	118,000

5 *Trade balance of the Reich and trade with France*[81]

	Products imported from France expressed as a % of the total imports	Products exported to France expressed as a % of the total exports
1938	3.7	4.5
1939	2.6	2.8
1940	4.6	0.3
1941	11.1	4.6
1942	16.6	7.3
1943	17.1	6.5
1944[82]	18.3	5.6

ber 1940, was a pseudo-agreement for 'clearing':[83] France's trade deficit has been estimated to have been 165,000 million francs (that is to say 40% of the overall deficit of the whole of occupied Europe).

On the whole this exploitation took place without much resistance from the French business bosses. Any generalisations would no doubt be unfair[84] in view of the fact that the sources of evidence at the disposal of the historian are sparse in this domain. The scanty evidence available[85] would seem to suggest that there were many businessmen and bankers who were not particularly choosy about the nationality of their commercial partners or about the nature of the services they were required to provide. At the Liberation, before judges who in many cases showed a most sympathetic understanding,[86] they based their defence on pleas of pre-existent commercial relations, the intricacies of the market and the need to keep business going in order to avoid unemployment. And up to a point there is some truth in all this. But it is perhaps worth brooding upon the following opinion expressed by one of Louis Renault's confidants,[87] who was in fact trying to defend his record:

> The errors of the last four years that he committed were for the sake of keeping it [his factory]. He did not like the Germans. Why should he like them? He never liked anyone. But he was afraid they would take his machines away from him. Faced with that fear he was as weak as a child. He let them have everything in order to keep everything and the result was that he lost the lot.[88]

There is nothing to prove that the managers of the Crédit Lyonnais did not comply easily enough in illegally financing the export of works of art to Germany. The Banque de Paris et des Pays-Bas, for its part, granted as much as a thousand million francs insurance to French businessmen working for Germany, not to mention the banking facilities it so generously provided. There can be no denying that this famous commercial bank did not suffer unduly from those hard times.[89]

As for the French State, it certainly strove to limit the effects of this exploitation, but it had always been implicitly recognised that all it could do, at the most, was retain some control over the economic collaboration. Furthermore, as usual, in order to protect one thing Vichy gave way over another. The 'other' even went as far as war equipment manufactured in French factories operating in both zones. First it was just a matter of so-called 'defensive' material (anti-tank shells and tank transporters pro-vided by Berliet – on the orders of Vichy – as from June 1941); but it very soon became a matter of more offensive material such as engines and fighter planes[90] which were produced following the signing of an agreement on 28 July 1941. Between 1940 and 1943, the French State delivered 31,000 million francs worth of war equipment to Germany (the sale of aircraft accounted for about half of this). All in all, Vichy was becoming an increasingly ineffective shield and the French economy was being increas-ingly drained.[91] Its exhaustion was not solely the result of the effects of economic collaboration and Nazi looting; the turbulence of the exchange market and the constraints inherent in any war economy also played their part, but it would not be exaggerated to say that the German demands represented the last straw. Although agricultural production somehow managed to keep up to scratch despite the reduced area under cultivation and the shortage of manpower, it was a different story where industrial production was concerned. This was being strangled by the inadequacy of coal supplies and the shortage of raw materials and means of transport (part of the SNCF rolling-stock had been transferred to Germany or placed at the service of the troops of occupation).[92] All in all, it was impossible to maintain financial equilibrium. The rise in official prices (let alone those of the black market) was steeper than in most other large nations involved in the war[93] and meanwhile wages were systematically being held down.[94]

Moreover it had proved impossible to close the 'circuit'. The deficit in public finances was increasing all the time and there can be no doubt that the burden of the tribute to be paid to Germany was one of the main causes: between June 1940 and August 1944 it amounted to 632,000 million out of the 1,466,000 million francs of budgetary expenses.[95] Taxation covered on average no more than 28% of these expenses.[96] As a result of the consequent need to soak up all available liquid assets, many loans were engineered, some of them short-term. But all this notwithstanding, it proved necessary to have recourse to advances from the Banque de France to cover, on average, 31% of expenses. Jean-Marcel Jeanneney has calculated that the public debt overall increased fourfold between 1940 and 1944. The men of the Liberation were to find themselves confronted with a most arduous economic and social situation. It was, indeed, even more dangerous than it appeared, given that technical and psychological conditions then further combined to set off a spiral of inflation which was being held in check for the time being only by the sustained pressure exerted by the Reich, for it was not in its best interests – commercial or political – to see France fall prey to galloping inflation.

The Parisian bogey

Laval was in difficulties all along the line: there was not going to be another Montoire and the regime was not going to find a second wind. His partisans have tried to show that he was at least able to contain the collaborationists. But that is a partly fabricated thesis, for Parisian collaboration operated above all as a political bogey used to frighten Vichy. Besides, as it became increasingly repressive, the French State played into the hands of the 'new gentlemen' of Paris.

By the end of 1941, the mystique of the national revolution was discredited. Bouthillier has written: 'Public opinion, initially so favourable, even enthusiastic, became doubtful, suspicious, distrustful and eventually, little by little, hostile. The divorce began slowly around the middle of 1941; at first it was imperceptible, a hair-line crack, but from 1942 onwards it became ever wider and more obvious.'[97] At all events, there was nothing much new left for the regime to try: there was no point in extending the black market or the fiasco of State collaboration which had never been popular and since the STO had become even less so.[98] Although Pétain may still have retained some of his charisma – especially in the northern zone – Laval was soon breaking all records for unpopularity.

This disaffection had gradually spread to all social levels. The regime had lost any chance of winning over the working class even though the workers had in the past flocked in large numbers to Montluçon, Commentry and Saint-Etienne to hear Pétain, who had then been enjoying a novelty's success. But the mountain had given birth to a mouse: the Charter of Work, which was incredibly complicated, operated solely to the employers' benefit while, on the other hand, real wages continued to fall, work loads increased and the young men were being sent off to Germany. Despite being cajoled and favoured by the regime, the peasantry had also begun to jib. It was becoming increasingly exasperated by the niggling controls, taxation that was considered to be unfair and the intolerable requisitioning, especially if it all went to keep the Wehrmacht fat. The Peasant Corporation had turned out to be no more than an instrument of coercion in the service of 'General Food Supplies'. From February 1941, the peasants had to fulfil 'agricultural contracts' for certain products (for every unit of production they would hand over the surplus of their harvests in return for subsidies and priority deliveries of fertiliser) or, failing this, they were obliged to comply with 'production orders' (receiving no subsidy). As for their other, so-called 'free' products, they had to declare how much seed was sown and how much it produced; any excess of the crop above a determined limit was placed at the service of 'General Food Supplies'. Despite increasingly strict measures introduced to make them toe the line, more and more of their products found their way onto the black market or were consumed at home (as we have seen above): all this was symptomatic. As for other social and professional categories, their attitude is harder to define. However, there is every indication that most civil servants were, at the least, waiting to see how things would turn out. The younger generation, too, was anything but won over by the national revolution. It was either sulking or becoming dissident and, despite the directives that continued to be issued by La Porte du Theil, who had remained a *maréchaliste*, some young men from the Chantiers de Jeunesse were going over to the *maquis*.

Discouragement – or prudence – was overtaking the Pétainists who had rallied from other positions. A number of diehard *maréchalistes* were also moving away. Some of the PSF, for instance;[99] its leader, while expressing a number of reservations with regard to one aspect or another of the regime, had nevertheless issued a strict order to place absolute confidence in Pétain and, after Montoire, had declared his personal approval of 'the principle of a collaboration'. But La Roque became disillusioned and entered into contact with a network working for the intelligence service.[100] Others, Pétainists won over by argument, did not go so far as that but were now inclined to favour the idea of Giraudism, which had appeared upon the scene at just the right moment to provide an impulse for the transition. The catholic hierarchy was also showing its ill-humour. It was still supporting the established regime and remained in favour of the ideology and advantages of the national revolution, but the STO[101] and, even more, the round-ups of the Jews[102] had made a number of bishops uneasy. Pétain retained the allegiance of the hard-core *maréchalistes*, who were still convinced that the victor of Verdun was a heaven-sent human shield for France; a large number of notables, particularly in the provinces, who were devoted to the national revolution and determined to savour their revenge for 1936; and long-established reactionaries whose front ranks were filled with Maurrasiens – those, that is, who had remained faithful to Maurras – who were carried along by their hatred of the 'enemy within'. Maurras himself continued to repeat his formula of 'France, and France only', but he had swallowed the bitter pill notwithstanding, not only State collaboration and Montoire but also the 'Relief' programme, which was certainly an act of positive collaboration. That, at least, is what is suggested by *L'Action Française* of 28 August 1942, in which he even went so far as to write: 'Together with all French people, the prisoners so happily liberated give thanks to Monsieur Hitler' and in the same article he attacked the 'terrorists' and applauded the creation of the Militia.[103] But no more than in the past did Maurras now represent the real country.

Faced with his increasing unpopularity, Laval was feigning indifference. On the other hand, he did admit to being far more worried by what was happening in Paris. In Vichy, Laval liked to pose as a kind of lightning-conductor against 'the new gentlemen' of Paris who, all unintentionally, helped to bolster his importance. In Paris, however, they were used as a bogey to scare Vichy.

Many writers of personal recollections and essays and film-makers have, as so often happens, been fascinated by the activist minorities and have embroidered much upon the theme of those whom Robert Brasillach, at his trial, dubbed 'the collaborationists'. That fascination is, in itself, not without interest. But we should distinguish[104] clearly between the myth and the reality.[105] For these people, who saw themselves as the triumphant revolutionaries of a new twentieth-century Europe, were in truth – at best – simply a bogey used to frighten Laval and – at worst – propagandists for a Hitlerian Germany, whose Pangermanism was far stronger than its desire to construct a fascist Europe.

It would be mistaken to see Parisian collaboration as a homogeneous whole entirely organised by a number of families of the extreme right. In reality the situation was far more complex and the 'leftist' variations of 'converts' deeply impregnated by pacifism and anti-communism should not be overlooked. However, it was certainly the extreme right that set the tone and, in the end, provided most of the big battalions. It should be made quite clear that to be collaborationist certainly meant favouring an alliance with the Axis powers but also – perhaps even more – it meant taking revenge on the old order and seeking to impose 'revolutionary' political practices. As early as the autumn of 1940, Déat, who was well ahead of the field, was writing in *L'Oeuvre*: 'So let France make her own revolution and let it be authoritarian, and then it will not be in Germany's interest to treat her badly. Annexation? That is not the point. As French people, it is in our true interest that there be no more frontiers and that we accept being a part of Hitler's Europe.'[106] Two years later, the collaborationists, while for the sake of appearances dealing tactfully with the 'old fool' (Pétain) as an individual, were launching a strong attack against Vichy. They claimed that it was *they* who were revolutionaries, *the* revolutionaries, wanting to set up a regime that would certainly be just as authoritarian and hierarchical as the French State but which would not be controlled by a 'reactionary' and clerical gerontocracy.[107] According to them, they were the embodiment of youth, a force for a new break, to be channelled into a single party or, failing that, into a united front capable of combining nationalist impera-tives with the need for social revolution. To tell the truth, very little was said positively about this social revolution (in principle the idea was a kind of neo-corporatism) and most of the collaborationists were not so much anti-capitalist as fundamentally anti-bourgeois. They claimed it was up to them to take over from that sick and decadent class. But for the time being all they could do was continue to try to outbid Vichy, condemning as derisory the repression being carried out by the French State ('Quickly and everyone' was the PPF slogan) and judging Vichy's State anti-semitism to be ineffective (see the unbelievably fatuous articles in the despicable rag *Au Pilori*) and the machinations undertaken to avoid the struggle against Bolshevism to be suicidal (Bolshevism being described as 'a Jewish undertaking, the most exorbitant undertaking of shitty lies ever cooked up by the Yids over the centuries': P.A.Cousteau – quoting Céline – in *Je Suis Partout*, 7 March 1942). Once France became fascist, they claimed, it would be able to occupy the important place it deserved in the new national-socialist Europe. State collaboration was no more than a stop-gap. Collaboration was something to be practised on a much wider scale and to be extended to include all domains, including military operations. With very few exceptions, however, the collaborationists were against 'denationalisation': 'We do not claim to have fought for the fascist or national socialist revolution but for the French popular revolution and the establishment of the French popular State', declared M.-Y. Sicard,[108] one of the leaders of the PPF. With rather more subtlety, Brassillach remarked on 11 April 1942, in *Je Suis Partout*: 'What we want, in so far as it depends upon us, is not collaboration but alliance.' But it was here, precisely, that the shoe pinched.

Since the defeat they had all travelled almost identical paths. Virtually all (Déat, Doriot, Rebatet and many others too) had proclaimed themselves, with more or less conviction and for varying durations, as 'the Maréchal's men'. Then, some rapidly, some more slowly, they reached the conclusion that Vichy held no future for their careers and left, to meet up again in Paris. But as late as the beginning of 1941, their feelings with regard to the Reich were still mixed. Déat was already a whole-hearted collaborationist but, to set against him, there were many 'leaders' who still had reservations and who at any rate still repudiated the German–Soviet pact. The invasion of the Soviet Union liberated their reticence and energies: total collaboration now became a priority objective since the Reich was undertaking the mission which justified its pre-eminence in the new Europe: the definitive crushing of Bolshevism. A certain Monsignor Baudrillart prophesied in the summer of 1942: 'Here comes the time of the new crusade. I declare that the tomb of Christ will be freed.'[109] Eugène Deloncle, more prosaically, remarked 'Since 22 June, I have found myself in agreement with the policy of the Reich, so I am once again fully active.'[110] If we look back a little further, we find that the individual paths travelled are rather more complex but not altogether inexplicable. Men such as Bucard and the Francists (a small fascist movement), who were already pro-Nazi, in the Franco-German Committee or militants in a 'White International' lost no time in becoming collaborationists. One might be more surprised by the evolution and position taken up by those who had formerly been supporters of Maurras but were no longer and who now fell prey to the temptations of fascism. They are represented well enough by the *Je Suis Partout* team.[111] Many of them had even before the war been seduced by the model of Nazi man and even by the Hitlerian system but, as Rebatet in his *Décombres*[112] recalls: 'However disconcerting we found Maurras, his authority was hard to dismiss; we did not dare to transgress his catechism all together and in public'.[113] The break was now definitive[114] and, encouraged by the struggle against Bolshevism, a transition took place from 'rational collaborationism' to 'heartfelt collaborationism'.[115] Brasillach[116] was to describe the latter well enough as follows: 'Like it or not we shall have lived together; all thinking people in France more or less slept with Germany during those years, not without a few quarrels, but the memories remain sweet'.[117] In the eyes of these repentant Germanophobes, the national socialist revolution, now promoted to the level of a universal mode, would regenerate decadent Europe. Others were unashamed 'converts': left-wing militants, erstwhile anti-fascists but simultaneously mostly anti-communists and pacifists of long standing. Most had, furthermore, been excluded from their party or had defended a minority line within it. They even included a few communists[118] who had broken with the PCF during the autumn of 1939 and now rediscovered Doriot, six years after his exclusion. Even more significant was the emergence of those who had followed Déat on his ideological peregrinations: the man who had opposed the tactics of the SFIO during the thirties had now come to favour an increasingly authoritarian type of socialism within a national framekwork. As early as 1940, he took the plunge. A number of former leaders of the CGT, most of them following the *Syndicats** tendency, did the same, disappointed by Vichy and its reactionary paternalism.[119] Finally, in a marginal position, there were also socialists who had still been militant SFIO members in 1939, but who claimed to be in favour of planning and pacifism, and who now intended to 'collaborate without opting out'[120] and build a truly socialist Europe. They produced a weekly paper, *Le Rouge et le Bleu*, under the direction of Charles Spinasse, a former minister in Léon Blum's government.

All in all, while commercial collaborationism[121] should no doubt be accounted an additional phenomenon, the fact remains that it is not easy to determine exactly the relative force of different factors: socio-political pressures, the desire for power and other stimuli peculiar to the circumstances. Those whom one might (following Gramsci) call 'organic intellectuals' (that is, who also favoured repressive action) had been deeply marked by an obsession with the decadence of the west, a fascination with

* A journal published by an anticommunist and pacifist faction of the CGT. [Trans.]

virile fascist man and by the hope they placed in a new Rome able to repulse the new Barbarians.[122] But in the last analysis, all of them were in the grip of a desire for power. Déat and Doriot, to mention only 'the big chiefs', had initially staked their bets on Pétain, then on Laval, before finally coming to play the German card for all it was worth. The various forms of servitude imposed by the total war were to operate a final sifting process, separating out those who drew the line at an 'inverted' kind of Maurrasism[123] (Brasillach) and those who committed themselves, with no hope of return, to the fate of the SS State. Almost all the socialists who had wanted 'to collaborate without opting out'[124] soon pulled out and tip-toed away. During the summer of 1943, clashes broke out in the Parti Populaire Français (PPF) as well as in the Rassemblement National Populaire (RNP) while at *Je Suis Partout* Brasillach, branded as a fascist in sheep's clothing, was obliged to leave the weekly together with those of his friends who did not want to be 'denationalised'. Most of the 'all-out' collaborationists boasted to whoever would listen that they were not 'quitters'; some even organised banquets for 'those condemned to death' (by the Resistance). Some of them, such as Déat, remained totally convinced that the Reich would emerge as victor in the end; some, Darnand for instance, were too far in to pull out; others allowed themselves to be ruled by their gut hatred for the 'enemy within' and nothing in the world could have prevented them from settling the old accumulated scores right to the bitter end. They all accepted the idea of civil war. Déat wrote coldly: 'France will, if necessary, be covered with concentration camps and the execution squads will operate without pause. The birth of a new regime is accomplished with the forceps and pain.'[125] Some of them acted as touts for the Gestapo. By September 1943, at all events, the break with Laval had definitely taken place. In a 'Plan for French National Rehabilitation' published on 17 September 1943, nearly all the Parisian policy-makers called for the formation of 'a truly socialist and revolutionary government', in other words, power. But their demand was premature; they would have to wait for Sigmaringen. For the moment, the Reich was not so desperate as to be driven to setting these extremists up in power.

Besides, what did they really represent at the time?[126] Relatively little. They certainly claimed to be active minorities but they were incapable of creating any mass movements and remained a minority imprisoned in an increasingly closed world. Let us pass rapidly over the lunatic fringe[127] and the semi-secret groups with plenty of blustering 'chiefs' but few rank-and-file members.[128] It was a different matter – to start with, at any rate – where Francism and the Mouvement Social Révolutionnaire (MSR) were concerned; these attracted more response but were soon torn apart by profound internal dissensions. Francism had been founded in 1933 by Marcel Bucard, a former combatant covered in medals and a good orator to boot, who became a member of the 'White International'. The Movement had been reorganised in 1941 but thereafter stagnated. Neither its leader, who was ill, not Paul Guiraud were able to check an obvious decline in 1943. As for the MSR, this was a resurgence of the CSAR, alias the famous 'Cagoule'. Its founder Eugène Deloncle had earlier created the RNP with Déat and when the two definitively split in the autumn of 1941, he managed to attract three-fifths of the movement into the MSR. He was at this point in a position to marshal between 12,000 and 15,000 militants and his paramilitary groups were much feared. But in May 1942 the MSR burst apart. Filliol and other extremists eliminated Deloncle and a number of other founding fathers by force.[129] Torn apart and absorbed by the PPF, it lost its clout. Two other movements, the Rassemblement National Populaire and the Parti Populaire Français, now monopolised the Parisian scene, each in its own way symbolising the fascist mode of action. The founder of the RNP,[130] Déat, was doctrinaire[131] and in search of a model. He had always nursed an ambition to leave his mark upon the age but in 1940 he was a marginal figure among the politicians: having been a great white hope for the SFIO, he became one of the rank-and-file leaders of the 'Néos' and ended up by being excluded from the party without succeeding in rallying enough militants to his support; as for his ministerial career (he was Minister for the Air in a Sarraut government), that had been extremely short. Déat remained convinced that in his clash with Blum he had been in the right, seeking to integrate the vulnerable middle classes into an anti-capitalist front that would be better adapted to the national framework, and he had inclined more and more towards an authoritarian type of regime. By 1940 he had become a fascist, favouring the one party idea and, thanks to Abetz's help (at the time Déat was urging the return of Laval), was able to found the RNP. After one false manoeuvre – the alliance with the MSR which, it is true, had brought its para-military groups with it as its dowry – he reasserted his independence of action[132] and applied himself to the task of forming a mass party within the framework of the middle classes. To this end, he created a Union of Teachers, a Social Front for Work, and Popular National Youth Groups, and also, of course, the Popular National Militia, which became operational in 1943. During the 'doctrinal congress' held in July 1942, he called for a socialism that would be modern, national, authoritarian, popular and corporatist, with a prime objective of 'purifying and protecting the race'. Doriot,[133] the head of the PPF, would probably have had no quarrel with the programme of his rival but the truth was that ideology had never been his strong point; he was above all a creature of action and fundamentally opportunist. Initially a vociferous supporter of the Maréchal,[134] he then took part in a press campaign with the aim of bringing back Laval and getting himself, Doriot, into the government. He had meanwhile become involved in some extremely complicated manoeuvres between various Hitlerian pressure groups, staking heavily on the LVF,[135] with the aim of becoming the Reich's preferred interlocutor. He wanted to make the PPF, founded in 1936, not so much a party for the masses, rather a movement of tried and trusted militants.[136] He also attached much importance to the media. So PPF men were very thick on the ground among the editorial staff of the Parisian press and Radio Paris.

There was a great profusion of these chiefs and furthermore they refused even to set up so much as a cartel of collaborationist movements. There is only one known instance of any lasting agreement, that reached in September 1941 between the PPF and Costantini's Ligue Française. Apart from this, the day-to-day story of Parisian collaboration was that of a complicated[137] and sterile guerrilla warfare which absorbed most of the energies of the militants involved. The extreme right was of course an old hand at this kind of thing but, spurred on by their lust for power, other leaders also threw themselves into it with abandon. Doriot and Déat sought to out-manoeuvre each other in terms of the support they could control: thus, in 1942 – a good year for the RNP – Doriot refused to allow the PPF to join a Revolutionary National Front but proposed a 'grassroots union' (he had retained a number of reflexes from his period in the PCF) and a 'front of French Labour'. A 'United Front of European Revolutionaries' even lasted for a full forty-eight hours – just long enough to pull in a decent audience for Darnand, who came to Paris on 19 December 1943 to sing the praises of the Militia. It should be added that in order to strengthen its own control, the German Embassy in Paris was only too happy to exacerbate the situation. This lack of unity was their first source of weakness. The failure to win a wider audience was another, and one just as asphyxiating. They could, no doubt, put on a show, fill meeting-halls for grand occasions and increase the sales of a few newspapers (*Je Suis Partout* increased from 100,000 copies in 1941 to 300,000 in 1944). But these relative successes should not mask their generally shrinking support. Overall, even taking into consideration the effects of the quota system for supplies of paper, the deeply committed collaborationist press failed to win new readers: the highest circulation figure for Déat's *L'Oeuvre* was 130,000. Militant membership was also in a state of stagnation: the RNP, which appears to have recruited the most members, would seem never to have numbered more than 20,000 active supporters and between the end of 1942 and 1944 the movements' membership shrank steadily.[138] Finally, of all this collaborationist crowd, really the only highly represented groups were the intellectuals and the journalists. Despite the fresh blood that came from the left, the Parisian fascists, as in the thirties, never managed to crack or get round the obstacle represented by the conservatives.

The last but not the least disappointment was their political failure. They swaggered about, thought they could gain power (Doriot even called a meeting of 7,200 delegates in November 1942 a 'congress of power') and would soon be ready to supplant the French State. But, almost to the end, they remained deluded on the score of the strategy of the Reich. True, they dominated the politico-literary life of the capital and controlled a fair portion of the Parisian press[139] and, above all, Radio Paris which attracted a considerable audience;[140] and furthermore they had paramilitary militia at their disposal. But right up to 1944, they never really had a free hand.

The men in power in Vichy, while making use of them from time to time, were distrustful of these candidates for power whose plans for a fascist society they did not share and whose activities they feared. As soon as Laval, who had used them, returned to the scene, he tried to water down the LVF, which he judged – quite correctly – to owe too much allegiance to the Parisians, by merging it with a 'Tricolour Legion' which he aimed to place under Vichy control.[141] But their main obstacle was to be the Germans. They could – or would – not understand that Hitler's strategy was aimed not at creating a national socialist Europe, as a federation of fascist nations, but rather at imposing a *Deutschtum*. Berlin had decided, for the time being, to let the Vichy regime survive rather than impose a quisling: to the collaborationists fell the thankless role of playing bogey-men. As Abetz put it, they were 'a political instrument which, when the time came, could be set up in open opposition to Vichy and could then proclaim a popular government which would suit us better.'[142] All the more reason for keeping a tight control upon all this rather too busy little world. Not only did Propaganda Abteilung issue orientations[143] to the Parisian press but, in 1943, the 'Hibbelen group', a dependant of the Reich's Pressegruppe controlled about 50% of the Parisian newspapers.[144] Abetz had no hesitation in prohibiting the demonstration that the head of the PPF had organised to round off his 'congress of power' in style; and meanwhile the Wehrmacht only granted leave in dribs and drabs to Lieutenant Doriot, who was thus virtually confined to the LVF barracks from March 1943 to January 1944.

The story of the LVF, the Légion des Volontaires Français (Legion of French Volunteers) against Bolshevism,[145] in itself symbolised the frustrations of the collaborationists. Yet the early days had been promising: less than one month after the Nazis entered the Soviet Union, all – or almost all – the various movements appeared to be competing in the vehemence with which they called for military cooperation to support the Reich in the decisive fight against Bolshevism. The outcome was a meeting held in common, amid great enthusiasm, on 18 July 1941. The Vichy 'reactionaries' had manifested a certain coolness at the sight of this new Legion under the control of the Parisians, but they had given authorisation for the creation of the LVF, as a private association. This relative coolness had not been altogether unexpected. However, the first of a number of unpleasant surprises awaited the Parisian 'Europeans'. Hitler limited the quota of volunteers to 15,000 men and at the same time Brauchitsch, one of the high-ranking Wehrmacht authorities, was declaring in private that he would 'have them unloading sacks of potatoes behind the lines.'[146] The next surprise was just as hurtful: there were no crowds stepping forward to repulse the detested Bolshevism in the steppes and the number of volunteers never even reached the figure set by the Führer.[147] It 'has been said that 'the head of the PPF was not exaggerating when he later compared the convoy of legionaries to a transfer of convicts'.[148] Placed under the command of Colonel Labonne, who was more of a chocolate soldier than a commando leader, it saw action near Moscow in a state of such unpreparedness that it had to be relieved within four hours of fighting. It was pulled right back and reduced to hunting down Soviet partisans. By the end of the year it had become first and foremost a political bargaining point. It eventually passed under the control of the Doriotists but some of the legionaries increasingly openly considered themselves simply as mercenaries in the pay of the Reich. And indeed, the LVF was known as the 630th regiment of the Wehrmacht and it wore the German army uniform distinguished only by a tricolour badge discreetly sewn on to one sleeve.

By now there were others, too, who had entered upon a similar mercenary kind of collaboration: the French Waffen-SS, for instance, for which the French State had authorised recruitment in July 1943 and which was organised as a *Sturmbrigade*; and the 'French Gestapistes',[149] every bit as pitiless as their Nazi masters. In 1944, most of these mercenaries were used for tracking down members of the Resistance. This was the last stage and it revealed clearly the profound contradictions of collaborationism: fascism needed a fund of exacerbated nationalism in order to develop; but the French fascists found themselves up against 'denationalisation'. In the early days, Drieu La Rochelle believed he had found the answer: in order to resist the expansionism of the fascist regimes, France must become fascist. But what happened? In the process of settling scores accumulated since the thirties, they donned the boots of the foreigner.

However, as the months passed, the collaborationists did become an embarrassment to Vichy. Laval made every effort to hold them in check. To a certain extent he was successful, but only by dint of playing a dangerous game. To pull the rug from beneath the Parisians' feet, he imposed increasingly coercive policies upon the Vichy government, which was scared by the spectre of a 'popular government' under Doriot's direction. In the struggle to put down the rebels, collaborationist militia found themselves shoulder to shoulder with the repressive forces of the French State. Vichy was to pay dearly for that collusion.

The institution of the Militia,[150] a political and paramilitary police force, is exemplary in this respect. As early as 1941, activists in the southern zone had decided that the Légion des Combattants – that is, the Vichy Legion – lacked power and impact. They proceeded to create a Service d'Ordre Légionnaire (SOL): it was composed of volunteers whose task it was to protect the demonstrations of the Légion des Combattants but also – as the founders of the group saw it – to fight effectively against the enemy within.[151] A number of Vichy ministers, led by Pucheu and Marion, gave the go-ahead to these initiatives and, in January 1942, overriding the misgivings expressed by François Valentin, the director of the Legion, the French State gave its official authorisation to the SOL[152] which then lost no time in expanding: it had its own training schools for leaders and its own hierarchy which tended increasingly to duplicate that of the Legion, and it also organised punitive expeditions.

Laval had inherited some shock troops, placed in reserve, but which he did not yet need. By the autumn of 1943, when Vichy had lost its army and was afraid of being left defenceless, with Paris outbidding it, the situation was quite different. The French State, with the endorsement of the Reich, thereupon decided to set up a police force which could be used against the rebels and, if the need arose, also serve as its own praetorian guard. The 'French Militia'[153] was thus created on 30 January 1943; it was described as an association 'recognised to be of public use', composed of 'volunteers . . . whose task was not only to support the new State but also to help to maintain order'. Its nature could hardly have been more clearly indicated. To be on the safe side, Laval declared himself its president. But, despite the fact that he did not trust him, he thought it tactful to appoint as its secretary general Darnand, who was already an inspector of the Legion and of the SOL of the south-eastern region. Darnand was first and foremost a man of action, a commando soldier known for the raids he had led in the course of both wars. He had felt humiliated in 1919 because he had not been accepted for promotion to officer. His was an early case of 'Plebeian fascism'[154] and he soon found himself on the extreme right wing, following which he became a deeply committed *maréchaliste* and a convinced supporter of the national revolution. Then, for a while, he hesitated: should he follow the Militia 'military faction' which advocated strong-arm Pétainism but were anxious to limit the Militia's functions strictly to policing, or should he throw in his hand with the 'political faction' (Gallet, Tissot, Bout de l'An), whose view was that 'the maintenance of order' was simply a transitional stage which would make it possible for the Militia, the hard core of the future fascist party, to assume wider functions? During the summer of 1943, Darnand made his choice: he swore allegiance to Hitler and became a *Sturmbannführer* (commander) of the SS. From that time onward, he sought to extend the Militia to cover the northern zone and to arm an active 'Franc-Garde'[155] which the Reich authorised him to do during the winter of 1943.

With the Militia, we truly do find ourselves at the crossing of the ways between the French State and the collaborationists. There can be little doubt that orthodox Pétainists were disturbed at the position adopted by Darnand and those who wished to impose a 'political' line. However, the Militia functioned as an official organisation and it was only in August 1944 that Pétain repudiated Darnand. Furthermore, the French State had no hesitation – with the endorsement of Pétain – in using the Franc-Garde against the *maquisards*, in particular at Glières.[156] Besides, the Militia should not be seen as exceptional: there were other concrete instances of the solidarity that had been established between Vichy and the gentlemen in Paris. Pétain did not trust the LVF but, all the same, in November 1941, he sent Labonne a letter that could hardly be interpreted as a repudiation. It ran as follows: 'I am happy to know that you are not forgetting that you hold in your hands a part of our military honour ... In taking part in this crusade which Germany has elected to lead, and thus eliciting the well-deserved gratitude of the whole world, you are helping to save us from the Bolshevik peril; it is our own country that you are protecting in this way while at the same preserving hope for a reconciled Europe ... '[157] The two groups still shared common hatreds. Finally, the evolution of certain individuals is significant. Take Philippe Henriot, for instance, – the son of an officer, a professor from the free university tradition of teaching, a militant catholic and an orator who spoke on behalf of a national catholic federation (FNC), a good enough representative of the catholic and conservative right which naturally enough became *maréchaliste*. Convinced, as he was, that the choice lay betwen Bolshevism and Christianity, he passed over to collaborationism, becoming one of the stars of the Militia while at the same time remaining an influential broadcaster on Radio Vichy, the official radio. So it is reasonable to suppose that, whatever their differences, a certain solidarity remained between the two types of collaboration.

The shadow army

During these two crucial years, the rebels considerably extended their audience and laid the foundations for an underground state. Admittedly, progress was halting and many new disagreements arose in connection with the incomplete unification of the internal Resistance. Nevertheless, the hardest steps had already been taken and the Resistance could quite justifiably be described as a shadow army: those whom Henri Frenay called 'soldiers without uniforms and citizens in revolt against the established power' were threatening the occupying power from the rear and were preparing for the political take-over, or relief, of metropolitan France.[158]

The Resistance gathers pace

The progress of the Resistance was by no means a linear one. It proceeded in spurts with three impulses of particular importance: the incorporation of the PCF, the political mutations of 1942 and the appearance of the *Maquis*.

The PCF's entry as a substantial presence into the Resistance had the most determining effect both in the short term, by acutely posing the crucial problem of 'immediate action', and in the middle term, by changing the internal relationships of the Resistance forces by reason of the new audience won over through the armed struggle.

On 22 August, 1941, at Barbès-Rochechouart *métro* station, the naval officer Alfonse Moser[159] was killed by a commando of three young communists led by Pierre Georges – the future Colonel Fabien – a veteran of the international brigades and an experienced militant from the Bataillons de la Jeunesse (Youth Battalions). Two days later, four Germans were struck down in the north. Two months after that, on 20 and 21 October, two teams from those same Bataillons de la Jeunesse killed the *Feldkommandant* in Nantes and a councillor of the military administration in Bordeaux. These young communists were introducing a new form of armed struggle in that they were attacking not just installations but also men of the army of occupation. Such action provoked – and still provokes – passionate controversy.[160] The 'individual gesture' certainly did not get a very good press from the public, communists included.[161] It was seen, at first, as a suicidal practice of doubtful efficacity in view of the system of hostages[162] adopted by the occupation authorities.

The first executions took place on 16 September 1941 but it was in October that the German repression struck French public opinion with violent force: within less than forty-eight hours, on 22 and 23 October, 98 hostages were shot.[163] More and more batches of hostages were shot by the occupying power up until the summer of 1942 (95 shot in December 1941, including Gabriel Péri and Sampaix, 93 in August 1942, among them Louis Thorez, etc). Then, as from the autumn of 1942, the number of executions decreased, as if the occupation authorities were losing confidence in this technique of intimidating the public.[164] It had initially been sufficiently effective for the communists of the Nantes region to insist that those responsible for the death of the *Feldkommandant* should give themselves up to the German authorities. And de Gaulle accurately expressed the feelings of most rebels when he declared on 23 October that it was altogether in accordance with the logic of war that German soldiers should be killed on French soil but 'tactics' dictated an end 'to the massacre of our combatants who are temporarily unarmed'.[165] Later on, the controversy came to turn not so much upon the moral or political legitimacy and effectiveness of the tactics favoured by the more aggressive communists, but rather upon the timeliness of the armed struggle as such. *Fabien* and his comrades pressed the Resistance to reply to one fundamental question: should it fling itself into 'immediate action' or wait, preparing itself for D-Day? *France d'Abord*, the FTP newspaper, for its part declared in February 1942 that 'French patriots proclaim that it is not enough to resist to save our honour; we must fight to save France'.

It is true that a number of the leaders of non-communist movements continued to suspect the French communists of closely modelling their strategy upon that of the Soviet Union. In October 1942, after all, *France d'Abord* had declared that to oppose the armed struggle was to 'delay the hour of the second front by deserting the front in France'.[166] More important still, the party's audience was growing.[167] While it had, in fact, more difficulties to face than is suggested by a historiography that is inclined to overdo the triumphal aspect, it certainly had once more set up an organisation which looked – in 1942 – a more serious proposition than many of the non-communist movements. The organisation was based on 'groups of three': cells, sections, regions and inter-regions were juxtaposed yet distinct in a pyramidical structure surmounted by 'triangles of leadership'. Its armed branch became operational as early as the winter of 1941; the FTP[168] was born in February 1942, an offshoot of the most combative groupings (the Organisation Spéciale, the Bataillons de la Jeunesse, and the Main-d'Oeuvre immigrée[169]). Once these became the military branch of the National Front, they were thrown open to admit non-communists, but the principal leaders were all well-tried communists.[170] The FTP soon adapted to guerrilla warfare – particularly the urban variety. The basic unit consisted of two teams, each of three men,[171] and sections, companies and battalions were supervised by a veritable underground general staff.[172] Under the vigorous leadership of Tillon, the FTP set itself to destroy the war potential of the enemy in an alternation of surprise attacks, sabotage operations and strikes at soldiers and officers of the army of occupation.[173] It was thanks to their multiform struggle that, according to Rémy, the FTP constituted 'the only underground armed organisation which fought successfully against the Germans'.[174] However, it should be pointed out that that is a value judgement that can be applied only to 1942 and mainly to the northern zone.[175] This dynamism in action was coupled with a political strategy with many targets, which also produced appreciable results. It was based on the Front National de Lutte pour l'Indépendance de la France (the National Front for the Fight for the Independence of France) which the PCF had created in May 1941 and over which it kept a careful control. This movement of national orientation[176] was remarkable not only in that it was implanted in both zones but even more in that it operated on a socio-professional basis.[177] Claiming to be the only patriotic and political organisation that was truly unificatory, it was exclusive in neither a religious nor a political sense (a number of clerics belonged to it) and it sought to attract fellow-travellers (in the strictest sense of the term), and also welcomed in a number of leaders from the southern zone (Georges Bidault, who had earlier been a militant with Combat, Yves Farge from Franc-Tireur)as well as political figures whose pasts certainly in no way predisposed them in favour of such a convergence (the radical Justin Godard, the christian democrat Max André, Louis Marin's friend, Jacques Debû-Bridel and Jacques Bounin, formerly of the PSF). In this way, not only did the PCF succeed in emerging from the political ghetto within which it had been confined since 1939: it furthermore managed to reorganise the Party apparatus, renew contact with the masses and at the same time associate Jacobin nationalism with the defence of the socialist land of the Soviets. All the conditions looked set for the PCF to repeat its success of 1936–7 and to take another leap forward.

Within the ranks of the non-communist movements such vitality was intimidating some fellow-travellers but simultaneously provoking as much if not more distrust and animosity. The distrust, which had been reanimated by the German–Soviet pact, was not disarmed: the PCF continued to be suspected of operating 'its own' Resistance, acting as a tool for Soviet strategy. It was therefore deemed necessary to be more vigilant than ever, especially as the communists were increasingly suspected of systematically infiltrating all the various movements, particularly those in the southern zone. That is why the National Front was rejected by so many organisers of the 'apolitical' movements in the northern zone and by almost as many of the leaders of Combat: thus initially Frenay was able to refuse to admit the National Front to the committee for coordinating the movements in the southern zone. Even those most in favour of harmony may well have subscribed to the lapidary sentiment expressed by Claude Bourdet in 1943: 'The communists should take their rightful place, but not *all* the places.'[178] There was certainly therefore a possibility – as can be seen from the example of a number of other European countries – of this communist upsurge provoking confrontations and conflicts. However, as we shall see, by 1943 the danger of such clashes had – to a very large extent – been staved off.

The *de facto* satellisation of the French State during the autumn of 1942 brought about changes which, while less crucial than the successes of the communists, should nevertheless not be underestimated.

The return of Laval and the sacrilegious desires he had expressed on 22 June had already scandalised many movement organisers who had hitherto behaved in a restrained fashion where the head of the French State was concerned. Combat now slipped its last mooring ropes,[179] adopted a much firmer ideological line and, in October 1942, attacked the criminal policies of the 'sinister old man'. The Défense de la France movement was in a similar fashion openly adopting an anti-Vichy position.

A few of the 'wait-and-see' brigade and ditherers had been even more upset by the dead-end evolution of State collaboration and were drawing progressively closer to the Resistance. Giraudism was, furthermore, offering the possibility of a convenient transitional position where necessary. Aimé Lepercq, chairman of the Comité d'Organisation des Houillères (the Organisational Committee for Coal Mines) went over to the OCM through the intermediary of Pierre Lefaucheux; François Valentin, an ex-director of the Légion des Combattants (Legion of Combatants) picked the third anniversary of the founding of the legion to issue an appeal to the Resistance. Similarly, some of the leaders of the defunct armistice army, who had been clinging to the belief that Philippe Pétain had been playing a double game, swung over and, urged on by General Verneau, regrouped themselves into the Organisation Métropolitaine de l'Armeé (Metropolitan Army Organisation)[180] under the leadership of General Frère. These people who rallied to the cause half-way through represented a whole spectrum of attitudes. For some, who now expected an Anglo-Saxon victory, the prime consideration was to refurbish their political virginity to profitable effect. But the motivation of others was less self-interested. Emile Laffon, for instance, reckoned that 'the moment had come for the elite to step forward from the ranks of the indifferent'[181] because, so far as he could see, the Resistance had by now proved itself to be a sufficiently serious and mature proposition; similarly, a number of nationalists at long last realised that giving priority to the struggle against 'the enemy within' at the cost of grovelling before the occupying power could only lead to a fatal impasse. Thus, on 29 August 1943, François Valentin declared: 'Our mistake has been to believe that it was possible to regenerate a country before liberating it.'

In this coming-of-age of the internal Resistance, the other decisive turning point was marked by the appearance of the *maquis* groups which sprang out of the rejection of the STO. Their importance has certainly been generally recognised; however, less has been said about the difficulties that had to be overcome in setting up this 'Saukel army'. Credit should be given both to the MUR and to the National Front for having first welcomed and then integrated men who, to start with, were no more than disorganised and, in many cases, bewildered rebels. The chronological record gives a clear indication of the difficulties of the enterprise. There were certainly a few, isolated, relatively early and effective instances of rebellion: thus, at Montluçon on 6 January 1943, only 20 out of the 60 men supposed to go to Germany did so. But, more generally, it was not until the summer of 1943 that the movement of defiance began to spread: in the Lot – a good enough specimen department – the number of rebels in June was still only 20 out of 168 drafted into the STO; by August it was 81 out of 85.

The task that both the Service National de Maquis, rapidly set up by the

MUR, and the National Front set themselves was 'to turn rebels into fighters'. During the winter of 1942, the first rebels were taken into improvised refuge camps set up, mostly, by local efforts. Thus, in the Ain, Henri Romans-Petit in December laid the foundations of what later became a model *maquis* camp. In the spring the movements made terrific efforts with only derisory funds to draw upon and a glaring shortage of leaders. Only a few – indeed, very few – officers from the ex-armistice army were, at this point, willing to offer their services to the future *maquisards*. Men such as Valette d'Osia and *Tom* Morel and their comrades from the 27th battalion of *chasseurs alpins* stand out as exceptions. But, despite everything, centres to welcome recruits were set up, training for leaders was organised and propaganda against the STO was increased tenfold. The Resistance reaped the rewards of its militant efforts during the summer. Its success redounds all the more to its credit given that London considerably underestimated what was at stake both from a political and a military point of view. Later on, the Free French leaders advocated setting up 'mobilising *maquis*' but – as we shall see – in order to promote strategies of quite a different kind. Even Jean Moulin, usually more receptive to the needs of the Resistance, tried to pare down the monthly budget allocated to the movements in the southern zone[182] and viewed the Service National des Maquis as a subterfuge devised by the movements to set up a secret army that would be quite autonomous from London.[183] For many *maquisards*, reduced to inaction for want of weapons, the winter of 1943 continued to be a trying one. But even if they could not operate militarily, they already counted for something from a political point of view. The rejection of the STO[184] not only undermined the authority of the French State, bogged down as it was in State collaboration, but above all it made it possible for the Resistance to absorb, in a practically unhoped-for fashion, many young and active men of a kind that had hitherto hardly come forward at all. This gave it a chance to widen its sociological bases while at the same time immeasurably increasing its possibilities of taking paramilitary action. At the same time, however, the appearance of the *maquis* altered the balance of power and relaunched the arguments about immediate action, in new terms.

Consolidation

As the months passed, the internal Resistance grew. And as it grew, proper organisation took over from the improvisations of the early days. In 1943, the year when it came to maturity, the foundations for an underground State were laid.

Over the past two years, its field of activity had widened considerably. New networks had grown up and the 'agencies' had multiplied. The new developments took many forms: there were, for instance, networks of direct action which specialised in strikes of a specific and particular nature, including meting out retribution to traitors; escape networks which had multiplied their channels to zones reputed to be less dangerous or to the sea, Switzerland and the Pyrenees[185] and which took charge of escapees, Jews on the run, 'burnt out' Resistance members who needed to be 'put out to grass', and Allied airmen; and intelligence networks, which were by far the most numerous and the most substantial. All intelligence received could be put to use but the most prized information concerned Kriegsmarine installations,[186] the large-scale movements of the Wehrmacht and the introduction of new secret weapons. As a general rule, such information was transmitted in coded form by radio, or else it was taken to London by the first available courier. The Intelligence Service still controlled a number of networks[187] and meanwhile the 'French section' of the SOE set up a number of well-trained sabotage and direct action teams. Most of these networks were now linked to the BCRA either directly or through movements which themselves almost all ran their own intelligence services. In the interests of both security and efficiency, Passy had decided in 1943 to install *centrales* (headquarters) to direct a number of large networks[188] in France itself. After the war, 266 were recognised (254 of which as fighting units) whilst 150,000 agents, (not counting 'irregular' ones) were listed.

The movements were also growing. Indeed, they grew so fast that it is almost impossible to do full justice to their complexity.[189] By now they were recruiting at all levels. We should take particular note of those in which non-communist supporters of the Resistance met with active sympathy right from the start. The trade-unionists still constituted a highly valued breeding-ground and Yvon Morandat was able to launch the Mouvement Ouvrier Français (MOF) (French Workers' Movement) with the hope of developing a specifically workers' resistance in the southern zone, drawing upon the CGT members who had remained loyal to the Jouhaux line and the Christian trade-unionists with Gaston Tessier at their head.[190] However, while the CGT and the CFTC were urging their militants to join the movements, they were still resolved to maintain a relatively autonomous confederal position – which in part explains how it was that the MOF did not produce all the hoped-for results. But at least the reunification of the CGT achieved in the Perreux Agreements[191] was, in general, to provide a new stimulus for the Workers' Resistance. The essentially Christian sector of the Resistance was also reaching a wider audience, although among the catholics it only won strictly minority support. It could draw upon the doctrinal rigour and firmness of the *Cahiers du Témoignage Chrétien* (fifteen numbers of which appeared between November 1941 and June 1944). These *Cahiers* (notebooks) were of a high intellectual calibre. Masterminded by Father Chaillet, in the name of the principles of Christianity, they vigorously denounced Nazism with all its amoralism and racism and, in December 1941, they declared that 'there can be no peace with Hitler with any French, human or Christian honour'. The persecution of the Jews had jolted a number of catholics and protestants out of their wait-and-see attitudes and these lent their support to the Amitiés Chrétiennes and Cimade organisations which strove to hide Jewish children. However, there were some Christian militants, such as Gilbert Dru, who believed it was necessary to go further. Most of them were young and came from the JEC or the JOC. They rebelled against the reticence and positions adopted by the hierarchy and against the cowardice of much of the ACJF and through them there emerged a new generation of catholics who were much more radical when it came to temporal commitments.[192] The older movements tried to diversify their recruitment as widely as possible. Some, however, continued to prospect particularly in relatively specialised milieux: thus, the OCM, under the joint leadership of Colonel Touny and Blocq-Mascart, aimed chiefly for the upper echelons of the administration and leaders in the private sector, at the same time making contact with anti-German military officers. Similarly, the remarkable cohesion of Libération-Nord stemmed from its high proportion of socialist and trade-unionist militants. New figures had also emerged: rising from the ashes of Combat, which had been decapitated in the northern zone, Lecompte-Boinet launched a new movement, Ceux de la Résistance, which, with the endorsement of Frenay, became completely autonomous; Dr Renet (*Jacques Destrée*), together with a few friends from *La Jeune République*, launched *Résistance* which assumed the mantle of the now destroyed *Valmy*. Overall, there can be no doubt that progress was made although it is difficult to give as precise details as we should like. Let us simply give some idea of the size of these organisations: in 1943, the OCM laid claim to some 100,000 members, although that is an estimate that seems to us very exaggerated even if, after the National Front, this was the most developed movement in the northern zone. More realistic perhaps are the 14,000 militants claimed by Ceux de la Résistance or the 50,000 men that the MUR declared it could assemble within the Secret Army alone. These figures may seem surprisingly low, but to them should be added a much larger number of sympathisers: take, for instance, Défense de la France which, according to Marie Granet, 'numbered about 2,500 really active militants and tens of thousands of sympathisers'.[193]

While numbers were increasing, certain internal changes were taking place which in the main favoured more radical attitudes. In a number of movements there emerged, so to speak, a second generation which was more determined to come to grips with the enemy immediately and did not feel itself to be concerned with the quarrels that divided the 'historical leaders'.[194] Thus Combat saw the arrival of Degliame-Fouché, Jean-Guy Bernard and others, in Libération-Sud there were Pascal Copeau, Pierre Hervé, Kriegel-*Valrimont*, Malleret-*Joinville*,[195] etc. When Lecompte-Boinet, the founder of Ceux de la Résistance returned to London in the

February of 1944, he felt lost within his own movement, now relaunched by a new team led by Voguë-*Madelin* and taking a much more radical political line.

The progress made is also explicable in terms of the repression that was now stepped up both by the French police forces and the specialised services of the occupying power: Abwehr, the security service of the Reich and, of course, the Gestapo, which had been officially set up in the northern zone during the spring of 1942. Carelessness and treachery took a heavy toll on many networks: by the summer of 1942, of all those set up by the BCRA, only Rémy's Confrérie Notre-Dame survived and it too had been much weakened by the information betrayed by Radio Phoebus and the liaison agent Capri. By 1943, all the main networks had suffered heavy losses. The movements were just as severely tried: between January and April 1942, of the communists, Danièle Casanova, Arthur Dallidet, Georges Politzer, Félix Cadras, Jacques Decour, and Yves Kermen and others 'fell'; in the spring of 1943, the OCM was undermined by the arrests of Touny, Simon and Farjon and in that October the leaders of Ceux de la Résistance were caught in a trap; and Combat, having already suffered the loss of its branch in the northern zone, lost a further number of remarkable militants: Bertie Albrecht, Jacques Renouvin, Edmond Michelet, Marcel *Peck*, etc.

However, this more and more relentless repression did not prevent the Resistance from establishing itself increasingly firmly and extending its militant activity. This took a number of different forms. Some of them made a deep impression upon public opinion – for instance, the indictments made at the Riom trial by Daladier and Blum. The latter, who declared himself flattered at being 'promoted to the ranks of the accused' turned himself during those days into an implacable prosecutor and more than fulfilled the contract he had fixed for himself: 'If the Republic remains as the accused, we shall remain at our posts as its witnesses and its defence.'[196] Similarly, the pastoral letter sent out by Monsignor Saliège, Archbishop of Toulouse, in August 1942, to protest against the persecution of the Jews who were being treated 'like a herd of beasts', which was read in every parish in his diocese, did not pass unnoticed. And there were other, less public gestures that deserve to be more widely known, such as the refusal of Judge Paul Didier to swear allegiance to a head of State who favoured collaboration.[197]

More and more, the Resistance was coming out into the open: it did so on 14 July and 11 November in 'patriotic' commemorative demonstrations[198] banned by both the French State and the occupying power (on 24 July 1941, the metal-worker André Masseron was shot for 'having sung the "Marseillaise"' on 14 July); the pupils of the Lycée Buffon[199] organised a demonstration in protest at the arrest of one of their history teachers, Raymond Burgard, the founder of *Valmy*. Celebrating Mothers' Day in their own fashion, on 31 May 1943, militant communist women invaded a shop in the rue de Buci which specialised in trade with the occupying power and distributed its stock to the public (the same operation was repeated on 1 August, in the rue Daguerre). In Lyons, following a recital given by the Berlin Philharmonic to an already angry crowd, the conductor Paray stepped forward to conduct an 'expiatory' concert of exclusively French music, rounding it off with the 'Marseillaise'.

The most important task for many members of the Resistance was collecting intelligence. It is quite true that the network of complicity was widening and that techniques were improving: thus, in April 1942, the engineer Keller established a tap on the line that linked the headquarters of the occupying troops with Berlin; it was known as the 'K-source'. Passy, for his part, estimates that the volume of correspondence from a network of average size represented about fifty pages of typescript at the beginning of 1942 and a good thousand pages twelve months later. It was following the precise recommendations that these provided that, in February 1942, British commandos blew up an anti-aircraft detection system at Bruneval and destroyed the large dry-dock at Saint-Nazaire. By 1943, the Channel coast held no secrets for the Allied general staff.

For other rebels, paramilitary action was the first priority. Sabotage action had become common.[200] In the 'battle for the railways', militants had now learned how to unbolt the rails over a long distance of track without cutting the current supply to the signals. The FTP, like other commando groups from other movements, concentrated their efforts against the industrial potential: in October 1942, men from Franc-Tireur put the Francolor business in Roanne out of action and in September 1943, others from the MUR sabotaged the electric power station of Chalon-sur-Saône. Others still made attacks against military installations: for instance, on 13 November 1943, Aimé Requet blew up the German army's artillery depot in Grenoble. Armed attacks against members of the army of occupation continued,[201] undertaken for the most part by the FTP, who also went in for grenade attacks against buses, restaurants and cinemas reserved for the occupying powers. Nazi heads were falling.[202] Renouvin had started by organising *Kermesses*[203] and went on to mount punitive expeditions against collaborationist leaders and over-zealous auxiliaries of the Vichy repression.[204] At the same time, there were spectacular raids to rescue comrades: thus, on 21 October, Lucie Aubrac launched an operation which succeeded in rescuing her husband and thirteen leaders of the MUR while they were being transferred from the Montluc fortress to the Gestapo headquarters in Lyons. Finally, there were the *maquisards*, who were responsible for guerrilla operations and were at the same time preparing for armed combat. Strictly speaking, they ought to have been regrouped into relatively small units of not more than fifty or so men, trained to carry out surprise attacks rather than for pitched battle. In practice though, a wide diversity reigned,

4 The Resistance in the department of the Tarn, November 1943–23 August 1944

Source: Reproduced by permission of M. Saulière from the map he produced in 1976 for the Comité d'Histoire de la Deuxième Guerre Mondiale

Key

- main roads
- railway
- wooded areas
- *maquis* groups
- battles
- railway sabotage
- sabotage
- parachute drops
- internment camps

to RODEZ

TANUS

MOULIN de Clary

to REQUISTA

VALENCE d'Albigeois

ERY

BERNAC

ASSAC

COURRIS

to MILLAU

RANCE d'Albigeois

ALBAN

PAULINET

TEILLET

BELMONT sur Rance

PONT ROC

SAINT PIERRE de Trivisy

MURASSON

LAC...

LACAUNE

DON Labessonnié

VABRE

...RAT sur Vèbre

ROQUECOURBE

BRASSAC

ASTRES

LE RIALET

ANGLÈS du Tarn

...VINTROU

to BEDARIEUX

PONT de Larn

SAINT PONS

MAZA...

LABASTIDE Rouairoux

SINT AMANS Soult

LABRESPY

...UE

LES ROUSSES

Pic de Nore 1 210 m

VERRERIES de Moussans

CARCASSONNE

N

depending upon the geographical and social environment, the weapons to hand and also the flair of individual leaders. Some *maquis* contained rebels who were lazy, undisciplined and in many cases ill-adapted to their new type of life. Others, in contrast, were models of their kind, emulating the example of the flexible yet rigorous organisation set on foot by Guingouin, the 'prefect of the *maquis*'. Another fine example is the 'Surcouf' *maquis*[205] set up in Normandy to the west of the Risle: in November 1942, a thirty-two year old grocer, Robert Leblanc, placed himself at the head of about a dozen rebels. By May 1943, there were thirty of them; by the following November they constituted seven groups, each of sixteen men, making surprise attacks on German communication lines. They numbered 250 by June 1944, rather more by July. 130 were to be lost (71 killed in action, 59 shot or dying in deportation).

This multiform activity had to be organised. All in all, the Resistance was successful in overcoming difficulties of all kinds and showed great creative imagination as it laid the foundations for an underground State.

The major intelligence networks were now organised in accordance with well-tried methods to the end of combining security with efficacy.[206] The backbone of the system was formed by general agencies placed under the direct control of the network leaders: supply (of false papers, lodgings etc); coding and decoding; the collection of information; sea and air liaison with London; radio transmitting. A large network would in general establish up to twenty or so 'agencies' which would cover several departments; each agency would be directed by leaders from five or six sectors using, for the most part, non-regular informers. The 'letter-boxes' would, as a general rule, be emptied each week by liaison agents.

The organisation of many of the larger movements was equally solid.[207] The model here was Combat, which had rapidly expanded beyond its original organisational core of the five general staff offices so dear to Frenay's heart. When the three large movements of the southern zone fused in January 1943, it was the structures of Combat[208] that the MUR to a large extent adopted. The basic force of militants was reorganised into groups of six or thirty, depending on the circumstances of the particular department. The regions (there were six in the southern zone)[209] constituted an essential means of liaison between the departments and the various 'national services' which, for convenience sake, had been distributed between the various services for 'action' and for 'civilian organisation'. 'Civilian organisation' included services which distributed the underground press, liaison services[210] and those responsible for supplying false papers,[211] lodgings, social aid[212] and for the Noyautage des Administrations Publiques (NAP) (the Infiltration of the Public Administration).[213] As for the 'action' services, they linked together the various intelligence 'agencies' incorporated within the 'Gallia' network, the Secret Army,[214] the commando groups that Renouvin had armed to carry out specific urgent missions, L'Action Ouvrière formed by Degliame-Fouché to set up industrial sabotage, the Résistance Fer,[215] the Service National des Maquis, and the teams that specialised in air operations and collecting parachute drops.[216]

In the northern zone, the non-communist Resistance was less well organised. But by 1943, five regions and a number of departments had at least managed to appoint a civilian leader and a military one. Alongside the creation of the CNR, the Secret Army was developing in the northern zone and meanwhile NAP was extending its ramifications in the north as well as in the south. That autumn a tune crossed the Channel, which soon became a rallying song, 'Ami, entends-tu?' (Friend, do you hear?).[217]

It should be noted that these improvements in the organisation of the Resistance often involved a concentration of authority. Claude Bourdet recognises that 'it was impossible to direct an underground movement in a democratic fashion'.[218] That observation holds good for all the larger movements, with the possible exception of Franc-Tireur which tried hard to maintain a fairly high level of general consultation in the interests of avoiding a situation in which authoritarianism might eventually provoke resentment and dissension.

Let us round off this panoramic description of the activities of the Resistance by considering counter-propaganda, which was the primary *raison d'être* for most of the movements. Newspapers were the most favoured means of counter-propaganda.[219] In most cases, the newspapers would consist of four small pages, containing a short editorial, a few leading articles, a summary of the principal news picked up from the BBC and an account of the operations being carried out by militants.[220] The list of underground periodicals – in all likelihood, an incomplete one – runs to no less than 1,034 titles. To be sure, many were stillborn or soon disappeared, but *Libération-Nord* managed to publish 190 numbers while, between December 1941 and June 1944, *Combat* brought out 58, *Défense de la France* 47, and so on. It is *Défense de la France* that holds the absolute circulation record: in January 1944, it printed 450,000 copies of one number; at this time the number of copies printed by *Combat*, *Libération-Sud* and *Franc-Tireur* varied between 125,000 and 150,000 copies. Considering the fact that the sale of paper, ink and stencils was forbidden and the close surveillance to which printers were subjected, the printing of such numbers of newspapers can be reckoned veritable exploits that were repeated every week or month, thanks in particular to the courage of small-scale printers,[221] many of whom paid for it with their lives.

All in all, the Resistance employed the cultural weapon to good effect, placing it under the aegis of militant commitment. It had its own underground publishing house of a kind – called, suitably enough, Les Editions de Minuit – set up by the novelist Pierre de Lescure and his friend, the engraver, Jean Brullet-*Vercors*.[222] It clandestinely published twenty-five slim volumes[223] including *Le cahier noir*, a lucid meditation by *Forez* (Mauriac), *Les amants d'Avignon*, the bitter-sweet trials and tribulations of a woman liaison-agent by *Laurent Daniel* (Elsa Triolet), a volume of *Contes*, short variations on the theme of the dark years by *Auxois* (Edith Thomas), *La marque de l'homme*, a drama of jealousy in an *Oflag*, written by *Mortagne* (Claude Morgan), and *Le temps de la mort*, the plunge into darkness, arrest and deportation depicted by *Minervois* (Claude Aveline). *Le silence de la mer*, which was the first in the series, was clandestinely distributed in February 1942.[224]

Members of the Resistance published committed literary reviews, the best known of which was the organ of the National Front writers, *Les Lettres Françaises*. The first number came out, after many difficulties,[225] on 20 September 1942, which was *Valmy's* birthday. Quite a few intellectuals decided 'to do something' in their own way.[226] Eluard's view was that poetry 'would certainly have to take to the *maquis*' and it was in the name of that same militant commitment that Aragon composed a new *Art poétique* inspired by his 'friends who died in May (1942)' and, in memory of Gabriel Péri, wrote the 'Ballade de celui qui chanta dans les supplices' (The ballad of one who sang under torture) and also 'La Rose et la réseda' (The rose and the reseda) – 'the one who believed in heaven and the one who did not' – which he dedicated, in December 1944, to 'Estienne d'Orves and Gabriel Péri and also to Guy Moquet and Gilbert Dru'. These militants were obliged to resort to many subterfuges and eventually take refuge in anonymity or even in total secrecy.[227] Aragon himself proved remarkably adept at exploiting every resource offered by history, in the pieces he wrote for *Crève-coeur* and also for *Aurélien*. 14 July 1943 saw the publication of *L'honneur des poètes*, 22 anonymous poems collected by Eluard;[228] in October, *Le domaine français*, an anthology of about sixty pieces, appeared. Being committed literature, it provoked both a chorus of adulation and also a storm of criticism. Among the critics we find a hotch-potch of wits with somewhat less than lustrous reputations in terms of political courage, sceptics, perfectionists, and so on.[229] It is not possible to generalise in such a domain[230] and it is well known that fine sentiments do not necessarily make for fine literature.[231] Nevertheless, we feel we should at least draw attention to the politico-cultural influence exerted by these committed intellectuals at this time, even if not all of them could aspire to lasting literary fame.

A time of convergencies

Between 1942 and 1943, 'fighting France' was at last emerging from the shadows: the internal Resistance and Free France were converging and their union prompted the various resistance movements to coordinate their action. The creation of the CNR in the spring of 1943 symbolised this double fundamental development. Of course, not everyone was in step and new difficulties arose. Nevertheless, the relative cohesion forged between the external and the internal Resistance – the communists included – made fighting France a quite unique element in European resistance.

As has often been pointed out, credit is incontestably due to the internal Resistance for having shattered the prevailing apathy, opposed adverse propaganda and prepared for a take-over from elitist groups that had proved themselves broken reeds. However, many of its leaders knew quite well that the Resistance could only become a mass movement if it offered adequate means of action. Rather than go cap in hand to the Allies, they judged it preferable to use Free France as a kind of intermediary, an external branch that could extend the internal struggle. For some, such strategic considerations were combined with deeper political concerns: Gaullism could be a rallying point for the post-war period and stand up not only to neo-Vichy Giraudism but also to communist pressure. As for the head of Free France, he was motivated above all by his 'particular idea' about the 'rank' that France should hold in a world conflict that was becoming increasingly complicated. As he saw it, it was of the first importance for him to be recognised by Vichy, by the Allies and by Giraud as the uncontested leader of all the resistance groups. To achieve this end de Gaulle had resolved to make the indispensable compromises, including going some way along with the PCF. But the head of Free France continued to regard the members of the Resistance as soldiers engaged in war, who must obey 'orders' – a view that was certainly not shared by most of the movement leaders, who considered the Resistance to have a greater political importance. Some compromises were going to have to be found.

The politicians did not find their tongues until 1942. Christian Pineau[232] was the first of the movement leaders to find his way to London, in March 1942, with the mission of sounding out the head of Free France. After him, many others made the same journey: d'Astier and Frenay for example, who held some crucial talks with de Gaulle in the autumn. Conversely, during the night of New Year's Eve, 31 December 1941, three men[233] were dropped near Saint-Andiol in the Bouches-du-Rhône. One was the ex-prefect, Jean Moulin[234] whose express mandate from the head of Free France was to act as his 'representative' in the southern zone.[235] In the spring of 1943, the 'Brumaire-Arquebuse mission' brought (to London) two emissaries of importance, Passy, with responsibility for paramilitary affairs, and Brossolette for political contacts.[236] Negotiations were forcefully pursued and resulted in agreements that were to mark a turning point in the northern zone.[237] Meanwhile, a number of political parties had been contacted or had made contact – the SFIO and the PCF for example. The SFIO sent Félix Gouin and Daniel Mayer to London and on 15 March 1943 Blum made his decision: the socialists would support the leader of Free France without reservations.[238] As for the PCF, with the twofold aim of increasing the efficiency of the internal Resistance and of speeding up the establishment of the second front, in January 1943 it delegated to Fernand Grenier powers to act as the official representative of the PCF and the FTP to Free France.[239]

All in all, Charles de Gaulle seems to have had the best of it with regard to achieving his ends: the BCRA had increased its efficiency and, above all, the rallying of the main resistance movements[240] and that of the now reorganised political parties gave Free France a wider audience among the Allies. As early as 9 November 1942, right in the middle of the negotiations between the Americans and Darlan, the movements of the southern zone sent a telegram, censored by the BBC, to the 'Allied governments', demanding 'with insistence that the destiny of the new liberated North Africa should immediately be placed in the hands of General de Gaulle'.[241] On 15 May 1943, Jean Moulin, in the name of the CNR, which was about to meet, cabled: 'The people of France will never accept the subordination of General de Gaulle to General Giraud.'[242] De Gaulle admits the 'decisive effects' of that statement and reckons that 'it had the immediate effect of strengthening [his] own position'.[243] However, to achieve the crucial rallying of all this support, the leader of Free France had had to compromise: not only had he removed all ambiguity from his condemnation of the practices of the Third Republic, but he was now no longer hesitating to take the initiative, as can be seen from his exhortation dated 14 July 1943: 'If there are still *bastilles* in existence, let them prepare to agree to open their gates. For when battle is joined between the people and the Bastille, it is always the Bastille that turns out to have been in the wrong!'[244] Free France and the major resistance movements had reached agreement on a programme of minimal action: to keep France in the war and participate actively in its liberation; and to give the French people their say once more. But there was more than one way of being 'Gaullist'. A fair number of Resistance members were *de facto* Gaullian Gaullists whose hope was that de Gaulle would federate the Resistance and control the communists. Others – and there were many among the leaders of the movements – regarded the head of Free France simply as a useful 'symbol' and intended, in any event, to preserve complete liberty of judgement where he was concerned for, as Frenay wrote to Moulin on 8 April 1943, 'these men want to be soldiers yet at the same time remain citizens'.[245] He went on to observe – quite rightly – that it was the Resistance 'that was the chief support' of 'Gaullism'. These movement leaders were certainly counting on receiving from Free France all the means they so sorely lacked – money, parachute drops of weapons etc,[246] but their intention was at the same time to turn the Resistance into a political force upon which it would be increasingly necessary to depend. That in itself explains how it was that complete cooperation was not achieved overnight. Jean Moulin had been entrusted with a twofold mission: to unite[247] the paramilitary formations of the movements in the southern zone and at the same time to place them under the authority of fighting France. The leaders of the big movements were certainly prepared to improve the coordination of paramilitary action by establishing a unified secret army and even to work towards fusion, but they wanted to preserve their freedom of manoeuvre and rejected the attempts of the London desk strategists who wanted to impose a strict separation between 'politics' and 'military matters'; for, as Frenay was at pains to point out in the letter cited above, 'the Resistance forms a single whole'.

However, the fusion of the movements proved an easier matter than had been supposed. The fundamental aspirations towards unity recognised by the second generation of organisers who had taken over from the earlier generation of 'historical chiefs', combined with the good offices of Franc-Tireur, overcame initial feelings of reluctance in the southern zone. During their visit to London in the autumn of 1942, Frenay and d'Astier agreed to the creation of a 'coordination committee' for the three big movements in the southern zone and by 26 January 1943, these set themselves up as the Mouvements de Résistance Unis (united movements of resistance).[248] In the northern zone, Brossolette, on 26 March 1943, was successful in setting up a 'coordination committee' which was less integrated but did include the National Front and also – and this was an important innovation – a diversity of political 'tendencies':[249] the CNR was about to be created. Although this unification of the movements remained incomplete[250] to the extent that a number of non-communist movements in the northern zone reproached the MUR for 'playing at politics' instead of war,[251] the decisive step had been taken.

All the more reason, in the view of the leaders, not to let themselves be overridden on the matter of the organisation of the 'Secret Army'. Many of the movement leaders opposed the typically London plan of turning the Secret Army into a strictly 'military' tool composed of carefully chosen men placed one hundred per cent 'under orders' and altogether cut off from 'politics'.[252] This was the cause of a violent conflict between Frenay and the first head of the Secret Army, General Delestraint,[253] who refused to countenance any 'revolutionary' aspects to his new army. This disagreement was also to affect the altercation over 'immediate action', a problem that was becoming increasingly acute as the months passed. According to the strategy of Free France, the Secret Army was to prepare itself methodically for D-day, within the strict framework of the general Allied plans and without putting the enemy on the alert. It was a schema that the most politicised part of the Resistance rejected: it refused to set up 'underground barracks', favouring instead more graduated forms of self-defence and immediate action. The leaders of the FTP and Libération-Sud believed that the merit of such a strategy would be to bring the rebels into the war and transform the movements into a mass organisation based on the working class, while the leaders of Combat considered that it would result in a veritable national uprising. The creation of the STO and the appearance of the *maquis* confirmed that analysis. De Gaulle came quite rapidly to recognise the danger of allowing a clash between the idea of a Resistance 'under orders', forced into immobility, and that of a Resistance that aspired to be 'insurrectional'. He decided to give ground: in a directive addressed to Delestraint on 21 May 1943, he wrote that 'the principle of the necessity for immediate action is recognised', adding that such actions would be set up 'almost always upon the initiative of the movements'.[254]

Finally, it was necessary to make preparations for the immediate post-war period and a Liberation which – as everyone, to a greater or lesser degree, recognised – would have to involve a profound transformation of the French political system. This led straight to a thorny preliminary problem: what place should be granted to the 'old' political parties?

Those parties certainly did not enjoy a good press, to put it mildly: those in London and many members of the internal Resistance too readily ascribed to them much of the responsibility for the collapse of 1940. Furthermore, many of those parties were conspicuous by their absence in the Resistance. Movements of the classical right had been deliberately disbanded and many of their erstwhile leaders had given their personal backing to the French State. The Radical Socialist Party had also adopted an extremely low profile and its self-effacement could scarcely mask a wait-and-see attitude which did not augur too well.[255] There were, however, three parties which had constituted or reconstituted themselves in secrecy and reckoned they had a right to be regarded as combatant. First, as we know, there was the PCF which had managed to emerge from the political ghetto in which it had been trapped in the autumn of 1939. It had steadily gained ground, had been recognised as of right by the head of Free France and certainly intended to take the place that was its due. As early as the summer of 1942, the socialists had also been successful in reconstituting their party and it was reborn officially in the spring of 1943.[256] They were all the more determined to be recognised given that there was a tendency to dismiss them as poor relations.[257] Finally, a third political group was emerging: the Christian Democrats; they included a number of former militants from the little PDP of pre-war days, who had been quick to commit themselves to the Resistance alongside Frenay. They had been joined by a number of young catholics formed by the Resistance, such as Gilbert Dru. Many of them reckoned that their struggle could continue within a large popular catholic party, which was to be profoundly restructured. In short, by 1943, the configuration of the triple party system of the immediate post-war period was already detectable. Furthermore, these parties which had won or rewon their spurs underground intended not only to make good their claim to participate in the underground fighting but also exploit that participation fully after the Liberation.[260]

This reawakening of the political parties provoked a fine outcry among those – and there were many of them – who opposed any return of 'the old political greybeards that had so carefully been preserved in moth-balls' (Passy). In London, where a solid spirit of anti-parliamentarianism prevailed and the old political formations had been over-hastily certified as dead, Brossolette was countering with an alternative, specifically Gaullian, strategy: 'People in France are either Gaullist or anti-Gaullist . . .; no third party is possible . . . all political faiths must be firmly based in the Gaullist movement.'[261] To that end, these Gaullians strove to attract to London figures from all parts of the political spectrum[262] who would commit themselves on a strictly personal basis. This deep distrust of the 'old party formations' was shared by many movement leaders who, for their part, wished also to promote 'revolutionary political expression' (Frenay) precisely through the movements themselves so that these would become the 'artisans of French renewal' (the manifesto of Ceux de la Résistance, published in 1943). However, this double offensive took a long time to get going and the critics of the political formations consequently found themselves obliged to accept their being represented within the institutions of the Resistance. Besides, the political formations did have some supporters, particularly amongst the Christian Democrats who had moved apart from Frenay, and they did overcome a measure of the reserve felt towards them. Thus Jean Moulin, for instance, who in June 1942 had still been opposed to the creation of a 'Resistance Parliament', was progressively converted to the idea of a CNR in which representatives of the various political formations would sit, on condition that such a body would have a purely consultative role and that action would remain under the control of the Resistance movements.[263] In February 1943, the head of Free France in his turn declared himself in favour of setting up 'as soon as possible' a single Resistance Council . . . under the chairmanship of Jean Moulin, the representative of General de Gaulle:[264] this would assemble representatives of the various movements and delegates of the political and trade-unionist groups, who would approve a common charter: to fight against the occupying power, overthrow dictatorships (including the French State) and pursue the struggle for liberty with de Gaulle.[265] Imperatives dictated by France's 'rank' had determined this choice: if France was to regain full credit in the eyes of the Allies it was necessary for the head of Free France to be seen as the undisputed head of a united Resistance in which political figures and groups known to the Anglo-Saxon politicians were represented.[266] Although Brossolette hit upon a 'transactional formula' which granted representation only to 'fundamental tendencies of French resistant thought', this amounted to no more than a rearguard action: on 27 May, at 48 rue du Four, in the 6th *arrondissement*, in the house of René Corbin, the treasurer and a friend of Pierre Cot, a meeting was held, attended by eight movement representatives, six delegates of 'political tendencies' and two delegates from the trade-unionist organisations.[267] The CNR had been born.[268] It created an institutional link[269] between the northern and southern zones, between communists and non-communists and between the old pre-war parties and the new groups which had grown up underground.

The birth of the CNR was the fruit of a number of compromises. There was a danger that these would have to be negotiated anew when, a few weeks later, Jean Moulin was killed. The question of a successor to the man whom Charles de Gaulle had praised as 'a man of loyalty and calculation ... an apostle as well as a minister'[270] was an extremely tricky one, particularly as he had, personally, carried extremely heavy responsibilities: he had been chairman of the CNR but also of the committee that directed the MUR, and at the same time the delegate general of Free France.[271] That delegation comprised forty or more permanent members at the head of 'general services' such as the Information and Press Bureau in the charge of Georges Bidault[272] and the Comité Général d'Etudes which was conceived as a planning committee for the post-Liberation period.[273] It was also Moulin who had been responsible for the distribution of funds to the various movements, and who controlled the services for liaison with London and for transmitting information to it. Claude Bouchinet-Serreules, who was appointed to take over for an interim period, was by no means inexperienced[274] but he was unfamiliar with the internal Resistance and, left without directions, had more or less to feel his way. He soon found himself up against the opposition of those movements which had accepted the official resurgence of the political parties only with reluctance. Under the patronage of the OCM and Combat, eight of these movements created a Comité Central de la Résistance (Central Committee of the Resistance) which, on 25 August 1943, declared itself to be 'the executive of the Resistance, responsible for the direction of all the activities of the Resistance within Metropolitan France' and sought to reduce the CNR to a merely nominal role. To counter this manoeuvre,[275] the interim delegate had the political wit to make a pre-emptive strike: he made no attempt to oppose the creation of the Central Committee but himself took the position of its chairman and, above all, he decided to split the functions that Jean Moulin had hitherto combined. Henceforth the CNR would have as its chairman a man who came directly from the internal Resistance.[276]

The head of Free France was certainly recognised as the head of a unified fighting France. Increasingly involved in the Algiers imbroglio and its consequent diplomatic manoeuvres, he left his loyal Gaullian followers to keep a watchful eye on the political evolution of the internal Resistance. The latter, having acquired a certain self-confidence, was now anxious to show that it had come of age politically and set up an underground State which would be ready to take over at the Liberation; but it was upset by a number of centrifugal forces. The general delegation and its services were going to have to act as intermediaries between Algiers and the Resistance of metropolitan France.[277]

The Algiers imbroglio

The political scene in Algiers was considered scandalous by almost all members of the internal Resistance. Liberated French North Africa had lived through six agitated months, starting with the provisional expedient of dyarchy under an American protectorate. But Gaullian Gaullism managed to come out of this Algerian interlude quite well.[278]

'Operation Torch' and the 'provisional expedient'

The Americans had been successful in landing in Algeria and Morocco, but at the same time they were floundering in a veritable political bog.[279]

The initiative was changing hands: the Anglo-Saxons were moving from defensive to offensive action in order to relieve the Soviet Union and satisfy public opinion which was by now starved of success. But where should the attack be launched? The Pentagon favoured a strategy of concentration: the principal foe – that is, the Reich – must be destroyed and annihilated in its entrenched position – that is, in Europe. The British, for their part, were pressing for a more peripheral strategy centring on the 'soft underbelly' of the Axis powers, which they regarded to be the Mediterranean: this presented the added advantage of being the main route to their own imperial possessions. Roosevelt, in some perplexity, eventually decided that to attempt a landing on the French coasts in the spring of 1943 would be altogether too risky[280] and, in July 1942, he opted instead for North Africa: this was 'Operation Torch'.

By reason of its size, it was an unprecedented operation and a difficult one, in which it was nevertheless necessary to succeed at all costs and, if possible, at low cost, by exploiting the neutrality of French North Africa. It was clear that military operations would have to take precedence over local political considerations. The great majority of local 'European'[281] notables[282] appear to have welcomed the national revolution with enthu-siasm (the Légion des Combattants in Algeria had mustered 150,000 members out of a total European population estimated at 1,200,000), since it was in favour of order and hierarchy and would have liked to bury once and for all the Blum–Violette project[*] and other dangerous pipe-dreams elaborated by the Popular Front. The army of Africa, approximately 120,000 men strong, was all the more *maréchaliste* given that, since Mers el-Kébir and the Syrian war, it had a number of scores to settle with the 'Anglo-Gaullists'. Weygand had managed to keep all those under his authority in a strict neutrality combined with a staunch loyalty to the Maréchal. But when he was recalled to France, his departure stimulated a number of activist groups which recruited their members in Algiers and Oran among the young and the Jewish community (José Aboulker is a good example here) – groups which believed they could count upon some sympathisers among the police, Commissioner Achiary for instance. They wanted to swing North Africa from a position of neutrality into the struggle against the Axis powers. But it should be noted that those who claimed to be 'Gaullists' had only a very restricted audience and their militant endeavours were limited to the task of propaganda.

Bearing in mind all these considerations, the Anglo-Saxons had decided that only American troops should take part in the landing and under no circumstances would any of the Free French be included. They had, furthermore, made a number of political contacts. That mission had been entrusted to Robert Murphy, a diplomat who had been Roosevelt's personal delegate in French North Africa since December 1940. His choice finally fell on a group of activists who were ready to bring North Africa into the war alongside the Americans. These men, usually referred to as 'the Group of Five', came from the right: Lemaigre-Dubreuil, a businessman who had earlier presided over the destinies of the Ligue des Contribuables (a small movement of the extreme right), was an organiser who was rather too turbulent for Murphy's taste but who had an entrée to all circles; his lieutenant, Rigault, was also markedly to the right; Henri d'Astier de la Vigerie, an aristocrat of great charm with royalist sentiments, also had many contacts; Van Hecke was an officer known for his direction of the Chantiers de la Jeunesse in Algeria; Tarbé de Saint-Hardouin, finally, was a diplomat, also with many connections. 'The Five' were looking for a 'big chief' who would be up to the task of rallying the army of Africa. In default of Weygand, who categorically refused to be party to any 'dissidence', they made contact with Giraud, whose escape from the fortress of Königstein, on 17 April 1942, had made quite a stir. His strategic megalomania was somewhat alarming[283] but he sported five stars, was available and was against all connivance with not only London but also the internal Resistance. By early autumn the conspiracy was shaping up nicely. The Five had made sure of both civil and military complicity.[284] After the neutralisation of all the potential opposition, a handful of high-ranking officers (Béthouart

---

[*] A proposal to grant more than 200,000 Algerians the right to vote without renouncing the Muslim law. [Trans.]

in Rabat, Mast and Jousse in Algiers) were to take command, respecting the existing hierarchical order, giving the Americans time to complete their landing operations. On 23 October, at Cherchell, the American General, Clark, made contact with the Five and, on 2 November, an agreement between Giraud and the Americans was concluded.[285]

On the Anglo-Saxon side, the operation was hailed as a success: three days after the landing, which took place on the night of 7–8 November 1942, the American troops were virtually in control of Morocco and Algeria, without having lost too many men,[286] although there had been fighting in Oran and in Morocco.[287] Not everything had gone according to plan, it is true. For one thing, by communicating the date of the operation extremely late in the day, the Americans had forced the conspirators into muddled and precipitate action. For another, they had taken pointless risks by changing their plans at the last moment: thus, in Casablanca, where they tried to land in force, they had come up against some extremely hostile marines. Finally, the Americans had failed to keep to the agreed schedule: in Algiers, the 400 civilians who had managed to gain control of the town for a few hours, were no longer masters of the situation by the time the vanguard of the American troops arrived. All these blunders and setbacks were not of a kind to encourage the French authorities to come over to them. Taken by surprise, shocked by the disorder unleashed here and there and above all by the unrest occasioned in certain fighting units, at first the military leaders stuck to the Vichy line, namely to respond more or less sharply to this violation of the neutrality of North Africa.

Two unpredictable political factors complicated the situation still further: the absence of Giraud[288] and the unforeseen presence of Darlan. As we have seen, the latter had initially adopted a loyalist position but, quickly seeing that the balance of forces was by the hour becoming increasingly unfavourable, he had – on the 9th – agreed to a 'suspension of hostilities' applicable in the first instance solely to Algiers, and then on the 11th also to Algeria as a whole and Morocco. Following the invasion of the free zone and the landing of the Axis troops in Tunisia, the Admiral of the Fleet, not without some wavering[289] and under pressure from the Americans who were declaring themselves ready to install Giraud over his head, had first committed himself to neutrality-come-what-may but then swung over into the Anglo-Saxon camp, covering himself by his 'intimate agreement' with the 'beleaguered Maréchal'.[290] By 13 November, Eisenhower and Darlan had already reached an agreement according to the terms of which the admiral would be recognised as 'High Commissioner'; the French administration – in particular the governors – would be maintained; and Giraud would be the commander of military forces in North Africa. There were two immediate consequences to the Algerian imbroglio. The first, of a military order, was that the Axis forces were to land without difficulty in Tunisia[291] and there embark upon a campaign which was to last until May 1943. The other consequence was political: Algeria and Morocco came under what Y.-M. Danan has termed 'a local Vichyism under an American protectorate'.[292]

This protectorate (of a sort) was based upon what the Americans called the 'Darlan deal' (meaning an operation which involved both going along with and at the same time blackmailing Darlan). It was the product of a combination of the admiral's fundamental opportunism and the pragmatism of the American military leaders, who had been left without any precise political directives and found themselves confronted by a hornets' nest for which they were unprepared. Unpleasantly surprised and resolved at all costs to ensure the security of their lines of communication, they played the Darlan card because he at least seemed to be in a position to command the obedience of the army of Africa.[293] Murphy, who was as much of a realist as he was politically conservative, had supported the Darlan deal with the approval of Roosevelt himself, who was all the less inclined to disown his generals given that he could envisage no alternative solution. Nevertheless, he was obliged to disarm the opposition provoked in some areas of American public opinion by this enthronement of Darlan: on 17 November, he announced that the 'Darlan deal' was, at most, 'a provisional expedient'.[294] It should be added that it was an expedient which won the support of Churchill (who overrode the opposition of part of his cabinet) and also of Stalin who, in a letter addressed to Roosevelt, congratulated him on the 'great success' of the Darlan operation.[295]

Whether they were provisional or not, Darlan tried hard to get dug into his new functions. Making specific reference to his status as heir-presumptive to the (now 'beleaguered') Maréchal, he gave himself the title of 'High Commissioner of France resident in North Africa' and created an 'Imperial Council'. Apparently on the advice of Murphy, he gathered around him some of the conspirators of November, making them members of a committee which functioned as a government.[296] As for the rest, nothing – or hardly anything – had changed. The admiral's experience of power had reinforced his penchant for order; besides, the fiction of the 'intimate agreement' prevented him – on pain of undermining his own legitimacy – from in any way altering the laws of the French State. In that sense it truly was Vichy that lived on alongside the benevolent neutrality of the local American authorities.

Despite all his political acrobatics, it was not only friends and allies that Darlan won himself. A number of very orthodox *maréchalistes* reckoned that the admiral was acting too high-handedly in respect of their venerable leader; the local Gaullists,[297] whose following was increasing, were not disarmed; some of the activists of 7 November, who had enrolled in a Corps Franc d'Afrique, regarded him as a dangerous impostor. It is from their ranks that Darlan's assassin emerged:[298] Fernand Bonnier de la Chapelle, who had belonged to the Chantiers de la Jeunesse before taking part in the events of the night of 7 November. He killed the admiral on 24 December, was tried hurriedly and in camera and executed at dawn on the 26th.[299]

Darlan's death ushered in a period of extreme confusion. Algiers, which was never again to return to being an uncomplicated town, was submerged in a quasi-Florentine atmosphere of plotting and kept in a state of high tension by the countless rumours circulating in the bars and in the Aletti hotel and relayed eagerly by 'Radio Grapevine'. It would be virtually impossible – and rather pointless – to follow all the complicated and tortuous interactions of these intrigues and 'conspiracies'. Only one factor remained constant: the determination of the American authorities, who were becoming increasingly disconcerted, no longer to accept just any political solution, especially as the Tunisian campaign was turning out to be more arduous than had been expected. It was probably American opposition that precipitated the failure of the attempt to seize power made by the Pretender to the French throne,[300] who had convinced himself that the 'Imperial Council' might invest him 'not as a pretender, but as a figure to provide a rallying focus'. The Americans similarly turned down the idea of Noguès, whom Bergeret now pushed forward, for fear of finding themselves with a second 'political expedient' on their hands. In the end it was Giraud who was set up in power on 26 December, with the quite unexpected title of 'Civilian and Military Commander-in-Chief in North Africa'. This outcome of the war of succession was logical: Giraud had American support and he was not marked by a Vichy past. He was therefore in a position to rally Darlan's adversaries without, however, being strictly classed as a 'dissident' and that, in its turn, could win him the support of those who were committed to neither the left nor the right. Furthermore, on the good advice of Darlan's entourage, which came over to him lock, stock and barrel,[301] he in his turn took great care to ensure his legitimacy through the intermediary of the Imperial Council, which produced an ordinance – necessarily a secret one – made in his favour by Darlan. Above all, on 28 and 29 December 1942, he offered reassurance to the reactionary camp by ordering the arrest and internment of those activists of 7 November and Gaullists who seemed likely to make trouble, meanwhile taking good care to respect the Vichy legislation. The prevailing conditions seemed to point toward a political variant of the 'Darlan deal'. However, Darlan's murder had made it possible for de Gaulle to intervene in the Algerian game: by 25 December, and in the name of the French National Committee, he had already invited Giraud to work with him.

The 'pas de deux'

Pas de deux is the term that usually refers to a ballet performed by a pair of dancers. Historians might prefer the word 'dyarchy',[302] that is, double power, to describe the situation when, after a number of further twists to events, de Gaulle and Giraud became co-presidents of a French Committee of National Liberation.

It would be mistaken to reduce this race for power to the egocentric ambition of two generals who had found their way into politics.[303] Although both were incontestably determined to fight the Axis powers, they differed on every count on points of fundamental importance.

General Giraud had had a fine career that had followed an extremely classic path.[304] His physical courage was undeniable and his integrity can be in little doubt; he was generally agreed to be most able from a professional point of view, although he was not very much at home when it came to mechanised warfare. There was an underside to these qualities, described – with considerable delicacy – as follows, by Jean Monnet: 'A man of great physical presence, with an unclouded, empty gaze, very conscious of his prestige as a heroic officer, intractable where military matters were concerned, hesitant in everything else. I will not pass judgement on his intelligence, which was that of a general long since formed by life in the desert and inclined to simplification'.[305]

He had one single aim: to fight the war, expressed in his slogan as 'One goal, victory'. But as he saw it, that meant reconstructing an army, not bringing the French nation back into the war; at the very most all he was in favour of doing was arranging for a kind of sacred union within the vaguest and most tenuous of political frameworks. For he would proclaim to all and sundry his horror of 'politics' – of politics of any kind. That is why he so strongly opposed the setting up of a provisional government. De Gaulle records the following significant exchange: ' "You are talking politics to me", he said. "Yes", I replied, "for we are fighting a war. And war means politics." He heard me but he was not listening'.[306] That distrust accounts for his lack of determination in November 1942.[307] His avowed apoliticism in fact masked deep and solid reactionary sentiments. All in all, he was close enough to the national revolution,[308] including its anti-semitism. Nor were his peers in the army of Africa of a kind to temper his views. Initially rejected by that army, he had become the willing enough prisoner of its most reactionary leaders, men such as Bergeret and Prioux.

The Gaullian Gaullists, for their part, had lived through the Algiers imbroglio with stupefaction. Their leader had not failed to denounce, even at this early stage, 'a proportion of guilty men' who symbolised 'dishonour and betrayal'.[309] He did so in the name of the precedence of Free France, which had brought France back into the war against both the Axis powers and State collaboration. And the negotiations now well under way with the leaders of the internal Resistance movements authorised him to speak in the name of 'fighting France'.

In its founder's view, Gaullism should persevere in its essential aims: he must indeed take charge of a nation at war. War certainly was being waged by the FFL:[310] Leclerc's men had seized the oases of Fezzan in the spring of 1942 and the brigade commanded by Koenig was known the world over for having held out against Rommel for fifteen days at Bir Hakeim.[311] They had also displayed the greatest firmness in defending French interests, even against the Allies, in the Levant and in Madagascar.[312] And what a nation at war needed to lead it was a government, not just a campaign general staff.

In the eyes of the Gaullians, that government already existed in the shape of the French National Committee, and they were certainly not prepared to scuttle it or to see it diluted in some vague and apolitical replacement. It is true that there was no lack of intrigue in London itself and the Gaullian government had had to ride out a number of crises, the most dangerous being that provoked by Admiral Muselier.[313] But the team by now secure at the heart of the National Committee (Cassin, Pleven, Dejean, Legentil-homme, Auboyneau, Valin, Diethelm, Soustelle, Catroux and Thierry d'Argenlieu) was relatively coherent and effective. Although he was by now exercising complete authority, the head of Free France was always careful to consult these men, to gain confirmation for the decisive choices he was making. On the advice of Passy, in whom he placed total confidence, he had widened the powers of his information services, these now becoming the Bureau Central de Renseignment et d'Action (BCRA), charged with responsibility for political action in France, and in the meantime contacts with the internal Resistance were increasing.

As for Roosevelt, having burned his fingers over the 'Darlan deal', he was resolved to keep the situation 'fluid' until the Liberation took place. Only when liberated could the French people decide on their own fate; meanwhile, they would obey 'local authorities' placed under the more or less discreet control of the American military authorities.[314] His mistrust of de Gaulle and of the overweening nationalism of Free France remained undiminished. But, as a pragmatist, he came round to the view that a division of power between the Gaullians and the Giraudists would make it easier to dispel the divisions among the French. Besides, Giraud and de Gaulle were to be simply 'trustees' of the liberated territories; their task would be to organise the war effort, not to play at being political leaders. He accordingly offered his good offices and 'invited' his two 'prima donnas', as he called them, to come to a meeting in Anfa – a suburb of Casablanca – where Churchill and he were meeting to decide on the follow-up to 'Operation Torch'. Like it or not,[315] de Gaulle was obliged to accept the 'invitation' but he refused to be taken in by the blandishments of Roosevelt and objected point blank to the Anglo-Saxon plan. The most he would do was make a sacrifice to protocol by offering his congratulations to Giraud in the presence of the necessary journalists and photographers.[316] Being convinced that de Gaulle would sooner or later be obliged to knuckle under, Roosevelt decided, despite his reservations with regard to Giraud's political intelligence, to nominate the latter as 'trustee for French military, economic and financial interests' for the liberated territories; and he undertook to equip ten French divisions. He nevertheless judged it prudent to provide him with a mentor: his choice finally fell upon Jean Monnet, a man of discretion but at the same time tenacious and effective, who, for his part, was also determined to get de Gaulle and Giraud to coexist.[317]

Jean Monnet saw clearly the necessity of improving Giraud's official image as soon as possible. The general would have to be dressed up as a liberal both in order to calm down his critics in some areas of American opinion and also to force the Gaullists to negotiate. His task was not an easy one: an ex-minister of Vichy, one Peyrouton, had just been appointed governor in Algeria, where thousands of political prisoners were still languishing in the prisons that the camps of Bossuet, Djenien bou Resz, and Djelfa etc. in effect were. Not only had the anti-semitic legislation never been abrogated but it had been decided that mobilised Jews should be concentrated in detachments of 'pioneers' so that they would not ever be able to claim the status of former combatants. However, with patience, and thanks to the fact that he could brandish the ultimate threat of the possibility of the sacrosanct military aid drying up, Monnet succeeded in provisionally overriding Giraud's reactionary entourage and persuading him to make a speech on 14 March.[318] It was what Giraud later, ingenuously, called 'the first democratic speech of [his] life' and it was constructed around three themes: the armistice was null and void; the French army would be born again from its ashes; French sovereignty would be safeguarded until such time as the 'French people' could express itself in conformity with 'the laws of the Republic'.[319] In consequence, the SOL was dissolved, dismissed civil servants were reinstated and republican slogans readopted. The ball was now in the Gaullian camp.

De Gaulle was not fooled. He confided to Catroux, his plenipotentiary in Algiers: 'The whole affair is being played out not between us and Giraud, who is nothing, but between us and the government of the United States.'[320] He acknowledged the 'republican turn' taken by Giraud but made three conditions for the conclusion of a lasting agreement: 1. a provisional government should be set up which would be responsible for directing the war, organising the Liberation and negotiating with the Allies; 2. in this government, the military authorities should be subordinate to the political leaders; 3. the regime born from the armistice should be unequivocally repudiated, and that implied a purge of all the high dignitaries who had served Vichy. On a tactical level, the leader of Free France pretended to be in no hurry to go to Algiers, reckoning that time was on his side in North Africa as well as in the milieux of the internal Resistance, which was proving a great help to him. Making full use of all the means,[321] both great and small, at his disposal and already, at this stage, making the most of that specifically Gaullian weapon, dramatisation directed at external opinion, he managed, in Jean Monnet's words, 'to avoid the irreparable while coming close to a split'.[322] Giraud, under pressure from an entourage which regarded the concessions made to Monnet as ridiculous, initially rejected the whole body of Gaullian demands: what *he* wanted was a military committee which he, as commander of the armed forces, would head; furthermore, as a man of order close to the national revolution, he opposed a purge which – he claimed – would shatter the vital sacred union. The combined efforts of Catroux, Jean Monnet and Harold Macmillan were needed to find a *modus vivendi*. Eventually Giraud was persuaded to come to an agreement and de Gaulle accepted a provisional compromise since it was now time for him to come to Algiers and operate 'from within': together they would be co-presidents of a provisional government.

On 30 May 1943, after two months of verbal guerrilla warfare, de Gaulle arrived in Algiers; that very day he plunged into his first heady encounters with the crowds. On 3 June, following some last-minute dramas, the Comité Français de Libération Nationale (CFLN) was at last born. It was to 'direct the French war effort everywhere and in all its forms ... exert French sovereignty over all territories beyond the enemy's power, manage and defend all French interests throughout the world.' Its founders undertook 'to re-establish all French liberties'. De Gaulle had scored a decisive point: what had emerged was certainly a 'French central power' and it would remain in place until such time as it was possible to form 'a provisional government constituted in conformity with the laws of the Republic'.

To make it possible for a fusion between those in London and those in Algiers to operate, a kind of institutional monster was created. In effect, the CFLN was directed by two presidents with identical powers who, together, fulfilled the functions of head of State. They took it in turns to act as president and their double signature was required to make valid all acts and decrees. Initially, the CFLN comprised seven commissioners: the two co-presidents each of whom co-opted two commissioners (Massigli and Philip for Free France, Monnet and General Georges for Giraud); the seventh, Catroux, was chosen by both Giraud and de Gaulle, together.

Gaullian Gaullism digs in

This institutional compromise did not last long. Within six months Giraud had been swallowed up, having failed to set up any Giraudist movement. By playing the nationalist card skilfully, de Gaulle, in contrast, had managed to get Gaullian Gaullism rooted. The Algerian interlude had come at just the right time to ensure a transition from the legitimacy born on 18 June 1940 to the consecration of popular legitimacy it acquired on 25 August 1944.

It is true that de Gaulle held some high trumps. In the first place, the institutional Resistance unequivocally recognised his primacy over Giraud and we have already mentioned the importance he himself attached to positions taken up within the CNR. Furthermore, those who were luke-warm or indifferent – the 'geographical Gaullists', as they were jokingly called – were not insensitive to the intransigent nationalism shown by the Gaullists both where 'betrayal' was concerned and in relations with the Anglo-Saxons, who were often short on political tact. Here at last was a statesman who, one could believe, might be up to the task of federating the various French political forces during the interregnum, always a delicate period.

In North Africa, the Gaullist movement was gaining in strength and putting down roots in popular circles. Political figures in the public eye were also offering their allegiance: Van Hecke (one of the Five), Couve de Murville – and let us not forget Peyrouton who, even before the founding of the CFLN had tendered to de Gaulle his resignation as Governor General. The committed also began to vote with their feet. It was in vain that the Giraudists denounced the 'enticement' practised by the FFL – movements which the latter preferred, more delicately, to call 'spontaneous corps movements'.[323] It is true that the majority of those who had escaped from Spain and of the young conscripts felt more attracted to the FFL, and the adventure that they represented then, than to the *Moustachis*, as the men of Giraud's dauntingly conformist army were known.[324]

Giraud's countless political blunders also made his rival co-president's task easier. Giraud nevertheless remained convinced that he deserved well by his country. It cannot be denied that he had obtained from the Americans complete equipment for eight divisions, which became operational in the autumn, and he restored the confidence of the army of Africa, which performed illustriously in the Tunisian campaign.[325] He had also recognised the opportune moment to lend logistic support to the insurgent Corsican resistance fighters and had thus facilitated the liberation of Corsica.[326]

At the same time, however, he was a poor politician and an unimpressive co-president. Impulsive, torn between a pseudo strong-arm attitude[327] and an inclination to cave in, he would seldom accept responsibility for the political consequences of measures which he had, nevertheless, counter-signed. In the long run, even his own supporters became discouraged by him. Furthermore, it soon became apparent that he had become some kind of a man of straw in the hands of the Americans:[328] in contrast to de Gaulle, he never made any protest against the clumsy interventions of Eisenhower who, acting on orders from Washington, on 19 June summoned the two co-presidents to give them a dressing-down. In July, Giraud left for the United States where, it must be said, his military contacts proved fruitful. During his absence, however, the CFLN was at last able to function in a normal manner and de Gaulle proved himself to be, in truth, a statesman. Giraud became more and more isolated and such councillors as remained faithful to him, such as the extremely conservative General Georges, were of little help to him. He himself realised that he had strayed out of line: his 'republican turn' had destroyed the fiction of legitimacy with regard to Vichy and had alienated a number of *maréchalistes*. And he had not proved capable of exploiting the consequences of that speech of 14 March to win support from new quarters.[329] The third path that he appeared to be advocating was vague, confused and spineless. He could at the most hope to win over a number of prudent members of the 'wait-and-see' school of thought, who regarded Giraudism as a practical and intellectually convenient means of making the necessary transitions as smoothly and painlessly as possible. Support of this kind was, by definition, fragile. A Giraudist state of mind certainly did exist but there was virtually no Giraudist movement.

Giraud very soon lost his footing within the CFLN,[330] which by mid-June comprised 14 commissioners.[331] Not that de Gaulle systematically strove to gain the upper hand, but those whose function was conciliatory, such as Monnet, René Mayer, Henri Bonnet and Couve de Murville, became convinced that it was indeed essential to 'play politics' and thus, for the most part, came to support the Gaullian options. The last altercations were over the competence of the commander-in-chief and the question of purges. Purges took place, not without opposition, but fairly soon.[332] But the other matter was more tricky: de Gaulle wanted the commander-in-chief – that is to say Giraud – to be subordinate to the political power. He was careful to base his claims upon those sacrosanct 'republican' principles, but what alarmed him most was that Giraud was hierarchically subordinate to the Anglo-Saxon command. It should perhaps be added that he was certainly not averse to putting Giraud in his place.[333]

De Gaulle's position improved once Giraud had gone off on his ill-timed visit to the United States. Three decrees passed on 31 July and 4 August by the CFLN – and counter-signed by Giraud – made changes in the way the Committee functioned. The alternating presidency was replaced by a specialised presidency;[334] in the event, Giraud was made responsible only as 'commander-in-chief' and 'for the direction of military operations'[335] whilst de Gaulle '[directed] the debates and [supervised] the execution of the Committee's decisions with regard to the other business and general policies of the Committee'. It was furthermore specified that 'as from the time when Giraud [assumed] effective command of all French forces in operation, he [would cease] to exercise his functions as president of the

CFLN': he was thus forced into a choice the consequences of which left no doubt in anybody's mind. On 2 October, the CFLN made the matter quite clear:[336] the 'CFLN elects its president; the president of the CFLN is appointed for one year; he is eligible for re-election'. Meanwhile, the 'commander-in-chief' would be appointed by decree. Tired and increasingly isolated, Giraud had accepted this setback, counting upon a big inter-Allied command. Even in this he was to be disappointed.

So it was the end of the road for the dyarchy which, anyway, never had been a very viable proposition. A few days later, there was a meeting of the Consultative Assembly. Then, after a few weeks, the CFLN integrated into its ranks a number of representatives from the internal Resistance. It now commanded enough authority to oblige the major Allied powers to recognise its *de facto* existence. The United States were the most niggardly of them, regarding it as a body 'administrating the overseas territories which recognised its authority'. The Soviets were more generous, defining it as representing 'the interests of the French State and Republic'.[337] These differing formulae were an indication of the fact that the CFLN had acquired a relative latitude of action in diplomatic matters.

The liberated and the insurgent

Churchill had not won his bet: the trees had already lost their autumn leaves before it proved possible to open a second front in the west. But 'Operation Overlord' had only been deferred; and the Anglo-Saxons were all the more determined that it should be a success in view of the progress of the Red Army in the east. The formidable war-machine forged over the Atlantic was set in position. Were the French going to have to wait passively to be liberated by the Anglo-Saxons or were they to participate actively in their own liberation?[1] The answer to this crucial question was one that would be of great significance during an interregnum that was likely to prove a difficult period. Our present story ends with the freeing of a Paris that was both liberated and insurgent. A good third of the country was still occupied, but the capital had recognised the legitimacy of the man of 18 June. It will be the task of Jean-Pierre Rioux, in the next volume in this series, to give an account of what became of the provisional Government.

The French kaleidoscope

Four years after the disaster of 1940, France once more became a battlefield and a political and military stake of capital importance from every point of view. It is that stake that we must now analyse.

The France of the Americans: a country that was a 'friend' but 'occupied'

In the Anglo-Saxon camp, the Americans had imposed their own strategy:[2] to attack the hard core of the German forces and destroy it. This implied a double requirement and it was to be fulfilled: namely, aerial and logistic superiority. Preparations for the landing as such had been made with the most painstaking care: an armada of 4,000 craft supported by 700 warships was involved. The first assault waves knew their objectives down to the smallest details. To avoid coming to grief against port fortifications – as had happened earlier at Dieppe – the troops were to land between the Orne and the Vire on gently shelving beaches of fine sand that were relatively poorly defended. Two artificial ports were to be constructed immediately to serve as logistic lungs.

Europe was about to discover a new style of war: war American-style, with the tactics of a dauntingly effective steamroller. In its planning, the Pentagon had put the civilian population to one side and had regarded as relatively negligible the forces of the Resistance, which it mistrusted. The FFI were to put into execution a number of scheduled plans to delay the arrival of German reinforcements and thus consolidate the bridgehead. After which, they might perhaps be used to carry out a number of specific actions under the control of specialised teams.[3] At all events, nothing that remotely resembled an armed and general insurrection was envisaged.

These military directives both justified and at the same reflected the policies decided upon in Washington. For most of the White House authorities France, since 1940, had been no more than a power of secondary importance and it was up to the United States to provide for its relief. Roosevelt was not well-disposed toward either de Gaulle or the internal Resistance, which had been described to him as owing allegiance to the communists and determined to unleash civil war. He thought, in all good faith, that the ex-occupied French people would be grateful to the Anglo-Saxons for ensuring an interregnum: 'until such time as the French people could vote', the liberated territories would be placed under the authority of a military administration known as AMGOT.[4] It had even been decided that the French should be allowed to see only 'Allied or inoffensive films'. But treating them like children in this manner was a mistake.

The France of the Germans: a vital battlefield and a conquered people to be mercilessly exploited as forced labour

By March 1944, Hitler had decided upon the main lines of a strategy propped up by 'fortress Europe'. The main confrontation was to take place in the West.[5] The Anglo-Saxons would take some time to recover from being thrown back into the sea, and German forces could then be deployed in the east in a colossal counter-attack until such time as the new weapons would be ready[6] to clinch the outcome.

The French coasts had therefore been shielded particularly carefully behind an 'Atlantic wall' that had been under construction since 1943. 10,000 forts were strung out between Dunkirk and the Spanish frontier. However, this defensive system had its faults, for the defences lacked depth. That is why Rommel, who was also bothered by the inferiority of the Luftwaffe, wanted at all costs to win the battle on the beaches. But his adversaries had criticised this 'obsession with fortifications' and he did not have at his disposal all the tank reserves that he could have wished for. Even more important, the German general staff had become convinced that the landing could only take place close to a big port, in all probability in the Nord or the Pas de Calais.

France had every reason to be alarmed at her promotion to the status of a vital battlefield. Those in charge had received orders to proceed 'regardless of French political considerations'. 'Lemon-squeezer collaboration'[7] was more than ever the order of the day. Over 4,000 *S-Betriebe* factories employing around one million workers were delivering 80% of their production to the Reich, which was also creaming off about one quarter of the meat produced and to whose service the SNCF devoted 57% of its freight traffic, etc.

Above all, repression was being considerably stepped up. The occupying power made preventative arrests of individuals reputed to be hostile and high-ranking civil servants;[8] it held in readiness for D-Day lists of hostages chosen from amongst local notables. The situation of France was increasingly coming to resemble that of Poland. The Wehrmacht was applying itself in particular to the decapitation of the Resistance movements and the 'pacification' of regions 'infested by bands'. The south-west was delivered over to the 'B division', the 'Jesser column', the tough 'Vlassov army' and the 'North African legion': Brantôme (in the Dordogne) was sacked, as was Montpezat in the Quercy, and many hostages faced firing squads. The terror was also unleashed in the Haut Jura[9] and in the Nord where, at Ascq on 1 April 1944, Waffen-SS (whose train had been held up for an hour following sabotage action) organised a veritable man-hunt that claimed 86 victims, some of them women and children.

The imminence of the Allied landings had not altered the Reich's political strategy: the Vichy government still remained its most useful tool. Its legitimacy made it possible to treat dissidents as outlaws and meanwhile it retained its hold over the hesitant and the luke-warm. The occupying power was determined to continue to exploit the State apparatus, in particular its repressive branches. In January, it had managed without great difficulty to get into the government two confirmed and collaborationist Pétainists, Darnand and Henriot, who now controlled the key posts of 'Maintenance of Order' and 'Propaganda'. From Philippe Pétain the Reich had extracted two further precious 'Messages': that of 28 April condemned without reservations all 'resistance groups' and issued a warning against the Liberation;[10] the second had been recorded in advance 'because he [Philippe Pétain] would probably be asleep when the landings took place'[11] and it insistently invited the French people to observe neutrality.[12]

The Reich decided to make greater use of those who still professed unconditional support for it, retaining, nevertheless, a tight control over them. The ranks of such people were thinning to the point where Henriot was even brought to declare, on 19 December 1943: 'We shall save the

French despite themselves' (exactly what Laval had proclaimed a few months earlier). Nevertheless, they still represented an effective means of exerting pressure upon Laval and, above all, they were becoming useful auxiliaries in the hunt for rebels against the STO and members of the Resistance. The occupying power now encouraged the creation of armed 'protection groups' within the principal collaborationist movements: thus Saukel urged Doriot on to set up 'action groups for social justice' within the PPF. The men the Nazis managed to attach to themselves often turned out to be mercenaries of a most ferocious kind.

The France of Vichy: illusions, time running out and a broken shield

Right up until the landings, the Vichy kingdom[13] could still appear to have some credibility: the administration functioned on the whole;[14] the urban police forces remained to a large extent loyal to the authorities in power.[15] Except for a handful of prelates (Saliège, Bruno de Solages, Théas and Rastouil), the catholic hierarchy, whatever its misgivings on the score of the STO and the anti-semitic measures, supported the established power.[16] In the occupied zone, Pétainism still attracted some strong support to judge from the welcome given to the head of State in both Nancy and Paris, although it is not possible to tell whether it was as the wonder-worker of the national revolution or as the shield of metropolitan France that he was acclaimed.[17]

In practice, however, the French State was less and less master of metropolitan France. The crisis of the autumn of 1943 was to deal the finishing blow to the Vichy government's aspirations towards autonomy. To disarm the increasingly pointed criticisms coming from certain politicians[18] and, above all, to pull the rug from under the feet of the Consultative Assembly that had just met in Algiers, the head of State decided to go ahead with the constitutional project introduced in 1940, get rid of Laval who was becoming increasingly unpopular, and play the wait-and-see neutrality card.

Forewarned by the precedent of Badoglio, Berlin reacted promptly. It forbade Pétain to broadcast[19] and awaited his full and complete submission. After refusing for a month to exercise his functions, the head of the French State caved in on every count. Henceforward the occupying power would *a priori* scrutinise all laws, whether or not they were constitutional. Pétain had to purge his own entourage and reshuffle his government 'so as to make it acceptable to the government of the Reich'. The Hôtel du Parc even acquired a new guest of note, the Führer's 'special diplomatic delegate to the head of the French State', Renthe-Fink.[20]

The French State was running to rack and ruin: its head of State was taciturn, morose, immured in solitude; its head of government was embittered, obsessed with his personal security[21] and increasingly authoritarian and isolated; it had a reshuffled cabinet known to observers from neutral countries as the 'Ministry of Civil War': Henriot, the new Secretary of State for Information and Propaganda, seeing himself as the preacher for a new crusade, devoted over half his 'radio chats' to exalting the hunt for 'stateless terrorists and criminal assassins'.

Vichy finished up as a police State and a cruel one: it gave itself a redoubtable legal arsenal, among other things installing, in January 1944, 'court martials' to judge 'terrorists' in accordance with a summary procedure. To increase their effectiveness, members of the Militia were promoted to posts of prefects and police superintendents. In April, in 'regions of operations' Militia leaders became 'superintendents for the maintenance of order', assisted by 'tribunals for the maintenance of order'; these were even more expeditive and introduced a system of terror modelled on those of Vaugelas in the Limousin and Di Costanzo in Brittany.

It was in the name of this legalised terrorism that the Militia Franc-Garde was launched against the Maquisards in the Glières region and that Militia leaders 'sifted out' the prisoners.[22] The Secretary of State for the Maintenance of Order and head of the Militia, Darnand in person, directed the repression in the prison of Eysses.[23] This legal and para-legal repression[24] was accepted not only by Laval, who justified the exceptional measures to the Council of Ministers, but also by Pétain.[25] It was extremely late in the day – on 6 August 1944, to be precise – that the head of State discovered and denounced 'these inadmissable and odious facts' – too late in the day to pull the wool over Darnand's eyes.[26]

Time was running out, then. Yet Philippe Pétain did not appear to harbour any doubts as to the correctness of his policies. He was the shield, he was the only legitimate power,[27] he would maintain order in the face of and despite everything. Furthermore, Pétain, as well as Laval, who was by now converted to a more circumspect attitude of wait-and-see, were convinced that they still had a certain room for manoeuvre for, as Laval explained on 9 November 1943 to the mayors of the Cantal: 'I do not wish disorder to become installed in our land and I should like to act in such a way that Germany is not so strong that it crushes us and Bolshevism, for its part, is not in a position to wipe us out. . .'[28] The last hope rested upon a compromise to be negotiated in the west, which would isolate the Soviets and allow the regime to survive while at the same time disengaging it from the imprudent State collaboration. Both Pétain and Laval considered themselves as the obvious mediators in these future negotiations. Emissaries set off from Vichy to Spain, charged with sounding out American officials and even convinced Giraudists.[29] But these would-be makers of a peace that was now to be an Anglo-Saxon one had an increasingly difficult case to plead once State collaboration had made it possible for the Reich to force France to further its, the Reich's, war interests.

Even before State collaboration collapsed pitifully into serving exclusively German ends, its record showed that it was becoming more and more crushing. The French could, it is true, give credit to the regime for having avoided 'polonisation' in the strict sense of the word. Those in authority and high-ranking civil servants of the French State had been able, over a greater or lesser period of time, to curb German demands, use their personal authority to save individuals directly threatened by the Gestapo and even mitigate the fate of particular categories of French people: thus, the French working in Germany had been relatively protected by the 'Bruneton mission'; similarly, the head of the French State had managed to prevent French women from being transferred to Germany in the STO; and finally, Jews – those, at least, with French nationality[30] – were relatively more protected than Polish, Dutch or Norwegian Jews. All these are points that have been made in the regime's favour. But they are far outbalanced by its passivity: in the first place, because of the remarkable extent to which France had officially allowed herself to be 'milked' by Germany. It has been calculated[31] that 42% of the 'special revenue' from abroad (covering – from 1943 to 1944 – more than 38% of the needs of the Reich Treasury) had been provided solely by France. An expert in this field, the German Hemmen, in December 1944 concluded his report with the following statement: 'Over four years of occupation, France has become the largest supplier of merchandise in Europe'.[32] We have already seen the extent to which Vichy France fed the Reich's war-machine.[33] It had supplied not only agricultural produce but also strategic raw materials and war equipment. The French State also allowed the use of its ports and supplied lorries, railway engines and trucks (20% and 64%, respectively, of all French rolling-stock). We have also seen how, thanks to Vichy, Germany was able to use French manpower in its war economy.[34] The Allies certainly had a right to ask for an explanation from the French State.

The famous metropolitan and Pétainist shield was, in truth, nothing but a colander with holes that grew larger and larger, and the first studies in comparative history that have appeared to date truly seem to show that France, far from having enjoyed a privileged position within Hitlerian Europe – as Vichy historiography would have it – was in effect one of its most exploited countries.[35] The exploitation was accompanied by a major political risk. All the time that they were engaging in State collaboration, Pétain and the men of Vichy had been trying to impose a new order upon the French people and to do so with the occupying power looking on. With such a combination, the men of Vichy were deliberately playing with fire and running the mortal risk of setting off a civil war.

The France of de Gaulle: a France united in the fight, sovereign and restored
The France of Charles de Gaulle's dreams was still a long way off. But now that Algiers was under the control of the Gaullians, he was – in the

autumn of 1943 – at least in a position to set about what seemed to him most fundamental: restoring the State. But how?

The restoration of the State implied the end of the dyarchy. That became official on 8 November 1943, when Giraud was forced to abandon the co-presidency. De Gaulle's idea was to tie Giraud down to military functions quite – or almost – devoid of all political responsibility. After a new clash over the control of the special services,[36] Giraud turned down the honorific post offered him, declined to accept any official functions and, in April, went off to sulk in Mazagran. Giraudism had faded away. Giraud's Vichy-type ideology, which he found it very difficult to disguise,[37] had alienated him from the great majority of members of the Resistance: they continued – and this was decisive – to prefer Charles de Gaulle. Giraud's lack of political firmness had done the rest.[38]

On 9 November 1943, the CFLN expanded,[39] making more room for men from the internal Resistance (Frenay, Emmanuel d'Astier de la Vigerie) and some former parliamentarians (Queuille, Le Troquet, Jacquinot). In April 1944, the communists Grenier and Billoux, in their turn, joined the government.[40] Meanwhile, however, a 'profoundly moving ceremony'[41] had already taken place in November 1943, namely the inaugural session of a 'Consultative Assembly' which, while it was not sovereign, nevertheless could be seen as a kind of national representation.[42]

Logically enough, on 3 June 1944, following the unanimous vote of the Consultative Assembly, the CFLN became the Gouvernement Provisoire de la République Française (GPRF) (the Provisional Government of the French Republic). A few weeks earlier, on 20 April 1944, an ordonnance had been published on the organisation of public powers at the Liberation; instituting, in particular, seventeen 'provisional secretary generals'.[43]

Meanwhile the now reborn State had acquired a more substantial army. The FFL had certainly always attracted much attention as they did honour to their flag stamped with the cross of Lorraine, but their forces had remained relatively small; by late spring 1944, the CFLN had at its disposal some 500,000 men armed by courtesy of the Allies. The major proportion of these troops were made up by the Algerian *pieds-noirs* (Algerians of European origin) and natives of AFN and AOF.[44] Most of the leaders came from the army of Africa that had remained pro-Vichy or Giraudist, and the merger with the FFL did not take place without a number of clashes (only Leclerc was given command of a large unit). In all, 8 divisions had been formed.[45] One – the 2nd Armoured Division – was to go to Great Britain, three were training under the rod of iron wielded by General de Lattre de Tassigny, who had escaped from prison in Riom; the other four saw hard fighting in Italy: they participated in the battle of Il Belvedere and in May 1944, while fighting in the Arunci mountains, made a decisive breakthrough that took the French troops to the outskirts of Rome, where they arrived on 4 June.[46]

In short, the provisional government had full recognition from the internal Resistance and the men of Algiers could feel satisfied that they had established an adequate organisation within metropolitan France. Its corner-stone was the General Delegation, with a delegate-general supported by a delegate for the two zones, and assisted by a number of technical committees. After the arrest of Bollaert, the General Delegation was entrusted to the charge of Alexandre Parodi-*Quartus*, a man after de Gaulle's heart: a high-ranking civil servant who had always rejected the French State and, very early on, had joined the Resistance as a militant, he belonged to a solid tradition of republican and patriotic lawyers. On the military side, a national military delegate (*Chaban*-Delmas) headed a pyramid of military delegates. All the armed forces of the Resistance were in principle regrouped within the Forces Françaises de l'Intérieure (FFI) and placed under the command (in London) of General Koenig. To oversee the interim period in the provinces, Algiers had appointed twelve 'regional commissioners of the Republic' and prefects[47] who were to hold themselves in readiness for D-Day.

On paper, then, the Gaullian restoration of the State was going well. But in the shifting game that was about to be played out, Charles de Gaulle was a long way from holding in his hand all the trump cards necessary to be in a position of control over the Liberation, as he would have liked. He needed to win the respect not only of the Allies – who had seen fit not to invite France to the Teheran conference, where the three major powers had, between 29 November and 1 December 1943, sketched in the post-war programme – but also of the politicians of the pre-war period and, above all, of the members of the internal Resistance.

To cope with the situation, the planners in Algiers had elaborated a strategy of concentration: 'mobilising *maquis*', covering extensive areas, were to pin down and 'chop up' the German troops, at the same time facilitating 'the liberation of large zones of the territory': this was of capital importance in terms of the political plan.[48] But did Algiers command the means for a politico-military strategy of this kind?

The members of the internal Resistance were not alone in harbouring in the back of their minds political plans for the post-Liberation period. The Gaullian Gaullists were also preparing for the post-war era. Men as diverse as Passy, Brossolette and Soustelle[49] shared in common not only a vigilant anti-communism but also a definite determination to dominate not only the 'old' parties of the Third Republic but also the resistance movements. They had at the time a prime instrument at their disposal in the shape of the BCRA, which had lost none of its pretentions to direct all operations from London or Algiers, short-circuiting all those who did not seem to it to be sufficiently orthodox.[50] De Gaulle, for his part, was careful to remain aloof from squabbles that were too partisan and he refused to sacrifice

Emmanuel d'Astier de la Vigerie, Commissioner of Internal Affairs, to the concerted and impassioned pressures exerted by Passy and Soustelle. But he placed his trust first and foremost in his Gaullian companions and was personally distrustful not only of the PCF but indeed of politicians of every colour. For the time being, it is true, he was governing as he saw fit, settling thorny questions in one to one conversations and manoeuvering within the CFLN without too much difficulty.[51] But the Consultative Assembly had appointed as its chairman F. Gouin, a well-tried parliamentarian, as well as former parliamentarians to head five of the seven commissions. And although he had managed to extract from the Assembly[52] a 'reservation of judgement' on the fate of various institutions,[53] there were by now flagrant disagreements in this domain which he judged to be of capital importance.

In the short term, however, it was with the main body of the internal Resistance that clashes looked likely to be the most serious. De Gaulle was certainly pressing forward, taking an increasingly hard line on the subject of a purge,[54] and by no means ignoring either economic or social problems.[55] But deep divergencies remained regarding the basis of the insurrection. On 18 April 1942, in a statement that had attracted some attention at the time, de Gaulle had suggested that 'the national liberation cannot be separated from a national insurrection'.[56] Two years later, the head of the provisional government was still anxious (despite the fact that the word 'insurrection' was now erased from his speeches) that the French should not remain passive in their liberation. However, he assigned very precise limits to any such insurrection:[57] its purpose would be to overturn the apparatus of the Vichy State and to restore a State that was unstained by any form of national compromise, and was sovereign, and to do so in an orderly fashion if possible, or at the very least, without any deep upheavals. No doubt what he had in mind was rather more than simply a prefectorial movement, but his programme was a very far cry from the expressed desires of the great majority of Resistance members.

In short, quite apart from his incontestable record as a Resistance fighter, Charles de Gaulle was in a position to provide a patriotic and reasonable alternative and also a federating principle that was not without attractions for a France that was becoming increasingly divided. However, he had yet to impose his will fully upon a number of Resistance movements which regarded themselves as having now come of age[58] and also to win over to himself, exile though he was, a French people traumatised by four black years.

The France of the Resistance: an insurgent, purified, new France

The main body of Resistance members were, for their part, altogether resolved to liberate themselves and not to serve simply as back-up forces in large-scale manoeuvres in which they would be regarded as of little account. On 24 May 1944, the CNR's Commission for Military Action spelt out their position: certainly, the priority for the Resistance forces was to carry out 'the measures decided by the inter-Allied general staff to ensure the success of the landing operations',[59] but equally – if not even more – they had to prepare for 'mass resistance action of an insurrectional nature'.

These directives reflected the determination of many Resistance leaders to set about intensifying 'immediate action' as from the spring of 1944. Measures of reprisal taken against traitors and agents of the repression had increased;[60] sabotage action was spreading (in the April of 1944, SNCF freight services were cut by a sharp 37% and meanwhile the secondary rail network was virtually paralysed); the Resistance was asserting its presence (Cajarc was occupied for forty-eight hours by the FTP of the Lot) or was 'pre-mobilising' (at the end of May, 3,800 men converged upon the Margeride area) or making effective surprise attacks;[61] in some regions, the Limousin in particular, the Resistance controlled the countryside with every nightfall.

In short – as the CNR proclaimed – the great majority of Resistance members made no secret of the fact that their activities 'would not come to an end with the Liberation'. They were certainly intending to become the militants of tomorrow who would make France a France not only restored but also purged, rejuvenated and – so to speak – new.[62] For all of them, the Fourth Republic was to be an antidote to the errors of the past which had led to the collapse of France in 1940. For almost all of them, politics were to be lived in a new fashion. For most of them, liberal capitalism was to be re-examined[63] and economic and social structures profoundly transformed in particular by means of nationalisation.

Such radical policies inevitably provoked clashes and tensions. In the short term disagreement focussed upon the question of the tactical timeliness and political legitimacy of 'mass resistance action of an institutional nature'. Broadly speaking (but there were a number of intermediary variants)[64] there was an opposition between two attitudes and simultaneously two strategies: one view favoured immediate and autonomous action which would not be geared simply to D-Day and, in one way or another, would mobilise the entire population (in particular through the creation of 'patriotic militia'); in short, a kind of 'popular war' leading to a carefully controlled but continuous insurrection. This line, defended by the communists among others, was opposed by those who favoured concealing their weapons in readiness for a D-Day programmed by Algiers and the Anglo-Saxons, within the framework of specifically military action controlled by the technical experts. This was the strategy defended by many movements in the northern zone which proclaimed themselves to be apolitical and by the ORA,[65] which regarded itself as the metropolitan branch of the army of Africa.

Another source of friction was the role that the political parties were to play. The problem was not a new one but those who were suspicious of the parties were able to exploit a spurt of anti-parliamentarianism prompted by the reappearance in Algiers of a number of somewhat worn out politicians and, above all, the resurgence of the PCF. The Party was in effect not only winning a fair number of supporters who were attracted by its offensive strategy and effective impact but was also appealing to a wider audience: the National Front, becoming increasingly diversified, could boast of recruits as widely differing as Bidault, Debû-Bridel, Justin Godart and Father Philippe; its military branch, the FTPF,[66] was making remarkable progress – especially in the northern zone; a number of movement leaders – such as Jean de Voguë-*Vaillant* (Ceux de la Résistance) were increasingly inclined to adopt the PCF's action strategy as their own. More important still, all the arrests and departures for Algiers had altered the balance of power within the Resistance apparatus and a number of key posts had fallen to members of the PCF: Villon was pursuing an active role within the permanent Bureau of the CNR and, together with Kreigel-*Valrimont* (the third member being J. de Voguë), controlled COMAC, which was its military commission, etc. At a local level, it seems likely that 30% of the members of the Comités de Libération (CDL) were either members of or sympathisers with the PCF; in the Parisian region, the chairman of the Comité de Libération Parisien (CLP) (Committee for the Parisian Liberation) was Tollet, who was a communist, and on 5 June *Rol*-Tanguy, formerly of the International Brigades, became the head of the FFI in the 'P' region (i.e., the Ile de France). While extreme cases – betrayal motivated by anti-communism – were, all in all, exceptional,[67] there can be no doubt that this undeniable progress, often exaggerated,[68] considerably contributed to the political dissension that divided communists from the majority of non-communists.

While it would be wrong to underestimate these tensions, it would be equally mistaken to exaggerate them for, in many respects, the Resistance presented an image of solidarity. It was a solidarity that was cemented by its Jacobin spirit and its patriotism. That all and sundry[69] were nursing political plans for the future in the back of their minds is quite obvious, but the leaders of the movements put the liberation of the country before their own particular interests, and that goes for the PCF too, although it was suspected at the time – and even today – of having been exclusively preoccupied with seizing power. The most recent works to have appeared on the subject[70] certainly tend convincingly to invalidate that persistent preoccupation. Admittedly, the Party adopted different styles depending upon whether it was expressing itself in Paris, Algiers or Moscow; but there were not two messages, one for the militants, another for the apparatus; first and foremost, it used one common language centred upon the (significant) order of the day proclaimed on 1 May 1944: 'Unite, arm, fight in the towns and in the villages, workers and bosses, farmers and landlords, parish priests and schoolteachers, to prevent looting and murder, for the liberty of France.' Besides, any other strategy would probably have been suicidal given not only the close Anglo-Saxon presence but also the motivations of the non-communists who had joined the Party primarily because they trusted it most in the struggle against the 'Boche'.

This prevailing patriotism is clearly reflected in the 'Resistance Action Programme' produced on 15 March 1944 and better known as the 'Programme of the CNP'. Its authors were guided by a twofold preoccupation: to mobilise all possible energies with a precise and methodical 'plan for immediate action'; and to win over and reorganise mens' minds with an eye to the future. The 'measures to be applied in the liberation of the country' are marked above all by a unificatory reformism which may have appeared revolutionary to some[71] because it favoured a 'veritable economic and social democracy', the 'eviction of great feudal landlords', the 'participation of workers in the direction of the economy', a 'complete social security plan', 'security of employment' and 'nationalisation measures'; all the same, it is quite clear that its authors had no intention of stirring up class warfare.

As has been said already, most Resistance members were keen to unleash a patriotic war. But while the Resistance had managed to set up a veritable underground State, its appalling poverty of means made it particularly vulnerable.

The underground State was still headed by the CNR,[72] the composition of which remained unchanged. But in the interests of greater security and effectiveness, the plenary meetings had been abandoned and effective power had devolved upon a Bureau of five members[73] who managed – up until mid-August, at least – to take their decisions with unanimity. This team which was relatively united was, thanks to Bidault's flexibility, on good terms with the delegate general. The Bureau was backed up by a number of commissions,[74] the most important of which was the Military Commission, COMAC. In the provinces, the various 'regions' with their hierarchical structures continued in every respect to provide an all-important framework for Resistance members. As for the Departmental Committees of Liberation (Comités Départementaux de Libération) (CDL) which, like the CNR, brought together representatives of both the movements and the political parties, their task was to coordinate action in respect of the Liberation process at a local level.

But this State was extremely poor. It found itself forced to levy dues, whilst the *maquisards* were, for the most part, obliged to 'live off the inhabitants', a circumstance which lay at the root of many mutual frictions. Above all, it lacked weapons. Furthermore, this scarcity was very uneven so that there were even instances of different *maquis* groups coming to blows in their desire to gain possession of revolvers and Sten guns. In December 1943, Emmanuel d'Astier de la Vigerie had thought he had won over Churchill to the idea of turning southern France into a kind of Yugoslavia. But in the end, the sceptical and mistrustful Anglo-Saxons had opted in favour of massive bombing raids – a mutilating strategy which for the most part was much less effective than the intermittent but precise attacks of the Resistance fighters.

There can be no doubt that the lack of weapons was deeply frustrating.[75] It certainly slowed down the recruitment of fighting men. In the autumn of 1943, the MLN leaders of six regions in the southern zone made their calculations: they had at their disposal 15,000 operational fighting men,[76] but they reckoned that that figure could have been quadrupled if the Resistance had been able to supply more weapons. By the spring of 1944 the total of combatants was probably larger but the proportion of men actually armed to potential combatants appears to have remained unchanged. On account of the shortage of weapons, *a fortiori* it proved impossible to constitute the reserves of forces that some leaders wanted to muster – in the form of patriotic militias, for instance. During the winter of 1943–44 inactivity and disenchantment were the causes of desertions and acts of indiscipline in a number of *maquis*.

A tragic foretaste of all the difficulties that awaited the insurgents was provided by Les Glières, in February–March 1944.[77] The incident was initiated by a promise of weapons to be dropped by parachute on the plateau of Les Glières, to the north-east of Annecy. Some 450 volunteers led by a young officer, *Tom*-Morel, went there to pick them up. Rumours of the affair broke out. Maurice Schumann mentioned it in a BBC broadcast. The Vichy government decided for political reasons to make an example. The Resistance men were vulnerable by reason of their concentration and lack of logistic support. They managed to fight off the attacks of the Militia but not of the Wehrmacht. Captain Anjot, who had taken over from *Tom*, chose confrontation as soon as the stakes became political, but the losses suffered and the semi-disastrous outcome should have provided a warning, in terms of tactics at least.[78]

For it would be wrong to be misled by the well-oiled planning and organisation of the institutional Resistance: the day-to-day reality on the ground was quite another matter. Whatever the importance of COMAC, it was in fact in control only in the Parisian region; in the southern zone the structure of the MLN was relatively solid, but in many of the regions of the northern zone many small, autonomous, often rival networks existed; and some *maquis* had even become self-sufficient enclaves of a kind. Furthermore, the massive offensives that the Gestapo and their French henchmen had been launching since the autumn of 1943 had sadly cut many communications, disorganising movements and networks, in fact disorganising the fighting Resistance.[79] Meanwhile, the super-NAP (which infiltrated ministerial circles) lost three of its successive leaders between March and June 1944; in November 1943 the Grenoble region lost its leadership; in March 1944, it was the turn of Toulouse, in May that of Lyons. It looked as if the insurrection would be an arduous one.

The France of the average man: freedom and survival

It is very difficult to construct a picture of the average Frenchman faced with the Liberation. It could be that – on the whole – while he certainly wished to be liberated, he was not necessarily willing to commit himself as deeply as de Gaulle and the Resistance would have liked.

To the difficulties inherent in commitment of any kind were added the pressures of a situation that was becoming increasingly limiting. City-dwellers who had not – or no longer had – the means to buy food on the black market[80] were wearing themselves out fighting destitution. There was no more coal, practically no sugar or fats and in some places milk products were unobtainable. Furthermore, France had ceased to be a national market and was dissolving into a collection of adjoining regions all trying to be more or less self-sufficient: in the Nord and the Pas-de-Calais, official rations for an adult had dropped to 25 grams of bread and 20 grams of meat per day; the situations in Marseilles and Bordeaux were also dramatic.

The economic situation was aggravated by political problems. Pétain-ism, though declining, could still count not only on the supporters of the national revolution and notables alarmed at the collapse of Giraudism, but also on the fantasies of ordinary French people for whom the Liberation – whether Gaullist or not – symbolised above all a triumph of 'Yids', 'good-for-nothings' and 'anarchists' organised into 'terrorist bands'. And there is nothing to prove that – as is so often claimed – it was the very same crowds that came out to acclaim Philippe Pétain in April and Charles de Gaulle in August. The fact is that a pro-Vichy public did still exist.

However, there are plenty of indications to suggest that on the whole public opinion had undergone a quite distinct evolution between the summer of 1943 and the spring of 1944. Simplifying, it could be said that the public in general had moved from a 'tacit complicity' (an expression much used by those writing their personal recollections of the period) to a more demonstrative kind of sympathy. And the fact is that, without that evolu-tion, the movements would have been totally decimated and far fewer *maquis* groups would have survived. There can be little doubt that Jacobin reflexes may well have counted for much from this time onward, for the people were exasperated by the increased requisitioning, the transfer of large sections of the population (especially the inhabitants of border areas), the hunt for STO rebels and the repression. One sign of the times was that 'L'Affiche Rouge'[81] elicited, on the whole, reactions of sympathy for those accused.[82] In the eyes of a growing number of French people, not only was Vichy incapable of liberating the nation from the 'Boche' but it had furthermore well and truly disqualified itself. Encouraged by the militant efforts of the Resistance, whole cantons in Britanny, the Limousin, the Haute-Savoie and the Jura had swung over into semi-dissidence. In the Lot, the Ain and the Morbihan nearly all the *gendarmerie* squads had disappeared or, if they remained at their posts, it was on the orders of the Resistance men.

But does that mean that all these sympathisers were ready to join the Resistance? No; in the first place, because such commitment was accompanied by very real risks, although these are systematically played down by those determined to regard the FFI simply as chocolate soldiers: even a symbolic strike could have fatal consequences.[83] It is not just by chance that there were so many young people among the insurgents: not only had they rebelled against the STO, they were also the adolescents who had been humiliated by the defeat and who, being less rigidly enmeshed in the social fabric, had revenge to take and adventures to seek. Average man's France itself, in this spring of 1944, was fearful of the future. People were afraid that the repeatedly postponed landings would be a fiasco, that reprisals exacted by the occupying power would be greatly increased, that France would be put to fire and the sword, just like all the towns decimated by the Anglo-Saxons' air raids which were becoming ever more murderous and ever more traumatising.[84] Some people, including most orthodox conservatives, were faced with measureless terror.

Blood, tears and dancing

On 6 June 1944, the longest day, the Anglo-Saxons were successful in establishing bridgeheads on the Normandy coast. After which, nothing – or almost nothing – went as had been hoped: for several weeks confusion mounted in a France that was becoming increasingly fragmented and at odds with itself. All the efforts of the combined Resistance forces were to be needed politically to cement together a France that was now liberated and insurgent but, at the same time, stunned by four years of darkness as well as the latest jolts.

The Germans clamp down and Resistance fighters are at risk in the open

The evolution of the situation depended to a large extent upon the speed of advance on the part of the Anglo-Saxon armies. During the early days, 'Operation Overlord' was a model of its kind: the advantage of surprise was fully exploited on relatively poorly defended coasts, the Allies gained total mastery in the air, and two artificial ports constructed in record time made it possible to bring up the necessary logistic support. Further-

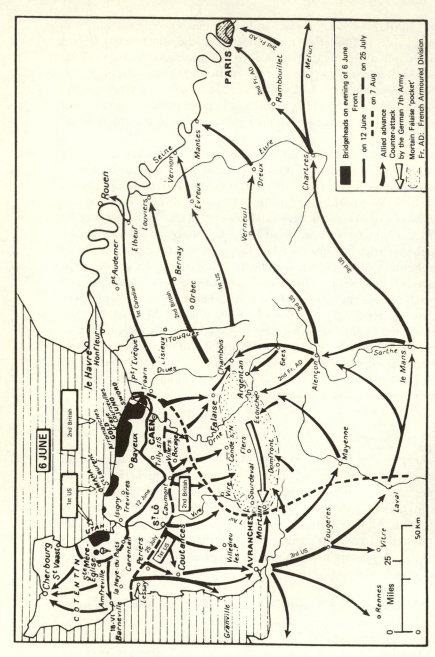

5 'Operation Overlord' and the breakthrough at Avranches

Source: R. Aron, *Histoire de la libération de la France*, 1959, vol. 1, pp. 22–3. Reproduced by permission of Editions Fayard

more, Hitler and his general staff interpreted Overlord as a diversionary movement and dithered for a while before providing tank reinforcements. By the evening of the 8th, Rommel had lost the battle in which he had wanted to retain the initiative, the battle of the beaches: the Americans, English and Canadians occupied a continuous stretch of the coast from the mouth of the Orne to the north-west of Carentan.

But very soon the Anglo-Saxon advance inland was blocked. Bayeux was taken but Caen could not be won; the German troops dug their toes in and put up a vigorous opposition. Hitler, who refused to envisage any compromise in the west, sent all the reinforcements available to the Normandy front. The Allied offensive became bogged down in a murderous, Italian-style war over positions. Then Eisenhower, leaving the task of containing the enemy's push in the east to Montgomery's British troops, mounted a wide flanking movement from the southern Contentin. Nevertheless, seven long weeks passed before a breach in the German line could be made.

All this marking time was to place many Resistance men in a cliffhanging position. On 5 and 6 June, the BBC had not only given the order to implement the plans aimed at neutralising or delaying the German reinforcements, it had furthermore pressed Resistance fighters to launch guerrilla operations throughout the country in order to distract the enemy general staff. De Gaulle, for his part, while emphasising that 'the struggle would be hard ... and long', on 6 June broadcast an appeal for a veritable national mobilisation: 'This is the battle of France, and it is also the battle for France! ... The sons of France, wherever they are and whoever they are, have one simple and sacred duty which is to fight the enemy with every means at their disposal.'[85] A few days later, on 10 June, faced with the development of the situation, Koenig, as supreme head of the FFI, was obliged to give 'the formal order to put the maximum curb on guerrilla activities'.

But it was rather late for that. Once the messages had been received, volunteers had flocked to the 'mobilising *maquis*'. 3,000 men went up into the Vercors, 7,000 converged or were about to converge upon Saint-Marcel in the Morbihan, into which region 'black-beret troops' under the command of Bourgouin and also weapons had been dropped by parachute. At the same time, a large number of the partisans of insurrectional action had mobilised themselves: the FTP of the Nord and the Pas-de-Calais judged that 'the objective conditions for the insurrection' now existed and proclaimed that 'the time [had] come to organise the mass rising and provide leadership for the millions of combatants';[86] the groups in the Lot and the Ardèche were marching on Tulle and Annonay; all over the place, the *maquis* were expanding with new volunteers and *maquis* groups were multiplying.[87]

This initial mobilisation took place with the problem of the scarcity of weapons still unresolved – indeed far from resolved. The Anglo-Saxons, absorbed in the Normandy front and still very much on their guard, continued throughout June to make only parsimonious parachute drops of arms. The result was that in certain *maquis*, overwhelmed by the flood of volunteers eager for action, it was not long before the situation became critical.

To accomplish their priority mission of maintaining the security of the major communication routes, the German forces had received the order to unleash a reign of terror[88] upon the regions that were 'infested by bands' and everywhere to destroy concentrations of armed men. With all the heavy means at their disposal, they inflicted considerable losses upon the *maquisards* of Saint-Marcel[89] and forced the insurgents of La Margeride and La Truyère into retreat following the battles of Mont Mouchet and Chaudes-Aigues. The balance of forces remained such that, during these early days, the Resistance fighters suffered heavy losses as soon as they exposed themselves too much or ventured beyond the elementary tactics of guerrilla warfare.[90] Like it or no, they found themselves obliged to adapt to a situation that was all the more uncomfortable given that France was in the process of splitting asunder.

France split apart

On the eve of the Liberation, the fact is that *de facto* situations of different parts of France varied enormously.[91] There was the liberated and Gaullian France of the Normandy coast, the insurgent but peaceful France of the 'Mauriac Republic', the hunted France of the Vercors, the martyred France of the Dordogne and the Corrèze etc.

In lower Normandy, now transformed into a battlefield, from the very first days an enclave of liberated France that was to become quasi-Gaullian had dug itself in. The Anglo-Saxons had eventually decided[92] to admit de Gaulle to the secret of D-Day, but the political problem remained unchanged.[93] Eisenhower had entrusted the provisional administration of French liberated territories to Montgomery, just as if the provisional government of the French Republic did not exist. De Gaulle thereupon refused to endorse the proclamation that Eisenhower delivered to the peoples of occupied Europe. But he still had to, prove the authority of his own government.

On 14 June, at dawn, de Gaulle, after four years of exile and accompanied by a dozen or so companions, landed on the beach of Courseulles and launched himself into the conquest of liberated France. From a political point of view, it was not the best region: the Resistance there had had no more than a modest success, the great majority of the local notables being firmly pro-Vichy (the bishop of Bayeux was even taken to task for having a *Te Deum* sung), and besides, the population had suffered from the fighting. Nevertheless, Charles de Gaulle passed his first test.

Later he was to enjoy more ardent welcomes from the crowds, but the recognition that he received here was, on the whole, warm – rather more chilly in Bayeux but more enthusiastic in Isigny. Jean Lacouture put it well enough: 'The plebiscite has not been won, but choices have been made'.[94] The real token of public support was to come from Rennes on 4 August, even before it was consecrated by Paris. By the time he returned to Great Britain on 15 June and once the authorities for the new administration had been installed, he had already accomplished the hardest part of his task.

The Commissioner for the Republic, François Coulet, had no difficulty in deposing the pro-Vichy sub-prefect[95] and gaining recognition for the new power. This *de facto* legitimation persuaded the British to adopt – locally – a flexible and realistic attitude and made it possible to score a victory on the monetary battlefront.[96] The Gaullian State had got off to quite a good start.

There were other parts of the territory too that were, in fact, free, such as the 'republics' immediately proclaimed by the resistants who controlled the towns and regions that had been evacuated by the Germans. It was thus that the 'Mauriac Republic' was born: it lived out its short life, from June to August 1944, without great restriction under the indulgent rule of a Liberation Committee set up as early as 7 June.[97] Similarly, in quite a few departments, whole cantons were ruled by the administration of the *maquis* whose control was all the more effective for being discreet. The Resistance men were getting ready to step into the prefectures when the time came.

Meanwhile, there were other 'republics' whose fate was dramatic in a different way. The Vercors, for one, may be regarded as a symbol of the brutal and incoherent side of the pre-Liberation period. 4,000 men converged upon the Vercors in implementation of the 'Montagnard plan',[98] the application of which had been supported in the face of all developments. The commissioner designate of the Republic there, Yves Farge, had issued a solemn proclamation: 'People of the Vercors, on 3 July 1944 the French Republic has in effect been restored in the Vercors; from this day forward the decrees from Vichy are abolished and all the laws of the Republic are again in force.'[99] But all this was premature. The Germans, worried about the security of their lines of communication with Italy, were methodically closing the sluice-gates of the north-east and preparing for a seige. After increasingly desperate appeals,[100] the encircled resistants,[101] having received none of the support counted upon, were forced to give in: in less than three days – between 21 and 23 July – German elite troops gained control of the plateau. About 650 *maquisards* were killed and the civilian population then suffered an atrocious repression. By reason of the scale of this drama, the 'Vercors affair' immediately provoked extremely strong reactions and remains – to this day – a matter of controversy.[102] Contrary to what may have been written, Soustelle and his services did not deliberately allow the Vercors resistants to be crushed. On the contrary, they tried hard to find helpful expedients but the BCRA and the COMIDAC of Algiers had, at the very least, shown negligence if not culpable dereliction of duty in showing itself incapable of providing the aid formally promised. It was a high price to pay for a military strategy that was less and less well adapted to the situation.

Finally there was also, equally, a martyred France – the France, for instance, that found itself in the path of the 2nd SS Panzerdivision 'Das Reich'.[103] The mission of this division, having left its bases in Montauban and Bordeaux, was to make its way to Normandy, annihilating all the 'bands' on its way. On 8 June, one of its columns retook Tulle and passed on leaving 99 hostages hanged from the trees, balconies and lampposts;[104] on 10 June, one of its detachments shot or burned alive 642 villagers and refugees in Oradour-sur-Glane, 240 of whom were women and children.[105] Similar Nazi soldiery slaughtered 51 hostages in Mussidan in the Dordogne, opened fire in Gourdon, terrorised Argenton-sur-Creuse where they massacred 54 people, shooting at random on peasants in the fields, torturing and killing Jews and gypsies, looting and raping.

These developments were causing the greatest alarm among national leaders of the Resistance, which was without weapons and impotent. On 14 July, the general staff of the FFI was drawing up a disturbing record: 'In many regions we are almost completely uninformed as to not only the strength of the enemy forces but also the state of our own and even the operations they are undertaking.'[106] On 10 July, Bourgès-Manoury – the extremely active delegate for the southern zone – for his part, cabled to London as follows: 'All regions struggling in a desperate financial situation; have for the second time in a month given orders to rob a bank.'[107] Here and there 'Chinese warlords' of a kind set themselves up as little tyrant chiefs; and here and there veritable bands of kidnappers appeared, claiming ransoms in the name of the Resistance. Such break-away units were as yet no more than fringe phenomena but it was high time the situation was opened up.

The Resistance blasts its way out

During the first days of August the locks were blown: the French were not only about to be liberated, but also to liberate themselves. But let us make no mistake about it: it was only very rarely that the process of liberation took the form of a triumphal progress lined by young women tossing flowers to the men of the 2nd Armoured Division perched on their tanks. More often, the Liberation took the form of fluctuating advances and retreats on the part of German troops, the FFI and the Allied forces. Nevertheless, by the end of the month, more than half of the French people found themselves not only free but also, thanks to the combined efforts of the various Resistance groups, spared a civil war.

The Anglo-Saxon forces were wearing down and undermining the German troops, who were overwhelmed by the air and logistic superiority of the Allies. Once the Cotentin had been conquered, the Americans blasted their way through Avranches and opened a 30 kilometre breach which the Germans' last counter-attack, launched on 6 August, proved unable to repair. Having lost 8 divisions in an infernal 'cauldron' between Falaise and Argentan, the Germans beat a retreat on 17 August. Two days earlier, 325 men – two-thirds of them French – took part in 'Operation Anvil', landing without difficulty along the Provençal coast.

These breakthroughs unleashed a great general resurgence of energy and dispelled any remaining hesitations. A new, imperious call came from de Gaulle on 7 August: 'Your simple and sacred duty is to take part immediately in this supreme effort. Everyone can fight. Everyone must. Stand up, Frenchmen! Fight!' It was answered by a second wave of mobilisation, a response which clearly had a political impact. But, despite what has sometimes been said, it was not without military effectiveness as well. It is true that with no heavy weapons the Resistance men were not, on their own, capable of barring the way to the German troops when the latter were numerous and well deployed (the capitulation of the 'Elster' column, 20,000 men strong, near Issoudun, stands out as an exception). But Resistance fighters certainly did liberate whole departments: Cahors and Annecy fell to them like ripe fruit and, in Limoges, Guingouin was rewarded for four years of sacrifices. They were also able to scout for, support and even reinforce the Allied forces: thus, it was they who – with the exception of a few coastal pockets – liberated Brittany; in Marseilles, the insurrection set off by the FFI forced the hand of de Lattre and precious port installations fell intact into the hands of the insurgents and the Montsabert troops. There were surprise attacks and ambushes all over the place; roads were cut, reopened and cut again; villages were liberated, reoccupied, reliberated.

Those whom the Liberation vanquished and a number of other fine wits have – once it was all over – poked considerable fun at the 'Fifis', the 'Bourbaki army' of chocolate soldiers. There can be little doubt that they were indeed a ragged lot but it was not so much their incorrect and 'folksy' turn-out that these people resented, more the festival atmosphere, the popular rejoicing that surrounded them. For those who had survived and those who were twenty years old, the dancing of the Liberation, dancing that had been forbidden by Vichy and that erupted spontaneously, was dancing unlike any other dancing had ever been.[108]

For the most part, it was only once the Liberation was already won that the resistance fighters of the eleventh hour arrived to swell the numbers of FFI, which suddenly found their ranks swollen by braggarts of every kind, waverers who had suddenly made up their minds, opportunists trying to get themselves into a favourable position, a number of shady characters with an eye to the main chance and – in greater numbers than is generally believed – Vichy men, even confirmed collaborationists, who were all the more inclined to boast of their courageous exploits given that they had memories of a doubtful past to cover up. The rallying of the notables was more discreet but certainly had greater effect. Jacques Bounin, honorary Commissioner for the Republic, who knew what he was talking about, describes Montpellier in 1944: 'The notables had been two years in coming ... that's all!, but now they were present too'.[109] Charles d'Aragon, president of the CDL of the Tarn, was now receiving many visits such as that of a sub-prefect – very much a supporter of the national revolution – who made no bones about declaring 'I want to become a prefect'; or that of a commissioner of police who had a very 'daunting' reputation and who had just rushed to join the Ajax network: 'The network, which was composed mainly of policemen, played a very useful role at the end of the Occupation; a number of civil servants with rather murky pasts can also be grateful to it for having made it possible for them to reacquire an easy conscience at no great cost.'[110]

Some had no wish, or no chance, to shift rifles from one shoulder to the other at the last moment. For some weeks it was not healthy to be classed as a 'Kollabo' whether what one had been – effectively or not – was a collaborator or a committed Maréchaliste. With feelings running high, a purge was taking place: men were arrested, molested, and some were executed. Women had their heads shaved or were paraded naked.[111] In the next volume this series, Jean-Pierre Rioux analyses the political bases and consequences of such behaviour. Let us limit ourselves at this point to giving some idea of its scope: the repression carried out by Resistance members – from the earliest days to the post-Liberation period – claimed about 10,000 victims.[112]

Nevertheless, the Liberation did not lead to civil war and the effects of Resistance groups working together were reunificatory rather than divisive. In the end, the power vacuum turned out to be of short duration. All the same, in many towns the Resistance men were not inclined to restore the State as such: they were not interested in the prospect of a State of just any kind, controlled by notables of just any kind. Charles de Gaulle was going to have to come to an understanding with them on this matter.

The occupying power, together with its mercenaries, in general exacted a high price for the insurrection. The German army,[113] retreating but in good order, fell fiercely upon the insurgents, leaving charnel-houses behind them.[114] In the Vercors, which had been retaken and combed, systematic repression clamped down between 28 July and 3 August, taking its toll of civilians as well as of Maquisards on the run.[115] It was horrific.[116] 201 civilians were massacred – 82 of them at Vassieux where nothing was left but the corpses of children with battered-in skulls, disembowelled women and emasculated old men. In Maillé, near Sainte-Maure in the Indre-et-Loire, on 25 August, 124 totally inoffensive villagers were shot like rabbits.[117] In the Loiret, a typical enough department, 82 people died in the fighting while 305 were shot by firing squads, 732 individuals were deported (617 men, 94 women and 21 children, 405 of whom were never seen again). And all Jews and Resistance members already in prison were systematically massacred.[118]

To carry out these operations, the occupying power used henchmen and others of their ilk among the Militia and the paramilitary groups set up within the collaborationist movements. These neo-extremists, whose entire energies were devoted to an exclusively Franco-French war, were out to settle political scores: they executed Jean Zay and Georges Mandel,[119] murdered notables reputed to be luke-warm[120] and set themselves up as torturers of the most appalling kind. The Militia was using torture in Lyons, Limoges, Bordeaux, Bourges, even Vichy. In Montpellier, which suffered under the prefect Rebouleau, a member of the Militia, Resistance men went through agony that defies description.[121] These executioners no doubt included a number of '*Lacombe, Lucien*'[122] figures, young men caught up, despite themselves, in the machinery of death. But the leaders, those with higher authority, were coldly settling the scores of a civil war carefully nursed ever since 1934: such were Filliol, a royalist and Cagoule member, Lecusson, also a Cagoule member and a frenetic anti-semite, and Dagostini, ejected from the LVF for 'cruelty'. The opinion expressed by the adjutant general secretary of the Militia, Francis Bout de l'An, is worth reflecting upon: 'The responsibility for the murders of J. Zay and G. Mandel should be laid at the doors of the leaders, not those who carried them out'.[123] The killing bound such men irretrievably to Nazi Germany;[124] Darnand's personal private secretary, Max Knipping, concluded the telegram he sent to Bout de l'An as follows: 'Not to have taken action in yesterday's affair (the assassination of Georges Mandel) would have resulted in our entirely losing the confidence of the SS.'[125] Now, all they could stand for was German France.

German France

Let us at this point briefly interrupt our chronological account to follow the final throes of collaboration all the way to Germany.[126] It was, from every point of view, a pathetic escapade.

Both Laval and Pétain clung to the last to the idea that they would be used as the indispensable mediators. Favouring an ambiguous wait-and-see attitude[127] and unequivocal anti-communism, they were hoping to turn to their advantage both the internal dissensions with the Reich, revealed by the failed assassination attempt against Hitler of 20 July, and also the divisions between the Allies. However, this theoretical strategy could hardly impinge upon reality now.

Laval was successful in carrying through only one operation: namely, containing the political offensive started by extremists who on 5 July published a 'Common Declaration of Political Orientation', signed by the cream of the collaborationists and by four ministers. But he was less and less in control of the situation. The French State was being washed away or was fading away, and the last big manoeuvres were doomed to failure. *Maréchaliste* emissaries sounded out the Abwehr in Nice, the Americans in Madrid, the Commissioner designate for the Republic in the Auvergne,[128] but all these advances met with failure. Auphan, to whom Pétain had given full powers as his 'representative to the Anglo-Saxon military command' and 'if the circumstances presented themselves' to make contact with General de Gaulle to find a 'solution of a kind to prevent civil war', was shown the door by the head of the provisional government all the more firmly in view of the fact that, right to the last, the French State had refused to encourage the struggle against the occupying power. Laval, for his part, had thrown himself into even more complicated deals. What he was after was a 'parliamentary solution'; he entered into many consultations in Paris, convincing himself that he would be able to call together both Chambers, and told Monzie that he did not rule out – in the medium term – seeing Queuille at the Elysée and Herriot in the Matignon; meanwhile he needed the latter to assemble the deputies. The most extraordinary aspect of the affair is that he was successful in persuading Abetz to release Herriot from the house-arrest under which he had been kept since July 1943. He then proceeded to install him at the Hôtel de Ville, assigning to him a role that was, to say the least, ambiguous.

Berlin brought this game of illusory politics to an end. Laval barely managed to hold a last Council of Ministers – with four members only – before he was summoned, on 17 August, to Belfort. Three days later, Pétain, under constraint and duress (the Germans had had to break down the door of the Hôtel de Parc) was also obliged to journey east. Although neither resigned ('I am and I remain your leader', Pétain declared on 20 August), they both embarked upon a strike, refusing to exercise their functions. In all logic, it was the only thing left for them to do.

By 7 September, they were transferred to the Sigmaringen castle perched up in the Swabian Jura. The Reich, which was determined to preserve the fiction of a free French State to the very last, on 1 October charged Fernand de Brinon with the task of setting up a 'governmental delegation' at Sigmaringen, 'the provisional seat' of the French State, making the most of the privilege of extra-territoriality and flanked, for good measure, by a German Embassy.[129] But the Nazi leaders soon set up, alongside this 'community reduced to gossiping' (A. Laubreaux), a 'Committee for

French Liberation' which had much more clout and which Doriot, finally, was promoted to head.[130] The Third Reich, which was demanding a *Volkssturm* (a mass rising) was using everything it could lay hands upon and insisting that all those who had come to Germany should be used in the most profitable way: those incapable of armed service had to work in factories, the rest – in principle, volunteers – were drafted into the Waffen-SS: these comprised survivors from the LVF, French Waffen-SS, Militia *franc-gardes*, etc. They were assembled in the Wildflecken camp and formed into a 'Charlemagne division', 7,500 men strong: on 12 November 1944, they swore allegiance to Hitler and were soon after in German uniform.[131]

Meanwhile, the Reich was collapsing. Pétain was playing a disillusioned hermit's game in a castle divided between 'active ministers' and 'sleeping ministers'. Laval, placed under house-arrest, was putting together some justificatory *mémoires*. Doriot never made it as the consecrated French Führer: on 22 February 1945, just as he was about to receive the endorsement of all the collaboration notables, his car was machine-gunned by two passing aircraft – probably German.[132] Three days later, the 'Charlemagne division' was crushed at Hammerstein in Pomerania losing, at the lowest estimate, 3,000 men. The remainder disappeared at Körlin or in the Belgard plain.[133]

In response to somebody who was singing the praises of the decimated Charlemagne division, Hitler had snapped: 'Those people are useless'.[134] It was a fitting last requiem for the collaboration. Those still in a position to do so now tried, by any means available, to escape the day of reckoning.

Insurgent Paris

'Paris! Paris violated! Paris broken! Paris martyred! But also Paris liberated! Liberated by itself! Liberated by its own people with the aid of the armies of France, with the support and aid of the whole of France, of fighting France, of the only France, the true France, eternal France ... France is coming back, coming home to Paris ...'[135] The date was 25 August, the place the Hôtel de Ville: there, de Gaulle found the right words to pay homage to the Parisian insurgents. The liberation of the capital[136] had, in fact, been carried out in an exemplary fashion. The establishment of a Gaullian State was looming on the horizon.

An insurrection that was not programmed

As we know, American strategy aimed to destroy the bulk of the enemy, not to take towns at all costs. General Eisenhower was all the more resolved to bypass Paris to the north and to the south since he was alarmed at the prospect of having to conquer it *quartier* by *quartier* and, besides, he did not think he had the means to supply it with food. Furthermore, he would then be able to put off until later the thorny problem posed by the establishment in the capital of the head of a provisional government to whom the United States refused legal recognition. The Anglo-Saxons reckoned that, once surrounded in the Parisian pocket, the German troops would end up by surrendering after two or three weeks.

The German general staff, for its part, was trying to stabilise the breakthrough in the Normandy front. Hitler's view was that the Parisian region should be a bastion to be held at all costs so that the retreating troops could be regrouped in good order. For this purpose, the command of *Gross-Paris* had at its disposal a hundred or more tanks and around 17,000 men. General Dietrich von Chiltitz had just been promoted to lead them. He had in the past been successful in cowing Sebastopol and had been involved in the plot of 20 July. Nevertheless, the Führer was under-estimating the effects of the failed assassination attempt upon the army of the occupation.

The Resistance men were faced with choices the consequences of which were all the more grave given that Paris was the seat of the institutional Resistance. While the principle of an insurrection was almost unanimously accepted, there was disagreement regarding both its ends and its means. There were some – the militant communists, the organisers of the National Front and also quite a few non-communists – who were pressing for pre-emptive action (with the help of parachute drops of weapons, the capital could be liberated before the Anglo-Saxon troops arrived), tough action (Paris was under no circumstances to provide a 'sanctuary' for the German troops) – action the decisive instrument of which would be popular guerrilla warfare. They controlled the military inter-connections, the COMAC, many of the FFI leaders in 'P' region, which was under the command of the communist *Rol*-Tanguy, and they were also influential both in the Parisian liberation committee and in the CNR Bureau. There were others, however, who aimed to apply a brake to the insurrection and set it off only in close liaison with the Allies, since the 20,000 mobilisable FFI were likely to have between them at most 2,000 rifles. Others still were fearful of a Paris of barricades and the emergence of a Commune controlled by the communists. However, nobody wanted to split the Resistance, and personalities who carried some weight, such as Georges Bidault and Alexandre Parodi, whom de Gaulle on 14 August appointed to be minister-delegate for the territories not yet liberated, were quite determined to prevent political breakaways, to the last.

Besides, after the breakthrough on the Normandy Front, the Resistance found itself united and ready to start the insurrection. As early as 18 August, the FTP, the general staff of the FFI, the elected communists and the trade-unionists of the Union Parisienne took the initiative and called for a general mobilisation[137] just a few hours before the unanimous CNR

Bureau announced: 'It is not possible for us to stand by as spectators of the victory. We have emerged from too great a trial, too grievous a betrayal for our hearts, too, not to be committed to performing our task at the hour appointed by History.'[138] During the afternoon of the 19th, the minister-delegate of the GPRF signed a decree mobilising all men aged between eighteen and fifty-five. The most pressing priorities of the internal Resistance had thus expressed themselves in pre-emptive action.

The American command, which was fairly well informed about what was happening in the capital, had been both irritated by this non-scheduled insurrection and also agreeably surprised by the relatively weak German riposte to it. The intelligence brought by Gallois-*Cocteau*, whom *Rol*-Tanguy had despatched across the German lines to ask for parachute drops of supplies, removed Eisenhower's hesitation: both politically and military, it was necessary to march on the capital. On 22 August, the supreme commander took it upon himself to launch upon Paris the only sizeable French unit to have landed in Normandy, the 2nd Armoured Division, 15,000 men strong and with 200 tanks. The 'Leclerc' men were to act as the necessary military link.

Seven eventful days

Since the landings, the Parisian Resistance had been biding its time. It had mounted punitive expeditions against collaborationists: Darnand escaped it, but a *corps franc* assassinated Henriot on 28 June.[139] In the suburbs and popular quarters it had organised demonstrations to culminate on 14 July. The public sector had become increasingly turbulent: on 10 August, the vast majority of railway workers in the Parisian region responded to the order of the day: 'Strike, to push the Boche back.' The post office workers were to follow suit ... it looked as if it was leading up to a general strike. One sign of the times was that virtually the whole force of the 20,000 *gardiens de la paix* in the prefecture of police went on strike on 15 August in protest against the disarmament by the Germans of the Saint-Denis police. On 19 August, the Resistance gave the order for mobilisation.

Between 19 and 22 August, the insurrection was feeling its way. Initially, the advantage of surprise played in favour of the FFI, and they laid their hands on a fair quantity of weapons. Meanwhile, resistant policemen were taking over the prefecture of police, resistants were in control of the Hôtel de Ville and occupying town halls, and provisional secretary generals were taking over the ministries. These successes – important from a political point of view – might well have turned into military traps had the German counter-attacks been sufficiently energetic, for clearly, in a pitched battle the insurgents would always have the worst of it.

That was why the idea of a truce was launched, on the initiative – apparently – of the prefecture of police, which was insurgent but vulnerable. Following negotiations between Nordling, the Consul General of Sweden, members of Choltitz's entourage and leaders of the Resistance, the truce was provisionally extended: it provided for a kind of territorial partition which left the German troops a number of retreat routes. In the eyes of some members of the Resistance this represented a semi-victory, taking into account the balance of forces and the uncertainty surrounding the immediate intentions of the Allies. Others saw it as a semi-betrayal grafted onto a strategy that had been disastrous in every respect for 'it was not a matter of holding on to public buildings but rather of spreading guerrilla warfare everywhere, in Paris and everywhere else too' (Villon).[140] The truce was approved by the CNR Bureau but, for the first time ever, only by a majority vote, not unanimously. To add to the confusion, on that same day, 20 August, Parodi was arrested, brought before Choltitz, to whom he presented himself as the head of the insurrection, the principles of which he firmly defended. And then, finally, he was released.

Two days later, the insurrection was relaunched. The truce had, anyway, been only partially respected. Certain German detachments – the SS in particular – had deliberately violated it. For the insurgents' part, it had been respected in a number of *quartiers* – to the relief, apparently, of at least some of the 'civilian' population. In others, however, it had been ignored. Then, on Monday 21 August, following a tense and bitter session in which a split was only narrowly avoided, the membership of the CNR in plenary session, that of COMAC, Parodi and Chaban-Delmas decided, first with a small majority, then unanimously, to break the truce.[141] On 22 August 1944, Paris was covered in barricades and insurrection flared up again in the streets. This new flashpoint appears to have taken the Germans by surprise. They were, in any case, venturing less and less out of their hiding places. They were regarded with much less fear now but, lacking heavy weaponry, the FFI were not in a position to overrun the dozen or so strongholds that were still firmly in German hands.

The 'Leclerc' forces were to bring the necessary fire-power. The 2nd Armoured Division had advanced 240 kilometres in less than forty hours and were trying to infiltrate between the pockets of German troops in the suburbs. On the evening of the 24th, three tanks and a few dozen men reached the Hôtel de Ville. On Friday the 25th, Paris had reason to believe itself liberated: the FFI and men of the 2nd Armoured Division were crushing isolated pockets of German resistance in fighting that was sometimes violent. Meanwhile, Choltitz had decided to capitulate: after a show of civility, he was made prisoner in the Hôtel Meurice and then went to the prefecture of police where he and Leclerc signed an 'agreement of surrender'. The time was 15.30. One hour later, he made out an order of surrender in Leclerc's headquarters set up in the Gare Montparnasse. In the meantime, *Rol*-Tanguy had persuaded Leclerc that the 'agreement of surrender' should be modified and that his own signature be added.

The apotheosis was to take place the following day, but there were some blunders. It began, as is well known, with a triumphal progress down the Champs-Elysées in the midst of happy crowds: first came some tanks, then a mixed company of motor-cyclists, an usher wearing insignia, de Gaulle with Leclerc, Bidault, Parodi, and various other personalities amid a great show of popular enthusiasm.[142] The arrival of the personalities of note at Notre-Dame set off a violent spate of gunfire.[143] Inside the cathedral, bereft of its archbishop and plunged in darkness owing to an electricity failure, instead of the planned *Te Deum* a *Magnificat* was sung, fervently no doubt but somewhat perfunctorily, against the din of another burst of firing. That evening the capital went to sleep sated with glory and drunk with relief. Just before midnight it suffered an air raid which claimed 50 or more dead and 400 wounded. Throughout the night, the men of the 2nd Armoured Division were fighting back German reinforcements who engaged serious battle with them the next day at Le Bourget. The war was not over yet.

Barricades and convergencies

Paris did not suffer the fate of Stalingrad nor yet that of Warsaw: the capital was not put to fire and the sword and the fighting never even disrupted the queues of housewives outside the bakeries.[144] Like everywhere else, the capital had its share of those who showed indifference or scepticism, its busybodies who spread alarm over the telephone and its many eleventh hour members of the FFI.

However, the strongest image is that of an insurgent Paris; the insurgents – to a large extent – rediscovered an identity with their revolutionary ancestors: many of them were pinned down in their native *quartiers* behind barricades that, in many cases, they defended with whatever came to hand.[145] The battle for Paris was first and foremost a complex of juxtaposed local situations controlled more or less efficiently by the institutional Resistance. But it was not lightweight warfare. Not only did the insurgents in Paris, like those elsewhere, suffer German reprisals[146] but, ill-equipped and inadequately armed as they were, their casualties were relatively heavy: some 3,000 killed and 7,000 wounded among the FFI and the 'civilian population'.[147]

Yet in this Paris of barricades, all parties worked together in the orderly manner so much desired by the Resistance: the efforts of the popular insurrection now joined with those of the external forces.[148] Indeed that amalgamation was so rapid that during the attack upon the Luxemburg Palace, the FFI and Leclerc together found themselves under the command of *Fabien* of the FTP. It was this cooperation – quite exemplary from every point of view – that 'saved' Paris. Although the activities of some intermediaries who were effective – Nordling,[149] for example – should not be underestimated, considerable circumspection seems called for when it comes to self-styled 'saviours' who (after the event) appeared to be extremely thick on the ground.[150] Chiltitz himself put on quite a show for posterity, although he appears at the time to have been simply living from day to day. Taken by surprise by the outbreak of the insurrection, he could have crushed it before it ever got going, on the 19th, but he appears to have both underestimated and overestimated the Resistance forces; by a few days later his room for manoeuvre had been considerably reduced. Having failed to apply to the letter Hitler's apocalyptic orders ('Either Paris must not fall into the hands of the enemy or the enemy must find it a heap of ruins'), he chose to surrender to regular troops.[151]

Within insurgent Paris, the institutional Resistance also managed to sidestep drama. It is true that a split was only narrowly avoided at the moment when the National Front realised that the truce[152] was not only a military error but also evidence of 'the fear inspired by the idea of a patriotic Paris taking its own destiny in hand'.[153] On 21 August, when, in the name of that Paris, Villon was threatening to post up an appeal to 'the people of Paris', denouncing the truce as a 'manoeuvre of the enemy', Parodi judged that it betokened 'total breakdown'. To avoid this, the session had to be suspended and considerable finesse deployed.[154] Did the truce win three precious days or did it all but undermine the insurrection? That is still a matter of controversy. At all events, through it two ways of feeling, if not two political attitudes, were brought into confrontation.

The fact remains that, despite everything, right up to the end and including the Liberation period, the will to maintain unity had eventually prevailed: nobody wanted a split or to see a rift developing between one part of the Resistance and certain groups among the fighting insurgents. Although many people were nursing their own particular political plans, nobody strictly speaking attempted to seize power. If the communists had really had the designs with which they are credited, it is hard to see why they did not gain control of the Hôtel de Ville or of many town halls. And, after all, Parodi displayed no hesitation at all in placing all the insurgent forces under the command of *Rol*-Tanguy.

Charles de Gaulle strides on

Since winning over the liberated portion of Normandy, de Gaulle had not been wasting his time. In early July, he had travelled to the United States[155] – where he had enjoyed an undeniable *succès d'estime*. His conversations with Roosevelt were sealed by a positive result: five weeks later the American administration abandoned its AMGOT project.

In mid-August, accompanied only by Le Troquer, his Minister for the Liberated Territories, he left North Africa for Brittany where he was treated to a very warm welcome. But what he was keeping his eye on was Paris, the seat of the State, particularly as he suspected that behind Laval's manoeuvres, American intrigue was at work, which he found most alarming. He gave his approval to the Parisian insurrection although, according to his *Mémoires de guerre*,[156] the truce made 'an unpleasant impression' upon him; nevertheless, he in no way underestimated the attendant risks of 'anarchy' which would irremediably have compromised the necessary restoration of the State. It was with undisguised relief that he learned of the advance of the 2nd Armoured Division, having already warned Eisenhower against 'the situation of disorder that might develop in the capital'.[157]

In the Gaullian canon of high deeds and symbolism, the day of 25 August must rate as one of its high spots: it had just about everything going for it. In the uniform of Brigadier-General, de Gaulle first stopped by at the Montparnasse station where he reprimanded Leclerc for having given in to *Rol*-Tanguy; he then 'went home' to the Ministry of War: France was, after all, at war and it was, after all, there that in June 1940 he had been carrying out his military functions. In his own words: '. . . not a piece of furniture, not a wall-hanging, not a curtain has been moved . . . Nothing is lacking except the State. My task is to replace it. That is why the first thing I did was install myself there'.[158] He was all the more inclined to linger there given that he had already made a decision – whatever he may have said later on – not to go on that day to the Hôtel de Ville where the CNR was resolutely awaiting him. Parodi and Luizet, the new prefect of police, managed to persuade him to make a gesture in the direction of the insurrectional rituals. So, not without a preliminary detour by way of the prefecture of police, he did after all pay his visit to the cradle of Parisian revolution. Once there, he was won over by the emotion of the occasion and paid insurgent Paris one of the finest pieces of homage it was to receive. He acknowledged and saluted the people who would make him king. Throughout his harangue, however, he never once mentioned the CNR and, with an acute sense of politics, he curtly refused to comply with Georges Bidault's pressing advice: he would not proclaim the Fourth Republic from the balcony of the Hôtel de Ville. 'No,' he said, 'the Republic has never ceased to exist.'[159] He did not intend to indulge in any Lamartinian sentiment nor to play the role of any sorcerer's apprentice in the mode of 4 September 1870, when the Republic was proclaimed under difficult yet moving circumstances.

But for his progress down the Champs-Elysées the following day, he preferred the jostling, popular crowds to a military parade. Popular legitimation – one of the keystones of Gaullian Gaullism – consecrated the original legitimacy, that of 1940, and entirely transformed his functions as head of the provisional government. Now he could strike while the iron was hot. To the members of the CNR and the leaders of the FFI whom he received, he made more or less the same declaration: 'Thanks to you, France will have a more glorious place in the world. Now hard work is needed, everything must once again be set in order . . .'[160]

Was the restoration already under way?

Conclusion. The exceptional or the normal?

In this volume, I have deliberately limited my efforts to setting out the facts. The method will perhaps be reckoned too 'positivist' and the account too 'circumstantial'. In my own view, however, it seemed correct to try to set in order a body of data much of which was in a disparate, unverified state. However, it would certainly be pretentious to claim that this analysis is exhaustive. For one thing, not all the archive documents relating to our study are accessible; for another, no study of a society at a particular period can be complete for the very reason that the curiosity about the past of successive generations invariably focusses upon a different set of questions.

Meanwhile, is it possible to superimpose a set of analyses in such a way as to yield a global explanation for the apparent chaos of these black years? In my opinion, there is to date no such explanation which can make sense of these war years that are full of so many contradictions.

What we are left with is a series of partial approaches – towards, for instance, the class struggle which the PCF regards as the alpha and omega of the entire situation. There can be no doubt that it did represent an important factor: we have stated repeatedly that it is impossible to understand the choices made by many men of Vichy without taking into account the political and social pressures; and it seems to us that, in the summer of 1944, a clear dividing line can be drawn between those notables who were determined to cling to their privileges, and the rest. But the fact remains that the Militia and paramilitary organisations set up by the collaborationist movements did recruit from popular milieux; also that the Resistance, for its part, throughout its history put down its roots in *all* the social classes and that the socio-professional distribution of its militants corresponds – broadly speaking – with that of the French population as a whole.[1] Furthermore, at the time, the PCF was so conscious of these facts that – except for the period between the autumn of 1939 and the spring of 1941, when talk of class against class was again to be heard – the communists consistently gave priority to a Jacobin line, more 'republican' than 'revolutionary' and based upon a 'National Front' that was open to all forces and social classes.[2] It was this unificatory policy that won 'the party of the

75,000 who were shot'[3] its position as one of the foremost political forces in France.

All in all, that same Jacobin reflex – detectable ever since the Revolution in every war in which the French have been involved – was the one that counted for most. I used the word 'Jacobin' advisedly, for the nationalists' version of nationalism proved a bankrupt one when it came to facing the ordeal. No doubt a small minority of right-wing nationalists joined the Resistance out of nationalist loyalty; but most of the dyed-in-the-wool nationalists for their part preferred – and how! – to fight a 'Franco-French war'[4] rather than one against the external enemy. At the end of his trial, Maurras exclaimed, 'It's Dreyfus' revenge!'. His words were an expression of the way in which the reactionary or 'revolutionary' right has forever exploited patriotism as a weapon for civil and social warfare.[5] But after 1945 it was at least no longer possible for Maurras' point of view to make a come-back after all its contradictions and bankruptcy.

But even if the Jacobin motivation was there, it operated only imperfectly. It would appear that the great majority of the French people had needed a more or less lengthy period to allow things to settle, to rise above and absorb the shocks of the thirties, the rise and fall of the Popular Front, the conclusion of the German–Soviet pact, the confusions, silences and retractions of all the political, social and cultural elites. It had certainly been a period fraught with complications, as can be judged from the following passage of dialogue which – in normal times – might have been written off as substandard Corneille. The interlocutors were Henri Frenay and his mother, herself the wife of an officer. She said: 'You are about to do harm to our country and you will make a thorough job of it, as you do of everything. So you cannot honestly believe that I am going to hold my tongue and let you do it! . . . I love you dearly, you know I do, my children are my life . . . but over and above a mother's love, there is one's country. I will go and denounce you to the police, to stop you from acting wrongly . . .' Frenay's reply was as follows: '. . . I respect your conscience; you must respect what mine tells me to do. If, however, you do as you have said, don't bother to call me to your death-bed for I shan't come.'[6]

There was thus a great need for political courage but also for lucidity, and that meant not confusing the order of one's priorities and not giving in to the temptation of settling old scores.

The difficulties that were experienced by people at the time are reflected in the complex feelings of French people forty years on: a mixture of secrecy, reserve (the genuine Resistance fighters were not an expansive lot) and lingering fascination (witness the success enjoyed by so many television programmes, books and films about the period).

Equally significant is the interpretation the politicians have tried to impose. We must clearly put aside those who took their places amid the ranks of the conquered and for whom history was over by 1944.[7] Close to them are the 'revisionists', those who survived the purges and thereafter exploited the cold war, still obstinately seeking, through a rehabilitation of the Maréchal, to provide a full justification for Vichy and State collaboration.[8] To date, such a political satisfaction has been denied them. What is more interesting in the context of this study is the view of those years that both the communists and the Gaullists have provided: a view of France rapidly overcoming temporary hesitations and – apart from a handful of 'collabos' and a minority of misled Vichy men – uniting, in the interests of the Liberation, around the working class and (according to the former) the party that represented its vanguard or (according to the latter) the man of 18 June. It is that kind of convenient but simplified interpretation that the film *Le chagrin et la pitié* tried to debunk, doing a good scouring job on the Gaullian myth and representing the French people in a less simplified and on the whole much less heroic manner.[9]

It should be added that, especially in deepest, provincial France, it is sometimes impossible to get through meals in a convivial spirit once the conversation turns to Pétain or the Resistance. That is not altogether surprising since – as I have pointed out – the choices that had to be made were first and foremost political ones[10] and, all things considered, the coherence and consistency of people's behaviour wins out over their diversity. It is worth stressing, yet again, the internal logic of the political road travelled by the majority of the French people from the time of the phoney peace up to the Liberation. But we should, at the same time, stop wondering at the fact that many of them quite rapidly chose to take refuge in a prudent wait-and-see attitude: they were accustomed to the guardianship provided by a governed democracy and to a society that had for generations been dominated by the notables, so there was no reason why they should suddenly have been transformed into political heroes. Nor should it be supposed that the crisis in the representative system can be accounted for solely by a catalogue of constitutional measures. The truth is that, as in 1958, the regime collapsed less as a result of an institutional bankruptcy and the attacks of its opponents than from the politicians themselves resigning from their responsibilities and an absence of champions willing to defend it.

By emphasising a continuity of evolution rather than a break, one perhaps lays oneself open to the charge of denying any originality to the Resistance. But the fact is that its record is not one that can be seen in terms of black and white. It was one of the first wars of liberation[11] of the twentieth century yet neither the military nor the politicians learned very much from it, as is shown by the convulsions of the decolonisation that followed. It is perhaps on a political level that its originality is most striking: through it, Christian Democracy emerged, the PCF became firmly rooted and Gaullian Gaullism acquired legitimacy. But it was not long before the 'spirit of the Resistance' was finding it hard to get its second wind. As we have seen, the movements which had had to step in to replace failing political party structures had already been constrained, like it or not, to admit to the reappearance of the 'old' political parties and make some room for them. It would not be long before they would have to give way to them altogether: within two years it was all up with the hope that many non-communist Resistance leaders had been nursing, namely that it would be they who would effect a political take-over. These Resistance men felt that the 'mystique' had been degraded into 'politics', to use the well-known distinction made by Péguy. And while the possession of the stamped card of a member of the Resistance helped a few people along the road to a fine career – particularly during the sixties – it must also be said that the generation that committed itself so deeply during the forties was, on the whole, sacrificed rather than 'rewarded'. The cold war was a determining factor in the way that the situation developed.[12] But it should also be recognised that some Resistance members were naïve enough to believe that the French people were ready for absolutely anything in 1945. Besides, how many of those who were so opposed to the parties had the talents to strike out away from the beaten track? In that respect, May 1968 was to be much more imaginative. By the time those four war years were over, the parliamentary panorama had changed considerably but as for the political system, that remained intact.

However, when all is said and done, these men and women of the shadows, of Free France, shared in common the feeling that tomorrow would be different and a time for singing. It is to salute their lucid commitment to the implications of what for most of them was a 'mystique' that this author now proposes to lay aside his deliberately aloof manner and end this volume with two quotations in homage to the militants, the leaders, the anonymous Resistance fighters and the dead. The first comes from the commentary on *Le chagrin et la pitié* by a Harvard historian of politics who, as an adolescent, lived through those dark years in France. His name is Stanley Hoffmann; he was an Austrian Jew:

> In Max Ophuls' film, Verdier and the two almost senile professors provide a disturbing, almost overwhelming contrast to the Grave brothers, Gaspard and Mendès. In my own memory, the professor, now seventy-three years of age and as energetic as ever, who taught me French history, gave me hope in the blackest days, dried my tears when my best friend and his mother were deported, made false papers for my mother and myself so that we could escape from a city infested by the Gestapo, where the complicity of friends and neighbours could no longer provide sufficient protection – that man obliterates all the bad moments, the humiliations and the terrors. He and his gentle wife were not heroes of the Resistance, but if there exists such a thing as the average Frenchman, it is that man who represented his people ...'[13]

The second text comes from a letter written by Jacques Bingen on 14 April 1944, just a few days before he 'fell' and swallowed his cyanide pill: 'On a *moral level*, I should like my mother, my sister, my nephews, my niece – who knows it already and will be my witness – and my dearest friends, both *men and women*, to be assured of how *prodigiously happy* I have been during the past eight months . . .'[14]

Notes

The number in brackets refers to the bibliography at the end of this volume. The place of publication of other works cited in the notes is, unless otherwise indicated, Paris.

Foreword

1 See (115), p. 409.

1 A phoney peace, a phoney war

1 The historiography of this immediately pre-war period has been quite revolutionised by the work of the colloquium of December 1975, organised by the Fondation Nationale des Sciences Politiques on 'France under the Daladier government'. Its proceedings have been published in two volumes (10); for the strictly parliamentary history, see also E. Bonnefous (13).
2 See, in the first instance, (4); then (120). See also (15).
3 See (20), vol. III, pp. 77–119; see also Prost's thesis (21).
4 Revolutionary defeatism was nevertheless advocated by the Marceau Pivert group. See (121); R. Gombin, *Les Socialistes et la guerre*, Mouton, 1970; and N. Greene, *Crisis and decline, the French Socialist Party in the Popular Front*, Ithaca, Cornell University Press, 1969. See also J.-P. Rioux, *Révolutionnaires du Front populaire*, 10/18, 1973.
5 See the analysis by R. Rémond (16); and the proceedings of the congress held at Strasbourg (11); see also (22).
6 On the Munich crisis, see (23).
7 Let us briefly recall the principal phases in the Czech crisis: it erupted at the beginning of September when Henlein, on the advice of Hitler, rejected the fourth 'statute concerning nationality' proposed by the Prague government and insisted that the Sudeten Germans – who found themselves in a 'state of legitimate defence' – should have the right to decide on their own fate. Tension was running so high that, on 15 September, Chamberlain flew to meet Hitler at Berchtesgaden. The crisis was now definitely engaged: Chamberlain's first capitulation was to accept that the 'mixed territories' should be attached to the Reich and he forced the hand of the French. Paris and London put pressure upon Prague to consent. But at Godesberg, on 23 September, Hitler produced new demands of a kind to bring about the effective dismantling of the Czechoslovak State. Negotiations were now broken off and between 23 and 28 September tension continued to mount. Paris called up some of its reservists 'to cover emergencies', the Home Fleet was put on a state of alert and meanwhile Berlin

delivered an ultimatum to expire on the 28th. It was at this point that the British government, exploring every possible alternative, seized upon a proposal put forward by Mussolini to organise a four-power conference – with neither a Czech nor a Soviet presence. At a meeting in Munich on 29 September, Hitler, Mussolini, Chamberlain and Daladier – 'the pork-butchers' club' – amended an Italian proposal in record time and during the night signed a protocol of agreement together with annexed clauses. On this series of developments, see H. Noguères, *Munich ou la drôle de paix*, Laffont, 1963.

8 Some have sought to lay the blame on the Czechs and Soviets. In Prague – as everywhere else – there were those who supported compromise at any price and it is not too hard to understand the moves made by the president of the Agrarian Party, Hodja, with respect to the French government during the night of 20 September – extraordinary though they were, to put it mildly. All the same, there can be little doubt that the vast majority of Czechs were preparing to resist. Stalin has been criticised sometimes for military bluffing since he knew – given that Poland and Romania were situated in between – that he would be incapable of coming to the aid of Prague, sometimes for having simply set up a first class funeral by proposing recourse to the League of Nations. The Soviets refrained from forcing the hand of Beneš (who was not in favour of such a move) but they advocated a 'conference' with French and Czechoslovak representatives and on 25 September gave Gamelin precise indications as to the military support that they could offer.

9 See the study by R. Girault (10), vol. 1, pp. 209–27.

10 His own exposition of his position, which is subtle but unconvincing, may be found in *Dans la tourmente, 1933–34*, Fayard, 1971. It is important to note that in French business circles – some of which had considerable interests in Bohemia – there appears to have been much more disagreement as to the advisability of the policy of appeasement than in Great Britain. See (103) and J.-N. Jeanneney, *François de Wendel en République. L'argent et le pouvoir, 1914–1940*, Ed. du Seuil, 1976.

11 The general staff exerted less influence here than has been generally suggested. General Gamelin was moderately optimistic throughout the crisis.

12 It is hard to conceive the animosity of this extremist press and the climate of civil strife that it fostered. *L'Action Française* – and it was not alone – insisted, bitingly, that the 'official Foreign Office declaration' of 26 September, which promised British support in the event of France being attacked, was a forgery perpetrated by the war party. On the day of the Munich declaration, the same daily newspaper called for bullets for 'Mandel, Blum and Reynaud', setting the words to the tune of the 'International'. A few months later, in March 1939, in *Je Suis Partout*, Brasillach wrote: 'But the cold dawn when Blum is taken to Vincennes will be a day of rejoicing for French families and champagne toasts will be in order for the occasion'. ('Pas d'union sacrée avec la canaille'. *Je Suis Partout*, 24 March 1939.)

13 See J. Colton, *Léon Blum*, Fayard, 1968; and Jean Lacouture, *Léon Blum*, Ed. du Seuil, 1977.

14 See his extremely revealing intervention in the Chamber of Deputies in the session of 9 December (*Journal Officiel*, p. 1708).

15 On 15 March 1939, Prague was occupied by the German army.

16 See (61), p. 172–97.

17 See the pertinent analysis by J.-C. Asselain, 'La semaine des quarante heures, le chômage et l'emploi', *Le Mouvement Social*, April-June 1966.

18 See the recent study by S. Berstein (10), vol. 2, pp. 275–306; and the shortly expected second volume of his *Histoire du parti radical*, Presses de la Fondation Nationale des Sciences Politiques.

19 See the well-documented article by G. Bourdé (14), pp. 89–233; also A. Prost (10), vol. 1, pp. 9–111.

20 Cited by S. Berstein (10), vol. 2, p. 297.

21 See P. Machefer, R. Sanson, J.-N. Jeanneney (10), vol. 2, pp. 307–57; and A. Prost (10), vol. 1, pp. 25–44.

22 See J. Becker (10), vol. 2, pp. 225–44.

23 At the end of 1938 these appear still to have included 10,000 graduates.

24 It is generally accounted for by a combination of factors: a reversal in the international situation, the massive repatriation of capital, the return to a liberal policy and the relaxation of the law on the forty-hour week. In the opinion of Alfred Sauvy (*Histoire économique de la France entre les deux guerres*, Fayard, 1967, vol. 2), the last measure was to prove decisive. However, his thesis is opposed: see *La politique économique française, automne 1938–été 1939*, Comité d'Histoire de la Deuxième Guerre Mondiale, 1976.

25 See the exhaustive study by G. Le Béguec (10), vol. 1.

26 See J.-M. Mayeur (10), vol. 1, pp. 243–54.

27 Daladier's intervention in the Chamber of Deputies, 9 December 1938 (*Journal Officiel*, p. 1708).

28 Cited by S. Berstein (10), vol. 2, p. 294.

29 See F. Goguel (10), vol. 1, pp. 45–54.

30 In June 1938, however, the supporters of Pivert were banned for lack of discipline.

31 See A. Prost, *La CGT à l'époque du Front populaire*, Colin, 1964 and J. Bruhat (10), vol. 2, pp. 159–88.

32 See his analysis (47), pp. 17–40.

33 On the evolution of French politics after Munich, see R. Girault (122).

34 See his particularly firm broadcast address of 29 March 1939.

35 There can be no doubt that the parliamentary procedure decided upon by the government and presidents of the various groups made things difficult for those who opposed them. But the latter were – at the time at least – cautious. On pacifism in 1939, see the remarks of G. Rossi-Landi (32).

36 The number of deserters was negligible. It is worth noting that German soldiers appear to have had similar feelings, more or less.

37 See (22); also H. Guillemin, *Nationalistes et nationaux*, Gallimard, 1974.

38 They used the channel of unofficial conversations involving important officials from the Foreign Office or from economic commissions. It is quite clear that there was still a powerful pressure group in favour of reaching accommodation with Nazi Germany; see (27), pp. 239–86.

39 The Ministry of Foreign Affairs of the Soviet Union published in 1976 *L'URSS dans la lutte pour la paix à la veille de la Seconde Guerre mondiale* (les Editions du Progrès, Moscow), a collection of documents of considerable interest, but they do not include any information concerning German–Soviet relations. On Soviet policy, see J. Levesque, *L'URSS et sa politique internationale de 1917 à nos jours*, Colin, 1980.

40 The Soviets had worked hard to obtain complete reciprocity of commitment, the advantage of the guarantee extended to the Baltic States and a strict interpretation of German aggression. They had insisted that any political agreement should be backed up by a military one.

41 It was the Soviets who, with reservations, took the initiative at the end of April.

42 See the work cited above, produced by the Ministry of Foreign Affairs of the Soviet Union, pp. 403–88: the accounts of the tripartite negotiations.

43 Daladier had entrusted to Doumenc the mission of bringing back 'an agreement

at all costs'. But he was hesitant when it came to forcing the hand of the Poles who, virtually right to the last, refused right of passage to the Soviet troops. See the account given by General Beaufre, *Le drame de 1940*, Plon, 1965.

44 The ambiguity here is such that the Soviets denied at first the existence of any secret protocol and later that it had been effective in any way. They also made the claim that it was their duty to 'liberate' minorities 'oppressed by the Poles'; but this thesis of liberation has no basis of convincing proof.

45 The deeper causes of the Second World War are still a matter of polemic: see (25). See also *Sommer 1939*, Stuttgart, Deutsche Verlags-Anstalt, 1979. There is a so-called revisionist Anglo-Saxon school of thought that has attempted to gloss over the question of responsibilities. Many of its theses are debatable, in particular its denial of any desire for power on the part of Hitlerism.

46 In a 'generous offer', Hitler proposed to the British that he should protect their Empire. As for the Poles, they were told to give up Danzig and to organise plebiscites in progressively extensive regions.

47 According to J. Zay (12), pp. 65–9, the second Council of Ministers had been very stormy. Bonnet and Daladier had exchanged some sharp words and Daladier had read out a telegram despatched by Coulondre, the French ambassador in Berlin on 25 August, which declared: 'It is essential to continue to resist, repeat resist, Hitler's bluff.'

48 Right to the last, Italophile pacifists clung to the hope of Italian mediation. During the night of 2 September, Bonnet proposed a 'symbolic retreat' on the part of the German troops, but Ciano refused to play the part of mediator.

49 See the excellent study by H. Michel (29); also the proceedings of the colloquium organised by the Comité d'Histoire de la Deuxième Guerre Mondiale (32); and the recent work by F. Bédarida (123).

50 In September 1939, two-thirds of the Belgian army were guarding the Franco–Belgian border.

51 Nevertheless, things were far from perfect: by deciding that the 7th army should move as far north as possible (this was the 'Breda manoeuvre'), Gamelin left himself without any reserve forces.

52 It was not until February 1940 that Hitler adopted the Manstein Plan which moved the axis of attack to the Meuse, in the centre of the Allied positions.

53 See (30); also (33).

54 Although it was not as extensive as was desired: it did not include the socialists and furthermore retained a number of notorious pacifists such as Bonnet, who had become Keeper of the Seals, and Monzie.

55 Some authors – quite mistakenly – represent the fifth column as a veritable Trojan Horse. Spies and other agents working for the Reich seem to have been relatively few on the ground.

56 See the bibliography in notes 129 and 130 of Chapter 3.

57 A number of historians stress the role of R. Guyot, who returned from Moscow around 20 September. Others emphasise the activities of Fried, one of the emissaries of the Third International, in France.

58 According to P. Robrieux, *Maurice Thorez, vie secrète et vie publique* (Fayard, 1975). It took a lot of persuasion to get Thorez to leave his Chauny retreat.

59 Compare the following recent statement made by G. Cogniot: 'Because of the role of fascism in the war, the conflict that broke out on 3 September harboured right from the outset the objective possibility of a just and liberating war, a war of the people against reactionary barbarity, a war for progress' (77), p. 44.

60 There is only one tract on record that preached active sabotage. Isolated acts of sabotage nevertheless did occur in the Farman factories of Boulogne and in a

number of other armament factories. But on the whole they were remarkably limited.

61 With its insistence upon frontier modifications, Moscow appears to have been trying to establish a defensive belt to protect Leningrad.

62 See the study by R. Girault (32).

63 The government of Finland had preferred to negotiate rather than become the battlefield of Europe. In the event, the Soviet conditions were relatively moderate.

64 See J.-L. Crémieux-Brilhac (32).

65 Expenses were covered as follows: 29% by budgetary receipts; 37% by borrowing; 34% by advances forthcoming from the Banque de France.

66 Index of industrial production (1938 = 100): December 1939 = 128, April 1940 = 154.

67 In April 1939, a skilled worker in the Paris region earned 400F for 40 hours of work compared to 420F (after deduction of tax at source) for 60 hours of work in March 1940.

68 R. Brunet, Chouffet, Froment, Rauzy and Rives.

2 The disasters of 1940

1 On the agony of the regime, consult (34) annotated by L. Noguères (35); see also (43) and the work of synthesis by J.-P. Azéma and M. Winock (44), pp. 316–441.

2 See (30), pp. 53–67.

3 See the successful portrait by E. Berl (43), pp. 53–61.

4 See the excellent account by F. Bédarida (10).

5 Germany was importing from Sweden 10 million tons (French *tonnes*) or more, transported by way of the Baltic or by Narvik (if the Baltic was ice-bound).

6 The declaration was made in response to a desire for such a document expressed by London on 19 December 1939. See (123).

7 See Chapman's detailed account of the French campaign (39); see also (38).

8 The operation had occasioned angry incidents between the French and the British Command which wanted to evacuate its own expeditionary force first. Churchill was obliged to intervene personally and order the embarkation solely of French troops on 31 May.

9 As a result of the French High Command's delay in giving the order to pull the troops out, 400,000 men were taken prisoner.

10 Bouthillier (36), vol. 1, p. 22, describes these ministers 'packed into the seats for general councillors, looking like students in an untidy classroom'.

11 See (75), p. 31.

12 See (31), p. 35.

13 His conduct was the focus of a number of disagreements. There can be no doubt that he was much less in command of the situation than he suggests in *Au coeur de la mêlée*, Flammarion, 1951. But the special pleading of his opponents' versions of the events should be regarded with even more distrust. The account given by P. de Villelume (*Journal*, Fayard, 1976), himself a notorious defeatist, should be read with the greatest circumspection; to counterbalance, see D. Leca, *La rupture de 1940*, Fayard, 1978.

14 Churchill had replaced Chamberlain on 10 May.

15 Chautemps had, on 15 June, suggested not asking for an armistice but instead addressing enquiries to Hitler concerning *conditions* for an armistice, a distinction that allowed for making a start on the process of negotiations while at the same time getting round the terms of the Franco-British agreement of 28 March.

16 On his extremely controversial resignation, see (37) and above all J.-N. Jeanneney (31), pp. 415–17.

17 Two years later, when the Resistance suggested arranging his escape, de Gaulle confided to Frenay: 'I have the greatest admiration for his intelligence ... but I cannot forget that it was he ... who turned to Pétain at a moment when the struggle could and should have continued, placing its reliance upon the Empire. It was not a mistake, rather a fault... His talents will be used in the position assigned to him' (see (71), p. 231).

18 See (40); and (41).

19 Cited by J. Vidalenc (40), p. 285.

20 (41), vol. 1, p. 35.

21 (31), p. 85.

22 'The unseeing town.' The German propaganda services tried – using photographs taken at a later date – to promote belief in quite a different story.

23 See (41), vol. 1, p. 30.

24 After the war this fundamental disagreement was obscured by a multitude of pseudo-problems: for instance, there were endless arguments as to the name of the man who first pronounced the word 'armistice' – a point that was really of very little interest. See (37), pp. 45–55; and (31), p. 397.

25 On 11 June, at Briare, he said: 'It will be impossible to continue the war if the British air-force is progressively dislocated.'

26 The 'defeatist' clan accepted at face value the account given by P. Baudouin of the meeting on 13 June between Reynaud and Churchill. Baudouin believed – mistakenly, as can be seen from accounts by other witnesses – or pretended to believe that Churchill had released the French government from its undertakings. See (31), p. 405–6.

27 See above, p. 38.

28 See (7), vol. 1, p. 45.

29 Alibert, the Under-Secretary of State for the President of the Council, persuaded those who consulted him – who, admittedly, must have been exceptionally gullible – that the German troops had not crossed the Loire!

30 Among the more famous names: Daladier, Delbos, Mendès France, Zay, Le Troquer, Grumbach, Mandel. The *Massilia* also carried Professor Perrin, J. Ibert, J. Cain, A. Maurois, etc.

31 Cited by A. Truchet, *L'armistice de 1940 et l'Afrique du Nord*, PUF, 1954, p. 99, a work that does much to set the record straight.

32 See (7), vol. 1, p. 45.

33 The archives of the Wilhelmstrasse – which are quite specific on the point – invalidate the retrospective evidence of Baudouin, the new Minister of Foreign Affairs and thereby ruin one of the claims made by the *maréchalistes*. See (28), pp. 310–11.

34 See the comparative assessment by H. Michel (29), pp. 264–89.

35 H. Frenay (71), p. 16.

36 *Autopsie d'une défaite* (L'Age d'Homme, 1973) is a well-documented and most pertinent study of French military doctrines by L. Mysyrowicz. The vast majority of high-ranking officers regarded tanks not as offensive weapons but as back-up forces for the infantry. As for the airforce, the most recent version of *L'Instruction sur l'emploi tactique des grandes unités* devoted to it no more than 4 out of its 177 pages. See also P.-M. de La Gorce, *La République et son armée*, Fayard, 1963.

37 See (28), pp. 333–4.

38 The French State handed over to the Gestapo, among others, Fritz Thyssen and his wife, Rudolf Breitscheid and Rudolf Hilferding, members of the SPD (the one

died as a deportee, the other committed suicide in prison) and Franz Dahlem of the Communist Party.

39 See Map 3.

40 See his speech of 25 June 1940.

41 M. Launay (*L'armistice de 1940*, PUF, 1972) gives a good description of this problem.

42 This statement was cited as exonerating evidence during Marshal Pétain's trial (34), p. 167. The British Prime Minister later saw fit to maintain that it was no more than an 'off-the-cuff' remark made in the course of 'desultory conversation'. And he went on to say: 'Now that all the facts are known to us, there can remain no doubt that France was saved no suffering by the armistice.' (See W. Churchill, *The Second World War*.)

43 Take, for instance, Hitler's remarks made in the course of a conversation with Mussolini on 28 October 1940:

It is in the interest of the Axis powers to see that the Vichy government retains control over the French Empire in North Africa. If Morocco fell under de Gaulle's command, we should be faced with a difficult task, for our action would have to depend entirely on our forces in the air. The best way of safeguarding these territories is to see that the French themselves are obliged to defend them against the British.

See *Les archives secrètes du comte Ciano*, Plon, 1948, p. 407; see also his *Journal politique, 1939–1943*, Neuchâtel, La Baconnière, 1946, 2 vols.

44 General Noguès reproached him bitterly for this at the time: 'The government, finding itself in an atmosphere of disorder, proved incapable of recognising the important element of morale and strength that North Africa represented ... it was bitterly to regret its failure to do so.'

3 There you stand, Maréchal

1 See (5); also (46); (124); and (45).

2 Of the fifty or so public announcements on the part of Philippe Pétain in 1940 and 1941, note the 'Messages' of 25 June and 13 August 1940, the 'Manifesto' of 11 October 1940, the speeches made at Pau on 28 April 1941 and at Commentry on 1 May 1941, and the statement of 8 July 1941. As a general rule, Pétain would recast a communication prepared by his entourage, giving it his own particular dry, didactic style and slant. We should also mention a couple of articles that appeared in *La Revue des Deux Mondes* in August and September 1940. On the ideology of Pétainism, see (16); J. Touchard, *Histoire des idées politiques*, PUF, 1967, vol. 2; and A. Slama, *Les messages, declarations et discours du Maréchal Pétain*, an account presented at the colloquium on 'The Vichy government and the national revolution' (45).

3 On Pétain before 1940, see (48).

4 My own view is that it would be mistaken to interpret the French State exclusively as a projection of Maurrasism as O. Wormser does (*Les origines doctrinales de la révolution nationale*, Plon, 1971).

5 The thesis defended by R. Bourderon, 'Le régime de Vichy était-il fasciste?' (8), 1973, is not convincing.

6 On this submission on the part of the parliamentarians, see in particular E. Berl (43), pp. 205–53; and his account of the debates, pp. 304–45.

7 Laval had made a false move when, on 16 June, he demanded to be given Foreign Affairs which Pétain, on the instigation of Weygand, refused him. On 23 June, he became Minister of State and Vice-President of the Council.

8 On the instigation of Badie, 27 parliamentarians had signed a motion recognising a delegation of power only on a temporary basis and within the framework of a republican regime. Badie was unable to defend it in debate; on these last parliamentary developments, see the excellent critical study by J.-N. Jeanneney (31), pp. 438–44.

9 58 deputies and 22 senators had remained staunchly republican. Not an impressive total. Many radicals failed to rise to the occasion as did many socialists (88 deputies voted full powers to Pétain as against 29). The situation was such that Léon Blum preferred to keep quiet rather than draw attention to this 'public spectacle of renegation'. It has often been claimed that it was a Popular Front Chamber that voted for full powers. That claim calls for correction on two counts: fifty or more communist deputies as well as the parliamentarians on the *Massilia* were absent and, above all, the 'National Assembly' also included a Senate which had already on two occasions brought about the downfall of Blum with massive majority votes. It was not from the right that most of the opposition came: 12 radical socialist deputies, 14 senators from the democratic left, 36 socialist deputies and senators. Of the eighty, 31 were later imprisoned or placed under surveillance; 10 were deported, 5 of whom died.

10 20 abstentions after a recount – among them those of Herriot and Georges Monnet.

11 See (34), pp. 77–8.

12 See the very pertinent analysis of S. Hoffmann (47), pp. 17–40.

13 See the study of M. Prélot (45), pp. 23–36.

14 René Cassin challenged the National Assembly's legal right to delegate its constituent powers. Specialists continue to argue about this.

15 Decree no. 3 stipulated that 'the Senate and the Chamber of Deputies be adjourned pending further orders'.

16 In 1934 he was Minister of War in the Doumergue cabinet; when that fell he told Lémery: 'One can do without the radicals, to govern: I would be glad to take on National Education as well as War. I would deal with the communist school-teachers...' (Cited by R. Griffiths (48), p. 237.) He returned to the Ministry of War in a stillborn Bouisson government in June 1935. In September 1939, after some wavering, he refused to enter the government.

17 See the detailed account by L. Noguères (35).

18 In 1934, *Le Petit Journal* had organised a referendum among its readers, the purpose of which was to select the most capable head of government: Pétain had topped the poll.

19 In September 1941 he had Darlan tell the Comte de Paris that the nature of the delegation of power was 'entirely personal'; in August 1942, Laval offered that same Pretender the Ministry of Supplies! [In 1660 General Monk declared for a 'free parliament' in other words, the restoration of Charles II. The loss of his support proved fatal to the Commonwealth cause.]

20 The ministerial run-down was gaining momentum right up until 1942. Under Darlan there were only 12 ministers: Hunziger, for his part, was not only in control of War but also held the Colonies, the Family and Health, and National Education.

21 A whole subtle diplomacy was involved in getting X invited to dine with the head of the French State and preventing Y from getting to meet him.

22 Belin – the Minister of Work – occupied (literally) the printing works of the *Journal Officiel* to prevent Colonel Cèbe – a member of the military cabinet – from getting in to alter the text of the Charter of Work at the last moment.

23 Those who had just been sacked usually learned of their disgrace following a meeting of the Council of Ministers. The sacking of Laval on 13 December 1940 was attended by positively grotesque circumstances: there were advance meetings of the plotters, physical interventions on the part of the ex-*cagoulards* now acting as 'protection groups', noisy remonstrations from Laval, who pulled out a penknife to defend himself. Even in her most extravagant moments, the Republic had not sunk to such burlesque depths.

24 Moysset told Darlan: 'Your ministry reminds me of the sign of a café in my old home town, Le Ségala; it was "The new cyclists and the ancient Romans"'.

25 It was under the proconsulate of Darlan that the invasion of the admirals assumed such excessive proportions. The Bishop of Lille, Cardinal Liénart, is reputed to have wondered 'where he [Darlan] would find another admiral to replace [him] when [he] died'.

26 On the professional army, see the well-documented work by R. Paxton, *Parades and politics at Vichy*, Princeton, 1966, and those of J. Nobécourt, *Une histoire politique de l'armee*, Ed. du Seuil, 1967, vol. 1 and P.-M. de La Gorce, *op.cit.*

27 See H. Ehrmann, *La politique du patronat français (1935–1955)*, Colin, 1959; the article by M. Lévy-Leboyer in *Le patronat de la seconde industrialisation*, a pamphlet produced by the Mouvement Social, 1979, and R. Kuisel, *Technocrats and public economic policy: from the Third to the Fourth Republic*, Rome, Banco di Roma, 1973.

28 Traditionalists and collaborationists violently attacked these promotions in which they detected the clandestine hand of 'a synarchic Empire movement' inspired by the Worms Bank and led by Barnaud and G. Le Roy Ladurie. The movement in question certainly did exist as an offshot of a Masonic society created at the end of the nineteenth century; but it was totally without any political or economic power. And the introduction in force of these 'modernist' and 'interventionist' technocrats can perfectly well be explained by the particularly difficult circumstances. See the completely convincing article by R. Kuisel, 'The legend of the Vichy synarchy', *French Historical Studies*, 1970.

29 On this project and its failure, see the complementary articles by A. Prost, 'Le rapport de Déat en faveur d'un parti national unique (juillet 1940)', *Revue Française de Science Politique*, 1973, and J.-P. Cointet, 'Marcel Déat et le parti unique' (8), 1973; it should be noted that in the spring of 1941 a 'provisional committee to organise support for the national revolution' had been created, which included a number of recognised *maréchalistes*. But its aims have never become clear and the venture soon came to nothing.

30 All the parliamentary ministers – with the exception of Laval – were sacked in September 1940.

31 The influence of Maurras should be neither under- nor overestimated. He seems to have gone to Vichy on ten or more occasions and was apparently consulted at least twice.

32 On 18 November 1940, in Dijon, he had, after all, declared: 'A new order is being born in Europe; it would be unforgivable if we did not participate in it.' See *Le procès Flandin*, Librairie de Médicis, 1947.

33 See G. Rossi-Landi (45), pp. 47–54.

34 There is no good biography of Darlan.

35 He was renowned for his *savoir-faire*: his opponents dubbed him 'the grovelling admiral'.

36 See (50), p. 326.

37 See J. Steel, W. Kidd and D. Weiss (45), pp. 55–64.

38 In line with the justice already dispensed, on 16 October 1941, Pétain decided to detain Daladier, Reynaud, Gamelin, Blum and Mandel in a fortress; Auriol,

Dormoy, La Chambre, Jouhaux and many others were also imprisoned or interned.

39 It was the prefectorial body that was the most seriously affected: between 1940 and 1941, 94 of its members were sacked and 104 compulsorily retired. The Prefect of Chartres, Jean Moulin, received the news of his dismissal on November 11. It fell to a German posted in Chartres to pay the respects that were his due: 'I congratulate you upon the energy with which you have defended the interests of your administration and the honour of your country.'

40 See D. Rossignol, *Vichy et les francs-maçons*, Lattès, 1981.

41 This measure can to some degree be explained by a desire to minimise Nazi looting.

42 The statute in fact went beyond legislation in the Reich which rested principally upon religious criteria.

43 Furthermore, in time, this legislation underwent further changes: in October all those with two Jewish grandparents married to a person also with two Jewish grandparents were classed as Jews. In June all those who practised the Jewish religion and had two Jewish grandparents were classed as Jews. See (62); also (92); see also pp. 110–15.

44 On family policies, see the study by A. Coutrot (45), pp. 245–63.

45 At least one woman who 'despatched a little soul to heaven' was guillotined.

46 But the authors most generally referred to were Proudhon, Maurras and Péguy. On Uriage, see P. Dunoyer de Segonzac, *Le vieux chef*, Ed. du Seuil, 1971; R. Josse, 'L'Ecole des cadres d'Uriage' (8), 1966; and J. Bourdin, 'Des intellectuels à la recherche d'un style de vie: l'école des cadres d'Uriage', *Revue Française de Science Politique*, 1959.

47 Pétain was its president; its successive directors were Héricourt, Valentin, Lachal. On the Légion Française des Combattants, see the excellent study by J.-P. Cointet (45), pp. 123–43.

48 On policies with regard to the young, see the study by A. Coutrot (45), pp. 265–84. On the Chantiers, see R. Josse, 'Les chantiers de la jeunesse' (8), 1964.

49 See A. Coutrot (45), p. 273.

50 See in particular (60).

51 In 1943 there were, over the whole of France, about 5,200,000 TSF receivers; between 1940 and 1944 the radio audience appears to have increased slightly.

52 Some were termed 'permanent' (more than fifty, relating in particular to State collaboration); others were 'temporary' (about 100 relating to the Riom trial alone), others 'daily' (at least 3,000 between July 1940 and August 1944). Thus on 23 April 1943 it was declared that 'daily' announcements should henceforth take account of the age of the head of State; on 10 December 1943 it was stated that 'it was forbidden to inform school prize-winners that their parents would be given leave to visit them'; all that could be suggested was that they were due for 'a nice surprise'; see P. Limagne, *Ephémérides de quatre années tragiques*, Bonne Presse, 1945–7, 3 vols., vol 3, p. 1633. See also the valuable evidence collected by this editor of *La Croix* who made a faithful note of all the pieces of information and all these 'requirements' and after the war published them as they stood.

53 39 Parisian newspapers had 'withdrawn'; 9 were dailies (*Le Figaro, Le Journal, Le Journal des Débats, L'Action Française, Le Jour-Echo de Paris, Le Petit Journal, La Croix, Le Temps* and *Paris-Soir*).

54 A number of departmental dailies were obliged to suspend publication for financial reasons. On the other hand, the larger regional dailies, in better financial circumstances, were consistently acquiring new readers. It would appear, in general, that under the occupation more people were reading

newspapers. (Of course, one reason for that may have been the need to keep informed of changes in the situation of general supplies.)

55 See (60), p. 85.

56 On agrarian policies, see P. Barral, *Les agrariens français de Méline à Pisani*, Colin, 1968, pp. 256–82; P. Barral and I. Boussard (45), pp. 211–33; on the Peasant Corporation, see (55).

57 Its field of application did not extend to either agriculture or the civil service, or to certain liberal professions that were covered by a special order. On the Charter of Work, see the exhaustive study by J. Julliard (45), pp. 157–94.

58 It should be added that some of this legislation survived the regime – the reorganisation of the banking profession, for example.

59 Here is one example: in 1944 only one 'professional family', that of the miners, was said to be run on the model provided by the Charter of Work.

60 The vociferous campaign centred on 'a return to the land' discredited itself by installing in the countryside 1,566 families, 409 of which quit after no more than a few months.

61 E. Dejonghe ('Problèmes sociaux dans les houillères du Nord et du Pas-de-Calais', *Revue d'Histoire Moderne et Contemporaine*, 1970) has given a detailed description of the reintroduction of the question of wage agreements, the worsening of the system of fines and the reinforcement of discipline and of the power of the *petits-chefs*, that is to say the foremen and overmen.

62 See the recent article by H. Rousso, 'L'organisation industrielle de Vichy' (8), 1979.

63 See the indictment of the representative of the Confédération des Moyennes Entreprises contre l'Etatisme et la Mainmise du Grand Patronat (Confederation of average-sized businesses against State control and take-over by the big businessmen), P. Nicolle, *Cinquante mois d'armistice*, Bonne, 1947.

64 See (45), p. 161.

65 See (56); and (57); also J.-C. Germain-Thomas, *Un exemple d'économie de contrainte: les idées et l'administration du gouvernement de Vichy en matière économique et sociale*, Law thesis, photocopied, 1969. See *L'annuaire statistique rétrospectif de la France*, INSEE, 1961. For the other side of the question, see pp. 129–33.

66 A number of technocrats devised two plans for the post-war period which were supposed to help the French economy to 'make its entry into the industrial era'; the model remained non-liberal, however. See R. Kuisel, 'Vichy et les origines de la planification économique', *Le Mouvement Social*, 1977.

67 In the Paris and Lyons stock exchanges which had reopened, access to the financial market became more difficult; however, that did not prevent a very steep rise in prices (index of French non-fixed interest securities, Paris Bourse: 1938 = 100; 1941 = 432; 1944 = 705).

68 There is still a lack of good regional studies; but we should at least mention those of Monique Luirard (130) and P. Laborie (129).

69 See pp. 135–44.

70 There is no good general work on worker trade-unionism between 1940 and 1944. See G. Adam, *La CFTC, 1940–1958*, Paris, Colin, 1964; and also (with a measure of circumspection) J. Montreuil (alias G. Lefranc), *Histoire du mouvement ouvrier en France des origines à nos jours*, Aubier, 1946.

71 This was the title of an article by Maurras which appeared in the *Petit Marseillais* on 9 February 1941. It included the following remarks: 'A divine part of the art of politics has been affected by the extraordinary surprise the Maréchal has given us. We expected everything of him, as indeed we might, as indeed we should. But our expectations have been answered in a more than human fashion. Absolutely

nothing is lacking. . .' The expression created quite a stir and in *L'Action Française* of 15 April 1941 Maurras produced a somewhat deprecatory interpretation.

72 On the men of the left in Vichy, see the analysis by F. Laurent in his contribution to the colloquium on 'The Vichy government and the national revolution' (45).

73 See J. Duquesne (52); that analysis has been refined in the course of the regional colloquia recently held; see the proceedings of the colloquia of Grenoble (October 1976) (53) and of Lille (November 1977) (54).

74 His sermon, published in *La Croix* on 28 June 1940, is of particular interest as the Archbishop of Toulouse was to show the greatest courage throughout the occupation.

75 Cited by R. Griffiths (48), p. 305.

76 See A. Prost, *L'enseignement en France, 1800–1967*, Colin, 1968, p. 475.

77 It was signed Georges Gérard; cited by J. Duquesne (52), p. 59.

78 R. Descouens, *La vie du Maréchal Pétain racontée aux enfants de France*, Nice, Ed. de la Vraie France, 1941.

79 The literature on Vichy collaboration is as abundant as it is variable and questionable. The painstaking analyses of the German archives undertaken by both R. Paxton (46) and E. Jäckel (63) discredit almost all the hypotheses of Robert Aron's *Histoire de Vichy* (Fayard, 1954) which was so highly regarded in the fifties. See the work of fundamental importance by S. Hoffmann (47), pp. 44–66, the syntheses by Y. Durand (5) and J.-P. Azéma (67), the controversial study by H. Michel (64). See also the study by A. Schérer (65), pp. 13–38, the number devoted to 'L'Occupation de la France' (8), 1964 and the work by A. Hytier (66).

80 In establishing the exchange rate at 1 Reichsmark = 20 francs, the Reich was certainly taking a lion's share (in 1939, the RM was rated at the equivalent of 6F on the exchange market) and the French State had to pay a daily tribute, initially of 400 million francs (a sum that would have made it possible to provide luxuriously for 10 million French soldiers, at the very least). At the height of State collaboration, in May 1941, this was reduced to 300 million but as from November 1942 the sum rose again to 500 million. Let us at this point indicate once and for all a scale by which to calculate the sums expressed in current French francs: the conversion indices to obtain 1970 francs are respectively: for 1940: 0.35; for 1941: 0.29; for 1942: 0.24; for 1943: 0.20; for 1944: 0.17; multiply these figures by two to obtain 1978 francs. To simplify, let us say that, by and large, one should multiply the prices of 1940 by 70, those of 1942 by 50, and those of 1944 by 35 to obtain 1978 prices expressed in *old francs*.

81 See Map 3.

82 Without giving any explanation whatsoever, the occupation authorities partially lifted this prohibition in September 1941 and altogether did away with this internal frontier in May 1943.

83 On the evolution of the 'attached zone', see E. Dejonghe, *Revue du Nord*, April–June 1978, pp. 233–52. In departments still traumatised by memories of the German occupation of 1914–18 and which in no way relished the idea of annexation, there were nevertheless virtually no attempts to follow the lead of the largest separatist movement, Vlamsch Verband von Frankrijk (The Flemish League in France) founded in 1942 by Abbé J.-M. Gantois, which offered allegiance to Hitler in December 1940. See E. Dejonghe, 'Un mouvement séparatiste dans le Nord et le Pas de Calais sous l'Occupation', *Revue d'Histoire Moderne et Contemporaine*, 1970.

84 Perhaps the organisers of these operations were hoping to make use, to the profit

of the Reich, of a number of Breton separatists who had taken refuge in Berlin and were now returned by general service waggon from Germany – F. Debauvais and O. Mordrel, for instance, two members of the movement favouring autonomy, Breiz Atao (Brittany first). However, these separatists represented such a minority trend that on 3 July 1940 they did not dare to proclaim an independent Brittany; and the National Breton Council that they set up encountered outspoken hostility from the catholic hierarchy ('Never has a Breton been a traitor', declared the Bishop of Quimper from his pulpit), and indeed from most autonomists, who – especially in the circles of the notables – put their trust rather in the policy of decentralisation favoured by the Vichy regime.

85 See the altogether explicit 'Message' of 30 October 1940. Here are a few phrases from it which made sensational news at the time: 'It is with honour and to maintain French unity, a unity that has lasted ten centuries, and within the framework of the active construction of a new European order that I am today setting out along the path of collaboration... The policy is my own ... It is I alone who will be judged by History...'

86 Judging a governmental crisis to be imminent, London had insisted on the afternoon of the 16th that 'the French fleet should immediately head for British ports'; but Reynaud, who shortly afterwards heard of the plan for a Franco-British union, did not pass the message on.

87 The British were in effect right out of the secret, for the orders of the Admiral of the Fleet concerned all aggression, 'enemy or foreign'.

88 As the British saw it, Hitler would lose no time in seizing the French fleet: as was proved by the fact that at Rethondes the Germans had refused to alter the clause stipulating that all warships should return to their peace-time anchorages; see above p. 46.

89 See the criticisms by A. Heckstall-Smith, *La flotte convoitée*, Presses de la Cité, 1964. It is nevertheless false to claim that 'Operation Catapult' was – from the beginning – an internal political manoeuvre set up by Churchill.

90 At Baudouin's trial, Gensoul declared: 'From the point of view of the honour of the French colours and as an admiral, my view was that under threat from guns, even English guns, I could not back down and accept the terms of this ultimatum.' He acknowledged that he had 'omitted' to pass on to the French Admiralty the clause that authorised the naval squadron to make for the Antilles where it could be neutralised under American control. The fact is that Admiral Gensoul had chosen on the spot not to retreat before the British; see J.-P. Azéma, 'Le drame de Mers el-Kébir', *L'Histoire*, 1980.

91 The 'mission of Professor Rougier' was the basis for speculations of the most fantastic kind. To judge from L.-D. Girard (*Montoire, Verdun diplomatique*, Bonne, 1948), Pétain not only possessed stupefying powers of second sight, but was also the finest double agent of all time. General Schmitt (*Les accords secrets franco-britanniques, histoire ou mystification*, PUF, 1957) has refuted many of the allegations made by L. Rougier (*Les accords secrets franco-britanniques*, Grasset, 1954). On Pétain's 'double game', see the pertinent study by H. Michel (64), pp. 151–56.

92 In July 1940, Weygand had issued a manifesto which exalted God, the Family and the Motherland; cited by E. Berl (43), pp. 282–83.

93 H. Michel has used German sources to support his rigorous demonstration of this point (64); see also (63); and (66).

94 It was this kind of embarrassment that Maurras conveyed in *L'Action Française*: 'Are you a partisan of this collaboration?' – 'There is no reason for me to be so' –

'Are you against it, then?' – 'No' – 'Neutral?' – 'Not that either' – 'You accept it then?' – 'I do not have to accept it or discuss it' (see (19), p. 513).

95 See p. 182.

96 Berlin, which was every bit as surprised, opted for firmness, to be on the safe side; Déat, who had been arrested in Paris, had to be set free immediately. On the 16th, Abetz, with an SS escort, went to the non-occupied zone to 'deliver' Laval, but he was not successful in getting him 'reinstated' at the head of Foreign Affairs. So he took him back to Paris, as part of his luggage.

97 Otto Abetz placed much reliance on Laval and it was he who raised the bids for him. Hitler, for his part, ascribed less importance to the sacking of a vulgar politician whom he distrusted. But the episode had the effect of reinforcing his distrust of the French. Besides, he was, at the time, altogether taken up with 'Operation Barbarossa' (the invasion of the USSR) and was losing interest in the unimportant affairs of France. On German reactions, see (63), pp. 180–225.

98 Thirty or more German aircraft landed in Syria. 20,000 rifles, 200 machine guns and twelve guns from the French army's stockpiles of weapons in Syria reached the Iraqi insurgents. See M.-C. Davet, *La double affaire de Syrie*, Fayard, 1968.

99 On the beginnings of the internal Resistance, see (68); see also the exhaustive survey by H. Noguères (6); and (125). Also (70); and the eye-witness accounts by H. Frenay (71) and C. Bourdet (72).

100 See D. Mayer, *Les Socialistes dans la Résistance*, PUF, 1968, pp. 12–13.

101 Such was the case in particular for a number of figures who emerged from the nationalist right and lost no time in becoming engaged in the Resistance.

102 Between December 1940 and April 1942, the militant socialist and CGT member, Christian Pineau, brought out the 70 first issues of the paper single-handed.

103 They were counting on the element within the general staff which was preparing for short-term revenge: in particular, for instance, the ex-5th Bureau which under the cover of 'bureau for anti-national activities' and 'rural works service', or of the CMD, gathered intelligence, eliminated spies in the pay of the Axis powers and hid away arms (65,000 small arms, 1,500 vehicles). On the activities of these secret services, see (46); and P. Paillole, *Services spéciaux*, Laffont, 1976.

104 To cite Philippe Viannay: 'In July 1942, at all events, I was still speaking of the "good faith and patriotism of the Maréchal" (see (6), vol 3, p. 478).

105 See (73), p. 87.

106 H. Frenay's expression (71), p. 12.

107 One illustrious victim was Loustaunau-Lacau, a former member of Pétain's entourage, who founded the 'Alliance' network. He was later interned, handed over to the Gestapo at whose hands he underwent 54 interrogations before cracking and surviving at Mauthausen. Vichy was progressively to get a grip on nationalist circles of resistance.

108 The line of demarcation represented a lasting division even more than an annoying obstacle. Only the National Front and – just for a few months – Combat managed to develop organisations in both zones.

109 It was in April 1941 that Loustaunau-Lacau, who was distrustful of Free France, made contact in Lisbon with an 'honourable correspondent' from the Intelligence Service and set up 'Alliance', a network that worked very efficiently for the English; on his story, see M.-M. Fourcade, *L'arche de Noé*, Le Livre de Poche, 1971, 2 vols.

110 We should beware of making unjust generalisations. The industrialist Marcel

Lebon provided the necessary funds for the Défense de la France movement to get started. The OCM numbered among its earliest supporters men of finance who were unstinting in drawing upon their private funds. It cannot be denied however that in general, in the very early days, the Resistance lacked patrons. Here is a quote from Frenay: 'The head of a big business who had been at the Ampère *lycée* with me and with whom I had remained on very friendly terms, gave me 5,000 francs. I had been hoping for ten times that amount; and the boss of a well-known shipbuilding yard offered me such a derisory sum that we refused it' (71), p. 69.

111 See (6), vol. 1, p. 442.
112 Compare F. and R. Bédarida, 'Une Résistance spirituelle: aux origines du *Témoignage Chrétien*, 1941–1942' (8), 1966, and M. Winock (61), pp. 203–38.
113 See (72), p. 73. Malraux made contact with the British SOE in 1943, operating there as Colonel Berger in March 1944 (see J. Lacouture, *Malraux, une vie dans le siècle*, Ed. du Seuil, 1976).
114 Let us cite a few historians: Marc Bloch, P. Brossolette, G. Bidault and also Lucie Samuel-Aubrac, Burgard, Morpain, etc.
115 See (72), p. 96.
116 See (70), p. 32.
117 See (60), pp. 97–176.
118 Cited by H. Noguères (6), vol. 1, p. 426.
119 This former young royalist of the Action Française group who had broken with L'Action Française when Maurras had become a neo-pacifist, had vigorously attacked Flandin when he sent a telegram of congratulations to Hitler.
120 On this demonstration which – later on – gave rise to many enquiries as to its original inspiration, see H. Noguères (6), vol. 1, p. 171–187, and R. Josse, 'La naissance de la Résistance à Paris' (8), 192.
121 The occupying power made no mistake about it. It made a few minor material concessions but also deported 224 'ringleaders' (126 of whom never returned from the camps) and took 94 hostages (9 of whom were shot).
122 A number of movements that had already put down roots by 1941 have been the object of interesting monographs: M. Granet and H. Michel, *Combat, histoire d'un mouvement de résistance* (73), M. Granet, *Défense de la France, histoire d'un mouvement de résistance, 1940–1944*, PUF, 1960; A. Calmette, *L'organisation civile et militaire* (76); D. Veillon, *Le Franc-Tireur* (74).
123 See M. Granet, 'Un journal socialiste clandestin pendant l'occupation, *Libération-Nord*', *Revue Socialiste*, April-May 1966.
124 See the account of this nonchalant aristocrat and political adventurer who was so eager for action (75).
125 See (107).
126 See (74).
127 See the complementary accounts by H. Frenay (71) and C. Bourdet (72).
128 In the face of all the evidence, the PCF started off by denying the existence of any secret protocol appended to the German–Soviet pact, all the approaches made to the Kommandatur to allow *L'Humanité* to reappear in June 1940 and the letter sent by François Billoux to Pétain, to provide evidence for the Riom trial etc. On the evolution of the PCF historiography (which has always insisted that the line it adopted was unfailingly correct), see the study by René Galissot, 'Les communistes et les débuts de la Résistance', *Le Mouvement Social*, January 1971.
129 As is well known, the archives of the PCF have not been opened to the public. We are, of course, bound to regret the fact. In 1975, however, Les Editions

Sociales did at least publish the complete collection of the underground *Humanité*, although Charles Tillon claims that it had first been purged by Jacques Duclos. Nevertheless, Claudy Delattre's painstaking study of this affair makes interesting reading: 'L'attitude communiste à travers *l'Humanité* clandestine pendant l'Occupation, juin 1940–juin 1941', *Le Mouvement Social*, January 1971.

130 For the PCF side, see above all the minutes of the colloquium organised in 1969 by the Maurice-Thorez Institute, published in 1971 (77) and vol VI of *L'histoire de la France contemporaine* (126). Of the anti-communist literature, see A. Rossi, *Les communistes français pendant la drôle de guerre*, Les Iles d'Or, 1951; R. Tiersky, *Le mouvement communiste en France*, Fayard, 1973.There are two convenient syntheses: one by J. Fauvet (18), the other by H. Desvages, 'L'attitude communiste face à l'occupant', *Politique Aujourd'hui*, November–December 1976. Charles Tillon's argued demonstration should on no account be missed (79).

131 Nevertheless, we should not overlook the approach made on 6 June by Politzer, however isolated it may have been. Politzer had retained contact with a member of the Central Committee and he approached Anatole de Monzie to assure him that the communists intended 'to defend Paris' and take part in 'the national war'; a second approach is said to have been attempted a few days later.

132 The underground *Humanité*, 7 July 1940.

133 It is in itself symbolic. Jacques Duclos ended up by admitting to the evidence. Although the text was claimed to have been written on 10 July, it had in fact been antedated. The internal evidence provided by the text itself (the faulty numbering of this underground issue of *l'Humanité*, allusions made to events which did not take place until after 10 July, etc.)invalidated the veracity of the date which had been ascribed to it, later and for symbolic reasons. According to Chaintron, (115), p. 532, on 10 July all that was in truth printed was a short tract of twenty lines later inserted into the *Appel au peuple de France* which was itself produced and distributed at the end of July.

134 It is well worth reading as a whole as it is reproduced in full by H. Noguères (6), vol. 1, pp. 459–67. V. Joannès' claim to have played 'a decisive role in the creation and organisation of the Resistance' is very dubious; see *De la guerre à la Libération*, Editions sociales, 1972, p. 49. All the more so in view of the fact that, in early August, there appeared another appeal entitled 'Long live the union of the French nation' which ventured no more than an extremely orthodox analysis of the imperialist war and excluded any patriotic Jacobin struggle.

135 The word 'German' is used twice ('the great German offensive'; 'the German army's occupation'); the terms 'Hitler' and 'Nazi', never.

136 Who was responsible for initiating these overtures? Tréand or Duclos? There is no easy way of deciding. At all events, they were not isolated: Belgian communists acted in a similar fashion; in France negotiations with the Germans, who were determined to have the last word, lasted almost two months, never – apparently – with the approval of Maurice Thorez. See the exemplary article by D. Peschanski, '*L'Humanité*: légale?', *Le Mouvement Social*, 1980.

137 It should, however, be pointed out that they were sometimes given a leg up by trade-unionists such as Frachon who did not go along altogether with the *Humanité* line but did favour a struggle for revenge.

138 The painstaking and enthusiastic work by C. Angeli and P. Gillet, *Debout partisans!* (Fayard, 1970), gives a good survey of anti-fascist activities.

139 François Billoux's letter, dated 19 December 1940, is cited in full by H.

Nouguères (6), vol. 1, pp. 483–6. It was first and foremost a justification of the pacifist line adopted by the PCF ever since October 1939. [The court of Riom was where those whom Pétain considered responsible for the defeat of France were tried.]

140 In its account of the miners' strike, *L'Humanité* of 20 June 1941 remarked: 'You should make no mistake about it: our common salvation will not come from the victory of one kind of imperialism over another.'

141 Officially, it was not yet a question of appealing for the beginning of a struggle against Germany, and the *Humanité* issue of 25 May which announced its creation ran the headline: 'Down with the imperialistic war! Long live the National Front's struggle for the independence of France!'

142 See (79), p. 326.

143 See (79), p. 326.

144 Perhaps interpreters of this phenomenon have not sufficiently stressed the explicit references to 1871 and the pre-Commune situation.

145 In a prophetic statement that appeared at the beginning of June 1941, Jean Epstein, the future leader of the FTP in the Parisian region, wrote: 'If the Soviet Union ever enters into war against Germany, it will carry with it the vast majority of the people of France.'

146 On 30 June 1941, *Liberté*, the newspaper produced by François de Menthon's movement, wrote: 'If Hitler meets his end in this adventure, so will Bolshevism. Hitler is unwittingly doing Europe a service. Destruction is the only thing the communists are good at.'

147 On 'war Gaullism', see (7) and (80); also (82) and J. Charlot, *Le phénomène gaulliste*, Fayard, 1970. On the beginnings of Free France, see (81); the study by J.-P. Cointet, *La France libre*, PUF, 1975; the evidence of R. Cassin, *Les hommes partis de rien*, Plon, 1974; and A. Gillois, *L'histoire secrète des Français à Londres*, Hachette, 1972.

148 Contrary to the generally held belief, the Appeal of 18 June did not contain the much quoted sentence: 'France has lost a battle but France has not lost the war.' This appeared on a poster in London in July, antedated to 18 June.

149 Its nine members were all, with the exception of René Cassin, either officers or colonial administrators.

150 This was created on 16 November 1940; on 23 January 1946, 1,057 crosses were distributed, 1,036 to FFL combatants and members of the Resistance the youngest of whom, Barrioz, had died under torture at the age of fourteen. 6 women were made Companions of the Liberation; 18 crosses were awarded to fighting units; 5 honoured the towns of Nantes, Grenoble, Paris, the village of Vassieux-en-Vercors and the Ile de Sein.

151 See (7), vol. 1, p. 219.

152 On this rallying of the AEF during the 'Three glorious days' (26, 27 and 28 August), read the piquant *Chroniques irrévérencieuses* of the first commissioner of the free AEF, J. Lacouture.

153 The most handy biography is the dashing one by J. Lacouture (83).

154 Pétain broke with his protégé when de Gaulle published *La France et son armée*, a series of studies on the French soldier, originally undertaken under the aegis of Philippe Pétain.

155 His first work, *La discorde chez l'ennemi* (1942) was a book of topical interest; the second, *Le fil de l'épée*, was an essay on military psychology; it was his third, *Vers l'armée de métier* (1934) that won him a certain notoriety in specialist circles. His fourth, *La France et son armée*, appeared in 1938.

156 He was quite quick to perceive what a decisive effect the armoured divisons

would have. It was only later (the first mention comes in a *mémoire* addressed to a number of leading figures in January 1940) that he realised the potential of a combination of tanks and aircraft.

157 Charles de Gaulle attached much importance to the battle of Moncornet. Without wishing to detract from his memory, it would seem fair to go along with the following judgement passed by Jean Lacouture on de Gaulle as a strategist: 'Despite his physical courage, attested on at least a score of occasions, his almost super-human sang-froid and his proverbial energy, Charles de Gaulle does not appear to have displayed in the field those qualities of immediate understanding and inventiveness which make a commander into a Masséna or a Rommel regardless of whether it is 1,000 or 300,000 men that they have at their disposal (83), p. 58.

158 Paul Reynaud had tried to appoint him secretary general of the War Committee as early as March 1940, but he had come up against strong opposition.

159 No more than 800 copies of *L'armée de métier* had been sold.

160 Raymond Aron wrote later: 'At the time I resented him turning the movement into a personal affair... I was exasperated by the aggressiveness of the little Gaullist circle that encouraged him to lose all sense of proportion.' (cited by A. Gillois, *op. cit.*, p. 101).

161 The junior officers were relatively numerous and provided the FFL with a number of remarkable leaders: Hautecloque-*Leclerc*, Koenig, Paris de la Bollardière, Petit, Brosset, Massu, Buis, Dewavrin-*Passy*, etc. The nonconformist and forthright account of Georges Buis, *Les fanfares perdues*, Ed. du Seuil, 1975, is recommended reading. We should like to make it clear once and for all at this point that italics are used to indicate the pseudonyms adopted both by the Free French and also by the internal members of the Resistance; if the latter chose to retain their wartime name, it has been retained here.

162 See M.-C. Davet, *op. cit.*

163 Of a total of 70,000 men (5,000 of whom were FFL), 6,000 men were put out of action: after the armistice of Saint-Jean-d'Acre around 6,000 men joined the FFL while 32,000 chose to be repatriated to France.

164 See (7), vol. 1, pp. 145–80.

165 Roosevelt had sent as his ambassador Admiral Leahy whose mission was to exert pressure upon Pétain and restrain State collaboration as much as possible. Leahy's relations with the head of the French State were cordial, while he considered 'the *maquis* people' as 'a bizarre lot' with 'strange ideas'. See Langer, *Le jeu américain à Vichy*, Plon, 1948; on the external policies of the United States, see (84).

166 Admiral Muselier's small fleet landed commandos whose rifles were loaded with blanks. Most of the islanders had no compunction in rallying to Free France.

167 The Secretary of State went so far as to speak of 'so-called Free French ships'. It is true that Muselier had conducted negotiations in a muddled fashion. But the real reason for this diplomatic war stemmed from the fact that the expedition breached the efforts of American diplomacy to neutralise – without entering into hostilities – the 'local authorities' of territories that neighboured the United States.

168 According to Passy, 'he was scarcely heeded'; see Colonel Passy, *Souvenirs*, Monte-Carlo, Solar, 1947, vol. 1, p. 233.

169 On 23 August 1941, following the execution of the hostages at Châteaubri-

ant, he declared: 'The war of the French will have to be conducted by those who are in charge of it, that is to say, by myself and the National Council' (7), vol. 1, p. 288.

170 See the evocative account by Rémy, *Mission d'un agent secret de la France libre*, Aux Trois Couleurs, no date; Rémy 'held out' for eighteen months in France and made for London in February 1942.

171 It is likely that de Gaulle – like so many others – came under the influence of Maurras during the twenties. However, his nationalism, which was by no means exclusive, owed much more to Barrès and to Péguy. At the end of the thirties he was moving a great deal in Christian Democrat circles. It is quite true that there was nothing to predispose him in favour of leftist feeling.

172 It seems quite clear that Passy and many of his comrades at the time were not especially sold on democracy. On the other hand, René Cassin, Pierre-Olivier Lapie, Maurice Schumann and Georges Boris were all staunch republicans.

173 See (7), vol. 1, p. 84.

174 The institutions of Free France reflected a very Gaullist view of power. Thus, right from the start, 'decisions [were] taken by the head of the Free French forces after consultation – if necessary – with the Council of Defence'. Later, Pierre Brossolette, who became a staunchly loyal Gaullist but also continued to speak his mind, remarked in a letter to de Gaulle written on 2 November 1942: 'On some subjects you will tolerate no contradiction, no discussion even. The immediate effect is that, within your entourage, the less good elements all agree with you; the worst are out to defy you; and the best are no longer willing to listen to you' (Cited by D. Mayer, *op.cit.*, pp. 189–190.)

175 On 23 June 1942 he was still drawing comparisons between the two regimes: 'A moral, social, political and economic regime has abdicated in defeat, having paralysed itself in licentiousness. Another regime, emerging from criminal capitulation, is exalting in personal power. The French people condemns them both.'

176 Cited by A. Gillois, *op. cit.*, p. 299.

177 They are mentioned, as such, for the first time in a speech delivered in May 1942.

4 France at the time of the Germans

1 See the model monograph by P. Laborie (129), the reliable study by M. Luirard (130); also C. Rougeron's pages on *Le Département de l'Allier sous l'Etat français, 1940–1944*, Moulins, Préfecture for the Allier, 1969.

2 On the lives and deaths of French men and women, see (86); also (87). A. Guerin (89), and F. Renaudot have compiled an impressive iconographical record, *Les Français et l'Occupation*, Laffont, 1975.

3 On life in Vichy, see (50); (86); and Maurice Martin du Gard, *La chronique de Vichy, 1940–1944*, Flammarion, 1948.

4 See (50), p. 20.

5 On life in Paris, see (86) and (100). Also, for complementary details, G. Walter, *La vie à Paris sous l'Occupation*, Colin, 1960 and (to be read with some circumspection) H. Le Boterf, *La vie parisienne sous l'Occupation*, France-Empire, 1974–5, 2 vols.

6 On the collaborationist episode, see pp. 135–44.

7 All the examples cited are borrowed from André Halimi, *Chantons sous l'Occupation*, Marabout, 1976.

8 This anthology set out to prove that 'the Europe baptised in 1940 had in fact

already existed for a long time' (p. iii), that French authors had made their own contribution to it since they had already 'treated national socialist themes' (*ibid.*). And one should make no mistake about it: the European ideal that Fabre-Luce was celebrating was in no way inspired by an enlightened liberalism.

9 *Combats*, the newspaper of the Militia, printed articles by Colette, Paul Morand, Jacques de Lacretelle and Pierre MacOrlan, etc.

10 See the 'German years' of Coco Chanel as reconstructed by Edmonde Charles-Roux, *L'irrégulière*, Grasset, 1974, pp. 489–556.

11 See *Les Zazous* by J.-C. Loiseau, Le Sagittaire, 1977. It is true that this movement was used as a vehicle to express inter-generation resentments as well as a subversive protest on the part of students in the Quartier Latin, while at the same time it also reflected the life-style adopted by the gilded youth of the Champs-Elysées.

12 Among the new cultural pundits, we should mention the drama critic of *Je Suis Partout*, A. Laubreaux, who came down like a ton of bricks on everything. Very few productions escaped his scathing comments, with which he was exceedingly free. One, however, called *Les pirates de Paris* (a very dud piece about the Stavisky affair) was well received and covered with praise: the author, who used the pseudonym Michel Daxiat, was in fact A. Laubreaux himself.

13 Some kind of intellectual life was kept up in Nice which was important for the cinema world and, even more, in Lyons where most of the dailies and reviews of the southern zone had established themselves. But Paris retained its pride of place.

14 After the event, a number of works of ingenious interpretation appeared – in many cases too ingenious to carry much conviction. Thus totally devoted admirers of Sartre would insist that *Les mouches* was a play about the Resistance since it attacked one feature of the prevailing ideology, namely its breast-beating. But in that case one might just as well make Anouilh out to be a hero of the Resistance on account of his *Antigone* in which it could be argued that the rebel sister wins a moral victory over Créon, who collaborates for reasons of State. My own, more prudent, view is that, despite the considerable differences between these two authors, they were both making use of themes that were in the air at the time. Then one can also play the game of 'patriotic allusions'. But although the line from *La reine morte*, 'the flower of the kingdom is in prison' often won a round of applause, it is not enough to turn the author of *Le solstice de juin* into a Jacobin of the Year II. Nor, in my opinion, is it very likely that the famous scene at the end of *Les visiteuses du soir*, in which the Devil (Jules Berry) flagellates Anne (Marie Déa), who though still living has become a statue, was understood by spectators at the time as symbolising the vanity of any struggle of Hitler's against a resisting France.

15 See in A. Halimi (*op. cit.*, pp. 179–82) a summary of varying Sartrian views on liberty under the Occupation. See J.-P. Sartre, *Situations II*, Gallimard, 1948, pp. 48–53, 120–22, 244–80.

16 On the intellectual Resistance, see p. 157–8.

17 See (131), R. Régent, *Cinéma de France*, Bellefaye, 1948 and Joseph Daniel (96); also G. Sadoul, *Le cinéma français*, Flammarion, 1962, pp. 88–100; also *Les cahiers de la cinémathèque*, Perpignan, December 1972 and summer–autumn 1973; and also the collection of articles edited by André Bazin, *Le cinéma de l'Occupation et de la Résistance*, 10/18, 1975; and the useful school textbook by J. P. Jeancolas and D.-J. Jay, *Cinéma d'un monde en guerre*, La Documentation Française, 'Documentation photographique', August 1976.

18 The Occupation authorities banned all Anglo-Saxon films and all films released after October 1937. A German company, 'Continental', not only financed thirty or more French films but also tried to distribute as many German and Nazi films as possible. The most notable were *Le Juif süss*, by Viet Harlan, *Le jeune Hitlérien* and *Président Kruger*, which were given a barely acceptable reception. On the other hand, Abteilung Propaganda managed to get its hands on the newsreels (actualités Mondiales, later France-Actualités) which it was compulsory to show in between the documentary and the main film and, furthermore, to do so with the cinema hall semi-lit so that any demonstrations of hostility could be immediately checked.

19 A few directors and actors had gone to Hollywood: Ophuls, Renoir, René Clair, Duvivier, Michèle Morgan, Jean-Pierre Aumont and Jean Gabin (who joined the FFL), etc. But on the whole the Resistance did not make much impact on the cinema world.

20 In the commercial sector there was a considerable decrease in the number of bankcruptcies (48 in 1943 as against 2,221 in 1937) and in business failures.

21 Alfred Sauvy (56) allows himself to be misled by the sources upon which he places most reliance, his dearly-loved *Bulletins Rouge Brique* which relate to the economic situation and were produced by the Institute of the day. In all fairness to Sauvy, I freely agree that they were not inspired by the Vichy authorities and that they may well have been of some use to the economic services of Algiers. However, the people who undertook these researches at the time were not in a position to learn all the facts, and the handful of other serious sources available testify to the incontestable reality of the black market.

22 See the very reliable study by A. Milward (99). Some idea of the semi-clandestine rake-offs of the Germans is given in the report by the administration of economic control published in vol 4 in the series produced by the Comité de l'Histoire de la Guerre (committee for the history of the war) (May 1950). See also the well-documented enquiry by J. Delarue (88). On German economic strategies, see pp. 129–33.

23 Szolkonikoff appears to have been assassinated in Spain in 1945. As for Joanovici, he was eventually brought to justice despite the precautions he had taken – somewhat late in the day – in financing a Resistance network.

24 See (88), pp. 99–100. Inspector Delarue was responsible for leading the enquiries concerning the aftermath of the Occupation.

25 On economic collaboration, see pp. 131–2.

26 See the enquiry cited, p. 52.

27 See (88), p. 139.

28 Crossing 'the line' is an adventure that is *de rigueur* in a whole body of romantic literature. It is true that the operation was seldom an easy one. It is not hard to understand how it was that Dr Petiot – who posed as the leader of a network of escape into the southern zone – was able to lure so many victims whom he then killed, cut into pieces and robbed. Search parties found more than one hundred blouses and skirts in his house.

29 There were official days 'without', interspersed with days 'with' (meat, alcohol. etc.) and the menus of restaurants were – in theory – subject to strict controls. In big cities it was definitely recommended to register with a particular retailer to have a better chance of getting one's vouchers for meat, tobacco etc. honoured.

30 They ranged from E (less than three years of age), to V (over 70 years of age), including J (for instance, J3 – between 13 and 21 years of age) and A (from 21 to 70 years of age). Two groups, heavy labourers and women who were pregnant or breast-feeding, were allowed supplementary rations.

31 To obtain approximations in terms of current prices, see note 80, Chapter 3. To give an equally eloquent standard of comparison: non-taxed eggs were on sale at 11 francs each (see (56), p. 127) which was more than the hourly wage of an unskilled worker in the Paris region. In 1978 an egg cost rather less than one-twentieth of the hourly wage of an employee on SMIC.

32 The free zone – especially in the Midi – came off the worst as, before the war, the occupied zone had produced about 70% of the wheat, 85% of the butter, 65% of the beef and veal, and all the sugar. The barrier of the demarcation line and an increasingly widespread tendency to aim for self-sufficiency created some extremely difficult local situations.

33 Although this was not the only cause of the shortages, as can be seen from sales of meat (see (56), pp. 130–1). Out of a total production of 1,150,000 tons (French *tonnes*), the peasants kept 250,000 from family slaughtering and a further equal quantity from secret slaughtering; but the Germans also carried off 240,000 tons, the middlemen 120,000. Once the priority groups had received their 100,000 tons, ordinary people were left with 190,000, that is to say 14 grams per day.

34 Ephraim Grenadou and Alain Prévost, *Grenadou, paysan français*, Ed. du Seuil, 1978, pp. 204–5 (1st ed: 1966). The book is already a classic and is highly recommended reading.

35 The normal ration for an adult was 350 grams of bread a day in September 1940. In April 1941 it fell to 275, then rose to 300 in November 1943. The sugar ration never – except for a few weeks – rose above 500 grams per month; the ration for fats was also 500 grams in 1940 and this fell to 150 in 1944.

36 They appear to have filled as many 'solvent' stomachs as family ones. The records for 1942 indicate that about 13,500,000 'family parcels' were sent, the equivalent of 279,000 tons (*tonnes*) of foodstuffs. But even so, they did not make up for the shortages.

37 The station of Toury (Beauce) saw its monthly total of travellers visiting the town rise from 700, before the war, to 12,000 in 1943.

38 See Table v in (56), p. 241 which shows that the relationship of money spent on food to the income of a couple depended on whether or not the wife went out to work. Depending on whether or not she was solely a housewife, the relationship was respectively 95% and 55% for a childless household, 126% and 91% for a couple with two children aged 10 and 14, 107% and 82% for a couple with three children aged 6, 10 and 14.

39 From a demographic point of view, losses by reason of the war were relatively moderate compared with those suffered by the Soviet Union or Germany. Overall, furthermore, the Second World War cost fewer lives and wiped out fewer age-groups than the First. 'Civilians' certainly paid a higher price: possibly as many as 170,000 (including those killed in air raids, French racial and political deportees, those who faced firing squads or were executed in other ways); 'military' losses however were far lower: around 230,000 (including the soldiers who took part in the 1940 campaign, the FFL and the FFI, and the men of Alsace-Lorraine drafted into the Wehrmacht); to this figure should be added some 100,000 prisoners of war and deportees for forced labour who died in Germany.

40 Mortality varied in different age, social and professional groups and also from one region to another. Thus the mortality-rate in the south was, relatively, higher.

41 While infant mortality (ie. up to the age of one year) did not increase more than 8%, adolescents were much more at risk. Adults did not suffer so much – north of the Loire at any rate – partly because there was a significant fall in deaths

resulting from alcoholism (table wine was rationed and the rights of still-owners abolished).

42 It is interesting that the proportion of illegitimate children increased by 20%.

43 Such an explanation based on the idea of a tenacious faith in life is supported by the appreciable drop in the number of suicides.

44 On the political evolution of the internal Resistance, see Chapter 5. On the lives and deaths of underground Resistance workers, see in particular (89), vol. 3; the extremely moving account of R. Pannequin, *Ami si tu tombes*, Sagittaire, 1976; and (72).

45 See (109), p. 165.

46 The official Pantheon of the Resistance certainly includes the names of a number of women: Danièle Casanova, the Jeunesses Communistes leader who died as a deportee; Bertie Albrecht, second-in-command of Combat who, when arrested in Mâcon in May 1943, shouted 'Mind out, friends, the Gestapo is here' and then, it would appear, chose to hang herself rather than go through the agonies of a second period of imprisonment. Others are perhaps less well known: Francine Fromond, the PCF militant who was abominably tortured but died without saying a word, or Princess Vera Oblensky who knew all the secrets of the OCM and was executed in August 1944 without having 'talked', or the militant socialist Suzanne Buisson arrested in March 1944 and never heard of again, or Emilienne Mopty who in May 1941 led the demonstration of the Hénin-Lietard miners' wives and was beheaded in January 1943. And there are many others too. Records and personal accounts have been collected by Nicole Chatel and Annie Boulineau, *Des femmes dans la Résistance*, Julliard, 1972; by Ania Francos, *Il était des femmes dans la Résistance*, Stock, 1978; and in the proceedings of the colloquium held in November 1975, *Les femmes dans la Résistance*, Ed. du Rocher, 1977.

47 A number of intelligence networks lived through dramatic 'affairs' most of which ended disastrously. For instance, the destruction of the 'Interallié' network can largely be accounted for by the complicated life of a double agent, Mathilde Carré, whose memoirs (*J'ai été la chatte*, Morgan, 1959) are not particularly convincing.

48 In theory those who were well and truly underground agents of the Resistance were supposed to lead solitary lives or at least sever all communications with their families. But there were plenty of exceptions: one, for instance, was André Ouzoulias who, despite the fact that he was an extremely disciplined militant, used to visit his wife once or twice a month.

49 To keep a comrade waiting for more than a quarter of an hour was greatly to increase the risk of his being arrested. In theory, a 'fall-back' rendezvous would have been arranged in accordance with a previously established calendar.

50 In the popular quarters of Lyons there were such warrens of dwellings that it was quite easy for rebels to slip from one to another.

51 See G. Guingouin (116). He insisted that anybody who did not belong to the *maquis* – including dignitaries of the PCF – should be brought blindfolded to his ultimate hideout in the forest of Châteauneuf.

52 For instance, that great member of the Resistance, Jacques Bingen, the civilian delegate of the southern zone, who had been arrested following an act of betrayal, could have given his guards the slip had not an employee of the Banque de France thoughtlessly named the fugitive to the occupants of a German lorry.

53 The head of the Secret Army, General Delestraint, was arrested on 9 June 1943 at the station of La Muette as a result of Aubry, one of the leaders of the AS, leaving an uncoded message in a letter-box that had been 'blown'. Using the

receipt given for a telephone message found on Roland Farjo, the Germans discovered a hiding place where they found the uncoded names and addresses of the leaders of the OCM. The movement was then decapitated. The reconstruciton of the 'Farjon affair' by G. Perrault (*La longue traque*, Jean-Claude Lattès, 1975) does not appear to have convinced most members of the Resistance.

54 It should be said that in what must be called 'the Hardy affair', the two court judgements of 1947 and 1950 acquitting René Hardy require the historian to abide by the 'verdict given'. For more details, see the clear and convincing study by Henri Noguères (6), vol. 3, pp. 410–73.

55 Henri Noguères has every right to point out that 'if one adopts the point of view of the rules implicitly accepted by all members of the Resistance, the mistake that René Hardy admits having made is inexcusable and beyond mitigating circumstances' (6), vol. 3, p. 466. Henri Frenay seems to have expressed the sentiments of many members of the Resistance when he wrote: 'Every Frenchman who knew about and lived through this affair has his own opinion. I have mine. I have already expressed it once and would do so again if the chance arose, by refusing to shake the hand of René Hardy' (71), p. 490.

56 On the calvary of Jean Moulin, see the painstaking enquiry by his sister, Laure Moulin, *Jean Moulin*, Geneva, Ed. de Grémille, 1970, 2 vols. The preface to this work contains the text of the fine speech made by André Malraux on the occasion of Jean Moulin's ashes being transferred to the Panthéon, on 19 December 1964. In his speech he paid honour to the work and sacrifice of *Max*: 'Poor tortured king of shades, behold your people of shades rising up in a June night shining with constellations of torture.'

57 André Devigny has written his own detailed account (Hachette, 1958) and Robert Bressen made a film quite remarkable for its restraint, from the book, *Un condamné à mort s'est échappé*.

58 See (108), p. 312.

59 See (63). For Alsace, see the fully study by L. Kettenacker (90).

60 During the twenties, the PCF had defended the right of Alsace-Lorraine to secede. A number of 'Alsation communists' (Hüber and Mourer among them) became men of straw for the Nazis during the Occupation. See P. Bankwitz, *Les chefs autonomistes alsaciens, 1919–1947, saisons d'Alsace*, Strasbourg, Istra, 1980.

61 Karl Ross was shot as a spy in 1940.

62 The first expulsions attracted a certain amount of attention: in November 1940 – barely three weeks after Montoire – 63 convoys deposited in the free zone refugees most of whom had been given no more than an hour to put together a maximum of 50 kilos of luggage and 2,000 francs.

63 The inhabitants of Mulhouse must inwardly have reflected that there was a certain irony in the renaming of the rue du Sauvage as rue Adolf Hitler.

64 In 1944, the Wehrmacht called up men born between 1910 and 1924 in Moselle and those born between 1910 and 1928 in Alsace. Most of these 'unwilling' conscripts were sent to the Russian front. This enforced mobilisation had repercussions some of which leave their mark even today.

65 Whole families were transplanted or even deported to Germany. There were some dramatic episodes at the time of their incorporation. Thus, in February 1943, 206 conscripts from Ballesdorf decided to escape to Switzerland. 183 reached their destination but of the 23 who decided to turn back, 17 were shot in the Struthof.

66 This paragraph owes a great deal to the account of Henri Dubrief. See P. Gascar, *Histoire de la captivité des Français en Allemagne, 1939–1945*, Gallimard 1967; and especially Y. Durand (132). See also R. Ikor's *Pour une fois écoute, mon enfant*, Albin

Michel, 1975, and the caustic account by J. Perret, *Le caporal épinglé*, Gallimard, 1947.

67 On the 'Relief' see p. 127. Following the failure of 'Operation Jubilee' that the Anglo-Canadians mounted near Dieppe, Hitler gave the order to liberate 1,580 prisoners who came from Dieppe or the Dieppe region.

68 About 5% of the prisoners remained in the base camps, employed on maintenance; a large number of *Kommandos* would return there for the night.

69 The 'reprisal' camps form a separate category: Colditz and Lübeck for officers. Ruwa-Ruska for escapees from the *Stalags* or hard cases. The punishment drills, with a selection of physical exercises, were much feared and food rations were reduced to the absolute minimum.

70 The French word means soup tureen.

71 As from 1944, escape became a very risky business. 3,000 made it in 1944, but the year before 33,000 had done so. There were two Resistance movements in France that recruited among freed and escaped prisoners: the MNPGD run by M. Cailliau and *Philippe Dechartre* and the MRPDG run by François Mitterrand who had made his own escape only after two abortive attempts.

72 In an attempt to increase their productivity, the Germans offered to 'transform' prisoners into civilian workers receiving a wage and enjoying more freedom of movement. They even allowed them periods of 'leave' but these were soon discontinued as many who had gone 'on leave' failed to return to Germany.

73 The description of 'labour deportees' that they are apt to claim is one denied them by many members of the Resistance and also by the courts; on the STO, see (91); and p. 128.

74 In the autumn of 1943 there were around 22,000 of these.

75 It is true that the 'Bruneton mission' set up in 1943 was more efficient than the 'Scapini mission' for prisoners, particularly where health was concerned.

76 Such as Grossbeeren, Spergau, Luxendorf.

77 It should be added that about 10,000 men from the STO chose to remain in Germany after the war.

78 See M. Marrus and R. Paxton (92); also (62); G. Wellers, *L'étoile jaune à l'heure de Vichy*, Fayard, 1973; and J. Laloum, *La France antisémite de Darquier de Pellepoix*, Syros, 1979. Much evidence and many works on the subject have been collected in Paris at the Centre de Documentation Juive Contemporaine.

79 They also played upon the prevailing atmosphere of anti-semitism. A French doctor, H. J., opposed his son Jean's projected marriage to a Jewish girl, Annette Zelman, so strongly that he went so far as to alert the Commissariat for Jewish questions which passed the matter on to the Nazi authorities. Despite the fact that the two young people decided to give up the idea of marrying, Annette Zelman was arrested on May 1942, deported on convoy 3 on 22 June 1942 and never returned from Auschwitz.

80 At the Liberation, some Jewish circles bitterly criticised the Union Générale des Israélites en France, set up by Vichy on 29 April 1941, which had considered it possible and necessary to go along with the Nazis a certain way in the hope of mollifying them.

81 On the measures taken by the French State, see above, p. 58.

82 See p. 127.

83 On this episode, see (88). Foreign Jews believed for a period of about ten months that they had found a relative haven in the Italian zone of occupation, after this had been extended in November 1942. While there, they were not mistreated in any way. However, in September 1943, the Gestapo carried out a huge round-up in Nice and the surrounding areas.

84 Almost all were Jews. The Nazis did not have time to transfer all the gypsies interned in France to the death camps.
85 See S. Klarsfeld, *Le mémorial de la déportation des juifs en France*, Ed. B and S. Klarsfeld, 1978; H. Langbein, *Hommes et femmes à Auschwitz*, Fayard, 1975; and L. Poliakov, *Auschwitz*, Julliard, 1964.
86 This is the figure that S. Klarsfeld arrives at, using German sources, in an altogether meticulous fashion. His book – a model of its kind – is the latest to appear on this subject. It should definitively discredit those who still dare to claim that Auschwitz and the final solution were simply fables dreamed up by 'international Jewry'.
87 Children under six years of age represented 2.7% of the Jews deported from France; children between 6 and 12 years, 5.8%, adolescents between 13 and 18 also 5.8%. The first deported children appear in convoy 19 of 14 August 1942.
88 14,469 of them came from old French stock, the rest had been naturalised more recently.
89 Let us cite the example of convoy 17 of 10 August 1942: it carried 997 racial deportees (525 women, 472 men). 766 were immediately eliminated. When the camp was liberated there was only one survivor from the entire convoy.
90 This is the estimate given by S. Klarsfeld.
91 See first the work by Olga Wormser and Henri Michel (93) which contains many personal accounts and references; also the accurate and sensitive thesis by Olga Wormser (94); also E. Kogon, *L'Etat SS, le système des camps de concentration allemands*, Ed. du Seuil, 1970, C. Bourdet (72); G. Tillon *Ravensbrück*, Ed. du Seuil, 1973; and *La déportation*, FNDIRP, 1967. The film *Nuit et brouillard* should on no account be missed.
92 Ruled with a rod of iron by Himmler and his SS men, the system included twenty or more camps upon which a large number of *Kommandos* were based; the distribution of these varied at different times. In theory, the following were classed as camps: Stutthof, Neuengamme, Bergen-Belsen, Ravensbrück, Orianenburg-Sachsenhausen (the main camp), Osnabrück, Esterwegen, Buchenwald, Gross-Rosen, Auschwitz, Maïdanek, Thereisienstadt, Flossenburg, Mauthausen, Dachau, Struthof, Schirmeck. The last two were situated in Alsace: Schirmeck was a re-education camp where some 15,000 Alsatians were interned, treated as convicts. Struthof-Natzwiller was a veritable extermination camp where 'political' prisoners of French nationality were sent from July 1943 onward. The deportees were assigned to *Kommandos* in which they were worked to death (the coffin with four places in it taken along with them every day seldom returned empty). They were finished off by spades or clubs, or hurled into the 'death ravine' where sentries shot 'escapees'. Political prisoners were exterminated quite systematically there, among them 108 members of the Alliance network, killed on the night of 1–2 September 1944.
93 In a letter to Himmler dated 30 April 1942, the SS General Pohl stressed that it was 'now necessary to direct all efforts to the economic side'. Deportees were used for anything and everything: draining marshland, quarrying stone, building roads, camps, factories, making tunnels, manufacturing war materials, etc. In the end this too was extermination: they were worked to death. The SS Commandant of Mauthausen would greet the deportees as follows: 'Germany needs your efforts, you will therefore work. But I should tell you that you will never see your families again. Once you have entered the camp, the only way out is through the crematorium chimney.' On labour in the concentration camps, see (94), pp. 294–402.
94 As early as February 1941, the Farben IG set up a 'Buna' factory in Auschwitz;

in 1942 the Krupp factories in Essen were using 5,000 'striped pyjamas' as well as 18,000 prisoners of war. Siemens, Roechling as well as other lesser captains of industry showed not the slightest compunction about using this slave labour force bought from the SS.

95 The decree of 7 December 1941 classed as NN (the correct interpretation seemed to be 'Nacht und Nebel', night and fog) those deportees all traces of whom had to be wiped out before their systematic extermination.

96 On 2 July 1944, 2,521 deportees left Compiègne on a journey which was, admittedly, particularly arduous. 984 were dead upon arrival. By 1945 only 121 survived.

97 This, in theory, was the infirmary. Occasionally, when the *Häftlinge* doctors were able to get their way, it might gain a breathing space for some. But just as often it was the antechamber of death. Sometimes it was even a laboratory for experiments (mutilations, sterilisations, inoculations of various diseases, etc.) carried out by SS doctors upon human guinea-pigs.

98 P. Vidal-Naquet, 'Un Eichmann de papier', *Esprit*, 1980, is essential reading.

99 In the women's camps it was based on *Aufseherinnen*.

100 Beneath them was a whole subordinate hierarchy of those in charge of a Block, secretaries, those in charge of particular huts, etc. There were about 25 intermediaries for every 1,000 deportees.

101 As a rule they could eat their fill and were not subjected to forced labour. Many of them – a few political, but mostly common-law deportees – behaved as brutal tyrants. If André Lacaze is to be believed (*Le tunnel*, Julliard, 1978), in order to satisfy their homosexual needs, common-law prisoners forced deportees to prostitute themselves. In some camps women deportees were prostituted in brothels reserved, in the main, for the SS and the *Kapos*.

102 Buchenwald could hold up to 40,000 deportees.

103 Every deportee wore a coloured triangle (green for common-law prisoners, red for political ones, violet for conscientious objectors, pink for homosexuals), and a sign indicating nationality. Some were used as pawns in the bitter struggle between the common-law and the political prisoners. As a rule, daily life in the camp was under the brutal rule of German common-law criminals.

104 The Committee for the History of the Second World War has identified, apart from members of the Resistance, just over 9,000 people taken in round-ups, about 8,000 'politicals' arrested on preventative grounds, about 1,000 common-law prisoners and 5,000 others.

105 It seems to have varied from one camp to another (fewer died at Buchenwald than at Mauthausen or at the Struthof) and also from one age-group to another; during the very last weeks, by which time epidemics were endemic, the last groups to be transferred suffered more deaths than ever.

5 Relief operations

1 See the summary by H. Michel, *La Seconde Guerre Mondiale*, PUF, 1975; for more profound studies, see A. Latreille, *La Seconde Guerre Mondiale*, Hachette, 1965; J. Vidalenc (2); H. Michel (3).

2 Enraged by the failure of the Protocoles de Paris, Hitler, despite the efforts of Abetz and Benoist-Méchin to relaunch political collaboration (see (63), pp. 304–8), maintained the status quo.

3 Blum and Daladier had already been condemned to detention in a fortified place by Philippe Pétain, legal justice being, for a time, suspended. They became, willy-nilly, the stars in a much publicised open trial that began on 19 February

1942; see P. Mazé and R. Génebrier, *Les grandes journées du procès de Riom*, La Jeune Parque, 1945, and H. Michel, *Le procès de Riom*, Albin Michel, 1980.

4 In Vichy, rumour had it that Romier and Barthélémy were still the court favourites. At this time Laval had had two interviews with Pétain, during which he had brandished the spectre of polonisation for France.

5 Basing their remarks upon German sources, E. Jäckel (63) and G. Warner (98) stress the evident misgivings of the Reich where Laval was concerned.

6 On Laval, see two useful works: F. Kupferman, *Pierre Laval*, Masson, 1976, and H. Cole, *Pierre Laval*, Fayard, 1964; the most carefully researched biography remains that of G. Warner (98). Laval's only daughter, José de Chambrun, piously assembled testimonies bearing credit to her father, in three thick volumes misleadingly entitled *La vie de la France sous l'Occupation*, Plon, 1957; only to be used with circumspection.

7 He was simultaneously pursuing a businessman's career which proved most lucrative. He used his profits from this to appropriate at no great cost a number of regional newspapers such as *Le Moniteur du Puy-de-Dôme*. Note that under the occupation inter-zonal passes were printed by one of his presses.

8 In his conversations with Mussolini in January 1935, Laval had intimated that France would allow fascist Italy 'a free hand'. The Duce took this as applying quite literally to the Ethiopian affair. He was offended by the prevarications of Laval and opposed the project of appointing him French Ambassador to the Quirinal in 1938; see F. Kupferman, *op.cit.*, pp. 65–6.

9 In mid-crisis, Laval extracted from Pétain Constitutional Act number 12 (17 November 1942), conferring new powers upon himself: 'Apart from constitutional laws, the head of the government may promulgate laws and decrees on his own signature...'

10 Pétain had made sure he retained some room for manoeuvre: it was Darlan who remained heir apparent and became the commander of military forces.

11 Pétain made an abundant show of their amical relations. Thus, in the presence of leaders of the Légion des Combattants, he declared on 10 June 1942: 'When Monsieur Laval speaks, he is in agreement with me just as I am with him as I speak to you now. He is the head of the government. He plots out the line to be followed. We enjoy a total communion in respect of our ideas and our actions.'

12 See p. 180.

13 Right up until the spring of 1944 the government team underwent no more than minimal changes.

14 Pierre Cathala, an 'independent radical' and lawyer who was close to Franklin-Bouillon, had become an intimate associate of Laval who had in the past made him a minister. Max Bonnafous, a product of Ulm, with a university degree and also a prefect, spent some time in the neo-socialist camp before rallying to Laval. Laval had also placed faithful supporters, J. Guérard, G. Hilaire, Rochat and R. Bonnefoy, in posts of political responsibility.

15 He had, on the other hand, systematically eliminated all those (who had not resigned of their own accord) whom he suspected of having been party to the 13 December cabale: Bouthillier, Belin, Caziot etc.

16 A small proportion of former Uriage pupils went off to the Vercors and later joined the *maquis* in the Montagne Noire region.

17 See F. Kupferman, *op cit.*, p. 143.

18 See (102), p. 372.

19 He had chosen as Belin's successor to the post of Minister of Work H. Lagar-

delle, a theorist of socialism who, during the early years of the century, had enjoyed some popularity among anarcho-syndicalist circles, but who had later proved a disappointment to all concerned.

20 Of all the councillors of State, only one refused to swear the oath. He was E. Blondeau, J. Jeanneney's personal private secretary.

21 De Gaulle, for his part, later wrote in his *Mémoires de Guerre*, vol. 2, p. 299: 'He did, no doubt, try to serve his country. Let us at least not deny him that...'

22 At the meeting of the Council of Ministers on the 24th, not a single member had any criticism to make of a statement which had, after all, scandalised or shocked the great majority of the French people. As for Darlan, he penned a letter of congratulations of the most whole-hearted kind: 'Allow me, dear President, to offer you my most sincere congratulations on your moving and courageous address'; his compliments are in direct contradiction to the thesis that would have it that the admiral too was playing a double game. As for Pétain, to whom this speech had previously been submitted, he raised only one small, formal, objection: 'You are not a soldier so you have no right to say "I believe..."'; you know nothing about it.' Laval, by now well schooled, hit upon a more civilian kind of expression: 'I desire...' What a find! On the composition of the text, see (35), pp. 397–406.

23 In a letter to Ribbentrop dated 12 May 1942, Laval made some dangerous offers: 'To win the great battle of history, Germany has mobilised the youngest and strongest of its people. It is consequently in need of men. I understand these needs and am ready to offer you my help'; see O. Abetz, *Pétain et les Allemands*, Gaucher, 1948, p. 158.

24 On Laval's bargaining, see pp. 124–33.

25 The *maréchalistes* – in particular Paul Auphan, in his book *Les grimaces de l'histoire* (Les Iles d'Or, 1951) – have tried to promote the thesis that Pétain encouraged Darlan to bring North Africa back into the war against the Axis. It is imperative to look back at the chronology and undertake the strictest analysis of the sources, those collected by A. Kammerer, *Du débarquement africain au meurtre de Darlan*, Flammarion, 1949 and, above all, by L. Noguères (35), pp. 407–547; the latter includes the day-to-day notes taken by Ménétrel, Pétain's doctor, who was also his confidant. They are indeed valuable, but one should be wary with regard to the interpretation given them by their author, *after* the event, in 1945. For instance, his interpretation of the notes he had made on 10 November 1942: 'Am. Auphan telegr. to D personally in agreement' (p. 448) ran as follows: 'From that moment onwards, the Maréchal approved of and encouraged Admiral Darlan, who had stopped the fighting and was getting on well with the Americans' (p. 449). He was, in fact, falsifying both the text and the chronology and it is easy to show that the telegram in question was one in reply to a cable in which Darlan expressed no more than a neutralist attitude. On this complex matter, muddled even further by the existence of 'secret telegrams' exchanged between Vichy and Algiers, it is essential to consult the clear, accurate and convincing work by P. Dhers (97).

26 This was ratified by Vichy in February 1941. The United States, which wanted to make sure that the Axis powers would not lay their hands upon the supplies delivered to North Africa, had meanwhile imposed the presence of twelve 'vice-consuls' who were, it must be admitted, better at collecting intelligence than at shining in terms of classical diplomacy.

27 The French Admiralty had initially thought that the two convoys which had got past the Straits of Gibraltar were bound for Malta.

28 On the development of the situation in North Africa, see Chapter 3.

29 It has been claimed (even recently, by P. Ordioni, *Tout commence à Alger*, Stock, 1972) that the presence of Darlan in Algiers could be explained by the launching of 'Operation Torch'. There is no evidence to support such a thesis. Darlan and, even more, his friend Admiral Fenard, had certainly been contacted by American emissaries, but nothing fruitful had emerged from these conversations. Darlan had been recalled to Algiers on account of a deterioration in the health of his only son, Alain.

30 In the text received by Vichy, this proposal was combined with the offer of an alliance 'durch Dick und Dünn' (through thick and thin). In the opinion of E. Jäckel, (63), pp. 344–9, this offer of an alliance was in all probability a suggestion added personally by Abetz.

31 That was the text of the first 'secret telegram', transmitted in an ultra-secret code that was to be used until 14 November. Its precise and limited meaning is clear but it was no doubt followed up by another secret telegram the gist of which it is impossible to know since it was, supposedly, destroyed.

32 Vichy then gave full powers to General Noguès.

33 It was to Abetz that it fell, in Munich, to awaken Laval at four o'clock in the morning, to break the news to him.

34 The Italian zone of occupation, hitherto a small one, was rounded out and extended to include the Alpes-Maritimes, the Var, the Hauts- et Basses-Alpes, the Savoie and the Haute Savoie, and the Drôme and took in parts of the departments of the Isère and the Vaucluse. The Wehrmacht eventually came to occupy the region on 8 November 1943, after Maréchal Badoglio had capitulated.

35 This order – on the directions of the government – annulled the orders of General Verneau, the head of the general staff and the future leader of the army's Resistance Organisation, who had directed the armistice army to leave its positions if the southern zone were to be invaded. Bridoux subsequently forced the officers to hand over to the Axis powers all stocks of secret weapons which – to a remarkable degree – they proceeded to do.

36 Vichy claimed he was a megalomaniac; he was sentenced to ten years detention but escaped from the Riom prison.

37 See (63), p. 357.

38 Since the invasion of the free zone and the penetration of Axis forces into Tunisia, Auphan, who had initially been a staunch supporter of the greatest firmness in respect of the Anglo-Saxons, had decided that it would now be better to restrict oneself to a strict two-way neutrality. Only a few days later he tendered his resignation, along with Gibrat and Barnaud.

39 At this point he was struck by a major excommunication order: 'Up until this day, I have refused to believe in the treachery of Admiral Darlan... I am not a man to give way before a difficulty, to suggest the contrary would be an injustice... By placing himself at the service of a foreign power, Admiral Darlan has put himself beyond the pale of the national community.' All these quotations are drawn from the work by P. Dhers (97)

40 Noguès, who was uncertain and alarmed, was pressing Vichy to give way a little, emphasising that 'the essential thing [is] to keep North Africa rallied around the Maréchal, not in the name of dissidence'. In his telegram of 12 November, he advised Vichy once again to entrust to Darlan the task of entering into negotiations on the spot. It was probably *that* recommendation that met with the 'deep agreement of the Maréchal and the President'. For more details, see Pierre Dhers' account which to date remains by far the most accurate one.

41 As for the 'occupation authorities', they were in all probability no longer interested in Darlan's machinations.

42 He continued, however, to alternate protests and professions of goodwill. As an example of the first, he dryly declared on 11 November: 'I solemnly protest against these decisions which are incompatible with the armistice agreement'; as an example of the second, on 5 December 1942, he wrote to Hitler as follows: 'In increasing the powers of President Laval, I have demonstrated my desire to see the establishment of relations of reciprocal confidence between our two countries, with the aim of reaching a political *entente*'; see (35), pp. 538–9.

43 Pétain had associated with Constitutional Act number 12, which granted Laval the power to sign for 'laws and also decrees', a restrictive counter-stipulation which definitely dotted the 'i's and crossed the 't's: 'You will not engage France, or allow it to be engaged directly or indirectly in a war against any power whatsoever; nor will you recognise any state of belligerence between France and any other nation or military power whatsoever.'

44 See (35), p. 479.

45 Hitler, who did not think that he would gain possession of it intact, had already offered it to Mussolini; see (63), p. 360.

46 See A. Kammerer, *La passion de la flotte française*, Fayard, 1951 and above all L. Noguères, *Le suicide de la flotte française à Toulon*, Laffont, 1961. In Vichy, Laval wanted to 'negotiate' and had a telegram sent to Toulon that ran as follows: '... avoid all incidents ... this overrides all orders previously received'; see H. Noguères, *op. cit.*, pp. 143–5. However, Admiral Laborde and his subordinates obeyed the previous orders and scuttled some sixty units, one battleship, 9 cruisers and 25 submarines. The crews of only four submarines decided to put out to sea: 3 of these, the *Casabianca*, the *Marsouin* and the *Glorieux* managed to reach North Africa.

47 See (63), p. 371.

48 Ciano, with some satisfaction, records the interview that Laval had with Hitler on 9 December 1942: 'After two days spent travelling by train, they sat him down first at a tea table, then at a dinner table, without allowing him to open his mouth; every time he tried to broach some subject, the Führer interrupted, to preach at him'; see Ciano, *op.cit.*, p. 501.

49 See (98), p. 368.

50 On the murders and executions of hostages, see pp. 145–6.

51 As is well known, the non-retroactivity of laws is a sacrosanct principle of French law; the Nazis, who were in no way embarrassed by such judicial quibbles, were delighted at this reversal. It is true that some Vichy officials went beyond even what the Wehrmacht demanded of them. Thus J.-P. Ingrand, speaking in the name of Pucheu, announced: 'the sentence passed by the special tribunal will be executed in exemplary fashion by beheading by the guillotine in a Paris square'; see (63), p. 270. Boemelburg was so astonished that – if we are to believe the evidence of H. Villeré (*L'affaire de la section spéciale*, Fayard, 1972, p. 201) – he exclaimed: 'And then he asked me if the Germans would be satisfied!' One of the five judges protested against this parody of justice but was not able to prevent the sentence and execution of Emile Bastard, Abraham Trzebrucki and André Bréchet; he managed – for the time being – to save the heads of three other communists who had been found guilty. Other special tribunals were set up in the two zones and functioned in an equally summary manner.

52 Pucheu always denied that he had 'trafficked in hostages'. However, at the Liberation the archives were found to contain the following conclusively damaging letter from the sub-prefect of Châteaubriant to the Kommandatur, which ran: 'Further to our conversation today, I have the honour of confirming that the Minister of the Interior has today made contact with General von Stulpnagel for

the purpose of indicating to him the communist internees that are the most dangerous of those at present interned at Châteaubriant' (cited by H. Giraud, *Un seul but, la victoire* Julliard, 1949, p. 279).

53 The 'special brigade' of Commissioner David alone made 2,071 arrests. It handed over to the Germans 495 members of the Resistance, 125 of whom were shot.

54 On 1 December 1942, Hitler exclaimed: 'There is nothing more hated in [that] country than the police . . . One day it will beg us not to leave'; see (63), p. 375.

55 3,031 men, 5,802 women and 4,051 children, according to the German statistics; a number of Jews had managed to escape the trap, thanks to indiscretions or to their having paid attention to the rumours going around. On these days of July, see C. Lévy and P. Tillard, *La grande rafle du Vel' d'Hiv'*, Laffont, 1967. Losey's film, *Monsieur Klein* (1976), is not without interest.

56 In the 16 camps situated in the southern zone, foreign Jews made up the majority of the interned 'undesirables'. At first the transfers were selective but from the autumn of 1942 onward, all considerations of age and health were suppressed.

57 Advocates anxious to whitewash the Vichy leaders appeared with remarkable regularity; see, for instance, in *Le Monde* of 11 and 23 September 1971, the claims of René de Chambrun and the refutations of those who contradicted him; see also the bibliography given in chapter 4, note 78.

58 See S. Klarsfeld, *op. cit.* Brasillach echoed Laval when he berated the Archbishop of Toulouse, who had made a spirited stand against these round-ups: '. . . for we must separate ourselves from the Jews *en bloc* and not keep the children; on this point humanity is in agreement with wisdom. But he [Mgr Saliège] forgets to mention that these brutalities are the work of police *agents provocateurs* trying to make us poor Aryan fools feel pity.' (*Je Suis Partout*, 25 September 1942); cited by P. Ory, *La France allemande* (100), p. 81. It is known that at least 10,000 Jewish children and adolescents were sent to the death camps. Only a few dozen returned.

59 185,000 French volunteers appear to have entered Germany; in June 1942 about 70,000 remained. By September there were 43,000, who were to remain in the Reich until 1945.

60 Those men given 'prisoner's leave' had, in principle, been selected from among the oldest, those in poor health and fathers with more than four children.

61 Only a few categories were exempted, such as miners, railway workers, firemen, policemen.

62 This top graduate of the Ecole Polytechnique, who had exceeded the points obtained even by Arago, was not gifted with much political acumen. He appears to have been drawn to Nazi Germany because it seemed to him the only system capable of creating the European technocratic order of his dreams.

63 Speer, the Führer's favourite architect, was not viewed with favour by the dignitaries of the Nazi Party. They were interested only in looting; he, on the other hand, did not rule out the possibility of a victorious Reich becoming the centre of a zone of European free trade. On the strategy and tactical choices of the Reich's Armaments Minister, see the excellent work by A. Milward (99); also *Au coeur du Troisième Reich*, Fayard, 1974, by Albert Speer.

64 Saukel tried to oppose Speer's action. And he retained supreme control over non-protected manpower. However, the fourth and fifth 'Saukel actions' brought in barely 80,000 men.

65 The French and the German statistics differ: the former take account of the official figures for departures from France while the latter are based upon the numbers of STO workers at one particular moment.

66 See the excellent critical analysis, 'La main-d'oeuvre française au service de l'Allemagne' (8), 1971; it corrects and raises the official figures submitted by France at the Nuremburg trial.

67 *R-Betriebe* was the description given to foreign businesses which were working 100% for the Reich. If we add to these those which were working for the Todt organisations, in 1942 they already included 850,000 employees (Todt was a German military engineer attached to military planning who was responsible for designing the Siegfried line and the Atlantic fortifications.)

68 580,000 employees in the autumn of 1943; in 1944, 770,000 were working in the *S-Betriebe*; 240,000 railway workers should be added to these.

69 They chiefly affected French possessions in central Europe and the Balkans (in particular the Bor mines in Yugoslavia, which were later bought back for a total sum of 4.5 thousand million francs). In France itself, German capital invested did not amount to more than 1,500 million francs. The paint industry was the one most affected, with the creation of Francocolor which involved Kuhlmann, the Société des Matières Colorantes et des Produits Chimiques de Saint-Denis, the Compagnie Française des Produits Chimiques et Matériaux Colorants de Saint Clair-sur-Rhône, 51% of which was controlled by IG Farben capital. Robert Aron, basing his findings on the report sent by Barnaud to Vichy, concludes that in all this affair 'the very least that may be said is that the attitude of French industrialists was not heroic' (see R. Aron, *Histoire de l'épuration*, vol. 3, book 1, *Le monde des affaires*, Fayard, 1974, p. 152).

70 Here are some examples drawn from the archives of the organisation committees (see H. Rousso, *op.cit.*): in 1942, 1943 and 1944 respectively, the French automobile industry provided the Reich with 65, 60 and 70% of its production, the mechanical industry, 72, 82 and 78%; the aeronautic industry, 57,100 and 100%.

71 See (99), pp. 273, 270, 271, 135, 76.

72 Gross domestic product.

73 In 1938 francs.

74 In millions of the current Reichmarks.

75 Between 31 March and 1 April of the following year.

76 In millions of current francs.

77 Including the deficit on the compensation agreement.

78 At the rate of exchange imposed during the war.

79 At the 1938 rate of exchange.

80 In (French) *tonnes*.

81 Including the French Empire.

82 From January to July.

83 The principle of the transaction was a classic one: the French government paid in French francs for purchases made in France by German businesses which settled up in Reichmarks with the German government. And vice versa. The French trade balance became very top-heavy, but it had judiciously been decided that in the event of imbalance it was up to the Banque de France to make the necessary advances to re-establish equilibrium.

84 Thus the Germanophobic fraction of employers in the north and east did – as a general rule – reject economic collaboration. François de Wendel provides a good example (see the epilogue to J.-N. Jeanneney's thesis, *François de Wendel en République*, *op. cit.*). Similarly, we may cite the effective ploys of H. Ardent, director general of the Société Génerale. A Union des Cadres Industriels de la France Combattante (Union of the Industrial Leaders of Fighting France) was later to be set up by Léon Blanchard, the director general of l'Energie Electrique

du Rhône et du Jura who, with the agreement of Charles Schneider, organised the sabotage of the Creusot electric plant, and by Eugène Roy, director general of the Longwy steel-works.

85 A certain amount of information is provided by the (systematically indulgent) work by Robert Aron, *Histoire de l'épuration, op.cit.*

86 Henry Ehrmann (*op.cit.*, p. 99) records the following Gaullian exclamation aimed at a delegation of employers who came to express their condolences to him in 1944: 'I did not see any of you gentlemen in London . . . good gracious, you are not in prison after all . . .' According to Robert Aron (*Histoire de l'épuration, op.cit.*, p. 332) barely one tenth of the businesses brought before the National Inter-professional Commission were condemned: the purge – the economic one at all events – was selective and kid-gloved.

87 See Fernard Picard, *L'épopée de Renault* (Albin Michel, 1976) for a good descrip-tion of the workings of economic collaboration.

88 See F. Picard, *op.cit.*, p. 265. Following each Allied raid, Louis Renault had one single obsession: to get production going again. 30,000 machines, at a conserva-tive estimate, were delivered to Germany (he was selling 3,500 in France). But Renault was not the only business caught in this involvement: Citroën was producing roughly the same number of vehicles for the Reich. It is also worth noting that in March 1944, the Berliet family council refused to go ahead with sabotaging its production lines that were working for Germany, as the Resist-ance was asking it to do. Two months later, the factories were half destroyed by the RAF. The same thing happened to the Michelin factories in Clermont-Ferrand. The management there told the future Commissioner for the Republic, Ingrand, that sabotage was 'an indecent and useless' operation; see (116), p. 85.

89 Between 1940 and 1944, the Banque de Paris et du Pays-Bas more than doubled its capital (increasing it from 300 to 675 million francs); that was not bad going, even taking into account the abundance of liquid assets on the financial market.

90 See the article by P. Facon and F. de Ruffray, 'Aperçus sur la collaboration aéronautique franco-allemande' (8), 1977; by September 1942, the French factories (admittedly without having honoured all orders received) delivered 1,540 aircraft. In 1943, the Reich transferred all machine tools to Germany and annexed the entire French aeronautic industry.

91 See the general statistical information and bibliographical references provided by A. Sauvy (56); P. Delouvrier and R. Nathan (57), A. Piatier (65), pp. 57–73, and J.-C. Germain-Thomas, *op. cit*; for the financial details, see the *Statistiques et Etudes Financières*, May supplement 1955 and December 1960.

92 Index of agricultural production (1938 = 100): 83 in April 1943, 78 in April 1944; index of industrial production (1938 = 100): 72 in May 1941, 61 in May 1942, 65 in May 1943, 43 in May 1944; in 1944 cloth production is estimated to have been less than 25% of what it was in 1938.

93 On average prices rose 50% in Great Britain, 30% in the United States, 10% in Germany. In France, between 1940 and 1944, the prices of wholesale industrial products rose 62%, wholesale agricultural produce rose 122% and retail prices rose 156%.

94 The occupation authorities exerted heavy pressure upon Vichy to keep wages frozen. Only two increases were authorised, one in 1941, the other in 1943. In Paris the hourly wage of a skilled worker rose from 1940 = 100 to 1944 = 163. Even taking into account the longer working day (with overtime payment), in real terms wages did not cease to fall.

95 To this sum, due 'for the German troops of the occupation's upkeep', should be added the further amount paid for the costs of billeting and various kinds of

requisitioning. The total comes to 680,000 million, not counting the 22,000 million francs paid to the Italian government. Since these figures are given in terms of the current franc and taking into account the franc's depreciation, it should, for the purposes of reference, be borne in mind that the budget for 1938 came to some 150,000 million francs and for that same year the national inland revenue has been estimated at 330,000 million: it is estimated (see (56), p. 98) that the tribute annually represented about 25% of pre-war production. To obtain a reading in terms of today's current franc, see note 80, Chapter 3.

96 The war had done nothing to alter the good old fiscal habits of the French. Note, in comparison, that in Great Britain, the revenue from taxation covered about 50% of public expenses.

97 See (36), vol. 2, p. 7.

98 Pierre Limagne (*op.cit.*, vol. 2, p. 1051) noted on 28 February 1943: 'Collaborationism developed among the bourgeoisie when the latter became discontented; now that there is talk of sending its children to work in the bombed German factories, a fine concert of indignation has arisen.'

99 See P. Machefer, 'Sur quelques aspects de l'activité du Colonel de La Roque et du *Progrès social français* pendant la Seconde Guerre mondiale' (8), 1965.

100 Apparently in 1942; La Roque was to be deported in 1943.

101 It was to be the subject of impassioned debates. It is significant that Cardinal Liénart – an anti-Nazi but a dyed-in-the-wool *maréchaliste* – declared in effect on 21 March 1943 that a catholic could in all conscience refuse to go to Germany. See H. Claude, 'La hiérarchie catholique, le gouvernement de Vichy et l'occupant, dans la zone réservée' (54), pp. 253–85.

102 See in particular F. Delpech, *La persécution des juifs et l'amitié chrétienne* (53) and *La France et la question juive, 1940–1944*, Ed. Sylvie Messinger, 1981.

103 He wrote in *L'Action Française* of March 1943: 'a third affair is envisaged: the Militia, oh, thank goodness for that . . . with the aid of a sure and good police we can, in our own land, deter all revolutionary impulses and all attempts to support the hordes of the east, and at the same time with our own persons defend our homes, our entire civilisation. That is what should be understood and what is all too little recognised.'

104 The works of P. Ory (100) and that of B. Gordon (133) should on no account be missed; see also (101).

105 It is striking that in this period which was, after all, one of buoyancy, French fascism did not produce any doctrinal work of note. Drieu la Rochelle, like Brasillach and many others, did no more than relate and illustrate the story of the collaborationist adventure. See, in particular, P. Sérant, *Le romantisme fasciste*, Fasquelle, 1960.

106 Cited by Raymond Aron (85), p. 41.

107 Nor had the technocrat 'young cyclists' found any more favour in their eyes: they were to be found in the ranks of the organisers of the well known and daunting Mouvement Synarchique d'Empire, see above, p. 56.

108 Saint-Paulien, *Histoire de la collaboration*, L'Espirit Nouveau, 1964, p. 259.

109 Cited by J. Duquesne (52), p. 169.

110 See P. Bourdrel, *La Cagoule*, Albin Michel, 1970, p. 259.

111 See (102).

112 The politico-literary event of the year 1942. It bears expressive witness to the growth of fascism. *Les Décombres* should, if possible, be read in the original Denoël edition, not in the more recent but expurgated edition produced by J.-J.Pauvert.

113 *Les Décombres*, p. 59.

114 The split had taken place in 1942, when Maurras disowned his iconoclastic friends whom he now classed as belonging to the '*Ja* clan'.

115 R. Brasillach, *La révolution nationale*, 4 September 1943.

116 This officer's son, a product of Ulm and a talented essayist, in his own way symbolises the angry young men of the extreme right during the thirties. Fascinated by the Alcazar and almost as much so by the Nuremberg rallies, he gives an account of those days in his *Notre avant-guerre*, published by Plon in 1940. He wrote literary articles for *L'Action Française* between 1931 and 1939 and in 1937 also became editor-in-chief of *Je Suis Partout*. He resumed that function when he returned from an *Oflag* in the spring of 1944.

117 *La révolution nationale*, 19 February 1944.

118 Among those who rejoined the PPF, we should mention Gitton, Clamamus, Albert Clément and Emile Nedelec.

119 They had set up the Centre Syndical de Propagande, whilst many of the ex-socialists were taking militant action in the Front Social du Travail. A weekly had been founded, *L'Atelier*, which included as contributors the old anarcho-syndicalist Dumoulin, P. Vigne, M. Roy, M. Lapierre, G. Albertini, and others.

120 They did not opt out of the Popular Front despite the fact that they reckoned it to be insufficiently 'social'; and they were opposed to the creation of a single party.

121 Countless seedy individuals gravitated into the collaborationist orbit, most of whom the Gestapo was to use to carry out its baser tasks. A sacked police inspector, Bonny, and a swindler, Chamberlain – known as Lafont or Monsieur Henri to his friends – had set up a formidable organisation that specialised both in racketeering and 'hard interrogation'. It was known as the 'Gestapo of the rue Lauriston'. On this collaborationist fauna, see the carefully documented work by J. Delarue (88). It should also be pointed out that important personages in the Parisian collaboration, such as Luchaire, were equally not above making some profitable deals. See (104), pp. 54–71.

122 In his *Journal d'un homme occupé* (Les Sept Couleurs, 1955), Brasillach wrote that it would have been criminal 'to deliver up the civilisation shared by Racine, Shakespeare, Dante and Goethe to Mongol hordes fanatically drunk on revolution and Judaism' (p. 190).

123 *Ibid.*, pp. 248–9; see the significant letter that Brasillach sent to Rebatet on 14 August 1943.

124 After ten months in print, *Le Rouge et le Bleu* was to scuttle itself in August 1942. It had, in all truth, not had an easy time with its new associates. In the *Appel* of 13 August 1942, Costantini, amongst other friendly gestures, suggested that 'Spinasse should be despatched to join his Jewish friends in a concentration camp or – better still – that he should be arrested and join his leader and friend, Blum'.

125 Cited by J. Delperrie de Bayac (105), p. 61.

126 For a socio-political approach, see (8), July 1973, January 1975, October 1977.

127 One of them was a relatively obscure deputy of the Third Republic, Maurice Delaunay, who in 1941 began to pontificate as 'the Master of Fire'.

128 Perhaps we should mention the Ligue Française set up by Costantini, an airforce officer whose only claim to fame was to have – personally – declared war on England in the August of 1940; the Parti Français National-Collectiviste formed by Clementi, a journalist of the extreme right; the Front Français created by Boissel, a violently anti-semitic architect; the Comité d'Action Anti-Bolchévique formed by Chack, an extremely anglophobic naval

officer; the Collaboration group comprised mainly intellectuals, its leader, the writer Alphonse de Châteaubriant, being better known as the director of *La Gerbe*. The autonomists who played the German card, such as the extremists who caused the rift in the Breton National Party, led by Le Coz, alias Laisné, or who enrolled in the 'Perrot Militia' of sinister memory, had just as limited an audience. See (100), pp. 168–200.

129 Deloncle was assassinated in January 1944 in circumstances that have remained mysterious to this day. Was he the victim of an internal vendetta within the MSR or of the struggle between the Gestapo and the Abwehr? See P. Bourdrel, *op.cit.*

130 The RNP has yet to find a historian. The work by Claude Varennes (G. Albertini), *Le destin de Marcel Déat* (Janmaray, 1948) is rather brief.

131 He had had a university training. A product of Ulm, he had taught philosophy before becoming a deputy. It is perhaps significant that Déat prepared all his editorials for *L'Oeuvre* one week in advance.

132 Déat was strongly suspicious of Deloncle, believing that it was he who had armed Paul Collette, who had wounded him quite seriously, as well as Laval, in August 1941.

133 On Doriot, see (103); also (but read with circumspection) two works written by two of the leaders of the PPF: *L'histoire de la collaboration, op. cit.* by M.-Y. Sicard and *Du communisme au fascisme*, by V. Barthélémy (Albin Michel, 1978).

134 He moved away from him in the spring of 1941; Doriot bitterly reproached Pucheu, an ex-member of the PPF, and Weygand for harassing his party both in the free zone and in North Africa.

135 His relations with Abetz were cool, for the latter did not trust him. On the other hand, we are told by D. Wolf (103), p. 335: 'By mid-May 1941, at the latest, Doriot was in contact with the SD (the Reich's security service) in Paris'. He was admitted to the LVF as a sergeant, then promoted to lieutenant and decorated with the iron cross.

136 He was not very particular when it came to methods; thus, Simon Sabiani and his henchmen got their grips on Marseilles.

137 A continuous succession of frustrated *coups*, scuffles and vendettas; mutual respect was not one of the collaborationists' outstanding characteristics. Drieu la Rochelle remarked, with moderation, that 'Chief Doriot was in effect no more than a politician of the same stamp as a radical socialist'.

138 In 1942, the RNP had managed to make some inroads among SFIO electors and had waged a vigorous and relatively successful campaign on the Prisoner Relief Programme. But it was losing ground as a result of the reversals suffered by the Axis powers.

139 Thus C. Jeantet and P.-A. Cousteau, both confirmed collaborationists, had become editors-in-chief of, respectively, *Le Petit Parisien* and *Paris-Soir* (Paris edition).

140 In 1943, Radio Paris was broadcasting ten daily news programmes of a very slanted kind. Its regular magazine programmes were equally biased (for example 'A neutral speaking to you', presented by Dieudonné (G. Oltramare), a Swiss by nationality and an extremist collaborationist). Jean Hérold-Paquis, who had been on the fringe of journalism prior to becoming a radio-man broadcasting over the Francoist wavelengths of Radio Saragossa, acquired a certain notoriety as from 1942 as a military commentator who signed off his reports with the words: 'The truth is that, if France is to live, England, like Carthage, must be destroyed'; the BBC and the internal Resistance had retorted with the slogan: 'Radio Paris lies, Radio Paris lies, Radio Paris is German.'

141 However, the Reich opposed this manoeuvre and in the autumn of 1942 the plan had to be dropped.

142 See O. Abetz, *op. cit.*, p. 148.

143 These 'orientations' were imposed in the course of two weekly meetings on the political and military situation. There were others that dealt with economic problems.

144 Between 1940 and 1944, 12 dailies and 18 weeklies came out in Paris: Propaganda Abteilung was the direct inspiration for *La France au Travail*; as for *Nouveaux Temps*, a daily founded by Luchaire, the president of the Corporation Nationale de la Presse Parisien, it was regarded as an unofficial organ for Abetz. See (104); and P.-M. Dioudonnat, *L'argent nazi à la conquête de la presse française*, Picollec, 1981.

145 See (88) and A. Merglen, 'Soldats français sous uniforme allemand' (8), 1977. The LVF has given rise to a considerable number of works, among others the novels of Saint-Loup (M. Augier), most of them smacking of hagiography.

146 At least, that is what Saint-Paulien maintains, *op.cit.*, p. 243.

147 If we are to believe the reputable statistics available, the LVF received no more than 13,400 applications to join up, between 1941 and 1944. Between June 1941 and May 1943, 11,000 men volunteered, about 6,500 were accepted, 170 were killed and 550 wounded; on 1 June 1944, of a theoretical force of 6,800 men, only 2,200 were prepared to fight in the front line. It should be noted that, with the exception of Doriot, the 'chiefs' who had in July 1941 declared their desire to perform their anti-Bolshevist duty in the field, soon adopted the view that they could strike their own particular decisive blows at Bolshevism by remaining in Paris and manoeuvring there.

148 See (103), p. 350. It proved necessary to guard the route taken by the first contingent of legionaries going to the station of departure.

149 See P. Aziz, *Au service de l'ennemi*, Paris, Fayard, 1971. A regular informer received on average 15,000 to 20,000 francs a month and a 'good capture' was rewarded with a bonus of 5,000 to 10,000 francs.

150 See the exhaustive work by J. Delperrie de Bayac (105).

151 The SOL developed principally in areas where rebels were active, in Haute-Savoie, Haute-Garonne, Montpellier – and in the Alpes-Maritimes, a stronghold of activists under the direction of Darnand, Bassompierre, Gallet, Gombert, etc.

152 See the 21-point programme of the SOL. See (105), p. 117; see also J.-P. Cointet (45), pp. 137–55.

153 Members of the Militia wore a (blue) uniform with a distinctive badge representing the γ, the symbol of the stubborn and tenacious ram; the Militia published *Combats*.

154 See B. Gordon, 'Un soldat du fascisme: l'évolution politique de Joseph Darnand' (8), 1977; also (105). Darnand was a royalist before he left *L'Action Française*, calling Maurras 'an old fool' ('un vieux con'). He then became an extremely active member of the Cagoule and for a short time belonged to the PPF.

155 From 1944 onwards, Darnand was developing the Franc-Garde, a militia stationed in barracks, composed of young volunteers, which included the sons of provincial notables, *déclassés* and young men avoiding the STO. The adult militants and sympathisers formed a kind of reserve whilst adolescents went into the Jeunesse de l'Avant-Garde.

156 See (105), pp. 308–53.

157 See the complete text in L.Noguères (35), p. 357.

158 On the development of the shadow army, see H. Noguères (6), vols. 2 and 3. Also the personal accounts of H. Frenay (71), C. Bourdet (72) and A. Vistel (108). On relations between the Free French and the internal Resistance, see (110); (71); and (109). See also J. Sweet, *The politics of resistance in France*, Northern Illinois University Press, 1976, in default of the work soon to appear devoted to *La Mission Rex* by Daniel Cordier, who was Jean Moulin's secretary.

159 Maurice le Berre had already fatally injured a German on 13 August, at the Porte d'Orléans.

160 A good analysis can be found in H. Noguères (6), vol. 2, pp. 147–65.

161 Marcel Cachin disowned such individual attacks in a letter written in September 1941.

162 'The Hostage Act', promulgated on 22 August 1941 made virtual hostages of all French people held by the Germans in the occupied zone. According to the 'Code of Hostages' of 10 July 1942, all close male relatives of a 'terrorist' could be shot, in order of age, working both upwards and downwards, if they were of 18 or more years of age – brothers-in-law and cousins included. The women were condemned to forced labour. See (63), pp. 265–84.

163 27 of them were shot at Châteaubriant (26 were communists; they included C. Michels, J.-P. Timbault and G. Moquet), 16 at Nantes, 5 at the Mont-Valérien, 50 in the camp of Les Souges near Bordeaux (42 of whom were communists).

164 Between 30 June 1940 and 31 May 1941, 14 Frenchmen had been executed for sabotage or espionage: by 23 October 1941, 123 hostages had been shot, 1,478 by 31 October 1942. Between June and December 1942, the number of victims fell to 254. But on the other hand executions in German prisons and transportations to concentration camps where prisoners were classed as 'Nacht und Nebel' continued to increase.

165 See (7), vol. 1, p. 228.

166 See C. Tillson, *Les FTP*, Julliard, 1967, pp. 123–4.

167 On the communist Resistance, see in particular (79); (78); (126); and (127).

168 This name comprehended both the snipers of the war of 1870 and the Soviet Partisans. On the FTP, see the impassioned work by C. Tillon, *Les FTP*, *op.cit.* (which bears the stamp of the cold-war period); this book should read in conjunction with his later work (79).

169 The MOI was able to preserve a number of autonomous units, mostly Jewish, such as the 'Deuxième détachement de Paris' (Second Paris Detachment), the 'Carmagnole' in Lyons and the '35th Brigade' under the command of M. Langer and B. Frankel in Toulouse; on this last, see *Les parias de la Résistance* (Calman Lévy, 1970) by C. Lévy; on the Jewish resistance of communist persuasion, see D. Diamant, *Les Juifs dans la Résistance*, Le Pavillon, 1971 and J. Ravine, *La Résistance organisée des Juifs en France (1940–1944)*, Julliard, 1973; (the Zionist Resistance was much less active; see A. Latour, *La Résistance juive en France*, Stock 1970).

170 The Valmy company had been given the task of protecting the leaders of the underground PCF and punishing renegades that it judged to be dangerous traitors: it was thus that Gitton was executed on 4 September, 1941.

171 To increase effectiveness, Epstein later expanded the basic unit to about twenty fighters. It should be noted that up until the spring of 1944, most FTP fighters led a double life, both a professional and a militant one.

172 It included, in particular, Charles Tillon, Eugène Hénaff, Dumont, Marcel Prenant, André Ouzoulias and Georges Vallet.

173 The leaders of the FTP stuck through thick and thin to the tactics devised by

Fabien. In October 1942, *France d'Abord* gave as the order of the day 'To each man his Boche'.

174 On the conversations between Rémy and the PCF, see (6), vol. 2, pp. 161–3, 654–7.

175 The FTP, like all the organisations of the National Front, were much less well implanted in the southern zone, partly on account of the long-standing existence of the movements regrouped within the MUR.

176 It was run by two organisational committees, the northern one directed by Pierre Gunsberger-*Villon*, the southern by Marrane.

177 The National Front had had no difficulty in setting up branches of a fairly classic kind such as the Front Uni des Jeunesses Patriotiques or L'Union des Femmes Française; it had also been able to develop in relatively well-disposed milieux, for instance among students (see the telling personal account by E. Morin, *Autocritique*, Julliard, 1959, pp. 27–62), university teachers, theatre people and writers; and it had put out feelers in professions that had hitherto been very hostile, for instance among doctors, tradesmen and the police.

178 See (72), p. 277.

179 Henri Frenay had until then kept up informal relations with intelligence officers in the armistice army. In particular, in February 1942 he had, with the approval of his organising committee, gone so far as to attend two meetings with Pucheu in Vichy. The head of Combat had in fact used those occasions above all to try to gain time and to negotiate the liberation of leaders of the movement who had been imprisoned; see his personal account (71), pp. 153–64. Nevertheless, his initiative had been sufficiently ambiguous to arouse some strong criticism from outside Combat.

180 The OMA – which later became the ORA – came into being during the winter of 1942. It regarded itself as a metropolitan branch of the army of Africa. It was from the first extremely Giraudist and immediately set itself apart from the movements (especially the MUR and the National Front) which it considered too politicised and confused.

181 Cited by C.-L. Foulon (117), p. 63.

182 Increasingly acute financial difficulties led the leaders of Combat to enter in negotiations with the American secret services installed in Switzerland. But these came to nothing when Free France firmly opposed them.

183 See the important report dated 7 May 1943 that he sent to London. It is cited in full by F. Closon (109), pp. 80–96.

184 One of the slogans was 'The new order! It means forced labour, far away from your families, against your country.'

185 On crossing the Pyrenees and all its perils, see (86), vol. 1, pp. 133–57.

186 Philippon-*Hilarion* was to leave Brest after supplying London with first-class intelligence; the engineer Stosskopf, who made a show of ultra-collaborationist sentiments also sent some remarkable intelligence on the Lorient submarine base.

187 For instance Alliance, which was always most effective and was now under the direction of Marie-Madeleine Fourcade; or the 'Gilbert' networks organised by Colonel Groussard from his base in Switzerland. A number of networks worked for American secret services. As for the Soviets, they used the services of the Orchestre Rouge whose story is skilfully told by G. Perrault (Livre de Poche, 1971).

188 Thus, the Centrale Coligny collected intelligence gathered by Rémy's CND,

Centurie (the OCM network), Cohors (the Libération-Nord network) and Fana (the National Front network).

189 See bibliography in notes 122–6, Chapter 3; also the excellent study by Marie Granet on Ceux de la Résistance (106) and the painstaking monograph by F. Bruneau (Yvette Gouineau), *Essai historique du mouvement né autour du journal clandestine 'Résistance'*, Besançon, SEDES, 1951.

190 Jouhaux, who had already been interned several times, was handed over to Germany and deported. His friends had moved right away from Vichy and the 'federals' who followed Belin. In the CFTC, those who remained loyal to the French State had lost influence since 27 June 1943, despite the pressure exerted by the Catholic hierarchy, the Charter of Work was repudiated by 63% of the votes. The CGT and CFTC were, nevertheless, determined to stand their ground and maintain a political presence, at the same time trying to gain control of a number of official organisms.

191 These agreements healed the rift brought about by the German–Soviet pact but also made more problematical the plan that some cherished to merge Jouhaux's CGT and the CFTC. Nostalgia for a lost unity and the attempts made at grassroots level to re-create it thus overcame the profound distrust that separated those who had formerly supported unity and those who had favoured confederation. The negotiations (which were long and difficult: the first contacts had been made as long ago as May 1941) bore fruit on 17th April 1943. The trade-union apparatus was to be reorganised in accordance with the voting of 1938.

192 Typically enough, Father Chaillet decided in May 1943 to launch a second underground paper, the *Courrier Français du Témoignage Chrétien* (12 numbers had appeared by the time of the Liberation) which would be accessible to a wider and less cultivated audience. He also paid more attention to temporal commitment and began to place a greater reliance upon young laymen such as André Mandouze. On the evolution of the *Témoignage Chrétien* movement, see the exemplary work by Renée Bédarida (107).

193 See (106), p. 133.

194 With remarkable cheek – for a neophyte – P. Copeau declares: 'When I arrived I felt rather as if I had landed in the middle of a veterans' organisation'; see (6), vol. 2, p. 547.

195 Some were militant communists. Nevertheless, it would be mistaken to regard this simply as a way for the PCF to infiltrate. On this problem as a whole, see p. 187.

196 See J. Lacouture, *Léon Blum, op. cit.*, p. 470.

197 Didier was a Judge at the Court of Paris. He was immediately arrested and then interned at the camp at Châteaubriant.

198 In particular, these gave them a chance for active propaganda: on 14 July 1943, young militants from the *Défense de la France* showed no hesitation in distributing some 5,000 copies of the newspaper in the *métro*. There were many dramatic moments: on 11 November 1942, at Brive, demonstraters led by Madame Michelet and her seven children only just avoided the German columns that were advancing into the southern zone. Some demonstrations turned into traps: in Grenoble, on 11 November 1943, in front of the Monument des Diables Bleus, German units made a bayonet charge, killing and rounding up demonstrators, 450 of whom were deported.

199 Of them, Arthus, Baudry, Benoit, Grelot and Legros were later arrested after having gone undergound, and were shot on 8 February 1943.

200 Abetz officially deplored 3,802 acts of sabotage carried out successfully between 1 January and 30 September 1943 (781 were against German army installations, 122 against French firms working for Germany, 1,262 against the railway network, and there were many more).

201 According to the same statistics supplied by Abetz, over the same period 281 strikes had been made against German soldiers, 79 against French policemen and 174 against collaborationists.

202 A detachment of the MOI missed Schaumberg, the commandant of Grosse-Paris, but struck down Julius Ritter, Saukel's delegate to France. In Dijon, the head of the Gestapo, Werner, was abducted, tried and executed.

203 These were planned as simultaneous attacks in a number of different towns upon collaborationist headquarters and kiosks that sold German newspapers.

204 The public prosecutor Lespinasse, who had shown great zeal in getting Marcel Langer guillotined, was assassinated in October 1943. Similarly, in December, so too was the president of the special tribunal in Lyons, Fauve-Pengali, and there were others.

205 Its story is told by M. Baudot, *Libération de la Normandie* (116), pp. 105–8.

206 See the precise description given by Passy in his *Souvenirs,op. cit.*, vol. 2, pp. 286–331.

207 A. Vistel provides a good overall view (108), pp. 122–350.

208 At the time, Combat comprised 14 'national services', employing a hundred or more permanent totally clandestine workers. They were organised by a *centre* under the direction of Frenay, B. Albrecht, J.-G. Bernard and C. Bourdet. See the well-documented work by M. Granet and H. Michel (73).

209 See the map provided by H. Noguères (6), vol. 2, p. 46.

210 These – as is well known – represented an essential cog in the machine. In the town of Lyons alone, the MUR in 1944 had forty or more liaison agents at their disposal.

211 Forgery of these had become a great art. Some, those for commissioners who were members of the NAP, were in effect 'real' false papers.

212 This provided material aid for prisoners and their families and also worked to set up internal relations inside the prisons.

213 M. Peck and C. Bourdet were the first to try to establish trusty networks within certain administrative departments. By the summer of 1943, the NAP had become a veritable Trojan horse within the State apparatus of Vichy, particularly in the prefectorial administration, the police, the PTT, and the transport department. A little later, Maurice Nègre undertook to suborn the ministers themselves: this was known as the 'super-NAP'.

214 On the problems posed by the secret army, see p. 161.

215 In order to be successful in the 'railway battle', J. *Lacroix* had laid the foundations for a veritable underground SNCF which was then further developed by René Hardy and Max Heilbronn.

216 First, flat, unploughed terrains had to be selected, away from electricity cables and houses; and then their whereabouts had to be made known to the RAF. These fields were used for parachute drops or, better still, landing areas for single-engined aircraft, Lysanders, which would bring in and carry out correspondence and three passengers. As from the summer of 1943, twin-engined aircraft were able to land, carrying about a dozen passengers.

217 A little later it was renamed *Le chant des partisans*. It was written by a musician-poetess Anna Marly; Kessel and Droun adapted the definitive text and in September 1943 d'Astier published it in the *Cahiers de la Libération*.

218 See (72), p. 134.

219 Some large movements (the OCM, Ceux de la Résistance, Ceux de la Libération), it is true, did not produce their own newspapers. On the underground press, see (70).

220 Some movements had professional journalists working for them: Georges Altman and Yves Farge at *Franc-Tireur*, Roger Massip at *Libération*, and later on Pascal Pia and Camus at *Combat*.

221 In the Lyons region we should mention Martinet, Pons, Chevalier, Agnel and Villemagne; in the Paris region, Geraerdt and De Rudder. As a safety precaution, the compositing was sometimes done at one address and the printing at another (usually on makeshift machines working flat out). Some movements managed to become self-sufficient quite soon: by December 1941 *Défense de la France* had laid hands on a Rotaprint machine which was installed in the cellars of the Sorbonne. Later on, under the direction of a young student from the Polytechnic, Bollier-*Velin*, who had learned the trade from Martinet, *Combat* set up a remarkable printing works for itself, with a large 'machine' in rue Viala in Villeurbanne. It was there that Bollier and his companions fell, with their weapons in their hands, on 17 June 1944. In February 1944 the entire personnel of the printing works of the Lion brothers were arrested in Toulouse, among them a young apprentice who was a member of the Resistance, who was deported. His name was Georges Séguy.

222 It later came under the direction of Vercors, Paulhan and Eluard, who were assisted by Aragon, Cassou, Chamson and Mauriac.

223 'Published under the oppression at the expense of a few patriotic men of letters.'

224 The appearance of this novel was delayed for six months, for security reasons. The delay caused a number of Resistance members to believe, mistakenly, that it was making a disguised plea for a 'wait-and-see' policy (the theme of the book being that silence is the only dignified response in the face of the occupying power).

225 It was Jacques *Decour*-Demanche, a scholar of German and a novelist, who had the idea of publishing an underground review both militant and at the same time open to people of all spiritual persuasions in the Resistance. He was closely supported by Paulhan and Jacques Debû-Bridel. After his arrest, the novelist Claude Morgan and the historian Edith Thomas had to produce the first few numbers on their own. Later on, the committee of directors expanded to include Aragon, Blanzat, Guéhenno, Mauriac, Father Maydieu and Vildrac. *Les Lettres Françaises* published 20 numbers, with articles by C. Bellanger, Cassou, M.-P. Fouchet, L. Parrot, R. Queneau, C. Roy, J.-P. Sartre, P. Seghers, J. Tardieu and E. Triolet, etc.

226 See in particular P. Seghers' (111) very valuable retrospective survey which is as informative as it is enthusiastic.

227 This militant literature also found support outside metropolitan France from Max-Pol Fouchet and his review *Fontaine* published in Algiers, and the Genevese publisher, François Lachenal, for example. Supervielle brought out his very fine *Poèmes de la France malheureuse* in Argentina.

228 Anonymity gave cover to, among others, Aragon, Desnos, Eluard, Guillevic, Francis Ponge, Pierre Seghers, Tardieu, Vercors; two of the poems have never been identified, written in all probability by unknown poets who disappeared in the Resistance.

229 Let us mention *Le déshonneur des poètes*, an inconoclastic pamphlet published in 1945. In it, Benjamin Péret expressed – legitimately enough – his opinion that 'these poems rose no higher than the lyrical level of pharmaceutical advertisements'. At the same time – but perhaps less legitimately – he seized the

opportunity to settle a number of old scores with Stalinists, clerics, Jacobins and many others, with a view to exalting a 'revolutionary poetry' which – possibly on account of its perfectionism – was conspicuous mainly by its absence.

230 It should be emphasised that a writer such as René Char, for instance, preferred to publish nothing at all once he had become Captain Alexandre. Picasso, in contrast, continued to paint more or less as if nothing had happened.

231 Nor do dark days necessarily make for noble behaviour. Thus, Gide spent these four years in a most circumspect manner, cultivating his beloved ego which dictated his behaviour so tyrannically that it even prevented him from associating himself with the petition organised against the Châteaubriant executions.

232 Pineau, who had been contacted by Rémy through Brossolette, was surprised, when he got to London, to find that he had to tell de Gaulle just about everything about the Resistance movements; he set off back to France with a political manifesto which the head of Free France only agreed to initial at the very last minute. See C. Pineau, *La simple vérité*, Julliard, 1960.

233 Moulin-*Mercier* (and even *Rex* or *Max*) had been parachuted in 'blind' together with a radio-operator, Monjaret, and Raymond Fassin-*Sif*, a schoolteacher who was to be responsible for liaison with Combat.

234 Brought up in a deeply secular and republican environment, Jean Moulin had chosen a prefectorial career which showed every sign of becoming a brilliant one. Although he was not officially a member of any party, he was known as a left-wing radical and a Jacobin who was close to Pierre Cot, whose principal private secretary he had been. After being dismissed in the circumstances by now well known, he decided to make for London, without joining any movement. The head of Free France soon came to regard him as just the intermediary that was needed between the external and the internal Resistance. See his enthusiastic biography by H. Calef, *Jean Moulin*, Plon, 1980; also H. Michel, *Jean Moulin, l'unificateur*, Hachette, 1964; soon to appear, Daniel Cordier's account (see above, p. 145).

235 His brief was worded as follows: 'I appoint Monsieur Jean Moulin, prefect, as my representative and also as the delegate from the National Committee for the zone of metropolitan France that is not directly occupied'; see (7) vol. 1, p. 647.

236 On the results of this mission which was well set up by the lieutenants of Moulin and Passy, see p. 161.

237 Pierre Brossolette, a product of Ulm and a graduate in history, had made his name as a militant journalist (he was the editor of *Le Populaire* and had also been a radio commentator, at least up until the time of Munich). In 1940, he had moved away from the SFIO. Sacked by Vichy, he had opened a bookshop, then become an agent for Rémy's network. He had been sent to London in April 1942, where he had been won over by the BCRA and its leader and became Passy's political mentor.

238 Félix Gouin had recommended a policy of remaining in France. In a long letter to de Gaulle, a few months later the old leader, now in prison, pledged the support of the SFIO and expressed his delight that the head of Free France had 'committed himself without reservation to democratic principles'.

239 This marked the culmination of the bargaining that had been going on for a full ten months. In the spring of 1942, Rémy contacted Beaufils, an FTP leader, and, in November, Fernand Grenier, who held a mandate from the underground central committee. He was succeeded in London by Waldeck Rochet.

240 Libération-Sud was the first to declare allegiance, in May 1942: 'We recognise that, at the moment, there is only one movement, that of Free France, and only one head, General de Gaulle, the symbol of the unity of France ...' Combat followed suit in August, Franc-Tireur in September and Libération-Nord in December. Défense de la France, which was highly suspicious of the authoritarianism of the head of Free France, did not come over until July 1943.

241 The complete text may be read in H. Noguères (6), vol. 3, p. 55.

242 *Ibid.*, p. 397.

243 See (7), vol. 2, p. 101.

244 *Ibid.*, p. 515.

245 This important text is cited in H. Noguères (6), vol. 3, pp. 277–82.

246 The internal Resistance received – relatively – more money than weapons. To give some idea of the sums involved: between January 1941 and May 1943, the movements of the southern zone received from Jean Moulin some 50 million francs.

247 He certainly deserves to be known as the man who achieved this unity. It was not an easy task: he had to win the respect of the 'historical leaders' and fight against individualistic tendencies. He did so resolutely, remaining Gaullian right to the end. But that did not prevent him from remaining close to the groundroots members of the Resistance whose personal advocate in London he became.

248 Those who were to become known as the MUR became, together with the National Front, the most important organisation of the internal Resistance. It was a decisive step: Combat, Libération and Frank-Tireur merged all their 'national services' – except those for propaganda – and their regional and departmental organisations: four of the five regions were placed under the authority of the head of Combat, assisted by lieutenants from Libération and Franc-Tireur. At the head of the MUR a 'directory' consisted of Frenay as first commissioner for military affairs, d'Astier for political affairs, Lévy in charge of intelligence and security, and Jean Moulin who acted as chairman.

249 It brought together Libération-Nord, the OCM, Ceux de la Résistance, Ceux de la Libération and the National Front. The PCF, the SFIO, the Christian Democrats, the CGT and the CFTC were indirectly represented.

250 In December 1943, the MUR became the Mouvement de la Libération National (MLN), integrating movements in the northern zone which had not found a place in the CNR or which were considered in the northern zone to be too 'political', namely Défense de la France, Résistance, and later on Voix du Nord and Lorraine.

251 It is important not to underestimate the weight carried by individualistic tendencies and pressures from the past. However, the political motivations renewed by the recharged energy of the PCF seem to have carried the day. The apoliticism that was professed quite often masked an ideology that was inclined to be technocratic or even authoritarian: it was shared by many of the leaders of the OCM – the largest non-communist movement in the northern zone – to such an extent indeed that the first of its four *Cahiers*, published in February 1942 and edited by Blocq-Mascart, was considered scandalous in many circles of the Resistance, especially in the southern zone. Running down the Third Republic was perhaps not so very shocking, but there were problems when it came to the animosity expressed towards the Popular Front in conjunction with an explicitly formulated anti-semitism.

252 They tried to apply some of the directives from London by improving the partitioning between the various intelligence services; but they came up

against considerable local resistance. As Copeau explains, 'they didn't want to have anything to do with it simply because it was impossible to distinguish a purely military resistance and a so-called political resistance which, as London saw it, should be occupied essentially with the distribution of small newspapers'; see (6), vol. 2, pp. 548–9.

253 General Delestraint, under whom de Gaulle had served, had felt some sympathy for the national revolution but had without hesitation condemned any policy of collaboration. Frenay, although he had himself recommended him, held against him the fact that Delestraint regarded the Secret Army as an army of the classic type that was simply to be held in readiness, and that he appointed to it officers who were inexperienced or were distrustful of the Resistance. In Frenay's opinion, 'a revolutionary army appoints its own leaders. Nobody imposes them upon it' (letter from Frenay to Delestraint dated 8 April 1943, cited by H. Noguères (6), vol. 3, p. 82).

254 The text is to be found in (110), pp. 189–91. Delestraint was arrested three weeks later. His successor was another professional officer, Colonel Dejussieu-*Pontcarral*, who knew the internal Resistance well.

255 Some of its 'chiefs' had, it is true, been reduced to impotence, either deported (Daladier) or interned (Herriot); the fact remains that no well-known figure made a mark in the Resistance and although Mendès France and Queuille both made their way to London, they did so of their own accord and carried no mandate from the party.

256 In the summer of 1942, after a rigorous purge of the party machine, Blum's loyal supporters set up a 'Socialist Action Committee' in each zone; in 1943, the reconstituted party was under the direction of an executive committee with eight members and a secretary general, Daniel Mayer, who was assisted by Verdier and Jacquet. According to D. Mayer, the SFIO could at that time muster 40,000 militants; see (121).

257 They had good reason to feel dissatisfied since, on Blum's advice, they had refused to create any partisan organisations and had instead joined in with a number of different movements (nearly all the earliest militants of Libération-Nord and Libération-Sud had been socialists). The progress made by the PCF and the fact that it had gained recognition from Free France had prompted the SFIO to change its strategy, particularly as links had slackened with d'Astier de la Vigerie and the MUR did not seem at all keen to make room for them.

258 The extreme left (see Y. Craipeau, *Contre vents et marées*, Savelli, 1977) did not have much influence.

259 It was on 16 October 1942 that there appeared for the first time, on a tract distributed in the Lyons region, the joint signatures of a party (the PCF) and several movements (Combat, Libération, and Franc-Tireur).

260 In his letter of March 1943 cited above, Léon Blum vigorously defended the political parties against the movements' expressed intention to remain in operation after the Liberation: he maintained that they would, at the most, be 'syndicates of egoistic and outdated interests'. See D. Mayer, *op.cit.*, pp. 211–17.

261 It was in opposition to the socialists who had taken refuge in London and who were anti-Gaullian, that Brossolette published in the *Marseillaise* of 27 September 1942 this vigorous declaration of his Gaullian faith. See the long case made out by the same author to André Philip, the future Commissioner of the Interior (cited by Passy, *op.cit.*, vol. 2, pp. 219–30).

262 We should mention Lapie, Pierre Bloch, Mendès France, Queuille, Jacquinot, Antier and Charles Vallin, the ex-president of the PSF and an ex-member of a

'Council of Political Justice' set up by Vichy, whom Brossolette had brought back in his luggage in September 1942, presumably with the consent of de Gaulle: this arrival provoked such an outcry among those whom Passy called 'the hardened sectarians' that the idea of giving him an official function was abandoned. He joined up and was killed during the Italian campaign.

263 Moulin had always taken a fairly prudent line and during the inaugural session of the CNR he made it quite clear that, in his view, the presence of delegates from political formations did not imply 'the reconstitution of parties as they functioned before the armistice'. That did not prevent Frenay from making out that Moulin, as the advocate of representation for the parties, 'was the grave-digger of the Resistance'; see (110), p. 412; as early as 1950 he produced an explanation which is amplified in his latest work (*L'énigme, Jean Moulin*, Laffont, 1977): 'Jean Moulin, a crypto-communist: that was the answer to my questions and with it everything became clear'; see (71), p. 565. Nevertheless, it should be pointed out that the only objective evidence for that thesis remains the links between Moulin and those close to Pierre Cot who later became progressivists or fellow-travellers. See the refutation to this thesis by Closon (109), pp. 102–12. It is possible that, in defending to de Gaulle the idea of a parliament of the Resistance which would include the parties, Moulin was seeking to avoid a rift between the 'apolitical' movements, those that were politicised but which rejected the old-style parties, and those that were in effect dominated by the parties.

264 See the *Instruction* to Jean Moulin on 21 February 1943 (7), vol. 2, pp. 445–6.

265 In his *Mémoires*, de Gaulle stresses that the CNR's 'character was one of representation, not of direction'; in 1943 however, the Gaullian directives were much more vague: with reduced national representation, the CNR would have to exercise full powers if the CFLN was no longer able to govern. See the analysis by R. Hostache (115), pp. 396–400.

266 The Democratic Alliance was highly valued by Churchill, for instance; it was thought necessary to include one Joseph Laniel who was believed not to have voted for full powers in July 1940; as for the delegate of the Republican Fédération, he was in effect chosen by Moulin on the eve of the meeting of the CNR: he was Debû-Bridel, a man close to Louis Marin.

267 The movements had delegated: C. Bourdet, P. Copeau, *Claudius*-Petit (for the MUR), J.-H. Simon (OCM), C. Laurent (Libération-Nord), Coquoin-*Lenormand* (Ceux de la Résistance), Villon (National Front); the political 'tendencies' had given their mandates to: A. Mercier (PCF), A. Le Troquer (SFIO), G. Bidault (Christian Democrats), M. Rucard (Radical Socialist Party), J. Laniel (Democratic Alliance), J. Debû-Bridel (Republican Federation); and for the trade-unionist conferations L. Saillant (CGT) and G. Tessier (CFTC).

268 According to all the participants, this inaugural session was a very moving occasion. Jean Moulin briefly set out the CNR's *raison d'être* and read out a message from the head of Free France; those present then voted on a motion presented by Bidault, which reaffirmed the political primacy of de Gaulle over Giraud but still recognised the latter as 'the commander of the resuscitated French army'.

269 On the structures of the CNR, see R. Hostache, *Le Conseil national de la Résistance*, PUF, 1958.

270 See the portrait of him given by de Gaulle (7), vol. 1, p. 233.

271 Appointed on 21 February 1943 as a full member of the National Committee of Free France, he was 'the sole personal representative of General de Gaulle and

of the National Committee for the entire metropolitan territory'; see (7), vol. 2, p. 445.

272 He was seconded by Rémy Roure, Louis Terrenoire, Yves Farge and Pierre-Louis Falaize amongst others.

273 It was in July 1942 that the first four 'sages' met for the first time: Paul Bastid-*Primus*, François de Menthon-*Secundus*, Robert Lacoste-*Tertius*, Alexandre Parodi-*Quartus*. On the CGE, see D. de Bellescize, *Les neuf sages de la Résistance*, Plon, 1979.

274 He had been personal private secretary to the head of Free France for two years and had asked to be sent on mission to France, where he arrived on 16 June 1943.

275 It is true that the partisans of a 'Central Committee' did not prove particularly skilful in their attempts to minimise the influence of not only the communists but also other movements. Meanwhile, the CNR organised itself with such efficiency that a man such as Blocq-Mascart, who had originally boycotted it, came around to attending its sessions.

276 This was to be Georges Bidault; the campaign for his appointment was led by Bouchinet-Serreules. Bidault was a history graduate who had already made quite a name for himself before the war as a journalist and militant catholic; he was considered by the movement leaders as one of their own men (he had been a militant in Combat after his return from captivity and had subsequently joined the National Front) and he also had the ear of both the christian democrats and the communists. He was to preside over the CNR with much flexibility (interpreted as opportunism by his adversaries).

277 The first intermediary, Bollaert, a prefect who was a patriot but relatively lacking in experience, considered himself as an ambassador. After his arrest, his successor Parodi, who had joined the Resistance very early on, proved himself a remarkably effective mediator.

278 Although the literature on the subject is abundant, there exists to this day no accurate and convenient summary; it is true that the facts themselves are not all clearly established; as guides see (112) and (113); also (7), vol. 2; and (80), vol. 2; the best documented (although fundamentally controversial) of the anti-Gaullian and pro-Algerian Vichy works is by Chamine (Geneviève Dunais), *Suite française* (Albin Michel, 1946–52, vols. 1 and 2); later works have in general plagiarised her, but have lacked her talent.

279 See J.-B. Duroselle and A. Kaspi, 'Considérations sur la politique et la stratégie des Etats-unis en Méditerranée' (114), pp. 359–84; also J.-B. Duroselle, 'Le conflit stratégique anglo-américain de juin 1940 à juin 1944', *Revue d'Histoire Moderne et Contemporaine*, 1963.

280 The failure of 'Operation Jubilee' mounted in August 1942, to probe the German coastal defences, seemed to justify his decision. The Anglo-Canadian troops, landed along a front of fifteen kilometres near Dieppe, suffered more than 1,200 killed and 2,300 taken prisoner.

281 See the bibliography with commentary by J.-P. Rioux (119); and in particular C.-A. Julien, *L'Afrique du Nord en marche, nationalisme musulman et souveraineté française*, Julliard, 1972; *Le Maroc face aux impérialismes, 1415–1956*, Ed. Jeune Afrique, 1978; also C.-R. Ageron, *L'histoire de l'Algérie contemporaine*, vol. 2 *1871–1954*, PUF, 1979.

282 A minority in Oranie, even 'phalangist' groups, had rallied to the SOL and the PPF.

283 He considered himself commander-in-chief of a Europe that would rise up at his call with the aid of the American forces which would be landed simultaneously along the Mediterranean coasts and in Brittany.

284 On the conspiracy and its ramifications, see Chamine, *op.cit.*; also the very technical work by General Mast, *Histoire d'une rébellion*, Plon, 1969.

285 The 'Murphy–Giraud agreements' reaffirmed the principle of the territorial integrity of France and its Empire, granted a kind of 'bailing-loan' and stated explicitly that Giraud would receive a very high command.

286 Although the fighting in Morocco claimed 1,500 victims from the two sides together, Algiers suffered less than 100 casualties: the Americans had landed 2,200 men at Sidi-Ferruch, whilst the French forces numbered 12,000.

287 In Oran, General Boisseau, who had imprudently been let into the secret, resisted vigorously for forty-eight hours; in Morocco, the conspiracy was also a failure. Béthouart was arrested and Noguès gave orders to repulse the aggressor. On the whole, however, with the exception of the Admiralty forces and judging by a telegram sent by Noguès to Vichy, the troops appear to have carried out orders 'without enthusiasm but out of duty'; see (35), p. 454.

288 Thanks to the Alliance network, Giraud had been taken to Gibraltar at a useful moment. There, however, he wasted precious time, wanting at all costs to be made the inter-Allied commander-in-chief. He did not reach Algeria until the 9th; finding himself confronted by Darlan, he took the course of self-effacement.

289 It is almost impossible to give a clear account of the complicated ballet executed by Darlan, Noguès and Juin. See in particular (97).

290 See above, p. 123–4.

291 The leaders on the spot, Admirals Esteva and Derrien and General Barré were, it is true, sorely tried. For instance, the commander at Bizerta, Derrien, having learned of the invasion of the southern zone, on 11 November at 18.00, gave the order to resist the Axis powers ('the Germans and the Italians are the enemy'); six hours later, having duly received a dressing-down from Vichy and recognising what was expected from Algiers, he was obliged to backtrack: 'Adopt an attitude of strict neutrality with regard to all foreign troops...' In the end, the Germans occupied Bizerta without a fight, while General Barré waited until 19 November before opening hostilities against the Axis powers. See (35), pp. 453–6.

292 See (112), p. 2.

293 Although Darlan had not managed to rally the Toulon fleet, his authority was not contested by the army of Africa; Giraud, on the other hand, was not kindly received by his peers ('You are nothing here', Juin had snapped at him). The 'Darlan deal' was made official by the Darlan–Clark agreements which represented a withdrawal from the Murphy–Giraud agreements since the Americans could claim their powers as 'occupiers'. On the American game in Algiers, see (with a measure of circumspection) R. Murphy, *Un diplomate parmi les guerriers*, Laffont, 1965.

294 Darlan then confirmed that he would certainly not remain in power indefinitely.

295 In this letter, dated 14th December 1942, Stalin added that 'Eisenhower's policy with regard to Darlan, Boisson, Giraud and others (was) perfectly justified'; cited by J.-B. Duroselle, 'Les grands alliés et la Résistance extérieure française', *European Resistance Movements*, Oxford, 1964, p. 499.

296 The Conseil Impérial was composed of his chief vassals (Bergeret, Chatel, Boisson and Noguès) and Giraud was to be called in under exceptional circumstances. Power was concentrated in the hands of the admiral and his political advisor, an ex-minister from Vichy, the extremely reactionary General Bergeret; these two were supported by a government of a sort which included two members of the 'Group of Five', Tarbé de Saint-Hardouin and

Rigault, who was a kind of Minister of the Interior; Henri d'Astier de la Vigerie, for his part, acted as chief of police in Algiers.

297 They were regrouped in the Algerian branch of Combat around René Capitan, Paul Coste-Floret, Viard, Fradin and Colonel Tubert.

298 Darlan's murder has given rise to countless theories. The most common interpretation is that of a 'monarchist conspiracy': it is suggested that the assassination was ordered – or suggested – by the Pretender and organised by Henri d'Astier de la Vigerie who was a royalist by inclination, and his second-in-command, Abbé Cordier. The two men were indeed arrested and charged but, on the orders of Giraud, the charges were never pressed. Some have added extra flavour to the theory and seen the plot as a 'monarchist conspiracy with Gaullist support'. The matter is still far from clear and the latest works on the subject, *Nous avons tué Darlan* (La Table Ronde, 1975) by Mario Faivre and the *mémoires* of an examining judge, A.-J. Voituriez, *L'affaire Darlan* (Lattès, 1980), do not shed as much light on the matter as could be wished. It seems likely that Bonnier de la Chapelle was convinced of the political need to strike down a man of the collaboration whose presence was blocking all evolution in North Africa. Bonnier may have believed that the murder of Darlan would give the Comte de Paris his chance and that he would become the man for the situation.

299 The murderer – who was twenty years old – hoped right to the last that he would escape the firing squad. His pardon was refused by both Noguès and Giraud, who justified the refusal on the grounds of reasons of State and the fear of disorders. As for Darlan, he was buried with great pomp.

300 After fighting in the Legion, the Comte de Paris had returned to Spanish Morocco, where he was normally domiciled; he had encouraged royalists to support the Vichy regime. He reached Algiers – on the sly – on 10 December, where he had a number of political contacts thanks to the efforts of Henri d'Astier de la Vigerie and Pose, the director of the BNCI, who had become a royalist convert late in the day and was a member of Darlan's government. It is perhaps exaggerated to use words such as 'irresponsibility and childishness' as Soustelle does (see (80), vol. 2, pp. 81–2), but the Pretender certainly does seem to have proved himself a weak manoeuvrer, committed a lot of blunders and at all events, failed to rally to his support the members of the Conseil Impérial, in particular Giraud.

301 Rigault, Lemaigre-Dubreuil and Tarbé de Saint-Hardouin accompanied him, as did Bergeret.

302 See (113); also (7), vol. 2; (80), and J. Monnet's interesting *Mémoires* (Fayard, 1976).

303 There is some truth in Jean Monnet's opinion: 'Giraud was every bit as egocentric as de Gaulle'.

304 Like many other Saint-Cyrians of his generation he had served for many years with the colonial troops. In 1936, he had been commander in Metz, with Colonel de Gaulle serving under him. As an army general he had been made prisoner of war in 1940 and had pulled off a dramatic escape in 1942.

305 See J. Monnet, *op.cit.*, p. 211. On Giraudism, see the very perceptive work by Jean Planchais, *Histoire politique de l'armée*, Ed. du Seuil, 1967, vol. 2, pp. 35–61. Giraud's own book, *Un seul but, la victoire, op. cit.*, is rather disappointing.

306 See (7), vol. 2, p. 145.

307 He had been indecisive and lacking in political courage. He even refused to cover the few high-ranking officers (Béthouard, Mast, Jousse and Baril) who had chosen to follow him in November.

308 In April 1942, he had sent a fine letter of allegiance to Pétain assuring him of his 'perfect loyalty' and declaring himself to be 'in full agreement' with him; but he had hardly any choice open to him at the time. On the other hand, it was on his own initiative that, in July 1940, while a prisoner of war, he had sent, also to Pétain, a diatribe directed against the Popular Front, lashing out in particular at 'pleasure seeking'; cited by A. Kaspi (113), p. 46; in 1936, admittedly, he had summoned the prefect to his presence to tell him that he would not tolerate any occupation of factories provoked by 'the parties of disorder'.

309 In a radio-address broadcast on 21 November 1942; see (7), vol. 2, pp. 406–7.

310 They appear to have mustered some 100,000 fighting men.

311 Bir Hakeim was no Stalingrad, but the battle certainly won considerable fame. The British had charged Koenig with the essential mission of delaying Rommel's offensive for a few days. The FFL dug in at a place known as Bir Hakeim, a crossroads, and there held out against the repeated assaults of the Axis forces from 27 May to 11 June 1942, before the latter managed to break through. A quarter of their men were lost.

312 To prevent a surprise attack from the Japanese, the British, without the endorsement of Free France, made a landing at Diego-Suarez in May 1942. After five months of talks with the pro-Vichy authorities, they continued with their fight for the island, winning it in November. The final political arrangement did meet with the approval of the Free French.

313 He had been considered a 'red admiral' before rallying in the very early days to Free France and becoming a member of the Comité National Français. Heterodox and supported by 'Londoners' who were hostile to de Gaulle, he clashed with Passy and other Gaullians and in September 1941 made an attempt to limit de Gaulle to purely honorific functions. After leading the Saint-Pierre-et-Miquelon expedition, he tried once again but without success. He left the CNF and subsequently rallied to Giraud. His work, *De Gaulle contre le Gaullisme* (Ed. du Chêne, 1946) was one of the first of quite a series of anti-Gaullian books.

314 Churchill, whom Roosevelt had delighted by adopting the British encirclement strategy with his action in North Africa, was even less than before inclined to fall out with the White House over Free France.

315 Initially, de Gaulle had refused to met Giraud in a territory that was virtually American. He only agreed to do so after what amounted to a veritable ultimatum from Churchill. In his *Mémoires de guerre*, he states that he thought that he was there 'in captivity'; see (7), vol. 2, p. 77.

316 Their relations had none the less been far from cordial. It was said that when Giraud was telling him with some satisfaction about his escape, de Gaulle asked him to describe the circumstances in which he had been taken prisoner!

317 After becoming distrustful of the political aims of Free France, Jean Monnet had become, in the United States, one of the architects of the 'Victory Program'. Wary of the 'egocentrism' of the two generals who were obliged, despite everything, to get along together, he wanted to set up a flexible and effective organisation which would also have the backing of the United States whose fundamental help, in his opinion, liberated France was going to be needing.

318 Cited by J. Monnet, *op. cit.*, p. 223. He is also credited with the following, significant, remark: 'If Paris is worth a mass, these American arms are certainly worth a speech.' All the same, Rigault, Lemaigre-Dubreuil and Bergeret tendered their resignations, judging Giraud definitely to be irresponsible.

319 The text is cited in full by Passy (110), pp. 285–388; see A. Kaspi's analysis (113), pp. 80–108.

320 Telegram to Catroux on 2 May 1943; see (7), vol. 2, p. 469.

321 He himself, in his *Mémoires de guerre*, speaks of a 'deliberate showmanship' and adds, in a more metaphorical vein, 'Before throwing the dice, I shook them hard'; see (7), vol. 2, p. 113.

322 See J. Monnet, *op. cit.*, p. 231.

323 Already in February, some of the crew of the *Richelieu*, anchored in New York, had gone over lock, stock and barrel to the FFL navy. During the summer, such movements accelerated to the point where one famous unit, created by Giraud, the Corps Francs d'Afrique, went over almost *in toto* to the 'enemy'. Many incidents, in effect, took place between the men in shorts and shirtsleeves on the one hand and the army of Africa on the other. (In the victory parade in Tunis, it was even the case that two, separate, French armies filed past.) Some of these clashes left lasting scars. (In the film *Français, si vous saviez* made thirty years later, Argoud still had it in for the 'Leclerc' men who had 'pinched his jeeps'.)

324 Giraud was proud of his moustache.

325 Of the 80,000 French and natives engaged in the Tunisian campaign – representing slightly under one-third of the inter-Allied forces – close on 13,000 were killed. They were deployed in difficult battles along the 'Tunisian backbone', while the American troops were coming under fire for the first time. It was only after the fighting along the Mareth line that the Axis troops, in April 1943, were forced to retreat, abandoning 150,000 prisoners.

326 Ignoring the advice from Algiers, which was to show prudence, the members of the Corsican Resistance rose up as soon as the news of the Italian capitulation became known, thus neutralising some of the Italian forces – which went over to them – and constituting a kind of bridgehead around Ajaccio. Giraud landed some of his best commandos there and, after some difficult fighting shared by the Resistance fighters and the army of Africa, Corsica was totally liberated on 4 October 1943; see General Gambiez (115), pp. 137–62.

327 Before the establishment of the CFLN, Giraud had made Muselier, who was eager to cross swords with de Gaulle, a kind of prefect of police for Algiers. Meanwhile rumours of conspiracies and *putches* swept through the town at regular intervals.

328 Yet he was not especially Americanophile. Nevertheless, right up until August, the State Department persisted in negotiating only with him and only on military matters, although they did not really provide him with fundamental backing.

329 It is significant that a delegation of parliamentarians from the Consultative Assembly, not a priori hostile towards him, were reprimanded for expressing their desire to hear him unequivocally condemn the Vichy regime.

330 We will spare the reader a description of the countless incidents that interspersed the life of the CFLN. Some had their funny side, such as the clash over Soustelle (whom Giraud detested). In reply to the latter, who was blustering: 'In the first place, he's a civilian', de Gaulle snapped: 'If that bothers you, we'll dress him up as a general'; see (80), vol. 2, p. 303.

331 Fighting France had nominated: H. Bonnet, Diethelm, Pleven, Tixier; Giraud had chosen: Abadie, Couve de Murville, René Mayer. François de Menthon joined them in September, at which point Pierre Mendès France, recalled from the 'Lorraine' flying group, replaced Couve de Murville.

332 As soon as the CFLN was set up, Catroux succeeded Peyrouton; Puaux was to replace Noguès as resident in Morocco and Bergeret was retired. A little later,

Boisson was to leave Dakar. In September, the CFLN decreed that all ministers in the Vichy regime would be sent for trial in the High Court.

333 De Gaulle seems to have been anxious to keep an important command for him, as indeed was the internal Resistance, communists included.

334 On these institutional changes, see the methodical analysis by Y.-M. Danan (112).

335 In compensation, Giraud received the command of all French armed forces, including the FFL (in June that command had been divided between the two co-presidents).

336 De Gaulle skilfully, if not with a positively Macchiavellian touch, had managed to get the liberation of Corsica to rebound against Giraud. There seems little doubt that de Gaulle was put out by the success of that operation. It is true, equally, that Giraud, in his usual way, had gone ahead as he saw fit, without keeping the CFLN properly informed. That provided fuel for his critics particularly as, on the spot, it had been the National Front, organised by Arthur Giovoni and François Vittori, that had retained political control of the island's liberation. Although the communist 'danger' was hardly credible (the PCF in Corsica totalled at the very most 6,000 militants in 1945) and de Gaulle received a very warm welcome a little later on, the latter nevertheless managed to make the most of the communist bogey.

337 The State Department had been at considerable pains to delay such recognition for as long as possible, continuing to deal only with Giraud. Moreover, Roosevelt did not consider himself bound by this *de facto* situation and according to American plans, France, during its Liberation, was classed among the 'militarily occupied countries'. The Soviets, on the other hand, had proved much more flexible as soon as the Comité National Français was formed.

6 The liberated and the insurgent

1 A totally new perspective on the historiography of this period has been provided by the colloquium held in Paris in October 1974, the proceedings of which were published in 1976 (115); see also the works in the 'La Libération de la France' collection (116) which often provide precious regional analyses; see also Claude Lévy, *La Libération, remise en ordre ou révolution?*, PUF, 1974.

2 See M. Blumenson (115), pp. 191–208. Churchill's declaration of 5 June, made in the presence of de Gaulle is well known: 'We are going to liberate Europe, but only because the Americans are there to help us. For, believe me, whenever it comes to a choice between Europe and the Atlantic, we shall always choose the Atlantic'; see (7), vol. 2, p. 224.

3 Preparations had been made for 'Jedburgh missions' composed of three officers and a radio transmitter. Some were dropped in by parachute before 6 June.

4 The Allied Military Government of the Occupied Territories had been tried out in July 1943 in liberated Sicily. The Anglo-Saxons had banned all political activity there.

5 On this strategy, consult H. Umbreit (115), pp. 243–60.

6 The V1s and V2s constituted the first generation of such weapons and were supposed to be followed by atomic ones. They were launched against London as from 13 June 1944.

7 On this economic exploitation see above, pp. 129–33.

8 Bouthillier and Borotra – both former ministers of the Vichy government – were deported. Between January and June 1944, 95 high-ranking officers and 22 prefects (14 of whom belonged to the NAP) were arrested and deported.

9 The toll taken on that 'Red Easter': 56 shot, 486 deported; see (6), vol. 4, pp. 579–80.

10 'This so-called liberation is the most misleading of mirages that you could be tempted to believe in'; see (35), p. 616.

11 See (63), p. 425.

12 'Do not listen to those who, seeking to exploit our distress, would lead the country into disaster.'

13 See R. Paxton and C. Lévy (115), pp. 323–56; also, with circumspection, A. Brissaud, *La dernière année de Vichy*, Librairie Académique Perrin, 1965.

14 An ever-increasing proportion of civil servants in positions of authority belonged to NAP and Super-NAP. During the autumn of 1943, however, Michel Debré whose task it was, together with Émile Laffon, to draw up lists of future commissioners of the Republic, went 'knocking on the doors of all and sundry but met with many who were hesitant'.

15 The forces that specialised in repression – the 'special brigades' in particular – under the leadership of a number of commissioners of sinister memory (Poinsot, David, Rigal, Rottée) were working more and more in collusion with the occupying power. The reports drawn up by the Reich Security Services stress the 'correct attitude' displayed by the average Parisian policeman – that is to say, up until May 1944. There were a number of policemen who were militants working for the Resistance networks – and often in extreme peril of their lives – but they were as yet only a small minority.

16 Charles de Gaulle was not successful in including a representative of the Church in the Provisional Government, as he would have liked to. On the choices made by the Church of France, see (52), pp. 279–316.

17 In Lyons and Saint-Etienne, in contrast, visits by the head of State were met with a polite indifference.

18 Anatole de Monzie wrote to the head of the French State in the name of the politicians who half-supported him, as follows: 'You have replaced elected representatives by notables and the traditional liberties by improvised abuses. Those notables and those abuses are now daily provoking revolt . . .'; cited by A. Brissaud, *op. cit.*, p. 54.

19 This radio ban produced a farcical situation: instead of the expected speech from the head of State, amazed listeners were treated to an excerpt from the operetta *Dédé*.

20 For the evolution of the autumn crisis, see in particular (63), pp. 415–29.

21 Every morning, his personal bodyguard would burst into the Hôtel du Parc, with their revolvers at the ready.

22 Philippe Henriot surpassed himself in ignominy on the radio (see his address of 25 March 1944, reported by J. Delperrie de Bayac (105), pp. 341–45): he went to great pains to present the *maquisards* as a 'rabble of deserters and urchins', quitters whose 'leaders had set them only one example, that of cowardice', and all the time he knew perfectly well under what conditions the officers of the ex-27th Battalion of Chasseurs Alpins had fought – men who were at that very moment being tortured by the Militia, one of whose pontifs he himself was.

23 This detention centre contained some 1,200 political prisoners from the southern zone. Following an abortive collective escape attempt, despite promises given, twelve 'leaders of the rebellion' were shot and all the other political detainees were handed over to the Germans for deportation; J. Delperrie de Bayac (105), pp. 303–6.

24 If necessary, they did without any legal cover: Maurice Sarraut, the director of *La Dépêche de Toulouse*, a notable who, to say the least, favoured a wait-and-see

attitude, was assassinated in December 1943 by hand-picked thugs from the LVF; one month later, Victor and Hélène Basch, aged 79 and 80, were slaughtered in the open by Lécusson, one of the most cruel leaders of the Militia.

25 See H. Cole, *op. cit.*, p. 275.

26 Darnand's reply to Pétain was: 'For four years I have received your compliments and congratulations. You have encouraged me. And today, because the Americans are at the gates of Paris, you turn round and tell me that I shall be a blot on the history of France. You might have got around to that rather earlier ...'; see (105), p. 527.

27 In November 1943, he decided that – in the event of his death – his constitutional powers would devolve upon the National Assembly and – provisionally – upon a directory of nine.

28 See F. Kupferman, *op. cit.*, p. 149.

29 Contacts with Gaullian and internal Resistance milieux were much more limited. Thus, in the autumn of 1943, Auphan sounded out Pierre-Henri Teitgen, but this approach did not lead to any concrete results since Vichy refused to give any undertaking whatsoever to put an end to Franco-German collaboration against the *maquis*. See the personal recollections of M. Debré and P.-H. Teitgen (8), April 1973, pp. 114–15.

30 See (46), pp. 344–5.

31 See the extremely pertinent account by A. Milward (99).

32 See P. Arnoult's analysis (65), pp. 55–6.

33 See above, p. 129.

34 In the autumn of 1943, French workers (including those of the Nord and the Pas-de-Calais) represented close on one-third of the male work force used by the Reich.

35 See (99) and, in particular, (46), pp. 333–55.

36 The merging of the various information services had favoured the Gaullians: Jacques Soustelle presided over the operations of the Direction Générale des Services Spéciaux.

37 In a letter sent on 28 April 1944 to one of his emissaries in Spain, he proposed the following significant comparison: 'The situation is now quite clear: General de G ... is tomorrow's dictator with a general staff of communists, socialists and Jews ... General G ... is a sincere supporter of the Republic but one which is based upon people who are clean and with no Jewry'; cited by J. Soustelle (80), vol. 2, p. 384.

38 Networks that were Giraudist or Giraud-sympathisers – Alliance, for example – declared their allegiance to the BCRA. The 'Pucheu affair' lost him all credit in many circles in Algiers, where the following slogan was going the rounds: 'A passport signed by Giraud takes you straight to the gallows': for Giraud, who had given the Vichy ex-minister a safe-conduct, was, at his trial, the most reticent of witnesses in his defence.

39 At the same time three Giraudists left it: Giraud himself, General Georges and Abadie.

40 Negotiations for their entry had been dragging on since September 1943. The PCF wanted to choose its delegates while de Gaulle intended to nominate his ministers. This relatively violent duel ended to the advantage of de Gaulle.

41 See (7), vol. 2, p. 153.

42 It could formulate opinions and exert a measure of control over the CFLN through its votes. In principle it was composed of 84 members, representatives of the internal and the external Resistance chosen by the CNR, parliamentarians who had voted against the delegation of full powers on 10 July 1940, communist

deputies and members of the General Councils of Algeria. It held about fifty sessions; see (112) and R. Hostache (115), pp. 372–4.

43 These were on-the-spot interim ministers; two of them were members of the PCF or sympathisers: Marcel Willard and Henri Wallon; see R. Hostache (115), pp. 380–7.

44 135,000 Algerian Muslims and as many Moroccans had been called up and partially regrouped in *Tabors* (Moroccan infantry battalions).

45 See P. Le Goyet (115), pp. 559–84.

46 See P. Le Goyet (114), pp. 403–39.

47 They had been appointed by Algiers 'after consultation with the Resistance'. Two prefects (Chaintron in Limoges and Montjauvis in Saint-Etienne) were members of the PCF. Most of them were civil servants of note. See (117).

48 The 'Calman plan' had provided for three 'offensive–defensive' hide-outs in the Massif central; the 'Montagnard plan' provided for the mobilisation of the Vercors. J. Soustelle himself (80), vol. 2, p. 399, admits that the Calman plan was 'an operation from which much was expected both from the military point of view and in the widest political sense'.

49 Jacques Soustelle, a product of the Ecole Normale and an anthropologist of note, came from the left. He had been appointed as head of the special services and secretary general of the Comité Chargé de Co-ordonner l'Action (COMIDAC) and had become a key figure in the Gaullian Gaullist clan. He was also a regular visitor to the Villa des Glycines, where Charles de Gaulle normally worked.

50 It had been divided between London (BRAL) and Algiers (BRAA). F. Closon, who had his own reasons for complaint, observes (p. 31) that 'while controversial, the BCRA was certainly an important set-up'. There is no point in maintaining that it was used as a scapegoat; nevertheless, it must be admitted that critics agree in their condemnation of this State within the State. Criticisms included those expressed by the FFL men sent on mission – Bingen and Serreules, for instance. Its opponents are quite justified in denouncing the systematic filtering of intelligence. (Closon, who was intending to hand a report from Jean Moulin straight over to de Gaulle, and not to Passy, had been told by the latter: 'Well, you will not be setting foot in France again, anyway'; see (109), p. 80.) It has also been justly criticised for partisan discrimination (particularly as regards the distribution of radio transmitters) and for a number of serious blunders (as in the Vercors affair).

51 On 5 June 1944, he told P. Viénot, with a certain amount of hurtful exaggeration: 'The CFLN does not exist; they are people of no substance'; see the personal recollections of A. Viénot, *Le Monde*, 6 June 1974.

52 He appears very soon to have become disappointed and suspicious: (7), vol. 2, pp. 153–9.

53 The status quo was to remain until such time as the territory of metropolitan France had been completely liberated and all prisoners repatriated; following which, electoral consultations would be organised. There was only one immediate change – one of great importance: the vote for women (decree of 21 April 1944)

54 On 3 September 1943, the CFLN decreed that ministers and high-ranking civil servants who held office under the Vichy regime would be brought to trial in the High Court. The Anglo-Saxons protested in vain against the arrests of Flandin, Peyrouton, Boisson ... As for Pucheu, arrested, condemned, and shot on 20 March 1944, de Gaulle refused him a pardon partly under pressure from the Resistance men; see (71), p. 406.

55 In his speech at the inaugural session of the Consultative Assembly on 3

November 1943, he exclaimed 'Once it is liberated ... France wants to see the end of an economic regime in which the great sources of national wealth escaped the nation, in which the principal activities of production and distribution eluded its control, in which the management of business excluded the participation of organisations of workers upon whom they nevertheless depended'; see (7), vol. 2, p. 546.

56 See C.-L. Foulon (115), pp. 31–54.

57 In his speech of 14 July 1943, after remarking that 'when battle is joined between the people and the Bastille, it is always the Bastille that turns out to have been in the wrong', he went on to say: 'But it is altogether in order for the French people to discuss their affairs and not emerge from the war only to engage in civil conflict'; see (7), vol. 2, p. 515.

58 De Gaulle, for his part, was willing to grant them a 'consultative role': that is the expression he used in his letter of 31 July 1944 to Parodi, to urge him to be firm in the face of the CNR. It is cited *in toto* by Jacques Soustelle (80), vol. 2, pp. 420–1. See in Henri Frenay (71), pp. 255–7, an account of the revealing conversation between de Gaulle and the head of Combat: '"Well", said de Gaulle, "we will try to get along together." "And if we do not succeed, we shall have reached an impasse", I said. The general remained silent for a few moments. He clearly regarded my remark as quite incongruous. "Well, *Charvet* [Frenay's pseudonym], France will choose between the two of us."'

59 There were a number of plans scheduled: the Resistance men were to give priority to the Green Plan (cutting rail tracks), the Violet Plan (cutting telephone wires) and the Blue Plan (destroying high tension wires), etc.

60 Here and there mistakes (some of them inadmissable) were made. In Voiron, on 20 April 1944, the safety of Resistance members in no way justified the massacre of the entire family (women and children included) of the Militia leader, Jourdan; see (105), pp. 266–7.

61 On 25 February 1944, with the aid of five men from the MLN commandos, Léo Hamon destroyed the STO records for category 42; see (6), vol. 4, pp. 410–11.

62 It is not possible here to enter into details – such was the wide diversity of resistance movements. Some idea of it can be gained from H. Michel and B. Mirkine-Guetzévitch, *Les idées politiques et sociales de la Résistance*, PUF, 1954. Let us limit ourselves to stating that in general – and in depth – differences of attitude between the right and the left certainly existed. However, what is so striking is not only the overall and unanimous reassessment of the Third Republic but also the fact that as the Liberation approached, a radicalisation took place. This phenomenon is particularly significant in the case of movements – such as Combat and Défense de la France – which had initially adopted a number of Vichy-type attitudes.

63 Voguë was insisting upon an 'economic revolution'. Combat was declaring its support for 'socialism', that is to say 'a distributive economy'. The OCM, which took a more prudent line, was nevertheless supporting the idea of a 'planned contractual economy'.

64 Individual reactions should not be overlooked. The 'mobilising *maquis*' had been accepted as whole-heartedly by Coulaudon-*Gaspard* (a man of the right) as by Yves Farge (a member of the National Front); in June, Guingouin, despite the pressures exerted upon him, refused, out of prudence, to launch 'his' FTP on Limoges, whereas other FTP groups under the command of Chapon had no hesitation in occupying Tulle.

65 L'Organisation de la Résistance de l'Armée, which was composed of reservist officers and half of the 4,000 officers on active service who were members of the

Resistance, did not enjoy a good press in many Resistance circles. Its 'D-Dayism' caused its members to be at best regarded as 'out of date', at worst suspected of being 'as much or even more concerned to maintain order as to expel the Germans' (a warning delivered by Bidault, as president of the CNR, in February 1944; cited by A. de Dainville (115), p. 470). Despite protests from Algiers and the flexibility shown by General Revers, the ORA was not allowed full membership of the Military Committee of the CNR. See the case put for it by Colonel de Dainville, *L'ORA, la résistance de l'Armée*, Lavauzelle, 1974.

66 The PCF was increasingly urging its militants to join the FTPF. Although composed of a majority of non-communists, the communists to a large extent controlled the leadership.

67 The most telling example is provided by the OCM leader for the south-west, Grandclément, who, having been arrested and 'turned' by the Abwehr, agreed, mainly out of anti-communism, to reveal arms caches, *maquis* locations, etc. He tried, although in vain, to convince Algiers of the desirability of a compromise peace in the west, before finally being executed by the British. His death caused the networks and movements of the Bordeaux region to be thoroughly disorganised.

68 The PCF was suspected of infiltrating the movements with many 'submarines' (militants who kept quiet about their political affiliations). They certainly existed, although probably not in such large numbers as has been claimed. It is at least worth meditating upon a recent declaration by Pierre Hervé, reputed to have been an influential 'submerged' communist: 'I was not a member of any party organisation and received no orders from any qualified representative of the PCF' (115), p. 427. Note the appearance, also, of counter-torpedoes (see the case made out by H. Noguères for the committedness of the SFIO (6), vol. 4, p. 223).

69 From the PCF, right across the spectrum, to the OCM and including the Christian Democrats. An entertaining description of the designs of the latter is given by a Resistance member of the early days, C. d'Aragon, *La Résistance sans héroïsme*, Ed. du Seuil, 1977.

70 See M. Agulhon (115), pp. 67–90; (127); and (128); also G. Madjarian, *Conflit, pouvoirs et société à la Libération*, Union Générale d'Edition, 1980.

71 Given that this programme referred explicitly to the model of a planned economy, it was – to say the least – at odds with the projects drawn up by the Comité Général d'Etudes (see above, p. 164). These had many recommendations to make on the subject of political institutions, but devoted not a single page to social questions; and the economic policies that they favoured stemmed from an extremely orthodox neo-liberalism; see D. de Bellescize, *op. cit.*

72 On the way that it functioned, see the painstaking analysis by R. Hostache (115), pp. 387–404.

73 In principle, Bidault represented the Christian Democrats, the Socialists and the Radicals; Saillant, the CGT, the CFTC and Libération-Nord; Villon, the PCF, the National Front and the Fédération Républicaine; Copeau, the MLN; Blocq-Mascart, the OCM, CDLL, CDLR.

74 We should mention the Comité d'Action contre la Déportation, the Noyautage des Administrations Publiques (NAP), the Comité Financier and the Agence d'Information et de Documentation.

75 In order to obtain a parachute drop of weapons, it was, in principle, necessary to possess a radio transmitting and receiving set; the *maquis* that were supported by 'Jedburgh missions' often did better than the others; thus, the *maquis* in the Ain, under the command of Romans-Petit, were kept well supplied.

76 These are the figures given by H. Noguères (6), vol. 4, pp. 54–6. According to the same sources, the FTP operational in the southern zone numbered close on 5,000 men.

77 See the recent convincing study by J.-L.Crémieux-Brilhac, 'La bataille des Glières et la "guerre psychologique" ' (8), 1975.

78 More than a third had been killed in the fighting; another third were taken prisoner in mopping-up operations: the more fortunate of these were deported, in most cases after torture.

79 The repeated trappings and round-ups destroyed the best networks linked to the BCRA (in particular the Confrérie Notre-Dame and the Alliance network); Bingen – that remarkable delegate for the southern zone – committed suicide rather than talk, as did Brossolette; the movements paid a heavy price: the Arrighis, both father and son (Ceux de la Résistance), Touny, the head of the OCM, Jean-Guy Bernard, Bollier, Bourdet (Combat), the historian Marc Bloch (Franc-Tireur), Marcel Prenant (head of the FTP general staff), Epstein, who had managed to 'hold out' for a year as head of the FTP in the Parisian region, and many more were killed or deported; very few lived to see the Liberation.

80 The discrepancy between official and black-market prices became excessive: a kilo of potatoes could cost anything from 3 to 22 or even 30 francs; 50 kilos of coal from 46 to 500 francs or sometimes even as much as 1,200 francs; A. Sauvy (115), p. 301, has calculated that a kilo of butter on the black market fetched 440 (old) French francs.

81 It singled out for public vilification the 'Armenian head of the band' and his comrades responsible for '56 murder-attempts, 150 dead, 600 wounded'.

82 A hundred or more partisans of the MOI had been arrested during the autumn of 1943. In February 1944, the occupying power put on a spectacular trial at which there appeared the Armenian poet Missak Manouchian and 23 of his companions (3 French and 20 anti-fascist foreigners). They were all condemned to death and immediately executed, with the exception of Olga Bancic, who was beheaded a few weeks later; see *La mémoire d'Hélène*, Maspero, 1977, by Hélène Elek.

83 Strikers from a factory in Romans, deported to an extermination camp, all died there in under a month. The underground CGT organised carefully limited action: on 1 May 1944, it launched a nationwide strike limited in principle – to one hour. In June and July, the insurrectional type of strikes that were prematurely started were failures almost everywhere.

84 On 20 and 21 April, wave after wave of 'Flying Fortresses' killed 650 Parisians; the raids at Whitsun took a particularly heavy toll: 700 victims in Lyons, 900 in Saint-Etienne, 2,000 in Marseilles where the raid brought to an abrupt end a strike that had started well enough.

85 See (7), vol. 2, p. 227.

86 Cited by E. Dejonghe and Daniel Laurent (116), p. 101.

87 In many regions the number of rebels increased three or fourfold.

88 Taking his inspiration from the directives that had been issued when in confrontation with the Soviet partisans, Rundstedt had called for 'the most energetic measures', declaring that 'a semi-success serves no purpose at all'. The FFI were to be considered as snipers and treated as such; see (63), pp. 459–60.

89 But they had at least managed to disperse after 5,000 weapons had been distributed amongst them.

90 Here are two striking examples: three companies of the northern FTP advancing in groups towards the Ardennes were intercepted and annihilated (34 killed in action, 68 shot, 86 died in deportation), see E. Dejonghe and D. Laurent (116),

p. 99. 150 volunteers from Revin suddenly joined the *maquis* set up by Paris de Bollardière; aware of the danger, the latter gave the order to disperse but the Germans, who were already alerted, were able to kill a hundred or more of those who were less experienced in warfare; see G. Grandval and A.-Jean Collin (116), pp. 133–6.

91 The Comité d'Histoire de la Deuxième Guerre Mondiale organised the production, department by department, of a series of extremely useful maps, in particular the 'Cartes de la Résistance', showing the positions of the various *maquis* and the location of attacks, sabotage action, parachute drops and major battles. See the map for the Tarn reproduced on pp. 154–5.

92 Ever since the spring, the Anglo-Saxons had – in the name of security – been criticising liaisons between Algiers and London. The result was further friction. In the end, Churchill took it upon himself to summon de Gaulle to London before the launching of 'Operation Overlord'.

93 The clash between de Gaulle and Churchill was so violent that the British Prime Minister is said to have ordered de Gaulle to be returned to Algiers 'in chains if necessary'. A. Eden and P. Viénot once again tried to patch things up.

94 See (83), p. 117.

95 Robert Aron (*Histoire de la Libération*, Le Livre de Poche, 1967, vol. 1, pp. 115–28) is quite mistaken in representing this as a simple and touching handover of power for which the French State should take the credit; the fact is that the Vichy administration by now had only one choice before it: to give in or to resign.

96 The Americans had decided to introduce in the liberated regions 'francs issued in France', the issuing of which should be placed under the control of the Anglo-Saxon authorities. François Coulet managed to arrange that – as from the month of August – the Treasury of the Provisional Government should take charge of the issuing and circulation of money.

97 See E. Martres, 'La République de Mauriac' (8), 1975.

98 Jean Moulin and General Delestraint-*Vidal* had in the past given their approval to the main lines of a plan devised by the Resistance men in the mountains. The COMIDAC in Algiers had elaborated it, and Descour-*Bayard* confirmed its validity to Vistel on 16 June: 'The Vercors constitutes a special case. I have received written orders, brought from Algiers by Clément, to put into execution General Vidal's plan which provides for the containment of the plateau'; see (108), p. 459.

99 Cited by Paul Dreyfus, *Vercors citadelle de la liberté*, Arthaud, 1969, p. 163.

100 One of the last messages received accused the authorities in Algiers of being 'criminals and cowards'. The *maquisards* had – in vain – asked for neighbouring airfields to be bombed and reinforcements to be dropped by parachute: barely fifty men were in fact parachuted in and weapons were in equally tragic short supply (one man in four had received, at most, a revolver).

101 A local, and inexplicable, weakness allowed the Germans, without striking a blow, to take possession of the key position of Pontaix, which should have been defended by 600 men.

102 Grenier, the Minister of the Air Force, was severely critical of COMIDAC and Jacques Soustelle who, whatever his claims, had not kept him informed. This caused a crisis that de Gaulle was obliged to get over as soon as possible. The controversy is by no means over. The most bitter attack came from C. Tillon (*op. cit.*, pp. 181–98), in answer to Jacques Soustelle's energetic justification (80), vol. 2, pp. 409–14. See the useful work by A.Vistel (108), pp. 453–60, 479–88, and Paul Dreyfus, *op. cit.* Note that de Gaulle devotes no more than a

few ill-informed lines to the Vercors; the head of Free France had, in general, very little to say about the internal Resistance.

103 This division, composed of Waffen-SS volunteers and *Volksdeutsche* (including some drafted Alsatians) was under the command of a full-blooded Nazi, SS General Lammerding who was noted for the cruelty he had displayed towards the Soviet partisans. On the routes taken and massacres perpetrated by the Das Reich division, see G. Guicheteau, *La 'Das Reich' et le coeur de la France*, Daniel, 1974; and, in particular, (88), pp. 279–482. On the repression, see also Gérard Bouaziz, *La France torturée*, FNDIRP, 1976.

104 After a serious hitch, the FTP had occupied Tulle on 7 June but then had to withdraw at the approach of a strong column of Waffen-SS. 600 able-bodied men were then rounded up and sifted by French and German Gestapistes. 99, classed as hostages, were hanged amid the most ghastly scenes of drunkenness. The Militia then sifted out the remaining hostages: 143 were sent to the death camps where 101 of them died.

105 The Oradour operation was carried out by the Dickmann company of the second battalion of the 'Der Führer' regiment. None of the pretexts (later) alleged by apologists of the SS stand up to an examination of the facts: not even the death of an SS officer, Kampfe, who had been intercepted by the *maquis* fifty kilometres away from Oradour-sur-Glane. There were certainly no *maquisards* holed up in Oradour. The men of the village were machine-gunned to death in barns, the women and children machine-gunned and burned in the church. Such high feeling was caused that the German commandant in Limoges, General Gleiniger, presented his regrets to Monsignor Rastouil who, despite threats, had publicly denounced the massacre.

The last underground number of *Les Lettres Françaises* carried the poem 'Oradour', by Jean Tardieu (cited by P. Seghers (111), pp. 353–4):

> Oradour n'a plus de forme
> Oradour, femmes ni hommes
> Oradour n'a plus d'enfants
> Oradour n'a plus de feuilles
> Oradour n'a plus d'église
> Plus de fumées plus de filles
> Plus de soirs ni de matins
> Plus de pleurs ni de chansons
> (Oradour has no more shape
> Oradour, no men or women
> Oradour has no more children
> Oradour has no more leaves
> Oradour has no more church
> no more chimneys no more girls
> No more evenings no more mornings
> No more tears and no more songs)

106 Cited by Colonel Jean Delmas (115), p. 457.

107 *Ibid.*, p. 455.

108 Stanley Hoffmann notes: 'Whoever has not lived in a town or village in France during the weeks immediately preceding and following the Liberation cannot know the sensation of delight at being alive at the end of an unimaginable trial, nor the joy of being happy amongst those with whom one has survived it, proud of one's companions' (47), p. 86.

109 J. Bounin (115), p. 553.

110 See Charles d'Aragon, *op. cit.*, p. 176.

111 Prostitutes were marked out and humiliated as well as women who had had love affairs with German soldiers (as depicted with sensitivity in Alain Resnais' *Hiroshima, mon amour*) or those reputed to have collaborated. The truth is that, in the guise of political morality, licence was given to the settling of old scores, voyeurism and male chauvinism. All the same, whether or not they were 'collaborators lying on their backs', there certainly were women who were deeply committed to collaboration or who were spies, or even torturers.

112 The Comité d'Histoire de la Deuxième Guerre Mondiale has undertaken a painstaking enquiry. Its known results make it possible to invalidate definitively both the extravagant fabrications on the subject of 'crimes committed in the name of the Resistance' (said to have claimed, at the lowest estimate, 300,000 victims) and also the 'revisionist' calculations (50,000 dead) of Robert Aron (*Histoire de l'épuration, op. cit.*, 1967, vol. 1). Among the 10,000 deaths there certainly were, nevertheless, a number of personally motivated 'excesses'; see (119).

113 It should be pointed out once and for all that pillorying the Germans – the 'Boche' – is obviously a way of avoiding the difficulty. Everybody knows that since then, in other wars of liberation, the armies of countries that fought against the Axis powers, the French army included, have committed their own share of atrocities. What is in question here is not just the Nazi system but also the place of the soldier-citizen in the army and in the nation. Having said that, two observations may be made: the SS units were not the only ones involved: the repression in the Vercors was carried out by regular regiments of the Wehrmacht; and, encouraged by the cold war, many West German politicians, emulating Achenbach, one of the leaders of the liberal party and a former councillor to Abetz, have sheltered behind legal quibbling to refuse the extradition of veritable war criminals. To take no more than the example of the executioner of Tulle (as well as of a number of towns in the Ukraine), namely General Lammerding: he became a prosperous and respected entrepreneur; on his tomb he was allowed the following panegyric: 'General Lammerding was a brilliant officer and a fine soldier; he was hounded to death after the Tulle affair, becoming its late victim'! Cited by G. Guicheteau, *op. cit.*, p. 58. We need obviously say no more.

114 Members of the Resistance, in their turn, used reprisals: 12 German prisoners were executed in the Ardèches after 45 *maquisards* had been slaughtered at Trassanel; 84 other prisoners were shot in Annecy following the massacre of Saint-Genis-Laval and after the Resistance men had in vain proposed to exchange them for Resistance members held in the Montluc fortress. There were, in all probability, other cases too. We nevertheless believe it can in all honesty be claimed that, as a general rule, the Germans who were taken prisoner were treated as such.

115 24 gravely wounded patients in the cave-hospital of the Luire were finished off; two of the doctors and one almoner were shot a few days later in Grenoble; the nurses were deported.

116 We will cite just one witness: the chief scout, M. Rouchy, who went to bury the dead. In the hamlet of La Mure, he counted 32 corpses, 'most had smashed skulls, some had their eyes torn out, two had been hanged, one of them having had his eyes torn out and his tongue cut off ...'; see Paul Dreyfus, *op. cit.*, p. 258.

117 Of these 124 victims, 44 were children of less than sixteen years of age; see Y. Durand and R. Vivier (116), p. 153.

118 Here are two examples: Jews who had taken refuge in Saint-Armand-

Montrond were rounded up by Militia men and Gestapistes: later, near Bourges, a well was discovered to contain the atrociously mutilated corpses of 38 men and women (see (105), pp. 409–14); about 500 Resistance members were taken from the Montluc fortress to be slaughtered near Lyons; in the locality of Saint-Genis-Laval alone, 110 people were machine-gunned or burned alive; see F. Rude (116), pp. 80–3.

119 Jean Zay, condemned by Vichy in October 1940 to criminal detention for life, was interned at Riom; on 20 June, he was taken away by three Militia men and killed. Mandel, who was handed over to Germany and deported, was sent back to France by the Nazis, to be executed. He was taken from the Santé prison by militia men and killed, on 7 July, in the forest of Fontainebleau; (105), pp. 496–525.

120 Thus Paul Laffond – a senator of moderate views – was slaughtered in his château in the Ariège, following a night of orgies organised by 'action groups' of the PPF.

121 The departmental head of the CDL – Guisonnier – was burned with a red-hot iron and then thrown into a bath of brine; Elise Pignol was beaten so badly that she could move neither arms nor legs; she was then hanged with a wire; see (105), pp. 469–75.

122 *Lacombe, Lucien* is the title of one of the most telling of the films made in the *mode rétro*, completed by Louis Malle in 1974. The young, non-politicised hero becomes a Gestapiste after getting into trouble for breaking the curfew. Such a development is by no means improbable, but others became Gestapistes with quite different, political, motivations.

123 See (105), p. 500.

124 That is why all Militia men captured bearing arms in the fighting at the time of the Liberation were – in principle – shot on the spot.

125 Cited by J. Delperrie de Bayac (105), pp. 513–14.

126 There are a number of works that are profuse, but inclined to special, *pro domo* pleading, for example: A. Brissaud, *Pétain à Sigmaringen*, Perrin, 1966. See in particular the recent work by H. Rousso (134). Two other accounts are of some interest: one, a vitriolic work and a classic of its kind is *D'un château l'autre*, by Louis-Ferdinand Céline, Gallimard, 1957; the other was written by Marie Chaix, seeking to understand her father, A. Beugras, one of the leaders of the PPF, *Les lauriers du lac de Constance*, Ed. du Seuil, 1974.

127 On 6 June, Laval declared: 'Those who ask you to stop working and incite you to revolt are your country's enemies.'

128 See the account of Henry Ingrand (116), pp. 144–8; on the vain manoeuvres of the *maréchalistes*, see G. Jeantet, *Pétain contre Hitler*, La Table Ronde, 1966.

129 A Commission Gouvernementale Française pour la Défense des Intérêts Nationaux (French Governmental Commission for the Defence of National Interests), limited to the defence of 'civilian internees', had received Pétain's endorsement. This had been transformed into a 'governmental delegation' which was regarded as null and void by the head of the French State.

130 Doriot had, as usual, tried to play a lone hand; first he had tried to make use of Bückel, the Gauleiter of Lorraine, and had then installed himself, together with his court, on Lake Constance. In the débâcle, the PPF remained the best-organised movement, controlling a radio transmitter and instructing commandos to make parachute landings in France.

131 The Germans who had taken care to eliminate Darnand as well as Doriot were pressing for a movement of denationalisation, which provoked a measure of resistance.

132 Doriot may have been the victim of a struggle that was taking place between a number of Nazi pressure groups; see (103), pp. 415–16.

133 Some hundreds of survivors opted to join a 'Charlemagne regiment' which took part in the battle for Berlin.

134 See (63), p. 430.

135 See the complete text of this famous address (7), vol. 2, pp. 709–10.

136 The fullest work is that by A. Dansette (118). See also the personal recollections of two talented writers, E. d'Astier de la Vigerie (75) and Charles de Gaulle (7). See also a collective work by a number of leaders of the insurrection, *La Libération de Paris*, Denoël, 1964.

137 The text can be found in the work by Dansette (118), pp. 372–3.

138 *Ibid.*, p. 374.

139 Despite pressure from the men of the Resistance, Cardinal Suhard had given absolution in the presence of the commandant of Gross-Paris. He was not forgiven for this by the Resistance men, who banned him from Notre-Dame on 26 August. Note also that Cardinal Gerlier, who held a requiem mass for Philippe Henriot, refused to preside over the obsequies of the great catholic militant and Resistance fighter, Gilbert Dru, killed on 27 July. On the attitude of the Church of France in 1944, (52), pp. 317–64, 431–43.

140 See his intervention in the session of the CNR during the afternoon of 20 August: (118), pp. 380–3.

141 See the account of this important plenary meeting, *ibid.*, pp. 387–90.

142 'Ah! It's the sea!': see (7), vol. 2, p. 311.

143 Much has been written on the subject of the shots that rang out outside and inside Notre-Dame. It is certain that the FFI and men of the 2nd Armoured Division were harassed by rooftop snipers, most of them Militia men. A truly psychotic mood had been created – which may explain the deadly fusillade (a number of dead and 300 wounded) prompted by a shot that was probably fired by accident. In his *Mémoires de guerre* (7), vol. 2, p. 315, de Gaulle accuses the communists of having started the firing in order to justify the maintenance of the insurgent forces. It is not a very likely hypothesis and there is certainly not a vestige of proof to back it up.

144 The situation threatened to become catastrophic: once the Germans had set fire to the Pantin mills, there remained, at the outbreak of the insurrection, barely seven days' supply of flour.

145 The most effective weapon against German tanks was still the petrol bomb made out of petrol, sulphuric acid and potassium permanganate.

146 Forty-two young Resistance fighters, whose average age was seventeen, fell into a trap laid by French Gestapistes: thirty-five of them were slaughtered in front of the waterfall in the Bois de Boulogne, the other seven were shot in Paris. At least two captured FFI convoys were shot at Vincennes; in the Jardin du Luxembourg eight horribly disfigured corpses were discovered with their hands totally skinned.

147 The losses of the 2nd Armoured Division totalled 130 dead and 319 wounded; the Germans lost 2,800 men killed.

148 Advance units of an American division passed through the east of Paris and were holding themselves in readiness to bring relief.

149 The Swedish Consul General, described by d'Astier as 'a cunning operator and a courageous philanthropist' (see (75), p. 177), expended many efforts on securing a truce. Credit also goes to him for having done much to organise the release of 3,400 political detainees.

150 Thus, the chairman of the municipal council appointed by Vichy, one Tait-

tinger, fancied himself – quite mistakenly – as a latter-day Saint Geneviève (the protectress of Paris – translator's note).

151 Later on, he liked to pose as a philanthropist who had fallen in love with Paris, despite the fact that he was generally notorious for his antipathy towards France and the French. It would appear that he and his entourage – as quite a few Wehrmacht officers – has lost faith in victory for Hitler and were preparing the way for future compromises.

152 In his book devoted to the FTP, Charles Tillon mounts a forceful attack upon the truce and its supporters. An eye-witness account is to be found in R. Massiet's *La préparation de l'insurrection et la bataille de Paris*, Payot, 1945.

153 See C. Tillon, *op. cit.*, p. 293.

154 See the account by A. Dansette (118), pp. 387–90.

155 He states explicitly that he '[had] nothing to request and would not negotiate' (7), vol. 2, p. 235.

156 *Ibid.*, p. 301.

157 (7), vol. 2, p. 300.

158 This extraordinary passage is well worth reading, *ibid.*, p. 306.

159· See (118), p. 311.

160 See R. Massiet, *op. cit.*, p. 218.

Conclusion. The exceptional or the normal?

1 See J.-C. Martinet, *Histoire de l'Occupation et de la Résistance dans la Nièvre, 1940–1944*, La Charité-sur-Loire, Ed. Delayance, 1978, and the unpublished theses by J. Girard, *La Résistance dans les Alpes-Maritimes*, Nice, 1973 and J. Sainclivier, *La Résistance en Ille-et-Vilaine*, Rennes, 1978.

2 See above, pp. 187–8.

3 The figure is clearly exaggerated since in all probability the number of those shot – including hostages – did not exceed 40,000. Nevertheless, it was not all that surprising for there can be no doubt that the communists were unstinting both with their efforts and with their blood in the fight against the occupying power.

4 I should like to repeat that this expression is attributable to Stanley Hoffmann (47), p. 43.

5 Maurras was – quite justifiably – accused of having provoked the assassination of Pierre Worms by writing in *L'Action Française* a few days previously, on 2 February 1944: 'It would be interesting to know whether the noble family is in a concentration camp or in England or America or Africa, or whether it has perhaps been allowed to cultivate the fine remains of its fortune in some – favoured or otherwise – corner of our own Côte d'Azur... If this nomad tribe has remained in France, an end should at all costs be put to such scandalous hospitality and to a tolerance that borders on madness.' In his own defence, Maurras retorted: '... at the beginning of 1944 the Jews in many countries were becoming arrogant'; cited by E. Weber (19), pp. 516–17.

6 Frenay adds: 'I kissed her and left. We did not meet again until the Liberation. I was a member of the government. She had not denounced me'; see (71), p. 117.

7 See the typical work by Paul Auphan, *Histoire élémentaire de Vichy*, France-Empire, 1971.

8 This 'revisionism' that developed during the fifties came into play at a number of levels. Most orthodox *maréchalistes* were anxious to differentiate strictly between a 'good' Vichy (Pétain's) and a 'bad' one (Laval's); that manoeuvre had already been attempted in Philippe Pétain's trial in which two of his counsel had pleaded that 'the old man had been misled'. Robert Aron's book, *Histoire de Vichy, op. cit.*,

which enjoyed considerable success during the fifties (it came out in 1954), aimed to support that thesis. In their *La Vie de la France sous l'Occupation, op. cit.*, José and René de Chambrun, for their part, attempted to show that Laval had been willing to dirty his hands (relatively speaking) simply in order to protect the French people from 'polonisation' and the excesses of the collaborationists. As for the collaborationists, their historiography is even more complicated: some of them congratulate themselves on having been the precursors – ahead of their own times – of an anti-Bolshevik Europe (more or less that of the Six) (that is the gist of the complacent line developed by Saint-Paulien, *op. cit.*).

9   The success of this film in 1969, when it appeared, launched the *rétro* style in which there were many pickings to be had. It is significant, however, that although initially intended for television, the film was banned from the small screen by the ORTF. It may also be significant that it was under the presidency of Georges Pompidou that the *rétro* style really took off.

10 That is probably why Valéry Giscard d'Estaing chose 11 November – rather than 8 May – as Remembrance Day for the two wars.

11 To deny that the Resistance had any military importance whatsoever, as some people continue to do, is purely and simply an instance of bad faith. Let us quote the well-known opinion of General Eisenhower: 'Our headquarters estimated that at certain points the value of the aid that the FFI brought to the campaign represented, in terms of manpower, the equivalent of fifteen divisions and, thanks to their assistance, the rapidity of our advance across France was greatly facilitated...'; see D. Eisenhower, *Les opérations en Europe des forces expéditionnaires alliées*, Lavauzelle, 1947, p. 28. It is, at all events, incontestable that, by delaying the arrival of German reinforcements, the Resistance fighters helped to consolidate the Anglo-Saxon bridgehead. All the same, as often happens in a war of liberation, the political impact proved more important in the short term.

12 Even as early as the fifties, the politicians were allowing those ostracised back into the fold; in 1947, Robert Schuman and René Coty, both of whom had voted for full powers on 10 July, were respectively President of the Council and minister in the government (to become President of the Republic seven years later); we might also mention Antoine Pinay who had also been a Pétainist in 1940: he became a minister in 1948 and subsequently the darling of all 'right-thinking' France.

In the same spirit, it could be pointed out that Georges Pompidou's only claim to fame over those war years was a critical edition of *Britannicus* and that Georges Marchais, admittedly not at the time a militant in the PCF, did service in the STO.

13 (47), p. 86.

14 Cited by H. Noguères (6), vol. 4, p. 630.

Bibliographical Guide

Every bibliography is by definition personal and debatable, and many of the works cited in the notes could well have been included in this guide. The first nine titles may be regarded as a general introduction to the period; the remainder are grouped within the chapter in which they appear.

1. G. Wright, *The ordeal of total war, 1939–45*, New York, Harper, 1968 (a clear and intelligent introduction to the European war, with a good bibliographical guide)
2. J. Vidalenc, *Le second conflit mondial*, Paris, SEDES, 1970 (a useful précis)
3. H. Michel, *The Second World War*, London, 1975 (a summary)
4. P. Renouvin, *Histoire des relations internationales*, vol. 8, *Les crises du XXᵉ siècle*, vol. 2, Paris, Hachette, 1967 (extremely clear)
5. Y. Durand, *Vichy 1940–1944*, Paris, Bordas, 1972 (outstanding)
6. H. Noguères, *Histoire de la Résistance en France*, Paris, Laffont, 1967–81, 5 vols. (a well-organised analytical study containing texts indispensable for any understanding of the internal resistance; readers in a hurry should consult H. Michel (68))
7. C. de Gaulle, *War memoirs*, London, 1955 (too Gaullian to be the work of a historian, but a talented *mémoire*)
8. *Revue d'histoire de la Deuxième Guerre mondiale*, Paris, PUF (very useful for its articles, its special issues and its reviews; a systematic table of nos. 1–100 appeared in 1977)
9. *Le chagrin et la pitié*, a film by Marcus Ophuls, 1969 (essential viewing)

Chapter 1

10. Proceedings of the colloquium organised in December 1975 by the Fondation Nationale des Sciences Politiques on 'La France sous le gouvernement Daladier d'avril 1938 à septembre 1939', published in two volumes: *Edouard Daladier chef de gouvernement* and *La France et les Français en 1938–1939*, Paris, Presses de la Fondation Nationale des Sciences Politiques, 1977–78 (these have completely transformed the historiography)
11. *Les relations franco-allemandes 1933–1939*, Paris, Editions du CNRS, 1976 (good analyses)
12. J. Zay, *Carnets secrets*, Paris, Les Editions de France, 1942 (all the more poignant given that it was published by Philippe Henriot with the purpose of pillorying the 'war-party')

13. E. Bonnefous, *Histoire politique de la Troisième République*, Paris, PUF, 1965–67, vols. 6 and 7 (a parliamentary account from the centre, senatorial in tone)
14. G. Bourdé, *La défaite du Front populaire*, Paris, Maspero, 1977 (contains many new insights)
15. F. Goguel, *La politique des partis sous la IIIe République*, Paris, Ed. du Seuil, 1958 (an important work, not to be missed)
16. R. Rémond, *The right wing in France, from 1815 to de Gaulle*, second revised edition, Philadelphia, 1966 (a classic, always worth rereading)
17. J. Touchard, *La gauche en France depuis 1900*, Paris, Ed. du Seuil, 1977 (a timely edition of a course of lectures given at the Institut d'Etudes Politiques de Paris)
18. J. Fauvet, *Histoire du parti communiste français*, Paris, Fayard, 1965, vol. 2; reissued in 1978 (the PCF seen from the outside with accuracy and precision)
19. E. Weber, *Action Française; royalism and reaction in twentieth-century France*, Stanford (Cal.), 1969 (meticulous)
20. A. Prost, *Les Anciens Combattants de la Société Française*, Paris, Presses de la Fondation Nationale des Sciences Politiques, 1977, 3 vols. (a very elegant thesis)
21. A. Prost, *Les Anciens Combattants*, Paris, Gallimard, 1977 (in the 'Archives' collection; essential reading)
22. C. Micaud, *The French right and Nazi Germany, 1933–39; a study of public opinion*, New York, 1972 (clear and useful)
23. G. Vallette and J. Bouillon, *Munich 1938*, Paris, Colin, 1964 (a very useful work in the 'Kiosque' collection)
24. *Enquête sur les événements survenus en France de 1934 à 1945*, Paris, Imprimerie de l'Assemblée Nationale, 1951, 9 vols. (uneven, but contains some interesting eye-witness accounts)
25. M. Steinert, *Les origines de la Seconde Guerre mondiale*, Paris, PUF, 1974 (a good analysis)
26. W. Hofer, *War premeditated, 1939*, London, 1955 (a skilful account)
27. S. Aster, *1939; the making of the Second World War*, London, 1973 (makes pertinent use of British source material)
28. *Les archives secrètes de la Wilhelmstrasse*, Paris, 1961, vol. 9, part 2 (a very useful antidote to the temptations of gallocentricity)
29. H. Michel, *La drôle de guerre*, Paris, Hachette, 1971 (a successful general enquiry)
30. G. Rossi-Landi, *La drôle de guerre*, Paris, Colin, 1971 (a good analysis)
31. J.-N. Jeanneney, *Journal politique*, Paris, Colin, 1972 (a model critical edition, with introduction and notes by Jean-Noël Jeanneney)
32. *Français et Britanniques dans la drôle de guerre*, Paris, Editions du CNRS, 1979 (extremely useful)
33. F. Fonvielle-Alquier, *The French and the phoney war, 1939–1940*, London, 1973 (a humorous work of considerable interest)

Chapter 2

34. *Le procès du Maréchal Pétain*, Paris, Imprimerie des Journaux Officiels, 1945 (the most revealing of the liberation trials, despite the reticence of the accused)
35. L. Noguères, *Le véritable procès du Maréchal Pétain*, Paris, Fayard, 1955 (a mine of hitherto unpublished information)
36. Y. Bouthillier, *Le drame de Vichy*, Paris, Plon, 1950, 2 vols. (the most impressive defence of Vichy and the armistice)
37. F. Avantaggiato Puppo, *Gli armistizi francesi del 1940*, Milan, 1963 (exhaustive)

38. A. Goutard (with a foreword by B. Liddell Hart), *The Battle of France, 1940*, London (some pertinent criticisms)
39. G. Chapman, *Six semaines de campagne*, Paris, Arthaud, 1972 (meticulous)
40. J. Vidalenc, *L'Exode de mai-juin 1940*, Paris, PUF, 1957 (a good retrospective enquiry)
41. H. Amouroux, *La grande histoire des Français sous l'Occupation*, Paris, Laffont, 8 vols. in preparation, of which 3 have so far appeared; *Le peuple du désastre*; *Quarante millions de pétainistes*; *Les beaux jours des collabos*, 1976–78 (uneven)
42. M. Bloch (with an introduction by Sir M. Powicke), *Strange defeat*, London, 1949 (the remarkable personal view of an historian and officer revolted by the capitulation)
43. E. Berl, *La fin de la IIIe République*, Paris, Gallimard, 1968 (contains some striking portraits and other useful information)
44. J.-P. Azéma and M. Winock, *La IIIe République*, Paris, Le Livre de Poche, 1978

Chapter 3

45. Proceedings of the colloquium organised, in March 1970, by the Fondation Nationale des Sciences Politiques on 'Le gouvernement de Vichy et la révolution nationale (1940–1942)', published in one volume as *Le gouvernement de Vichy, 1940–1942*, Paris, Colin, 1972 (contributions of particular quality on a 'taboo' subject)
46. R. Paxton, *Vichy France; old guard and new order, 1940–1944*, London 1972 (an excellent work of synthesis)
47. S. Hoffmann, *Decline or renewal? France since the 1930s*, New York, 1974 (a collection of essays by an American political historian which convey a remarkable understanding of France and the French; the wartime subjects are models of subtle perception)
48. R. Griffiths, *Marshal Pétain*, London, 1970 (the best biography of Pétain before 1940)
49. J. Isorni, *Philippe Pétain*, Paris, La Table Ronde, 1973 (contains the most important Pétain texts, with a commentary by a convinced Pétainist)
50. H. Du Moulin de Labarthète, *Le temps des illusions*, Geneva, A l'Enseigne du Cheval Ailé, 1947 (a not untalented defence by the director of Philippe Pétain's civil cabinet)
51. H. Michel, *Vichy année 40*, Paris, Laffont, 1966 (a solid and convincing analysis)
52. J. Duquesne, *Les catholiques français sous l'Occupation*, Paris, Grasset, 1966 (an early work of synthesis, still mainly convincing)
53. Proceedings of the colloquium organised in 1976 by the University of Grenoble-II, published in one vol. as *Eglises et Chrétiens dans la Deuxième Guerre mondiale*, Lyon, Presses Universitaires de Lyon, 1978 (solid monographs introducing the necessary complexities)
54. Proceedings of the colloquium organised in November 1977 in the University of Lille-III, published in two issues of *La Revue du Nord*, Lille, April–June and July–September 1978 (a sound regional approach)
55. I. Boussard, *Vichy et la Corporation paysanne*, Paris, Presses de la Fondation Nationale des Sciences Politiques, 1980 (an illuminating investigation of the complicated functioning of the corporation)
56. A. Sauvy, *La vie économique des Français de 1939 à 1945*, Paris, Flammarion, 1978 (uneven but stimulating)
57. P. Delouvrier and R. Nathan, *Politique économique de la France*, Paris, Librairie de

Droit, 1958 (a clear and methodical course of lectures delivered at the Institut d'Etudes Politiques de Paris in 1957–58)

58. M. Cépède, *Agriculture et alimentation en France durant la Deuxième Guerre mondiale*, Paris, Génin, 1961 (a well-informed thesis)
59. P. Durand, *La SNCF pendant la guerre*, Paris, PUF, 1968 (a good monograph)
60. C. Bellanger, H. Michel et C. Lévy, *Histoire générale de la presse française de 1940 à 1958*, Paris, PUF, 1975, vol. 4 (an excellent work of synthesis)
61. M. Winock, *Histoire politique de la revue 'Esprit', 1930–1950*, Paris, Ed. du Seuil, 1975
62. J. Billig, *Le Commissariat général aux questions juives*, Paris, Centre de Documentation Juive Contemporaine, 1955, 3 vols. (exhaustive)
63. E. Jäckel, *La France dans l'Europe de Hitler*, Paris, Fayard, 1968 (radically transforms the historiography of state collaboration)
64. H. Michel, *Pétain, Laval, Darlan, trois politiques?*, Paris, Flammarion, 1972 (an excellent analytic enquiry)
65. *La France sous l'Occupation*, Paris, PUF, 1959 (a collection of vigorous and well-documented studies; see in particular those by P. Arnoult, A. Piatier, A. Schérer)
66. A. Hytier, *Two years of French foreign policy, Vichy, 1940–1942*, Geneva, Droz, 1958 (solid and convincing)
67. J.-P. Azéma, *La collaboration, 1940–1944*, Paris, PUF, 1975
68. H. Michel, *Histoire de la Résistance en France*, Paris PUF, 1972 (a useful summary but over-influenced by a 'London' point of view)
69. H. Michel, *The shadow war, resistance in Europe, 1939–45*, London, 1972 (a good overall view of the internal resistance)
70. C. Bellanger, *La presse clandestine 1940–1944*, Paris, Colin, 1961 (a work in the 'Kiosque' collection providing a useful insight into the internal resistance)
71. H. Frenay, *The night will end*, London, 1976 (the disappointed passion of one of the historic leaders of the Resistance; essential reading)
72. C. Bourdet, *L'aventure incertaine*, Paris, Stock, 1975 (a remarkable personal account; also essential reading)
73. M. Granet and H. Michel, *Combat, histoire d'un mouvement de résistance*, Paris, PUF, 1957 (a well-organised early monograph)
74. D. Veillon, *Le Franc-Tireur*, Paris, Flammarion, 1977 (excellent)
75. E. d'Astier de la Vigerie, *De la chute à la libération de Paris*, Paris, Gallimard, 1965 (a work of considerable talent)
76. A. Calmette, *L'OCM, l'Organisation civile et militaire*, Paris, PUF, 1961 (a solid study)
77. Proceedings of the colloquium organised in October 1969 by l'Institut Maurice-Thorez, published in one vol.; *Des victoires de Hitler au triomphe de la démocratie et du socialisme, origines et bilan de la Deuxième Guerre mondiale*, Paris, Editions Sociales, 1970 (contributions of uneven quality but which herald a thawing and revision of PCF historiography)
78. A. Ouzoulias, *Les fils de la nuit*, Paris, Grasset, 1975 (a classic by a leader of the PCF)
79. C. Tillon, *On chantait rouge*, Paris, Laffont, 1977 (a remarkable personal account; unbeatable for 1939–41)
80. J. Soustelle, *Envers et contre tout*, Paris, Laffont, 1947–50 2 vols. (excellently informed, but cannot resist settling old scores dating from the days of the RPF)
81. H. Michel, *Histoire de la France libre*, Paris PUF, 1972 (a useful summary)
82. J. Touchard, *Le Gaullisme 1940–1969*, Paris, Ed. du Seuil, 1978 (published

version of a course of lectures delivered at the Institut d'Etudes Politiques de Paris, including a pertinent analysis of Charles de Gaulle before 18 June)

83. J. Lacouture, *De Gaulle*, London 1970 (stylish and subtle)
84. J.-B. Duroselle, *From Wilson to Roosevelt; foreign policy of the United States, 1913–1945*, London, 1964 (extremely useful)
85. Raymond Aron, *De l'armistice à l'insurrection nationale*, Paris, Gallimard, 1945 (an extremely perspicacious account by a non-Gaullian 'Londoner')

Chapter 4

86. H. Amouroux, *La vie des Français sous l'Occupation*, Paris, Le Livre de Poche, 1971, 2 vols. (a wealth of accurate detail)
87. *Vie et mort des Français, 1939–1945*, Paris, Hachette, 1971 (valuable personal recollections, assembled by Jacques Meyer)
88. J. Delarue, *Trafics et crimes sous l'Occupation*, Paris, Fayard, 1968 (an extremely well-documented enquiry)
89. A. Guerin, *La Résistance: chronique illustrée 1930–1950*, Paris, Livre-club Diderot, 1972–76, 7 vols. (uneven in quality but valuable for its description of the life and death of an underground militant, a piece of iconography without parallel)
90. L. Kettenacker, *La politique de nazification en Alsace, Saisons d'Alsace*, Strasbourg, Istra, 1978–79, 2 vols. (an excellent analysis)
91. J. Evrard, *La déportation des travailleurs français dans le IIIe Reich*, Paris, Fayard, 1971 (exhaustive)
92. M. Marrus and R. Paxton, *Vichy France and the Jews*, New York, 1981 (a welcome work of synthesis of lasting value)
93. O. Wormser and H. Michel, *Tragédie de la déportation, 1940–1945*, Hachette, 1954 (many detailed, distinctive, personal recollections)
94. O. Wormser-Migot, *Le système concentrationnaire nazi 1933–1940*, Paris, PUF, 1968 (a thorough exposition)
95. *Nuit et Brouillard*, 1955 (a remarkable film by Alain Resnais based upon a very fine text by Jean Cayrol; not to be missed)
96. Joseph Daniel, *Guerre et cinéma*, Paris, Colin, 1972 (an interesting political point of view)

Chapter 5

97. P. Dhers, *Regards nouveaux sur les années quarante*, Paris, Flammarion, 1958 (the most carefully researched and convincing analysis of the events of November 1942)
98. G. Warner, *Pierre Laval and the eclipse of France*, London, 1968 (the best biography of Laval)
99. A. Milward, *The New Order and the French economy*, Oxford University Press, 1970 (a thoroughly researched analysis of the Reich's exploitation of occupied France)
100. P. Ory, *Les collaborateurs, 1940–1945*, Paris, Ed. du Seuil, 1977 (a brilliant essay, and see also by the same author, *La France allemande*, Paris, Gallimard, 1977, a volume in the 'Archives' series that collects together a number of well-chosen texts and provides a lively commentary)
101. M. Cotta, *La collaboration, 1940–1944*, Paris, Colin, 1965 (a good overall view of the collaborationist press)
102. P.-M. Dioudonnat, *Je Suis Partout, 1930–1944*, Paris, La Table Ronde, 1973 (an indulgent analysis of a heretical Maurrasian offshoot)

103. D. Wolf, *Doriot, du communisme à la collaboration*, Paris, Fayard, 1969 (meticulous and convincing)
104. C. Lévy, *'Les Nouveaux Temps' et l'idéologie de la collaboration*, Paris, Colin, 1974 (methodical and finely judged)
105. J. Delperrie de Bayac, *Histoire de la Milice*, Paris, Fayard, 1969 (a thorough enquiry, not easy to refute)
106. M. Granet, *Ceux de la Résistance (1940–1944)*, Paris, Ed. de Minuit, 1964 (an excellent analysis)
107. R. Bédarida, *Témoignage Chrétien, 1941–1944*, Paris, Editions ouvrières, 1977 (an excellent monograph)
108. A. Vistel, *La nuit sans ombre*, Paris, Fayard, 1970 (a deeply-felt and well-informed personal recollection)
109. F. Closon, *Le temps des passions*, Paris, Presses de la Cité, 1974 (a fine work)
110. Passy, *Missions secrètes en France*, Paris, Plon, 1951 (may be considered the third volume of the memoirs of the father of the BCRA. A personal account of great importance, it manages – usually – to overcome the prejudices of the RPF militant)
111. P. Seghers, *La Résistance et ses poètes*, Paris, Seghers, 1974 (a fine anthology with a profoundly-felt commentary, although not perhaps for pure aesthetes)
112. Y.-M. Danan, *La vie politique à Alger de 1940 à 1944*, Paris, Librairie Générale de Droit et du Jurisprudence, 1963 (a pioneering study of solid worth)
113. A. Kaspi, *La Mission Jean Monnet à Alger, mars–octobre 1943*, Paris, Publications de la Sorbonne, 1971 (new and stimulating)
114. Proceedings of the colloquium organised in November 1969 by le Comité d'Histoire de la Deuxième Guerre Mondiale, published in one volume as *La guerre en Méditerranée*, Paris, CNRS, 1971 (contains some pertinent analyses, in particular of the development of various forms of nationalism)

Chapter 6

115. Proceedings of the colloquium organised in October 1974 by the Comité d'Histoire de la Deuxième Guerre Mondiale, published in one vol. as *La libération de la France*, Paris, CNRS, 1976 (lengthy but fundamental)
116. 'La libération de la France' collection, Paris, Hachette (a series of regional studies of uneven quality but very frequently irreplaceable). Among the works most pertinent for our purposes are : M. Baudot, *Libération de la Bretagne*, 1973, and *Libération de la Normandie*, 1974; R. Bourderon, *Libération du Languedoc méditerranéen*, 1974; E. Dejonghe and D. Laurent, *Libération du Nord et du Pas-de-Calais*, 1974; Y. Durand and R. Vivier, *Libération des pays de Loire*, 1974; H. Ingrand, *Libération de l'Auvergne*, 1974; G. Guingouin, *Quatre ans de lutte sur le sol limousin*, 1974; P. Guiral, *Libération de Marseille*, 1974; G. Grandval and A.-Jean Collin, *Libération de l'Est de la France*, 1974; F. Rude, *Libération de Lyon et de sa région*, 1974
117. Ch.-L. Foulon, *Le pouvoir en province à la Libération. Les commissaires de la République*, Paris, Presses de la Fondation Nationale des Sciences Politiques, 1975 (new and well-organised)
118. A. Dansette, *Histoire de la libération de Paris*, Paris, Fayard, 1966 (a creditable systematic account of the Parisian insurrection)

Supplementary bibliography

The following works have appeared since the first French edition was published:

119. J.-P. Rioux, *La France de la Quatrième République*, vol. 1 *L'ardeur et la nécessité, 1944–1952*, Paris, Ed. du Seuil, 1980 (outstanding)

120. J.-B. Duroselle, *La décadence 1932–1939*, Paris, Imprimerie nationale, 1979 (a valuable work of synthesis)

121. M. Sadoun, *Le parti socialiste des accords de Munich à la Libération*, Paris, Panthéon-Sorbonne, 1979, 2 vols. (a methodical recent thesis)

122. Proceedings of the Franco-German colloquium held in Bonn in 1978 on Franco-German relations from 1936 to 1939 (useful)

123. F. Bédarida, *La stratégie secrète de la drôle de guerre*, Paris, Presses de la Fondation Nationale des Sciences Politiques, 1979 (a critical edition that is a model of its kind)

124. H. Michel, *Pétain et le régime de Vichy*, Paris, PUF, 1978 (very handy)

125. H. Kedward, *Resistance in Vichy France*, Oxford University Press, 1978 (an original approach)

126. *Histoire de la France contemporaine 1940–1947*, vol vi, Paris, Editions Sociales et Livre-club Diderot, 1980 (a recent analysis by communist historians)

127. S. Courtois, *Le PCF dans la guerre*, Paris, Ramsay, 1980 (new and stimulating)

128. J.-J. Becker, *Le partie communiste veut-il prendre le pouvoir?*, Paris, Ed. du Seuil, 1981 (unfailingly intelligent)

129. P. Laborie, *Résistants, vichyssois et autres, l'évolution de l'opinion et des comportements dans le Lot de 1939 à 1944*, Paris, Editions du CNRS, 1980 (an outstanding study of public opinion)

130. M. Luirard, *La région stéphanoise dans la guerre et dans la paix 1936–1945*, Saint-Etienne, Centre d'Etudes Foréziennes, 1980 (a solid regional study)

131. J. Siclier, *La France de Pétain et son cinéma*, Paris, Veyrier, 1981 (contains a wealth of information and is quite convinced that no Vichy-slanted cinema actually existed)

132. Y. Durand, *La captivité. Histoire des prisonniers de guerre français 1939–1945*, Paris, FNCPG-CATM, 1980 (a very fine work in every respect)

133. B. Gordon, *Collaborationism in France during the Second World War*, Ithaca and London, Cornell University Press, 1980 (a useful work of synthesis)

134. H. Rousso, *Un château en Allemagne. La France de Pétain en exil, Sigmaringen, 1944–1945*, Paris, Ramsay, 1980 (stylish)

135. Proceedings of the colloquium organised in Lyon in 1978, published as *Eglises et chrétiens dans la Deuxième Guerre mondiale*, Lyon, Presses Universitaires de Lyon, 1981 (contains some good analyses)

Index

The index does not include the names of authors of works or articles cited in the notes. The war pseudonyms of members of the Resistance who kept these after 1945 have been retained.

Thomas, Édith, 158, 255 n. 225
Thorez, Louis, 145
Thorez, Maurice, 26, 37, 216 n. 58, 228 n. 136
Thyssen, Fritz, 218 n. 38
Tilden, Robert, 105
Tillon, Charles, 81, 82, 84, 146, 227 n. 129,
    251 n. 172, 227 n. 152
Timbault, Jean-Pierre, 251 n. 163
Tissot, Noël de, 143
Tixier, Adrien, 264 n. 331
Tixier-Vignancour, Jean-Louis, 28
Tollet, André, 187
Touny, Colonel, 77, 151, 152, 271 n. 79
Tréand, Maurice, 82, 228 n. 136
Triolet, Elsa, 158, 255 n. 225
Trzebrucki, Abraham, 243 n. 51
Tubert, Colonel, 262 n. 297

Vaillant-Couturier, Paul, 106
Valentin, François, 143, 148, 222 n. 47
Valette d'Osia, Colonel, 149
Valin, General, 171
Vallat, Xavier, 55, 59, 111, 126
Vallet, Georges, 251 n. 172
Vallin, Charles, 258 n. 262
Van Hecke, Colonel, 166, 174
Vaugelas, Jean de, 181
Védy, Gilbert, 106
Vercors, 158, 255 n. 228
Verdier, Robert, 258 n. 256
Verger, Jules, 63
Verneau, General, 148, 242 n. 35
Viannay, Philippe, 80, 226 n. 104
Viard, Paul-Émile, 262 n. 297
Vieljeux, Léonce, 79

Viénot, André, 268 n. 51
Viénot, Pierre, 42, 268 n. 51, 272 n. 93
Vigne, Pierre, 248 n. 119
Vildé, Boris, 80
Vildrac, Charles, 255 n. 225
Villemagne, 255 n. 221
Villeré, Hervé, 243 n. 51
Villon, Pierre, 187, 204, 206, 252 n. 176, 259
    n. 267, 270 n. 73
Viollette, Maurice, 166
Vistel, Alban, 272 n. 98
Vittori, François, 265 n. 336
Vlaminck, Maurice de, 94
Vlassov, General, 179
Voguë, Jean de, 152, 187, 269 n. 63
Vorochilov, General, 21
Vuillemin, General, 214 n. 11

Wagner, Robert, 107
Wallon, Henri, 268 n. 43
Weil, Simone, 11
Weizäcker, Ernst von, 22
Werner, General, 254 n. 202
Weyer, General, 69
Weygand, General, 33, 36–7, 38, 41, 43, 55,
    70, 71, 74, 75, 86, 87, 117, 121, 123, 124,
    166, 219 n. 7, 225 n. 92, 249 n. 134
Willard, Marcel, 268 n. 43
Wiltzer, Alexis, 42
Worms, Pierre, 277 n. 5

Zay, Jean, 42, 199, 218 n. 30
Zelman, Annette, 237 n. 79
Zyromski, Jean, 8